Israel's Lord

Israel's Lord

YHWH as "Two Powers" in Second Temple Literature

David E. Wilhite
Adam Winn

LEXINGTON BOOKS/FORTRESS ACADEMIC
Lanham • Boulder • New York • London

Published by Lexington Books/Fortress Academic
Lexington Books is an imprint of The Rowman & Littlefield Publishing Group, Inc.
4501 Forbes Boulevard, Suite 200, Lanham, Maryland 20706
www.rowman.com

86-90 Paul Street, London EC2A 4NE, United Kingdom

British Library Cataloguing in Publication Information Available

Library of Congress Cataloging-in-Publication Data

Names: Wilhite, David E., author. | Winn, Adam, 1976– author.
Title: Israel's Lord : YHWH as "two powers" in second temple literature / David E.
  Wilhite, Adam Winn.
Description: Lanham : Lexington Books, Fortress Academic, [2024] | Includes
  bibliographical references and index. | Summary: "Israel's Lord reviews Second
  Temple Jewish literature, finding that many texts describe a concept known as 'two
  powers' in heaven. The two powers concept provides a helpful paradigm for reading
  New Testament texts and their varying depictions of Jesus as the 'Lord' of Israel"—
  Provided by publisher.
Identifiers: LCCN 2024012705 (print) | LCCN 2024012706 (ebook) | ISBN
  9781978712300 (cloth) | ISBN 9781978712317 (epub)
Subjects: LCSH: God (Judaism)—Name. | Judaism—History—Post-exilic period, 506
  B.C.—210 A.D. | Jews—History—586 B.C.–70 A.D.
Classification: LCC BM610 .W55 2024 (print) | LCC BM610 (ebook) | DDC
  296.3/112—dc23/eng/20240530
LC record available at https://lccn.loc.gov/2024012705
LC ebook record available at https://lccn.loc.gov/2024012706

∞™ The paper used in this publication meets the minimum requirements of American
National Standard for Information Sciences—Permanence of Paper for Printed Library
Materials, ANSI/NISO Z39.48-1992.

Contents

Acknowledgments

Well over a decade ago we began discussing the idea central to this book. At first it was a debate, wherein we could not see eye-to-eye. Then, at some point, we convinced each other. In doing so, we realized that we had so refined each other's thinking that we had something to contribute to the wider conversation.

In considering the best format and venue for this material, we consulted many helpful advisors, but we especially need to thank Neil Elliot, who was with Fortress Academic. Neil gave us a contract for this and two other books, enabling us to provide a detailed argument in three stages. We thank him for his confidence in us and in our project.

We would also like to thank our respective institutions, Baylor University and the University of Mary Hardin–Baylor. Our administrators and colleagues have supported us in various ways, including providing travel funds and research leaves. We especially thank our research assistants, Amanda Becker, Solomon Svehla, and Sara Patterson, for the help they provided throughout this process.

We also need to thank friends and fellow scholars who have dialogued with us about this issue at various stages. Special thanks go to Michael Bird, Brian Gamel, Lidija Novakovic, and Marianne Meye Thompson, for providing us with feedback on earlier drafts of our manuscript. While any flaws in the current version remain our own, these individuals helped us sharpen our work.

Last but not least, we thank our families for their love and patience. As we said, we have been talking about this idea—relentlessly at times!—for over a decade, and in the last few years we especially devoted a significant portion of our energy and time to this project. Amber, Charlie, Rena Evelyn, Molly, and Brennan, your support means the world to us, and we dedicate this book to you.

Abbreviations

All abbreviations for ancient texts follow the guidelines from *The* SBL
Handbook of Style (Atlanta: SBL Press, 2014).

AB	Aramaic Bible
ABRL	Anchor Bible Reference Library
AJSR	*Association for Jewish Studies Review*
AnBib	Analecta Biblica
BBR	*Bulletin for Biblical Research*
BTB	*Biblical Theology Bulletin*
BZAW	Beihefte zur Zeitschrift für die alttestamentliche Wissenschaft
BZNW	Beihefte zur Zeitschrift für die neutestamentliche Wissenschaft
CBCA	Cambridge Bible Commentaries on the Apocrypha
CBQ	*Catholic Biblical Quarterly*
CBQM	Catholic Biblical Quarterly Monographs
CBR	*Currents in Biblical Research*
DCLS	Deuterocanonical and Cognate Literature Studies
DJD	Discoveries in the Judean Dessert
DSD	*Dead Sea Discoveries*
ETL	*Ephemerides Theologicae Lovanienses*
ETR	*Etudes théologiques et religieuses*
FAT	Forschungen zum Alten Testament
HTR	*Harvard Theological Review*
HUCA	*Hebrew Union College Annual*
JAJ	*Journal of Ancient Judaism*
JANES	*Journal of the Ancient Near Eastern Society*
JBL	*Journal of Biblical Literature*
JCTCRS	Jewish and Christian Texts in Context and Related Studies
JJS	*Journal of Jewish Studies*

JQR	*Jewish Quarterly Review*
JRR	*A Journal from the Radical Reformation*
JSHRZ	Jüdische Schriften aus hellenistisch-römischer Zeit
JSJ	*Journal for the Study of* Judaism
JSJSup	Journal for the Study of Judaism Supplements
JSNT	*Journal for the Study of the New Testament*
JSNTSup	Journal for the Study of the New Testament Supplements
JSOTSup	Journal for the Study of the Old Testament Supplements
JSP	*Journal for the Study of the Pseudepigrapha*
JSQ	*Jewish Studies Quarterly*
JTS	*Journal of Theological Studies*
NovTSup	*Novum Testamentum Supplements*
NTS	*New Testament Studies*
RevQ	*Revue de Qumran*
RThom	*Revue Thomiste*
SBLDS	Society of Biblical Studies Dissertation Series
SBLEJL	Society of Biblical Literature, Early Jewish Literature
SHR	*Studies in the History of Religion*
SJLA	*Studies in Judaism in Late Antiquity*
SJT	*Scottish Journal of Theology*
SNTSMS	Society for New Testament Studies Monograph Series
SPB	*Studia Post-Biblica*
SR	*Studies in Religion*
STDJ	Studies of the Texts of the Desert of Judah
STNC	Studien und Texte zu Antike und Christentum
SVTP	Studia in Veteris Testamenti Pseudepigrapha
TDNT	*Theological Dictionary of the New Testament*
TSAJ	Texts and Studies in Ancient Judaism
TynBul	*Tyndale Bulletin*
WMANT	Wissenschaftliche Monographien zum Alten und Neuen Testament
WUNT	Wissenschaftliche Untersuchungen zum Neuen Testament
VC	*Vigiliae Christianae*
ZNW	*Zeitschrift für die neutestamentliche Wissenschaft*

Introduction

The expression, "Jesus is Lord," is arguably the earliest Christian confession.[1] What did this expression imply for those who confessed it? In particular, how does Jesus relate to the "Lord" of Israel? It is abundantly clear that from the first century forward, many Christians understood their confession to be a claim that Jesus was divine. But how they did so has been, and continues to be, a matter of great debate. Did the earliest Jewish Christians understand Jesus to be divine or was such divinity the product of Christian expansion among Greeks and Romans? And in what sense did these Christians understand Jesus' divinity? Was he a divine being under the God of Israel or next to the God of Israel? And in what sense could such a commitment regarding Jesus' divinity fit within what has long been understood as a strict monotheistic conviction of Jews and their refusal to worship any God but one? In light of such commitments, can one conclude that Jesus is the God of Israel and if so, how? These questions and others plague our modern efforts to understand early Christian commitments regarding Jesus' divinity.

As our starting point, we begin by considering Christian commitments to Jesus' divinity in the early Christian movement, particularly those from the second century onward, a period for which we have much greater and clearer evidence than is available from the first century. Today, when most Christians—whether they be practitioners or professional scholars—read their Old Testament, they tend to assume that the God described therein is God the Father, the God to whom Jesus prays in the New Testament. For such modern readers, Jesus, or God the Son, is only present in the Old Testament by way of prophecy, typology, and foreshadowing. This assumption, however, is almost completely the opposite of how most Christians in the second century and beyond read their scriptures. Ancient Christians tended to assume that the primary person encountered in Israel's scriptures God was God the Son, or the pre-incarnate Jesus. It was the pre-incarnate Jesus who walked with Adam and Eve in the garden, who appeared to the patriarchs, who called Moses in the burning bush, and who appeared to Elijah on Mt. Horeb. Such

1

an understanding of Jesus as the God of Israel's scriptures is pervasive and well established in Christian literature of the second century onward,[2] but it is largely foreign to how modern thinkers approach the Christian Old Testament. Therefore, it will prove helpful to review a few brief examples to illustrate this ancient approach before returning to contemporary debates and to the argument we wish to contribute to the current climate.

ANCIENT CHRISTIAN READINGS OF THEOPHANIES

Around the year 155,[3] Justin Martyr published his *Dialogue with Trypho, the Jew*.[4] In this exchange, Justin and his Jewish interlocutors debate the proper interpretation of the scriptures, especially as they relate to Jesus of Nazareth. After much discussion, Justin—allegedly—convinces his opponents that the scriptures did in fact predict the Messiah must first suffer and die, before returning as a victorious king. Nevertheless, Trypho and company still do not concede that these prophecies refer to Jesus, and they insist that Justin offer proof: "But prove to us that Jesus Christ is the one about whom these prophecies were spoken."[5] In a somewhat shocking response for modern readers, Justin refuses to do so—at least immediately. Instead, he explains that he must first show how Jesus is not just the fulfillment of prophecy. Jesus, Justin claims, was the "Lord" who appeared to the patriarchs: "I will supply the proofs you wish [that Jesus is the prophesied messiah], but for the present permit me to quote the following prophecies to show that the Holy Spirit by parable called Christ *God*, and *Lord of hosts* and *Lord of Jacob*."[6] In what follows, Justin reviews key examples of when the "Lord" appeared in the scriptures, showing these encounters to be with none other than the pre-incarnate Jesus.

Of course, since Justin continues to differentiate between the God who spoke and the Word who was heard, or between the Father and Jesus, Trypho thinks Christians like Justin must believe in "another God besides the Creator of the world."[7] In response, Justin attempts to clarify his "paradoxical (παράδοξος)" answer,[8] since he believes the scriptures speak of both the Father and Jesus as the "Lord" of Israel. In short, any appearance of God, especially under titles like Angel, Word, and Wisdom, are understood by Justin and his community as appearances of the pre-incarnate Christ.

This way of reading the scriptures becomes ubiquitous in later Christian texts. By the time Augustine writes his *On the Trinity* beginning in the early 400s,[9] the reading is so prevalent he feels compelled to offer a correction. The bishop fears that the common portrayal of an invisible Father sending a visible Son would lead to "Arianism," or subordinationism.[10] Instead of assuming all theophanies are Christophanies, Augustine insists that any given passage could depict the Father, or the Spirit, or even the one triune God.[11] To make his case, he reviews virtually every instance where the "Lord" appears in the scriptures, such as when the Lord appears in Eden (Gen.3),[12] to Abram/ Abraham (Gen. 12 and 18),[13] in the burning bush (Exod. 3:2),[14] as well as an assortment of similar scenes.[15] In each case, Augustine first admits that the consensus of fellow Christians from his day reads these passages as referring to the Son, but he—often by way of special pleading—claims they could refer to other persons of the Godhead.[16] In so doing, Augustine betrays how ubiquitous the opposing view is in his day: most Christians continued to read all theophanies as Christophanies (while still differentiating the Father and the Son).

In our present project, we investigate the historical context of this early Christian view. While Justin is the first to explain his reading explicitly (writing in response to Jews who contested it), we believe that we can demonstrate that Justin inherited his practice from an earlier generation of Christians.[17] Namely, we believe that this form of reading can be found in texts from the New Testament itself. Before we can make such a claim, however, we must see if there is any precedent for thinking of a second divine entity in Second Temple Jewish literature. Obviously, such a claim raises numerous questions related to Jewish monotheism and contemporary debates regarding the origins of claims about Jesus' divinity. It is to those debates that we now turn.

CONTEMPORARY NEW TESTAMENT STUDIES

Scholars of the New Testament and Christian origins have largely deemed the view outlined above to be a creation of second century Christianity and a concept that is completely foreign to the earliest Christian writings. Thus, various theories have been proposed for understanding the evolution of Christian commitments regarding Jesus' divinity from the time of the earliest Christians in Jerusalem to those held by Christians in the second century described above. These theories can be largely grouped into two categories, one that sees commitments to Jesus' divinity originating in the Greek world, and another that sees such commitments originating in the Jewish world. The first theory is a product of the *religionsgeschichtliche Schule*, the History of Religions school, which generally argued that the early Jesus community would have been limited to a low Christology because of its Jewish commitment to monotheism. It is argued that such a monotheistic commitment would have made any commitment to Jesus' divinity impossible. Thus, this theory contends that Jesus was initially understood to be merely a human messiah figure, one sent by God, yet who was in no way identified as God.

Adherents to this theory then assume that the belief in Jesus' divinity came from Greek and Roman converts to Christianity who, from their more fluid way of understanding "divinity," attributed divine status to the Jewish human messiah.[18] It is then somehow through the combination of this attribution of divine status granted to Jesus and the monotheistic convictions of Judaism that the christological convictions of second century Christians conclude that Jesus is the God of Israel's scriptures.

In response to this approach, a school of thought has arisen that locates Jesus' divine status within the context of Judaism rather than Hellenism and thus allows for an early rather than late high Christology.[19] This approach generally begins with Jewish convictions regarding the God of Israel and then demonstrates how the Christian writings of the first century attributed such convictions to Jesus. With this evidence, it is concluded that the earliest Christians in some way perceived Jesus as sharing in the divine identity of the one God of Israel or being closely associated with God in an utterly new and unprecedented way. Scholars advancing such an approach then claim that there was no christological development from low (a mere human messiah) to high (a divine messiah), but that the earliest Christology of the Christian movement was a divine one. Yet, those scholars who advance such a position fall short of finding in first century Christian writings the christological convictions that, as demonstrated above, are clearly present in the second century of the Christian movement, namely that the pre-incarnate Jesus is understood as the very God of Israel who is active in the narrative of Israel's scriptures. For these scholars, such a view of Jesus is still to be understood as a christological innovation of later Christians, even if it is one with a more substantial precedent than what is provided by the former History of Religions approach. These second century Christians do not need to bend Hellenistic convictions about Jesus' divinity to fit with Jewish monotheistic convictions, rather they merely adapt christological convictions that are already at home in Jewish monotheism and retrofit them to reread the scriptures.

Both of these approaches suffer from the need to rely on dramatic and often unexplainable innovation within the movements they are observing and seeking to explain. The History of Religion's approach must explain the innovation of a Hellenistic Christian movement, one that seems to have roundly rejected pagan worship, drawing on the religious convictions related to that worship to understand the figure of Jesus. They must then explain the innovation of those Hellenistic convictions being blended with the convictions of Jewish monotheism, convictions the History of Religions school itself perceives as so rigid they cannot allow for a divine messiah. These proposed innovations have been thoroughly criticized by those proponents of an early high Christology that finds its roots in Judaism rather than Hellenism. Yet, this latter position must posit its own questionable innovations. It often must propose a radical innovation within the earliest Christian movement that brings the human figure Jesus into what they often argue is the presumably unassailable sphere of Israel's God. Additionally, it must also propose the innovation of second century Christians of moving from a Jesus that is in some way identified or closely associated with the God of Israel to understanding Jesus actually to be the God of Israel and arguably the primary divine actor in the scriptures.

While these innovations are not impossible, they do undermine the strength of the theories that propose them, at times even running contrary to convictions upon which the theories themselves are often built. A theory that does not require such challenging innovations but rather is able to draw a line of continuity from the Judaism in which the early Christian movement originated, through the Christian writings of the first century, to the christological convictions of the Christian writings of the subsequent centuries, would arguably have greater explanatory power. It is just such a line of continuity that we seek to establish. We intend to argue that the very christological convictions that dominated the Christian writings of the second century and beyond were not a major innovation, but rather were shared by many of the writings of the first century and are evident in the Christian New Testament. That is to say that like second century Christians that followed them, many authors of the New Testament understood Jesus to be the YHWH of Israel. We also contend that this christological conviction of these New Testament authors was not a radical innovation, but rather one that found its origins quite naturally in the first century Jewish world. Such a claim indeed runs against the grain of most, but not all, scholarship concerning early Judaism and Christianity and will require significant evidence and argumentation to substantiate it. Yet, if the case can be made, it would provide a more plausible explanation of the development of Christian convictions regarding Jesus' divinity than has been offered in recent scholarship.

THE CURRENT ARGUMENT

The present volume is a meager first step in that monumental effort just described. Its focus is the world of Second Temple Judaism and, in particular, Jewish convictions regarding the God of Israel within that world. While the ultimate goal of our project is to understand the nature and development of Christian convictions regarding Jesus' divinity, it is of first importance to understand Jewish beliefs about divinity in general, and the God at the heart of Jewish religious devotion in particular. Thus, while first century Christian convictions are a concern of the project and we fully recognize that such convictions are evidence concerning Second Temple Judaism itself, the present volume intentionally brackets out such Christian material and focuses exclusively on Second Temple (non-Christian) Jewish sources. In this way, we attempt to demonstrate what ideas were available to the earliest Christians in the formulation of their commitments regarding Jesus' divinity.

This book's primary concern is the nature of what has often been understood as Jewish monotheism, that is Jewish practices and convictions regarding YHWH, the God of Israel. It considers various paradigms for understanding such convictions and makes a case for one paradigm over and against its competitors. The book does this by carefully examining Second Temple literature's depictions of divine and exalted figures (e.g., God's Word and Wisdom) and assesses the relationship between these figures and the God of Israel.

In what follows, we will argue that many Second Temple Jews understood the one God of Israel in terms of "two powers in heaven." This expression comes to the foreground in the rabbinic period. However, we will argue that this concept describes the beliefs of at least some Jews of the earlier Second Temple period, thereby making it important context for New Testament texts. In order to make such a claim, we will first revisit the debates about ancient Jewish monotheism, especially as they relate to the rise of Christian claims about Jesus' divinity. After engaging the contemporary scholarship on these issues, we will offer a more extensive set of criteria to help assess whether any given figure in Second Temple literature could be understood as a "second power."

With these criteria in place, we will then turn to the various candidates considered as "divine" in the Second Temple period. We begin with one of the most discussed figures, God's Word, which will require two chapters in order to cover the range and complexity of the primary sources: in chapter 2 we consider the primary sources themselves, while in chapter 3 we assess the various ways in which God's Word in Second Temple Jewish sources has been understood by scholars. Next, in chapter 4 we turn to discussions about God's Wisdom, finding that Wisdom often has the same features as the Word, and in some texts the two are equated. Along these same lines, we then devote chapter 5 to a figure known in scripture as "the Angel of the Lord," who seems to appear under various names and headings in Second Temple literature. Since this figure is also often equated with God's Word/Wisdom, we then follow this chapter by examining other titles that seem to be devoted to this figure, namely God's Spirit, Name, and Face. The debate over these involves questions about how concretely and personally they should be understood, or whether they are abstractions, and whether they are interchangeable. This debate, however, is not a concern for the next figure, the Son of Man, whom we study in chapter 7, although other concerns arise in attempting to identify this seemingly heavenly figure. Likewise, in chapter 8 we see how the shadowy figures of Melchizedek and Enoch are treated in later texts of the Second Temple period. Along these same lines, we then in chapter 9 consider a number of characters who appear to be humans exalted to divine status, namely Adam, Moses, and the high priest. Finally, in chapter 10 we will assess the overall findings of this study and offer our own conclusions.

NOTES

1. Cf. Rom. 10:9; 1 Cor. 12:3.

2. For the evidence that theophanies were read as Christophanies in the second century and beyond, see D. Georges Legeay, "L'Ange et les théophanies dans l'Ecriture Sainte d'après la doctrine des Pères," *Revue Thomiste* 10 (1902): 138–58, 405–24 and *Revue Thomiste* 11 (1903): 46–69, 125–54; Charles A. Gieschen, "The Divine Name in Ante-Nicene Christology," *Vigiliae Christianae* 57, no. 2 (2003): 115–58.

3. For the date, see Craig D. Allert, *Revelation, Truth, Canon and Interpretation: Studies in Justin Martyr's "Dialogue with Trypho"* (Supplements to Vigiliae Christianae 64; Leiden: Brill, 2002), 32–34.

4. As for the historicity and context of this work, see discussion in Michael Mach, "Justin Martyr's *Dialogus cum Tryphone Iudaeo* and the Development of Christian Anti-Judaism," in *Contra Iudaeos: Ancient and Medieval Polemics between Christians and Jews*, eds. Ora Limor and Guy G. Stroumsa (Tübingen: Mohr Siebeck, 1996), 35; and Judith M. Lieu, *Image and Reality: The Jews in the World of the Christians in the Second Century* (Edinburgh: T&T Clark, 1996), 104–9.

5. *Dial.* 36.1, εἰ οὗτος δέ ἐστι περὶ οὗ ταῦτα προεφητεύξη, ἀπόδειξον. Text = Philippe Bobichon, *Justin Martyr, Dialogue avec Tryphon: edition critique* (Fribourg: Departement de Patristique et d'Histoire de l'Eglise de l'Universite de Fribourg, 2003), 272; trans. = T. B. Falls, T. P. Halton, and M. Slusser, *St. Justin Martyr: Dialogue with Trypho* (Washington, DC: Catholic University of America Press, 2003), 56.

6. *Dial.* 36.2, ἐλεύσομαι πρὸς ἃς βούλει ταύτας ἀποδείξειζ ἐν τῷ ἁρμόζοντι τόπῳ ἔφην. τὰ νῦν δὲ συγχωρήσεις μοι πρῶτον ἐπιμνησθῆναι ὧνπερ βούλομαι προφητειῶν, εἰς ἐπίδειξιν ὅτι καὶ Θεὸς καὶ κύριος τῶν δυνάμενων ὁ Κριστὸς καὶ Ἰακὼβ καλεῖται ἐν παραβολῇ ὑπὸ τοῦ ἁγίου πνεύματος (T. Falls, T. P. Halton, and M. Slusser, *St. Justin Martyr*, 56, original italics; P. Bobichon, *Justin Martyr*, 272). Italics original, indicating citations from scripture.

7. *Dial.* 50.1, ἄλλος Θεὸς παρὰ τὸν ποιητὴν τῶν ὅλων (Falls, Halton, and Slusser, *St. Justin Martyr*, 76; Bobichon, *Justin*, 310). Also, cf. *Dial.* 55.1, ἕτερος Θεὸς παρὰ τὸν ποιητὴν τῶν ὅλων.

8. *Dial.* 48.2 (Falls, Halton, and Slusser, *St. Justin Martyr*, 73; Bobichon, *Justin*, 304).

9. For the dating, see Eugene Teselle, *Augustine the Theologian* (New York: Herder and Herder, 1970; reprint = Eugene, OR: Wipf and Stock, 2002), 294–309; and Marie Hombert, *Nouvelles recherches de chronologie augustinienne*, Collection des etudes

augustiniennes, Série Antiquité 163 (Paris: Institut d'Études Augustiniennes, 2000), 45–80.

10. For Augustine's tendency to interpret scripture in a Trinitarian framework (even beyond *Trin.* 2), see Jaroslav Pelikan, *"Canonica Regula:* The Trinitarian Hermeneutics of Augustine," in *Collectanea Augustiniana,* ed. Joseph C. Schnaubelt and Frederick Van Fleteren (New York: Peter Lang, 1990), 329–43.

11. For a detailed study of Augustine's responses to earlier commentators, especially in light of the "Homoian" debates, and for Augustine's own developments in understanding the theophanies, see Kari Kloos, *Christ, Creation, and the Vision of God: Augustine's Transformation of Early Christian Theophany Interpretation* (Leiden: Brill, 2011).

12. *Trin.* 2.17.

13. *Trin.* 2.19–22.

14. *Trin.* 2.23.

15. *Trin.* 2.24–32.

16. His one clear victory is for Dan. 9:17–14, wherein the Son of Man (= Jesus) approaches the Ancient of Days (= the Father); *Trin.* 2.33. Augustine, however, does not address the fact that this is an apocalyptic vision, and not an actual theophany.

17. E.g., *The Epistle of Barnabas* (written c.135) frequently speaks of the "Lord" acting in the scriptures in ways that clearly refers to Jesus (cf., *Barn.* 2.5, on Isa. 1:11–13; 6.14 on Ezek. 11:19; 6.16 on Ps. 41:3LXX; 7.3 on Lev. 23:29; 7.11–8.7 on "Jesus" commanding all Israel in the scriptures; 12.10 on Ps. 109:1LXX; 21.3 on Isa. 40:10.

18. Older key figures in this school of thought include Adolf von Harnack, *History of Dogma,* 7 vols (Gloucester: Peter Smith, 1976 [German original = 1894–98]); and Wilhelm Bousset, *Kyrios Christos: A History of the Belief in Christ from the Beginnings of Christianity to Irenaeus,* trans. John E. Steely (Nashville, TN: Abingdon Press, 1970 [German original = 1913]).

19. For a diversity of views on this subject, see the essays in Carey C. Newman, James R. Davila, and Gladys S. Lewis, *The Jewish Roots of Christological Monotheism: Papers from the St. Andrews Conference on the Historical Origins of the Worship of Jesus* (Leiden: Brill, 1999). Most who hold to the Jewish roots of Jesus worship follow Martin Hengel, *The Son of God: The Origin of Christology and the History of Jewish-Hellenistic Religion* (Philadelphia: Fortress, 1976 [German original = 1973]). It is worth noting for our purposes how Hengel treats the title *"Kurios":* the proponents of the History of Religion approach believed that the title *Kurios* derived from the mystery religions, a conclusion that Hengel calls "a quite senseless undertaking" because of the overwhelming evidence that the New Testament authors applied the descriptions of YHWH in the Hebrew Bible to Jesus (*Son of God,* 77).

Chapter 1

Re-assessing Monotheism in Light of a Two Powers Paradigm

Over the past thirty years, the notion of Jewish monotheism in the Second Temple period has been the center of significant debate. Can the Judaism of this period rightly be identified as monotheistic? Is there anything that creates a clear boundary marker between the God of Israel and all other entities? Does the Jewish affirmation of and devotion to one God equate to an affirmation of the oneness of that God? These questions and others like them have generated a variety of competing answers, answers that seek to account for tensions in the existing literary evidence in various ways. Two basic models have emerged for addressing these tensions in order to understand the God at the center of Jewish devotion, models that are often described as exclusive monotheism and inclusive monotheism. As will be demonstrated below, both of these models have strengths and weaknesses, with one model resolving existing tensions in the other only then to be plagued by tensions that the other model resolves.

It is in response to these conflicting strengths and weaknesses that we consider a new emerging model, one in which finds its grounding in the "two powers in heaven" heresy of the later rabbinic period. The aim of the present volume is to assess the plausibility that this later belief in two powers in heaven was both present and non-heretical in the Second Temple period. We achieve this aim by closely examining the depiction of divine attributes (Word of God, Wisdom of God, Name of God, etc.), supernatural figures, and exalted human agents within Second Temple literature. In this examination, we use a number of criteria to assess the likelihood that these various entities could have been understood as a second power in heaven. After making a case for and against identifying such entities as a second power, we then consider the explanatory power of a two powers model for explaining the entirety of Second Temple and relevant rabbinic data regarding the God of Israel. While we recognize that definitively proving any one model is not possible, we attempt to demonstrate that a two powers model offers a more compelling explanation of the evidence than alternative proposals. Yet, before we engage in assessing Second Temple understandings of Jewish monotheism, an assessment of the term itself is necessary.

DEFINING JEWISH MONOTHEISM

Throughout the history of modern biblical studies, it has largely been accepted as axiomatic that Judaism of the Second Temple period was monotheistic.[1] Yet, over the last three decades serious questions have been raised about the appropriateness of this long-held assumption.[2] Many have noted that the term is a product of modernity, one that was used in the field of religious studies to categorize, analyze, and evaluate religious movements past and present, and thus using the title to describe the religion of Second Temple Judaism risks significant anachronisms. Additionally, the term monotheism generally refers to a belief in the existence of one and only one God, making it a dubious descriptor of Second Temple Judaism. Overwhelming evidence demonstrates that at least a significant strand of Judaism, if not all Jews, affirmed the existence of other supernatural beings, beings that they would even identify as "gods."[3] This widespread recognition of other gods within Second Temple Judaism has led a number of scholars to argue for dispensing with the descriptor of monotheism altogether.[4] But others have seen value in maintaining the term if it is adequately nuanced.[5] The reason for such assessments is that, though Jews of the Second Temple period affirmed the existence of other supernatural powers or "gods," overwhelming evidence supports the conclusion that the vast majority of Jews, if not all, offered singular devotion to and worship of the God of Israel. Closely associated with this devotion was the deep commitment that the God of Israel was superior to and sovereign over all other supernatural powers. To be sure, Jews likely disagreed over what constituted a transgression in violating the demand to worship Israel's God alone. There is evidence, though rather scant, of Jews who sought advancement among Gentiles by making financial contributions to pagan institutions such as a local gymnasium and possibly pagan temples/shrines.[6] While surely some Jews would have perceived such an action as a transgression, these Jews presumably did not.[7] But despite these exceptions, explicit engagement in the worship of a pagan god would have been regarded by most Jews, if not all Jews, as a violation of Jewish faith and identity. Thus, while the modern label "monotheism," might not accurately describe the faith commitments of Second Temple Judaism, if properly nuanced (e.g., "ancient Jewish monotheism," as suggested by Hurtado) the term could be used in a fashion to describe Second Temple Jews' unique (or almost so) singular devotion to one and only one God and the belief that this God was distinct from and superior to all other supernatural beings. For the sake of simplicity, we will move forward using the phrase "monotheism" or "Jewish monotheism" to describe these religious commitments of most Second Temple Jews.

THE NATURE OF JEWISH MONOTHEISM

Beyond the debate related to terminology, many questions remain. Of particular importance is the question of the uniqueness of Israel's God, or put another way, what set the God of Israel apart from human beings or other supernatural beings or gods? As noted above, answers to this question have fallen into two broad categories, what we call an exclusive monotheism and an inclusive one. Proponents of an exclusive monotheism find what seem to be well-established beliefs about and commitments to the God of Israel within both the Hebrew Bible and Second Temple literature. From these beliefs, they contend that clear and distinct boundary markers, usually understood in terms of divine prerogatives and functions, separated the God of Israel from all other entities within the Second Temple period. Proponents of an inclusive monotheism find in this same body of literature what appear to be clear exceptions to the boundary markers proposed by exclusive monotheist, and as such reject the notion of absolute boundary markers between the God of Israel and all other entities. While proponents of inclusive monotheism do affirm that Jews conceived of their God as a unique entity, the boundary between that God and other entities is conceived as permeable, so that any and all divine prerogatives and functions of Israel's God could be shared with other exalted or intermediary figures. Here we examine these competing understandings of Jewish monotheism, noting prominent proponents and assessing both strengths and weaknesses.

Exclusive Monotheism: Maurice Casey and James Dunn

Both Maurice Casey and James Dunn are strong examples of scholars who affirm an exclusive understanding of Israel's God, an understanding particularly grounded in both the Hebrew Bible and Second Temple literature regarding the worship of Israel's God, and that God's creation of, and sovereignty over, the cosmos. To this end, Casey states, "In the second Temple period, Jews gradually committed themselves to a strict form of monotheism according to which only the LORD himself was regarded as genuinely God."[8] After citing a sampling of evidence regarding Jewish worship of YHWH alone, he states, "There is ample evidence of this kind. It is straightforward and unambiguous. Being monotheistic was Jewish, and being polytheistic was

Gentile."[9] James Dunn shares similar sentiments when he says, "Certainly the oneness of God, or the conviction that only Yahweh was worthy to be designated God and worshipped as God, is well established by the first century CE."[10] The difference in Casey's and Dunn's respective positions on Jewish monotheism differ little. Only a slight difference in their understanding of the strictness of this monotheism can be seen when they attempt to explain Christian commitments to Jesus's divinity. For Casey, Jewish monotheism is too strict and exclusive to ever allow a human such as Jesus to be recognized as divine or a proper object of worship, and thus, one must look outside of Judaism to find the origins of such a development.[11] While Dunn finds any commitment to identifying Jesus as the God of Israel absent in the earliest expressions of the Jesus movement, an absence primarily due to the movement's Jewish roots, he ultimately allows for an identification of Jesus as God's divine Logos to originate in a Jewish context at the end of the first century CE.

Exclusive Monotheism: Larry Hurtado

Larry Hurtado is one of the leading proponents of an exclusive monotheism in Second Temple Judaism.[12] While Hurtado is quick to acknowledge Jewish recognition of other divine beings (beings that could even be called "gods") and highly exalted intermediaries, he contends that there existed for Jews a clear and fixed boundary between these figures and the God of Israel. Hurtado examines the literary and material evidence of the Second Temple period and focuses particular on Jewish practice as the best window into assessing Jewish understanding of the God of Israel. From this analysis, Hurtado offers compelling evidence that Jews gave cultic devotion (including temple worship, cultic sacrifice, and prayer) to the God of Israel alone: the existence of a temple cult for Israel's God alone,[13] tradition in which worship of angels or beings other than the God of Israel is forbidden, the testimony of Greeks and Romans regarding the singular worship practices of Jews, the willingness of Jews to suffer and die rather than offer cultic and religious devotion to anything other than the God of Israel, and the absence of evidence that any deviation from such a pattern of cultic and religious devotion existed. Thus, he concludes that in the Second Temple period, receiving such cultic worship was the prerogative of Israel's God alone and that it was not granted to any other entity. Cultic worship, then, becomes a boundary marker that sets the God of Israel apart from all other entities. The one exception to this is early Christian devotion to Jesus, which Hurtado argues was unprecedented in the world of Second Temple Judaism. Hurtado's reconstruction of Jewish monotheism is quite similar to that of Casey and Dunn, though perhaps more nuanced. It is at the point of their assessment of Jesus devotion in the early Christian movement where their paths depart in significant ways.

Hurtado's case for an exclusive monotheism, one that rests largely on the single criterion of cultic devotion, is not without its critics. In response to Hurtado's claim that cultic worship and devotion was restricted for the God of Israel alone, many have put forward examples that seem to undermine such a claim, including the possible worship of the Jewish high priest, Adam, Moses, angels, and the Enochic Son of Man.[14] In light of such examples, it must be asked how worship or devotion can function as the criterion that sets the God of Israel apart from all others, if there are examples of such worship being granted to beings that are not the God of Israel. Hurtado responds to these examples in a variety of ways. He often contends that what some have regarded as the worship of these figures is merely veneration, and not true "cultic" worship or devotion.[15] He also notes that these examples are often only literary descriptions of worship (if they can actually be affirmed as "worship") and that they do not offer evidence of what Jews actually did in their practice of cultic worship or liturgical devotion. Finally, Hurtado regularly notes that central to his argument is the establishment of a *pattern* of cultic worship and devotion, and because no such pattern exists for the examples offered, they do not, in fact, undermine his position.

Determining whether these figures do indeed receive cultic worship will be considered below. For now, it only need be recognized that legitimate debate exists on this matter between Hurtado and his opponents. Yet, related to such debates is Hurtado's firm distinction between "cultic" worship and worship that, in his assessment, is nothing more than honorific veneration. Loren Stuckenbruck has pushed Hurtado on this issue, noting that distinguishing between cultic devotion and mere veneration is not a simple task.[16] There are indeed traditions in which angels reject human prostration before them, signaling that such an activity would indeed be regarded as an inappropriate act of worship. Yet, other traditions exist in which such prostration before an angelic or human figure is allowed.[17] We might also consider hymns of blessing and praise sung to angels as to God.[18] Hurtado assesses these as mere veneration, but when he applies them to Jesus, they seemingly amount to cultic devotion. What makes one example appropriate "cultic" worship and the other mere veneration? Might Second Temple Jews, themselves, disagree on such distinctions, and if so, how can clear boundaries be drawn? It certainly seems plausible that acts deemed as mere veneration by Hurtado, could have been seen as acts of religious and cultic devotion by certain worshipping Jewish communities.

Hurtado's claim that these examples are strictly literary and do not reflect actual Jewish practice does seem to have some merit, as imaginary literary depictions are indeed different than worship "on the ground" so to speak.

But it must also be recognized that a literary description quite likely has its origin in the real-life experience of Jews or at the very least evinces what would be deemed as theologically appropriate. Thus, the way in which such literary examples might fit within actual Jewish practice requires further consideration.

Finally, what is to be made of Hurtado's insistence on a clear pattern of devotion, and that such a pattern only exists for the God of Israel alone. The evidence that Hurtado puts forward for such a pattern is noteworthy and cannot be ignored. Yet, if there are indeed noteworthy examples of figures or entities receiving worship that appear distinct from Israel's God, then the means by which they might actually be included in this larger pattern of devotion should be considered.

Exclusive Monotheism: Richard Bauckham

Another prominent voice for an exclusive monotheism in Second Temple Judaism is that of Richard Bauckham.[19] Rather than focusing on religious praxis as does Hurtado, Bauckham focuses on divine functions that distinguish the unique identity of Israel's God from all other reality. Bauckham particularly focuses on the act of creation and the sovereign reign over creation, with this latter function closely associated with sitting on the divine throne. For Bauckham, Second Temple Jews reserved both of these functions for their God alone, and as such they could not be shared with other entities. Thus, Bauckham argues that if an entity is depicted to be engaged in either of these functions, one must conclude that such an entity is rightly included in the unique identity of Israel's God. While Bauckham might arrive at his understanding of an exclusive Jewish monotheism by different means of argumentation than Hurtado, Casey, or Dunn, the end result looks quite similar. Though similar to Hurtado and contra Dunn and Casey, Bauckham uses the evidence to conclude that the earliest Christian movement included Jesus in the identity of Israel's God and for this reason granted him worship.

Yet, Bauckham's case for an exclusive monotheism runs into a problem that plagued Hurtado, namely examples of entities that may be distinct from the God of Israel yet engage in the activities that Bauckham claims are reserved for Israel's God alone. A number of examples can be offered here. The Enochic Son of Man seemingly sits on God's heavenly throne and from there seemingly exercises sovereignty over the entire cosmos. God's Word and Wisdom both engage in the act of creation as well as sovereignty over that creation.[20] In the Exagogue of Ezekiel the Tragedian, some conclude that Moses sits on God's throne and from it, may exercise authority over the cosmos.[21]

Bauckham rejects many of these examples, arguing that while they might be representatives of God's rule or agents that enact aspects of it, they do not exercise sovereignty over the entire cosmos.[22] Bauckham dismisses the example of Moses from the Exagogue because he interprets it as a dream that represents Moses' role as ruler over Israel, not the cosmos. While Bauckham previously accepted the Enochic Son of Man as an exception to his argument, an exception he claimed proved the rule, he has now revised this position, arguing that this figure does not sit on God's throne or exercise sovereignty over the cosmos.[23] While this case will be addressed more thoroughly below, it only needs to be recognized now that not all of Bauckham's detractors are convinced. However, Bauckham's treatment of God's Word and Wisdom requires further attention.

Regarding God's Word and Wisdom, Bauckham concludes that both share in the unique identity of Israel's God because both engage in the act of creation. But here Bauckham has been criticized for circular reasoning.[24] He contends that the act of creation is a clear boundary marker for the unique identity of Israel's God and explains a possible exception to this contention in terms of the contention itself. While Bauckham may ultimately be right in identifying God's Word and Wisdom with the God of Israel, he cannot do so solely on the basis of the assertion he is trying to prove, namely that only the God of Israel engages in the act of creation.

In addition to noting figures/entities that undermine Bauckham's attempts to establish an exclusive monotheism, many critics have noted the ambiguity surrounding Bauckham's language of inclusion in the divine identity.[25] Bauckham uses the concept of identity to refer to *who* the God of Israel is, contra the ontological question of *what* the God of Israel is. He is intentionally seeking to move past debates over functional and ontological divinity. Yet the notion of a figure/entity being included in the unique identity of Israel's God creates ambiguity. Does such inclusion mean that Jesus is to be equated with the God of Israel, that is,which is to say, Jesus is the God of Israel? Bauckham rejects such an understanding.[26] Does such an inclusion mean that there are two Gods? Bauckham rejects this conclusion as well. Does such an inclusion mean that the included is simply closely associated with but also subordinate to the God of Israel? Again, Bauckham demurs. Bauckham seeks to clarify his language by claiming that the included figure (for Bauckham, Jesus) is intrinsic to the identity of Israel's God, but such an explanation seems to leave the reader with a mysterious and vague category for which there seems to be no precedent in Second Temple Judaism.[27] While Bauckham claims that his language is a more precise way of speaking of Jesus's relationship to the one God of Israel, his critics have found it to be quite the opposite for the reasons outlined here.

Finally, Bauckham has been criticized for an anachronistic understanding of creation, one that lies at the heart of his argument for an exclusive monotheism, namely creation *ex nihilo*. Bauckham seeks to understand that which sets Israel's God apart from all other reality, and he uses creation as a primary boundary marker, claiming that Israel's God alone creates and that all else is created. Yet, such an understanding of creation is built on the presumption that Second Temple Jews understood the God of Israel to have brought the entire creation out of nothing, ex nihilo. Contra this presumption, many have argued that creation ex nihilo was a foreign concept in both Second Temple Judaism and the larger ancient Mediterranean world.[28] Instead, it is argued that Jews conceived of creation in terms of God ordering and organizing the raw matter of the cosmos into its present form. Such an understanding of creation would undermine Bauckham's attempt to use the categories of created and creator as a basis for establishing an exclusive boundary marker for the God of Israel. To be fair to Bauckham, whether a belief of creation ex nihilo existed in the Second Temple period is the subject of ongoing debate, with important voices arguing on both sides.[29] But this uncertainty destabilizes any attempt to separate reality into the neatly defined categories of created and creator. It may still be that the action of creation can function as an identity marker for the God of Israel, perhaps even an absolute one, but the case for such an identity marker would need to be disentangled from the debate over creation ex nihilo.

Exclusive Monotheism: Strengths and Weaknesses

The greatest strength of the exclusive monotheism model is that it finds incredibly strong support in both the Hebrew Bible and the Second Temple period. That the God of Israel alone should be worshipped is attested in the foundational texts of Judaism, the Torah, and is reiterated throughout the Hebrew Bible. It is affirmed over and over again by both religious and secular Jewish texts of the Second Temple period and it is also attested to by non-Jews. The material evidence of temple and cultic devotion granted to the God of Israel alone in the Second Temple period only confirms what is widespread in the literary evidence. Similar strength of literary evidence supports the claim that YHWH alone creates and is sovereign over creation. That from this seemingly ubiquitous evidence scholars would conclude that Jewish monotheism was exclusive is not surprising. And yet, despite the strength of the literary evidence, noteworthy exceptions within that same body of literary evidence exist. It is with regard to these exceptions that the greatest weaknesses of the exclusive model emerge.

While, above, a number of weaknesses were noted regarding specific articulations of an exclusive monotheism, one particular weakness is common to all. Many scholars do not feel that proponents of an exclusive monotheism adequately account for the noteworthy exceptions that stand in tension with the very boundary markers on which the exclusive paradigm is built. Many see in depictions of God's Word and Wisdom more than poetic or philosophical circumlocutions for Israel's God or God's activity and instead see distinct entities. Some are not persuaded by the claims that the Enochic Son of Man receives mere veneration rather than worship or that he merely sits on an earthly throne. Some reject the conclusion that the prelapsarian Adam is also merely venerated rather than worshipped. With these and other examples that violate the so-called boundary markers of exclusive monotheism, dissenting scholars perceive an attempt to shoehorn these exceptions into a paradigm that simply does not fit them. For these scholars, the square peg of the Enochic Son of Man or the prelapsarian Adam will simply not fit into the round hole of exclusive monotheism.

Inclusive Monotheism

While exclusive monotheism does well accounting for what appear to be well supported boundary markers within both the Hebrew Bible and Second Temple literature, they have been criticized for their failure to properly account for the notable exceptions within that very literature. These very exceptions have led many to reject the notion of an exclusive model altogether for understanding Second Temple commitments regarding the God of Israel. Other scholars have instead used these very exceptions as evidence that Jewish monotheism of the Second Temple period was not exclusive at all but rather inclusive. Proponents of such an inclusive monotheism would affirm the distinct identity of the God of Israel, a Most High God who was indeed central to Jewish worship, created the cosmos, and reigned over it. Yet, at the same time, they would also contend that the boundary between that God and all other entities was permeable. That is to say, that prerogatives and functions that rightly belonged to the God of Israel could be shared by that God with other entities and that no such prerogative or function could be regarded as the unique property of Israel's God or a boundary marker that could be used to strictly identify that God. Figures that share in such prerogatives and functions could rightly be identified as "gods" or as "divine" in some sense, but they would not be rightly equated with the Most High God of Israel. One of the leading voices for this approach is William Horbury, whose work focuses on angelic/spiritual messianic figures who were closely associated with the God of Israel and shared in his functions and prerogatives.[30] Such figures include Melchizedek who in one of the Dead Sea scrolls enacts the eschatological judgment of God (11Q13) and the Enochic Son of Man who apparently receives worship and exercises cosmic sovereignty.[31]

Another important proponent of inclusive monotheism is Crispin Fletcher-Louis, who focuses on human figures that seemingly share in the prerogatives of Israel's God, with particular focus on receiving worship.[32] Like Horbury, Fletcher-Louis sees the Enochic Son of Man as an important example, as he seemingly receives cultic worship.[33] He also notes Second Temple texts in which it appears both Adam and the high priest are objects of such worship.[34] For Fletcher-Louis, the ideal human figure was rightly understood as the image or idol of God, and thus could be regarded as a proper object through which the God of Israel could be worshipped. In this way, certain human figures are then included in the worship of Israel's God. Loren Stuckenbruck has argued that while no official cult is devoted to the worship of angels, there is evidence of angels being granted veneration that parallels the veneration granted to Israel's God, and which might be regarded as "cultic" by some in the first century.[35] These voices are representative of those who would reject the notion of a strictly exclusive monotheism within Second Temple Judaism in favor of an inclusive one.[36]

Inclusive Monotheism: Strengths and Weaknesses

The strength of the inclusive paradigm is the ability to explain well the notable exceptions to what seem to be well-established rules regarding the God of Israel. Without denying that Israel's God is the highest God, that this God created and rules over the cosmos, and that this God, rather than other pagan deities, is the proper object of worship, they are able to reconstruct a Jewish monotheism flexible enough to incorporate other figures, natural or supernatural, into these prerogatives of the high God. Yet, the plausibility of this flexibility is questionable when one considers how widespread and pervasive the general rules outlined above are in Second Temple literature. For example, would the Jews who authored or read the book of Daniel, a book in which three Jews are willing to give their lives rather than worship the statue of a human being, perceive the worship of a figure like the Enochic Son of Man permissible? Would the Jews described by Josephus, who were willing to give their lives over the presence of standards bearing Caesar's image, be comfortable with the granting of worship to a human like Adam or Moses (see Josephus, *Jewish War*, 2.169–174)? Given the overwhelming amount of evidence that supports the exclusive worship of YHWH alone in the Second Temple period and without some direct evidence to explain this proposed flexibility, it seems difficult to answer either of those questions in the affirmative.

Additionally, if such flexibility existed to include, in the worship of YHWH, entities that were decidedly not YHWH, why did such flexibility never manifest itself in the form of an official cult? If worship of such entities was acceptable, what would prevent Jews from behaving like their pagan neighbors and offering powerful and exalted figures, both human and supernatural, some form of cult? If such figures could be included in the worship of Israel's God, it is incredibly difficult to explain why evidence of their inclusion in such worship can only be found in literary sources and not in cultic practice. Here Hurtado has a strong argument against the existence of such an "inclusive" monotheism.

One might also ask, if nothing is the sole prerogative of Israel's God and all could be shared with lesser entities, what is able to explain the pervasive commitment to worshipping Israel's God alone among Second Temple Jews. In the ancient Mediterranean world, it is hard to explain the existence of such a unique expression of cultic devotion without their being unique prerogatives of Israel's God. While some might simply point to the local identity of Israel's God as the explanation, that is, Israel worshipped their God alone because that God was *theirs*, this hardly seems adequate. Many of Israel's neighbors had their own local deities, but this did not stop them from adopting and worshipping the gods or even rulers of their neighbors. What made Israel unique if not a unique understanding of their God? Others might argue that YHWH's identity as the Most High God may be enough to explain unique worship practices. Yet, again, this explanation also falls short. Virtually all ancient Mediterraneans affirmed the existence of a most high and most powerful God, with Zeus/Jupiter being a prime example. But this identity as the most high and powerful god was not enough to lead any of Israel's pagan neighbors to restrict cultic devotion to the high god alone. Why would such an identity lead Israel to such a unique practice of worship when it did not lead any of their Mediterranean neighbors to the same outcome? Here it seems that Bauckham has yielded a crucial insight, namely that the unique worship practices of the Jews require grounding in a theological uniqueness. Without a unique understanding of Israel's God, it becomes very difficult to explain how Israel was able to keep its people from assimilating into the worship practices of the world around them, particularly when there was significant pressure to do so. Relatedly, if all prerogatives of the God of Israel could be shared with other entities, the uniqueness of that God would seemingly weaken and with it the uniqueness of Israel's worship. That the uniqueness of Jewish worship practices was largely unwavering, strongly suggests that at least some prerogatives of Israel's God were perceived as unsharable.

To address some of these tensions, Horbury has proposed that Second Temple Judaism held within it, both inclusive and exclusive understandings of the God of Israel.[37] In this way, the evidence put forward by proponents of an exclusive monotheism is explained by Jews who were indeed "exclusive" in their understanding of the one God of Israel. In the same way, the evidence put forward by proponents of an inclusive monotheism is explained by Jews who were "inclusive" in their understanding of that same God. While such an explanation may at first glance seem an adequate solution, it carries with it a number of problems. First, it does not adequately explain why those Jews who favored an inclusive monotheism never sought to include "lesser" entities into the formal cultic worship of Israel's God. We see no evidence that any Jew pursued such a path. Second, we see no evidence of conflict between Jews over this issue. If one group of Jews was deeply committed to an exclusive monotheism and another were including lesser figures into the prerogatives of Israel's God, including the worship of that God, would we not expect to see evidence of such a conflict in the existing literature? Third, many of the texts which proponents of an inclusive monotheism rely on to advance an inclusive paradigm either include the type of evidence that supports an exclusive position or are clearly relying on texts that do so. For example, perhaps the most prominent figure within the inclusive/exclusive debate is the Enochic Son of Man. The *Parables of Enoch*, in which proponents of an inclusive monotheism perceive the Enochic Son of Man sharing in divine prerogatives, is clearly an interpretation and expansion of the book of Daniel, a fact that suggests its author(s) and readers are supporters of Daniel and the traditions therein. Yet, Daniel is a book that strongly supports the exclusive worship of Israel's God alone. In it, Israel's heroes risk death rather than grant worship to an entity other than the God of Israel. The book is written in response to the actions of Antiochus IV, who forced Jews under the penalty of death to worship Zeus in the Jerusalem Temple. It seems questionable that later interpreters of a book that clearly defended the worship of YHWH alone, would advance the worship of an entity that is distinctly not YHWH. While Second Temple Judaism was indeed diverse and it is possible that some Jews had a more inclusive view of Israel's God than others, such an explanation does not seem to account for what is seen in the literary record, the record from which the only evidence of an "inclusive monotheism" can be found.

Ultimately, the inclusive model is clearly able to better explain the "exceptions" than the exclusive model. However, while it explains the "exceptions" well, its explanation of them makes it difficult to explain what seem to be rather deeply engrained boundary markers within the literary evidence. Thus, the inclusive paradigm does not seem to explain the existing data any better than the exclusive paradigm, as it merely exchanges one set of tensions for another. A paradigm that would explain both the apparent, seemingly well-established boundary markers, as well as the notable "exceptions," would, in our estimation, be the stronger interpretive solution.

AN ALTERNATIVE PARADIGM FOR
JEWISH MONOTHEISM

Both the exclusive and inclusive models considered above focus primarily on the Hebrew Bible and the literature of the Second Temple period—and for good reason. Surely, these two spheres of literature are the most important for reconstructing Second Temple Jewish commitments regarding the God of Israel. However, when one comes to an interpretive impasse, it may prove fruitful to look elsewhere for a solution. To break this impasse, we look to the writings of the later rabbinic period. While these writings certainly reflect a Judaism that is in many ways significantly different than that of the Second Temple period, one can also find continuity between them. If proper cautions are taken, evidence from the later rabbinic period can be drawn upon to aid in understanding Jewish commitments of the Second Temple period. It is to these very writings that we look for a possible way forward in breaking the impasse between the exclusive and inclusive models, hoping that they will offer a way forward that is able to better account for the existing evidence.

Throughout rabbinic literature, there are numerous references to "two powers in heaven," with the belief in such a reality consistently condemned as a heresy.[38] The literature is adamant that there is indeed only one power in heaven and that the God of heaven is one rather than two. For quite some time, scholars of rabbinic Judaism, as well as early Christianity and Judaism, understood this heresy has been understood strictly in terms of Christianity and Gnosticism. Thus, the rabbis were understood to be stomping out an alien idea that these two emerging religious movements had introduced to the Jewish world. Yet, this position was significantly challenged by the landmark work of Alan Segal, *Two Powers in Heaven: Early Rabbinic Reports about Christianity and Gnosticism*. Segal argued that while Christianity and Gnosticism were surely within the purview of rabbinic censure of a belief in "two powers in heaven," they were not the only focus of the censure. Segal contended that Jews themselves (non-Christian and non-Gnostic) were included in the rabbinic censure, and thus there were Jewish proponents of a belief in "two powers in heaven" during the rabbinic period.[39] On this point, Segal has persuaded many, and his conclusions are widely recognized.[40]

Building on this conclusion, Segal also argues that this belief found its origins not in the rabbinic period where its critique is prevalent, but rather in the late Second Temple period.[41] Additionally, Segal concluded that, like the rabbis of the later rabbinic period, Jews of the late Second Temple period deemed this belief in two powers a heresy. Again, many have widely followed Segal in both of these conclusions. Yet, some have embraced the former while rejecting the latter. That is, some have fully accepted that the belief in two powers in heaven is a product of the later Second Temple period but have rejected the conclusion that such a belief was regarded as a heresy. Rather, they have contended that the belief in two powers fit comfortably within the world of common Judaism in the Second Temple period.

Representative of this position is Daniel Boyarin, who argues that a robust theology of God's Word (*Logos* in Philo and *Memra* in the Targums) was prevalent in both Palestinian and Hellenistic Judaism, with the Word being understood as a distinct divine second power.[42] Boyarin grounds such a theology in Jewish efforts to navigate two theological poles, namely a growing Jewish commitment to the utter transcendence of Israel's God and biblical traditions in which that God is clearly immanent.[43] Daniel Orlov has also recognized the prominence of a two power theology in late Second Temple Judaism, yet, instead of understanding it in terms of transcendence and immanence, he proposes categories of ocular versus aural.[44] For Orlov, the second power is that which can be visibly ascertained and could be equated with the notion of God's *Kavod*, while the first power is that which is invisible and is primarily manifested through the divine voice.[45] Such a notion of two powers offers explanatory power for conflicting traditions regarding the visibility and invisibility of Israel's God. The first power is that which if seen brings death, while the second power is that which is described by Ezekiel and Isaiah or appears before Israel as a cloud descending on the tabernacle.

Like Boyarin and Orlov, we believe that such a two powers paradigm has significant explanatory power for understanding the literary evidence of the Second Temple period and the Jewish commitments regarding the God of Israel to which that evidence bears witness. Thus, taking our lead from the condemnation of the "two powers in heaven" heresy present in the rabbinic period, we turn to Second Temple literature to see if we can detect within it, entities that could reasonably be identified as a "second power." Yet, this raises the question of what in particular we are looking for, or put another way, what is meant by a second power. Unfortunately, rabbinic literature never directly explains what precisely is meant by "two powers in heaven," what the heretics believe about them, or what precisely they are rejecting. Daniel Boyarin understands this heresy in terms of the one God of Israel comprised of two distinct entities, a "dual godhead."[46] While that most seem to understand the two power heresy in the same manner as Boyarin, Daniel Orlov seems to understand the second power as a supreme heavenly agent that essentially acts as God, yet would ultimately be distinct from God. Orlov can even envision the position of "second power" exchanging hands from one divinely exalted figure to another (e.g., from Satan to Adam), whereas for Boyarin, the identity of the "second power" seems more inherent and not exchangeable. Thus, Orlov's understanding of a two powers theology is in some ways similar to that of the inclusive model described above, with the second power being the highest agent of the God of Israel who is able to stand in the place of the God of Israel, but is not necessarily identified as the God of Israel. What distinguishes Orlov's position from the inclusive monotheism seems to be his belief that only one entity can hold the position of second power at a time, and that sharing of God's divine prerogatives is not limitless. Here, we will refrain from favoring one of these understandings over the other until our concluding chapter, where we will consider the viability of both positions in light of the analysis we offer throughout this book. What seems common to both understandings is that the second power acts as and is both recognized and treated as Israel's God. Thus, in our attempt to detect the presence of a "two powers" paradigm in Second Temple literature, we will focus on figures that meet such a description.[47]

Throughout this book, we will use the phrase "second power" to describe a figure that acts like YHWH, is recognized as YHWH, named YHWH, or is treated as YHWH. The precise identity of such a figure—that is, whether the figure is best understood as an exalted agent of YHWH or is in some way actually understood as YHWH—will be assessed in our conclusion.[48] Regardless of the precise identity of the second power, we believe that with a two powers paradigm the current impasse between the exclusive and inclusive views of Jewish monotheism might largely disappear, particularly if this new paradigm is able to account for both the strengths and the weaknesses of these respective positions.

PERSONIFICATION OR HYPOSTASIS: IDENTIFICATION AND LANGUAGE

When seeking to identify a second power figure within Second Temple literature, a particular challenge arises in assessing what figures should be considered for such an identification. Not all scholars agree on whether certain entities are rightly identified as a distinct entity as opposed to a mere figure of speech. For example, some scholars perceive God's Word and Wisdom performing certain functions or activities, and conclude from these texts that as such, they should be understood as distinct figures that share their own distinct identity. Yet other scholars conclude that these are nothing more than mere figures of speech or poetic ways to speak of God's own activity or presence, perhaps in an attempt to protect God's transcendence, and that they do not identify as distinct figures. The former view tends to use the word hypostasis to identify these figures,[49] while the latter often uses the word personification.[50] Thus, for entities such as these, we will first have to properly identify them before determining if they should be considered as a possible second power figure.

Yet, there remains much confusion with the term "hypostasis" because it is not always used as consistently as we have just delineated it. First, there are those who offer an imprecise definition of the term. Many modern scholars define a hypostasis as a "quasi-independent" agent, which seems to do little to clarify things. For example, Bousset and Hugo Gressmann unhelpfully defined it as "between" an abstraction and a personal being.[51] And yet, Bousset and Gressmann immediately proceed to list Wisdom as the premier exemplar of this category, only to stipulate that Wisdom is an actual being who is more than a poetic personification.[52] Similarly, Sigmund Mowinckel defined a hypostasis as, "halb seltbständige," that is, "half autonomous," and as such the hypostasis is a personification of a higher deity's action.[53] Since so many early modern scholars lacked precision for this term, in his 1947 book entitled *Word and Wisdom*, Helmer Ringgren uses hypostasis in such a way that it covers a range of referents:

> the hypostases represent a personification . . . But the personal character should not be stressed too much. In fact there are cases when a divine quality is spoken of as in independent entity without it being personified, and I should like to use the term "hypostasis" in these cases as well. But it should also be kept in mind that the result of a personification is not always a hypostasis; it may very well be an allegory or a poetical metaphor.[54]

In other words, for Ringgren, "hypostasis" can refer to a personification of a divine attribute, to impersonal independent entities, and to mere literary depictions. Then, adding to the confusion, Ringgren studies the figure of God's Wisdom in various ancient texts and concludes that Wisdom is more than "an abstraction or a purely poetic personification but a concrete being, self-existent beside God."[55] Therefore, in Ringgren's way of thinking, Wisdom is not a "hypostasis," or at least not merely a hypostasis, because a hypostasis is a literary device and not an ontological reality, but Wisdom does have its own existence.

Unsurprisingly then, more recent scholarship has continued to use the term in ways that are ambiguous at best.[56] For instance, Dunn speaks of a "quasi-personification," that is something "between personalities and abstract beings."[57] Even Gieschen, who champions a form of two powers theology, demurs when it comes to the concept of hypostasis for some figures: any one of them can be "depicted with independent personhood of varying degrees."[58] Following Gieschen, Ruth Tuschling attempts to offer a nuanced definition: "By hypostasis I understand a figure which is in some ways a projection or extension of God, the instrument of his will, and not fully separate from him, although the degree of independence can vary."[59] She adds that "a 'separate hypostasis' is a contradiction in terms."[60] These scholars cannot be wholly faulted: the term has become so common in the secondary discourse that it cannot be ignored, and yet it is used to describe an array of figures that do not all seem to have the same level of "personhood," independence, or existence.

From where did this term arise? The Greek word ὑπόστασις originally functioned as a rough equivalent to "substance" or "being (οὐσία)," but then in the Trinitarian debates of the fourth Christian century the pro-Nicene party eventually redefined this word to serve as a stronger form of πρόσωπον (cf., the Latin, *persona*).[61] In other words, a hypostasis came to be understood as a distinct, personal entity—an entity just as distinct as Jesus was from the Father, for example.[62] Therefore, in modern studies of Christian origins and early Christology, New Testament scholars were especially keen to ask about a given "hypostasis" from pre-Christian Jewish sources in terms of whether said figure could serve as a conceptual precursor which Christians could have accommodated to depict Christ's preexistence.[63] As used by most biblical scholars, the term is to some extent anachronistic, but it is apparently inextricably ingrained in the scholarly discourse.[64] The term, if rightly defined, could prove useful. In its pre-Nicene usage[65] the term did not (necessarily) mean a "person," but instead it was roughly equivalent to "being" or substance.[66] In this way, historians can speak of a "hypostasis" in Second Temple Jewish sources meaning that a figure is a distinct "entity" with its own reality of some sort, regardless of whether it is "personal" or a "person" in any modern sense.

For our purposes where possible, we will avoid the term, given its ambiguity and problems. And yet, in conversation with contemporary scholarship we wish to insist that when we use *hypostasis*, we mean that a certain figure in Second Temple literature is spoken of as a distinct entity. The alternative would be a *personification* of an abstract aspect of God,[67] spoken of as if said figure were a personal entity but only as a euphemistic means of avoiding blasphemy by speaking of God too directly and familiarly. The latter may be motivated by a view of God that sees divinity as too spiritual or holy to interact with the material and the mundane. And yet God is still thought to be ultimately responsible for certain events and so God's "Word" or "Wisdom" (or "Hand," "Name," etc.) is invoked as if it were a distinct agent when, in fact, the means through which the transcendent God acts is left unexplained and mysterious.

Thus, before assessing whether an entity such as God's Word should be identified as a second power, we will first need to address whether they are truly a hypostasis or merely a personification of a divine attribute. If it is determined that such a figure is indeed a hypostasis, we can then consider whether it could be identified as a second power figure. We now turn our attention to the means by which we will make this latter assessment.

THE CRITERIA FOR IDENTIFYING A SECOND POWER

In our effort to identify second power figures in the Second Temple period, it seems the best way forward is to consider certain features that could communicate to a Second Temple Jew the identity of their God. Thus, we put forward a number of criteria that are based on features that are closely associated with Israel's God in both the Hebrew Bible and Second Temple literature. In putting forward and using these markers, we seek to avoid what we perceive as a weakness in previous efforts to use such markers for identifying the uniqueness of Israel's God, namely, the overdependence on one or two criteria. Daniel Boyarin addresses this very weakness when, in response to Hurtado, he states, "While in general I find Hurtado's argument bracing and important, his exclusive reliance on only one criterion, worship, as determining the divine nature of a given intermediary seems to me overly narrow and rigid."[68] We concur with such an assessment. While cultic worship might be an indicator of the identity of Israel's God for many, if not most Jews, it does not necessarily follow that the absence of cultic worship given to an intermediary would preclude such an identification. Where cultic worship of an intermediary is lacking perhaps other identity markers such as engagement in creation, sovereignty over creation, or attribution of the divine name could function as means of communicating an identification as Israel's God. There are a variety of functions, divine prerogatives, and specific actions in Israel's story that Jews associated with their God, and all of these markers could be, and thus should be used, to identify an entity as a divine, and thus potentially as the second power in heaven. We contend that the more criteria attributed to an exalted being the stronger the case that an identification as a second power is intended and would be perceived by a Second Temple Jew. Thus, the following criteria are proposed for assessing an exalted figure's relation to, and identification as, a second power in heaven.

Receiving Worship

As noted above, a significant amount of evidence supports the conclusion that the vast majority of Second Temple Jews, if not all, regarded the reception of cultic worship to be the prerogative of the God of Israel. Thus, the reception of such worship must be acknowledged at the very least as a possible marker for identifying a figure as the second power in heaven. We leave open the possibility that such worship could be shared by the God of Israel with other exalted beings, and thus, worship is not necessarily an absolute boundary marker that identifies one as a second power. Yet, it is an important marker nonetheless. The degree to which this identity marker might be absolute can be reassessed after all the evidence is examined.

Creating the Cosmos

Both the Hebrew Bible and Second Temple literature clearly recognize the creation of the cosmos as the prerogative of the God of Israel, with some texts explicitly declaring the God of Israel as the sole creator.[69] Above we addressed the weaknesses of Bauckham's claim that the act of creation was a strict boundary between God and all other entities, namely the circular reasoning Bauckham must use regarding God's Word and Wisdom as well as his dependence on a possibly anachronistic concept of creation ex nihilo. To avoid such pitfalls, two caveats are necessary. First, here we only recognize creation as a possible marker for identifying a figure as the second power in heaven, not a marker that demands such an identity. Second, for the sake of argument, we restrict our understanding of creation to the notion of Israel's God organizing the cosmos (an act that indeed involves the creation of life, including human, plant, and animal) and in this way we avoid the unresolved debate over creation ex nihilo. The degree to which this identity marker is absolute can be reassessed after the examination of all the evidence.

Ruling over Creation

The depiction of Israel's God as sovereign over the cosmos is widely attested both in the Hebrew Bible and Second Temple period literature.[70] Closely related to God's sovereign reign is the imagery of God's throne, from which God is depicted as ruling.[71] Thus, we propose that sovereignty over creation is a possible marker for identifying a figure as the second power in heaven, though contra Bauckham not necessarily an exclusive one.

Bearing the Name

The Tetragrammaton, the name YHWH, was regarded by Jews as the personal and proper name of the God of Israel. There is evidence that by the late Second Temple period, this name is treated with extreme reverence and that the practice of refraining to speak this name was already widespread among Jews.[72] Thus, the attribution of, or even close association with, this name could function to identify an exalted figure as a second power.[73] Yet, we cannot ignore the possibility that some Jews might allow for an exalted figure to share in some way in the divine name without being rightly identified as Israel's God.[74] In light of such possibilities, we put forward use of the divine name as a possible marker for identifying a figure as the second power.[75] Yet, in our review of the sources, we will examine whether the divine name is merely shared with a certain figure or whether a figure is depicted as rightly and fully bearing the divine name.

Taking the Role of YHWH

This criterion considers citations or translations of the scriptures that replace the God of Israel with an exalted figure. For example, in 11QMelch of the Dead Sea Scrolls, the exalted figure of Melchizedek is described. In this description, there is an apparent citation of Isaiah 61:2a, "To proclaim the year of the LORD's favor."[76] Yet, in the scroll's citation, the name of YHWH is replaced with the name Melchizedek. On the surface, such an exegetical move seems to be a remarkable one indeed, and we contend it could be interpreted as a means by which the exalted figure that is substituted for the one God of Israel is, in fact, being identified as Israel's God—a second power in heaven. While this conclusion is shared by a number of interpreters, it has been resisted by others who have sought to offer examples for which they contend an identification with the one God of Israel is not possible.[77] For now, we simply move forward under the premise that such an exegetical move could, even if it does not always, function to identify a figure as the second power. Yet, after assessing the existing evidence, we will consider the examples that have put forward as exceptions to determine whether this identity marker could be regarded as absolute.

Holding Additional Titles

This criterion considers a figure that might only meet a small number of criteria but is also explicitly identified with a figure that meets a larger number of the criteria. Because the two figures are explicitly identified with each other, the criteria met by one figure can be assumed to be applied to the other figure, even if no tradition directly applies those criteria to the latter figure. For example, the "Angel of the Lord" may only meet a small number of the criteria laid out above, but the "Angel of the Lord" is explicitly identified as God's Word (*Logos*) by Philo. Through such an identification, the many criteria met by God's Word can be understood, for Philo, to apply to the "Angel of the Lord" as well. In this way, the above criteria can be assumed for a figure that does not directly meet them.

MOVING FROM TEXT TO PEOPLE

The focus of this project is primarily the literary evidence that is relevant to the Second Temple period. As such, it must be recognized that while this literature is certainly a window into the beliefs and practices of Second Temple Jews, it is a window with noteworthy limitations. During the late Second Temple period, there were millions of Jews spread across Rome's empire. It is widely recognized that these Jews were marked by significant diversity. Thus, the degree to which any one text can speak to the specific beliefs of this numerous and diverse group of people is significantly limited. First, it must be recognized that the sources themselves are biased toward the perspective of the literate and educated, those who would, to a certain degree, be regarded as elite. They cannot be counted on to provide the perspective of the common Jewish farmer or peasant. While there is evidence that the religious views of the educated Jews did influence and shape the views of the less educated, the degree and scope of this influence is uncertain (see, for example, Josephus, *Antiquities,* 18.15). Second, it is possible that any one text, or even perhaps a group of texts represents a sectarian expression of Judaism and that the theological commitments expressed therein are not shared by the majority of Second Temple Jews (see certain writings of the Dead Sea Scrolls as just such an example). Third, even if a particular commitment can be established in wide variety of Second Temple literature, it must be recognized that such a commitment might not be held by certain segments of the Jewish population.

However, we return to the truism that literature is a window into what real people believed, even if a limited window. Thus, the presence of a belief within Second Temple literature is evidence of the presence of that belief in the world of Second Temple Jews, though perhaps only a limited presence. Even so, we contend that the more pervasive a belief is within Second Temple literature the more likely it was that the believe was pervasive among Second Temple Jews. Due to the considerations noted above, the pervasiveness of the former and latter need not be proportional, but some level of correlation ought to be acknowledged. If a belief communicated in Second Temple literature is pervasive, we contend that it is best recognized as fitting comfortably within what E. P. Sanders described as "common Judaism."[78] Such a conclusion need not mean a belief was held by all or even the majority of Jews but that the holding of such a belief would, at the very least, not be recognized by most Jews as problematic or inconsistent with fidelity to a Jewish identity. For our present purposes, we need not show what "most Jews" believed, but rather only the presence of a particular belief within the world of the "common Judaism" of the Second Temple period. The acceptable presence of such a belief within the Second Temple Jewish world would then be readily available for the earliest members of the Jesus movement (a movement begun by Jews) to draw upon for the formation of their own evolving theological commitments.

PRELIMINARY CONCLUSIONS AND STRATEGY

In the chapters that follow, the criteria outlined above will be applied to the following divine attributes and exalted figures: God's Word and other possible hypostases, including God's Wisdom, Name, and Face; angels, with particular attention given to the Angel of the Lord; and various exalted humans, such as the Son of Man, Melchizedek, Adam, Moses, and Israel's high priest. After carefully examining these entities, we will consider the significance of our results and their implication for the nature of Second Temple Jewish monotheism. To be clear, the primary sources do not invite a rigid application of these criteria, and so instead of offering a predetermined grid forced onto the ancient material, we will analyze each of the figures mentioned above as they develop historically, carefully examining the context of the various bodies of literature in which they appear. Not every criterion will be relevant to every entity we consider, and where irrelevant a criterion will be omitted from our analysis. As we proceed, we will consider the interplay between our analysis and the criteria provided above.

With these criteria in mind, we can now turn to specific figures who appear in Second Temple Jewish texts, figures which some have claimed either to have divine status or to be God's self-manifestation. In particular, we are especially interested to see if any of these figures rises to the status of what some could have considered the second power in heaven. The first candidate is the "Word" of God, and so it is to that entity we will devote the next two chapters.

NOTES

1. See, for example, the statement made by Maurice Casey, *From Jewish Prophet to Gentile God: The Origins and Development of New Testament Christology* (Louisville, KY: Westminster/John Knox, 1991), 169, "You could not both generate belief in the deity of Jesus and remain within the Jewish community."

2. For examples of works engaged in this debate, see P. Hayman, "Monotheism—A Misused Word in Jewish Studies?" *JJS* 42 (1991): 1–13; Paula Fredriksen, "Mandatory Retirement: Ideas in the Study of Christian Origins Whose Time Has Come to Go," *SR* 35 (2006): 231–46, esp. 241–44; Larry Hurtado, "'Ancient Jewish Monotheism' in Hellenistic and Roman Periods." *JAJ* 4 (2013): 370–400; Richard Bauckham,

Jesus and the God of Israel (Grand Rapids, MI: Eerdmans, 2008), esp. 60–106; Nathan McDonald, *Deuteronomy and the Meaning of "Monotheism"* (FAT 2/1; Tübingen, Mohr Siebeck, 2003); Michael Mach, "The Concepts of Jewish Monotheism during the Hellenistic Period," in *Jewish Roots of Christological Monotheism: Papers from the St. Andrews Conference on Historical Origins of the Worship of Jesus*, eds. Carey C. Newman, James R. Davila, and Gladys S. Lewis (Journal for the Study of Judaism Supplement vol. 63; Leiden: Brill 1999), 21–42; Michael S. Heiser, "Monotheism, Polytheism, Monolatry, or Henotheism? Toward and Assessment of Divine Plurality in the Hebrew Bible," *BBR* 18, no. 1 (2008): 1–30.

3. See William Horbury, "Jewish and Christian Monotheism in the Herodian Age," in *Early Jewish and Christian Monotheism*, eds. Loren T. Stuckenbruck and Wendy E. S. North (JSNTSup 63; New York: T&T Clark 2004), 16–44; Fredriksen, "Mandatory Retirement"; Matthew V. Novenson, "The Universal Polytheism and the Case of the Jews," in *Monotheism and Christology in Greco-Roman Antiquity*, ed. Matthew V. Novenson (NovTestSup 180; Leiden: Brill, 2020), 32–60.

4. See, for example, Fredriksen, "Mandatory Retirement," 241–44, who has called for its "mandatory retirement."

5. Hurtado, "Ancient Jewish Monotheism," 370–400, offers a defense of such a position. For similar assessments, see Bauckham, *Jesus and the God of Israel*, 60–106; James F. McGrath, *The Only True God: Early Christian Monotheism in Its Jewish Context* (Champaign: University of Illinois Press, 2009), 2. Ruben A. Bühner, *Messianic High Christology: New Testament Variants of Second Temple Judaism* (Waco, TX: Baylor University Press, 2021), 11, comments on how the range of terms "clearly shows that the early Jewish worldview has a place for various heavenly beings. Yet the ancient sources do not give a unified classification or terminology for all those beings, and it often remains unsettled how they relate to each other."

6. For these examples and discussions of them, see E. S. Gruen, *Diaspora: Jews Amidst Greeks and Romans* (Cambridge: Harvard University Press, 2002), 122–26. Contra such conclusions, see M. H. Williams, *The Jews Among the Greeks and Romans: A Diasporan Sourcebook* (London: Bloomsbury, 1998), 148, who determines that "evidence for the involvement of real, as opposed to fictional, Jews in Roman cultural and religious life is severely limited."

7. For such an assessment, see Gruen, *Diaspora*, 122–26.

8. P. M. Casey, "Monotheism, Worship and Christological Development in Pauline Churches," in *Jewish Roots of Christological Monotheism: Papers from the St. Andrews Conference on Historical Origins of the Worship of Jesus*, eds. Carey C. Newman, James R. Davila, and Gladys S. Lewis (Journal for the Study of Judaism Supplement vol. 63; Leiden: Brill 1999), 214.

9. Casey, "Monotheism," 215.

10. James D. G. Dunn, *Did the First Christians Worship Jesus? The New Testament Evidence* (Louisville, KY: WJK, 2010), 64.

11. P. M. Casey, *From Jewish Prophet to Gentile God: The Origins and Development of New Testament Christology* (Louisville, KY: WJK, 1991), 168–78.

12. See Hurtado, "First-Century Jewish Monotheism," *JSNT* 71 (1998): 3–26; idem, *Lord Jesus Christ: Devotion to Jesus in Earliest Christianity* (Grand Rapids,

MI: Eerdmans, 2005); and idem, *One God, One Lord: Early Christian Devotion and Ancient Jewish Monotheism*, 3rd ed. (New York: Bloomsbury/T & T Clark, 2015).

13. While the primary cultic center for the worship of Israel's God was in Jerusalem, a second temple did exist in in the city of Leontopolis in Egypt. It was established in the second century BCE by a Jewish priest named Onias, under the reign of Ptolemy VI. This was a fully functioning cultic temple which offered sacrifices to the God of Israel, and it remained in use until its destruction was ordered by Vespasian in 73 CE. For discussion of this temple and its history, see Abraham Wasserstein, "Notes on the Temple of Onias at Leontopolis," *ICS* 18 (1993): 119–29. See also, E. S. Gruen, *The Construction of Identity in Hellenistic Judaism: Essays on Early Jewish Literature and History* (DCLS 29; Berlin: De Gruyter, 2016), 359–82.

14. For High Priest, see Margaret Barker, "The High Priest and the Worship of Jesus," in *Jewish Roots of Christological Monotheism: Papers from the St. Andrews Conference on Historical Origins of the Worship of Jesus*, eds. Carey C. Newman, James R. Davila, and Gladys S. Lewis (JSJSup vol. 63; Leiden: Brill 1999), 93–111; and Crispin Fletcher-Louis, "Alexander The Great's Worship of the High Priest," in *Early Jewish and Christian Monotheism*, eds. Loren T. Stuckenbruck and Wendy E. S. North (JSNTSup vol. 63; New York: T & T Clark/Continuum, 2004), 71–102. For Adam, see Fletcher-Louis, *Jesus Monotheism: Christological Origins—The Emerging Consensus*, volume 1 (Eugene, OR: Cascade, 2015); Andrei Orlov, *The Glory of the Invisible God: Two Powers in Heaven Traditions and Early Christology* (JCTCRSS 31; New York: T&T Clark/Continuum, 2019), 24–27. For Moses, see J. R. Daniel Kirk, *A Man Attested by God: The Human Jesus of the Synoptic Gospels* (Grand Rapids, MI: Eerdmans, 2016), 77–87; Orlov, *The Glory of the Invisible God*, 28–31. For Son of Man, see Fletcher-Louis, *Jesus Monotheism*, 171–205; Kirk, *A Man Attested by God*, 139–57; Adam Winn, "Identifying the Enochic Son of Man as God's Word and Wisdom," *JSP* 28.4 (2019): 290–318; Orlov, *The Glory of the Invisible God*, 10–23; Peter Schäfer, *Two Gods in Heaven: Jewish Concepts of God in Antiquity*, trans. Allison Brown (Princeton: Princeton University Press, 2020), 45–53.

15. Hurtado, *One God, One Lord*, 51–56.

16. Loren T. Stuckenbruck, "'Angels' and 'God': Exploring the Limits of Early Jewish Monotheism," in *Early Jewish and Christian Monotheism*, eds. Loren T. Stuckenbruck and Wendy E. S. North (JSNTSup 63; New York: T & T Clark 2004), 68–70.

17. See Stuckenbruck's discussion of Joseph and Aseneth 15.11–12, in which Aseneth prostrates herself before an angel; "'Angels' and 'God,'" 55.

18. Stuckenbruck, "'Angels' and 'God,'" 45–70.

19. Bauckham, *Jesus and the God of Israel*.

20. See discussion below in chapters 2, 3, and 4.

21. For additional examples, see the discussion in Kirk, *A Man Attested by God*, 84–86.

22. Bauckham, "Is 'High Human Christology' Sufficient? A Critical Response to J.R. Daniel Kirk's *A Man Attested by God*," *BBR* 27.4 (2017): 503–25.

23. For Bauckham's previous treatment of the Enochic Son of Man, see *Jesus and the God of Israel*, 15–16. For Bauckham's new assessment of this figure, see *Son of Man: Early Jewish Literature*, vol. 1 (Grand Rapids, MI: Eerdmans, 2023), 17–106.

24. See, for example, Andrew Chester, *Messiah and Exaltation: Jewish Messianic and Visionary Traditions and New Testament Christology* (WUNT 207; Tübingen: Mohr Siebeck, 2007), 24–25; and Chris Tilling, *Paul's Divine Christology* (WUNT II, 323; Tübingen: Mohr Siebeck, 2012), 20.

25. See, for example, Fredriksen, "How High Can Early High Christology Be?," in *Monotheism and Christology in Greco-Roman Antiquity*, ed. Matthew V. Novenson (NovTestSup vol. 180; Leiden: Brill, 2020), 293–320, at 294; Kirk, *A Man Attested by God*, 17–21.

26. Bauckham, "Is 'High Human Christology' Sufficient?," 514–15.

27. For a similar conclusion see Fredriksen, "How High Can Early High Christology Be?," 294 n. 4.

28. See Frances Young, "*Creatio ex Nihilo*: A Context for the Emergence of the Christian Doctrine of Creation," *SJT* 44 (1991): 139–51; Fredriksen, "How High Can Early High Christology Be?," 299–303; Gerhard May, *"Creatio ex Nihilo": The Doctrine of "Creation out of Nothing" in Early Christian Thought* (Edinburgh: T & T Clark, 1994); Henry Chadwick, *Early Christian Thought and the Classical Tradition* (Oxford: Oxford University Press, 1984), 46–47.

29. For those arguing that creation ex nihilo was at home in the late Second Temple period, see Jonathan Worthington, "*Creatio ex Nihilo* and Romans 4.17 in Context," *NTS* 62.1 (2016): 49–59; Marcus Bockmuehl, "*Creatio ex Nihilo* in Palestinian Judaism and Early Christianity," *SJT* 65.3 (2012): 253–70. For an overview of the current debate, see Gary A. Anderson and Markus Bockmuehl (eds.), *Creation Ex Nihilo: Origins, Developments, Contemporary Challenges* (Notre Dame: University of Notre Dame Press, 2018).

30. William Horbury, *Jewish Messianism and the Cult of Christ* (London: SCM, 1998); idem, "Jewish and Christian Monotheism," 16–44.

31. 1 En. 37–71.

32. Fletcher-Louis, "Alexander The Great's Worship of the High Priest," 71–102; idem, *Jesus Monotheism*.

33. Fletcher-Louis, *Jesus Monotheism,* 171–205.

34. Fletcher-Louis, "Alexander The Great's Worship of the High Priest," 71–102.

35. Stuckenbruck, *Angel Veneration and Christology: A Study in Early Judaism and in the Christology of the Apocalypse of John* (Tübingen: Mohr Siebeck, 1995); idem, "'Angels' and 'God,'" 45–70.

36. For a similar voice that notes many of these same figures participating in what are often identified as divine prerogatives, see Andrew Chester, *Messiah and Exaltation: Jewish Messianic and Visionary Traditions and New Testament Christology* (WUNT 207; Tübingen: Mohr Siebeck, 2007).

37. See William Horbury, "Jewish Christian Monotheism in the Herodian Age," in *Early Jewish and Christian Monotheism*, eds. Loren T. Stuckenbruck and Wendy E. S. North (JSNTSup 63; New York: T&T Clark 2004), 43–44.

38. *m. Sanh.* 4:5; *t. Sanh.* 8:7; *m. Ber.* 5:3 (compare w. *b. Meg.* 25a and *Ber.* 33b); *m. Meg.* 49 (compare w. *j. Meg.* 4:10 75c); *b. Hag.* 15a; b. Ber. 6b; *Mek. R. Simeon Yohai, p.* 81. *Bashalah* 15; *Mek. R. Ish. Bahodesh* 5 and *Shirta* 4; *Pesiq. Rab. Piska* 21 100b; *Tanḥ.* 8; *Sifre Deut.* 379; *Sifre Zuta Shalah* 15:30. See review and discussion of these sources in Segal, *Two Powers,* 33–146; and Schäfer, *Two Gods,* 70–133; also, see Boyarin, "Two Powers in Heaven; or, The Making of a Christian Heresy," in *The Idea of Biblical Interpretation: Essays in Honor of James L. Kugel,* eds. Hindy Najman and Judith H. Newman (Leiden: Brill, 2004), 331–70. And see our discussion of Enoch and Metatron at the end of chapter 8.

39. Segal, *Two Powers,* 260–67.

40. See, for example, McGrath, *Only True God,* 81; Orlov, *The Glory of the Invisible God*; Schäfer, *Two God's in Heaven*; Michael S. Heiser, "Co-regency in Ancient Israel's Divine Council as the Conceptual Backdrop to Ancient Jewish Binitarian Monotheism," *BBR* 26, no. 2 (2015): 195–225; Boyarin, *Border Lines*; idem, "Two Powers in Heaven"; S. R. Scott, "The Binitarian Nature of the Book of Similitudes," *JSP* 18, no. 1 (2008): 55–78.

41. Segal, *Two Powers,* 260–67.

42. Boyarin, *Border Lines,* 112–27.

43. Boyarin, *Border Lines,* 112.

44. Orvlov, *The Glory of the Invisible God,* 1–9.

45. Orvlov, *The Glory of the Invisible God,* 8–9.

46. Boyarin, *Jewish Gospels,* 158. For a similar position, see Schäfer, *Die Geburt des Judentums aus dem Geist des Christentums: Fünf Vorlesungen zur Entstehung des rabbinischen Judentums* (Tübingen: Mohr Siebeck, 2010); idem, *The Jewish Jesus: How Judaism and Christianity Shaped Each Other* (Princeton: Princeton University Press, 2012); and, idem, *Two Gods.*

47. Adiel Schremer, "Midrash, Theology, and History: Two Powers in Heaven Revisited," *Journal for the Study of Judaism* 39 (2008): 230–54, focuses on the tannaitic sources instead of the later amoraic ones in order to claim that the issue was primarily "existential" and not "theological." Even if we were to accept this distinction, we find that the point does not affect our claim that some version of the two powers paradigm was present earlier in the Second Temple period. We do agree with Schremer and others that the "theological" debate is not simply one of Jewish reactions to Christian or Gnostic groups.

48. Benjamin D. Sommer, *The Bodies of God and the World of Ancient Israel* (New York: Cambridge University Press, 2009), has argued that the fluidity that some ancient Israelites applied to the YHWH of Israel, a fluidity that allowed their God to be present in different "bodies," continued to influence Jewish traditions well into the Second Temple and rabbinic periods. While Sommer's work on ancient Israel is strong, we would contend that his treatment of the way in which the Israelite notion of divine fluidity influences later Jewish conceptions of God is indeed of greater nuance. We contend that a two powers theology could be understood as a developmental step beyond the notion of divine fluidity of ancient Israelites and a means by which later Jews explained traditions in their scriptures that reflect such notions of fluidity.

49. Cf., Bauckham, *Jesus and the God of Israel*, 17, who seems to endorse this view when he says, "Jewish writers envisage some form of real distinction within the unique identity of the one God" and that "Second Temple Jewish understanding of divine uniqueness does not define it as unitariness and does not make distinctions within the divine identity inconceivable."

50. E.g., Hurtado, *One God, One Lord*, 41, who sees Wisdom, Word, etc., as "the personified divine attributes . . . basically vivid ways of speaking of God's own powers and activities."

51. With Hugo Gressmann, *Die Religion des Judentums in späthellenistischen Zeitalter* (Handbuch zum neuen Testament 21; Tübingen: Mohr Siebeck, 1926), 342–43, "Die 'Hypostasen' sind wie die Engel Mittelwesen zwischen Gott und Welt, die sein Wirken auf die Welt ermöglichen. Sie sind nur abstrakter, schemenhafter, schwerer zu fassen, als die derben und anschaulichen Gestalten des volkstümlichen Engelglaubens. Sie erscheinen als Mitteldinge zwischen Personen und abstrakten Wesen, nicht so losgelöst von Gott wie die konkreten Engelgestalten, mehr mit seinem Wesen verschmolzen und zu ihm gehörig, aber doch wieder gesondert gedacht, seltsame Zwitterbildungen eines kindlichen, zur vollen Abstraktion noch unfähigen Denkens."

52. *Die Religion des Judentums*, 343, "Hier ist die Weisheit die weltdurchwaltende schöpferische gesetzgebende Vernunft Gottes fast eine Eigenschaft und ein Besitz oder auch das Werk Gottes doch auch wieder ein für sich bestehendes Wesen Gottes Werkmeisterin und Gehilfin Sie ist die Lehrmeisterin und Führerin der Menschen zu einem vernunftdurchwalteten gottesfürchtigen Leben und wiederum besitzen die Frommen und Gottesfürchtigen Weisheit und Einsicht Ganz anschaulich und lebendig tritt uns ihre Gestalt hier kaum zum erstenmal entworfen in den Sprüchen Salomos c 8 entgegen Es ist mehr als dichterische Symbolik und Personifikation."

53. "Hypostasen," in *Die Religion in Geschichte und Gegenwart*, 2nd ed. (Tübingen: Mohr, 1928), 2:2065: "eine halb selbständige, halb als Offenbarungsform einer höheren Gottheit betrachtete göttliche Wesenheit, die eine Personifizierung einer Eigenschaft, einer Wirksamkeit, eines Gliedes uslo, einer höheren Gottheit darstellt."

54. *Word and Wisdom: Studies in the Hypostatization of Divine Qualities and Functions in the Ancient Near East* (Lund: Håkan Ohlssons, 1947), 8.

55. *Word and Wisdom*, 104.

56. Gerhard Pfeifer, *Ursprung und Wesen der Hypostasenvorstellung im Judentum* (Stuttgart: Calwer, 1967), 14–16, offers helpful nuances for the terminology.

57. James D. G. Dunn, *Christology in the Making: A New Testament Inquiry into the Origins of the Doctrine of the Incarnation* (Grand Rapids: Eerdmans, 1980), 168.

58. Charles A. Gieschen, *Angelomorphic Christology: Antecedents and Early Evidence* (Leiden: Brill, 1998), 45.

59. R. M. M. Tuschling, *Angels and Orthodoxy: A Study in their Development in Syria and Palestine from the Qumran Texts to Ephrem the Syrian*, STNC, 40. (Tübingen: Mohr Siebeck, 2007), 93.

60. Tuschling, *Angels and Orthodoxy*, 104.

61. More could be said about Origen's influence, but it would not help the present discussion. The best introduction to this matter remains J. N. D. Kelly, *Early Christian Doctrine*, rev. ed. (San Francisco: Harper, 1978), 126–36 and 252–71. For a more

thorough treatment, see John Behr, *The Way to Nicaea: Formation of Christian Theology*, vol. 1 (Crestwood, NY: St Vladimir's Seminary Press, 2001); Behr, *The Nicene Faith: Formation of Christian Theology, Part 1*, vol. 2 (Crestwood, NY: St Vladimir's Seminary Press, 2004); and Behr, *The Nicene Faith: Formation of Christian Theology, Part 2*, vol. 2 (Crestwood, NY: St Vladimir's Seminary Press, 2004).

62. We suspect that the theological background for the term in fact offered modern New Testament scholars a positive way forward: it could be read as offering an "orthodox" interpretation (i.e., one God in three hypostases) while simultaneously being used by scholars in a way that fit the Tübingen School's paradigm of a low-to-high Christology (i.e., using hypostasis to mean personification).

63. See bibliography in Eva Günther, *Wisdom as a Model for Jesus' Ministry in the "Lament over Jerusalem"* (Matt 23, 37–39 Par. Luke 13, 34–35) (WUNT 2.513; Tübingen: Mohr Siebeck, 2020), 37–41.

64. Saul M. Olyan, *A Thousand Thousands Served Him: Exegesis and the Naming of Angels in Ancient Judaism* (Tübingen: Mohr Siebeck, 1993), 89–91, suggests the term "hypostasis" and its cognates be discarded entirely.

65. By pre-Nicene, we mean before the Nicene doctrine became normative, not before the council of 325. The term was actually used in the original Creed of Nicaea in its more ancient sense (i.e., as a synonym of "being"): the last anathema is against those who say, "that he came to be from things that were not, or from another hypostasis or substance (ἢ ἐξ ἑτέρας ὑποστάσεως ἢ οὐσίας)." (Text/trans. from Norman P. Tanner [ed.], *Decrees of the Ecumenical Councils: Nicaea I to Lateran V*, volume 1 [London and Washtington, DC: Sheed & Ward and Georgetown University Press, 1990], 5).

66. E.g., Heb 11:1.

67. We should note that ancient writers were well acquainted with the literary practice of personification (i.e., what was called *prosopopoiea* in classical rhetoric) and could explicitly describe how God spoke through a "personified" attribute or even through another "person"; cf., Philo, *Mos.* 2.187–88. The fact that Philo and others do not make such stipulations for Word, Wisdom, and other such hypostases will be important in the chapters that follow.

68. Boyarin, "The Gospel of the Memra: Jewish Binitarianism and the Prologue of John," *HTR* 94, no. 3 (2001): 257 n. 53.

69. See, for example, Gen 1; Exod 20:11; Job 38:4–11; Prov 8:22–30; Isa 40:26, 28; 42:5; 44:24; 45:12; Neh 9:6; Hos 13:4 (LXX); 2 Macc. 1:24; Add. Esth. 13:10; Bel. 5; 3 Macc. 2:3; Jub. 2; 12:4; Sib. Or. 3:20–35; 8:375; Josephus, *Ant.*, 1.155; Philo, *Mut.* 22; *Conf.* 170; *Vit. Mos.* 2.100. For texts that speak of Israel's God as the sole creator, see Isa 44:24; Philo, *Mut.* 22; *Conf.* 170; *Vit. Mos.* 2.100.

70. See, for example, Deut 10:14; 1 Chr 29:11–12; Ps 103:19; Dan 4:34–35; Add Esth 13:9–11; 16:18, 21; Bel 5; 3 Macc 2:2–3; 6:2; Wis 12:13; Sir 18:1–3; Sib. Or. 3:10; 1 En. 9:5; 84:3; 2 Bar 54:13; Josephus, *Ant.* 1.155–56; Philo, *Mut.* 22.

71. See, for example, 1 Kgs 22:19; Pss 2:4; 9:7–8; 29:10; 55:19; 93:2; 102:12; 103:19; see Bauckham 2008: 161–64.

72. In the DSS, vocalization of the divine name is punishable by excommunication from the community (1QS VI, 27-VII, 2; 1QIsaᵃ). Both Josephus and Philo suggest

strong restrictions on vocalizing the divine name (Josephus, *Ant.* 2.275–76; Philo, *Mos.* 2.114–15). For a thorough discussion of the evidence for such a practice, see Sean M. McDonough, *YHWH at Patmos: Rev. 1:4 in its Hellenistic and Early Jewish Setting* (WUNT 2/107; Tübingen: Mohr Siebeck, 1999), 58–122; Robert J. Wilkinson, *Tetragrammaton: Western Christians and the Hebrew Name of God* (Leiden: Brill, 2015), 61–64 and 79–83; and Gieschen, "The Divine Name as a Characteristic of Divine Identity in Second Temple Judaism and Early Christianity," in *Monotheism and Christology in Greco-Roman Antiquity*, ed. Matthew V. Novenson (NovTestSup 180. Leiden: Brill, 2020), 62–65.

73. For similar conclusions, see Gieschen, "The Divine Name," 65–73; Bauckham, *Jesus and the God of Israel*, 24–25.

74. See, for example, Jarl E. Fossum, *The Name of God and the Angel of the Lord* (WUNT 36; Tübingen: Mohr Siebeck, 1985); Gieschen, "The Divine Name," 81–83.

75. For further discussion and instances when the "Name" acts as a distinct agent, see our discussion in chapter 6 of this book.

76. All scripture citations are NRSV unless otherwise noted.

77. For interpreters who support this criterion, see David B. Capes, "Jesus' Unique Relationship with YHWH in Biblical Exegesis: A Response to Recent Objections," in *Monotheism and Christology in Greco-Roman Antiquity*, ed. Matthew V. Novenson (NovTestSup vol. 180. Leiden: Brill, 2020), 85–98; idem, *The Divine Christ: Paul, The Lord Jesus and the Scriptures of Israel* (Grand Rapids, MI: Eerdmans, 2018); Bauckham, *Jesus and the God of Israel*, 186–91; Hurtado, *Lord Jesus Christ*, 108–18. For an interpreter who resists, see Kirk, *A Man Attested by God*, 137–38.

78. See E. P. Sanders, *Judaism: Practices and Belief, 63 BCE to 66 CE* (Philadelphia: Trinity Press, 1992).

Chapter 2

God's Word in Second Temple Literature

The concept of God's Word features prominently in both the Hebrew scriptures and the religious and philosophic literature of Second Temple Judaism. While at times it is clear that this concept is being used merely to describe an aspect or action of Israel's God, there are many instances in which it seems to be a distinct entity with personal traits and actions of its own. Here we seek to assess the concept of God's Word in Second Temple literature. Is it merely a trait or divine attribute of Israel's God prone to being personified through vivid literary artistry? Is it merely an idiomatic means of saying "God"? Or does it reflect the belief in a distinct divine entity that is also rightly identified as a second divine power in heaven? To answer these questions, we will first survey the use of God's Word in both the scriptures as well as in Second Temple literature.

THE WORD OF GOD IN THE HEBREW SCRIPTURES

The concept of God's word (דבר; cf. the LXX use of λόγος or ῥῆμα) is ubiquitous throughout the Hebrew Bible. God creates through speaking. He speaks often to his people, including the patriarchs, judges, kings, and prophets. There are some texts that might imply that God's Word has an independent existence from God himself. For example, Psalms 33:6 states, "By the word of the LORD, the heavens were made."[1] And Psalms 107:20 says, "He sent forth his word and healed them" (cf. Ps 147:15, 18; Isa 9:8; 55:10–12).

While these examples might be interpreted as God's Word being a distinct entity, most would conclude that they are nothing more than vivid depictions of divine communication. However, at certain times it seems that God's Word might more clearly be depicted as a distinct entity, perhaps even an entity that can take on physical form. Several examples are discussed by Charles

Gieschen, with perhaps the best example coming from Genesis 15:1.[2] Here we are told that the "word of the LORD" came to Abram in a vision, and presumably, the Word speaks to Abram promising him great reward and protection (15:1). Abram responds, directing his speech to the "Sovereign LORD" (NRSV), or the "Lord GOD (יְהֹוִה אֲדֹנָי)," questioning why he has not yet been given offspring (15:2). Then again, the text claims that the "word of the LORD" came to Abram, and this time no vision is mentioned. Again the "word of the LORD" speaks, promising Abram a son of his own (15:4). Then "the word of the LORD" leads Abram outside where the dialogue continues and culminates in the sealing of the covenant between God and Abram. After Abram has divided various animals in half and set the halves opposite each other, the text describes a pot of fire and flaming torch passing through the divided animals. Within the context of the passage, that which passes through the animals could easily be identified with the Word of the Lord, which is to say the Word is physically manifest.

Certainly one could conclude that "the Word of the Lord" is simply a way of referring to a message from God that comes to Abram in a vision, and in some sense is simply another way of referring to God. However, it is also possible to see in this text a distinct entity, the Word who acts on behalf of God. In this story the "Word of the Lord" is twice described as coming to Abram, speaking to Abram, leading Abram outside; and finally the Word seems to manifest itself in the form of a pot of fire or a torch. Though not the only interpretive option for this narrative, it is easy to see how this text could lend itself to the interpretation that "Word of the Lord" was a distinct entity that in some way represents God himself.

Gieschen also notes the narrative of Samuel's call, in which "the Word of the LORD" could be understood as a distinct entity.[3] While it is clearly God that calls to Samuel (1 Sam. 3:6, 10), the narrative opens by telling the reader that the "Word of the LORD" was "rare in those days" and that visions were infrequent (3:1). The text also explains that Samuel did not yet know YHWH at the time of his calling, and the reason given is that "the word of the LORD had not yet been revealed to him." Shortly after the call narrative, the text says, "The LORD continued to appear at Shiloh, for the LORD revealed himself to Samuel at Shiloh by the word of the LORD" (3:21). Here the text could be read as making a distinction between the "Word of the Lord" and the Lord himself. The fact that the Lord is not known by Samuel because the "Word of the Lord" had not yet been revealed to Samuel may imply some distinction between the two. If such a distinction was not intended, why would the text not simply say that the Lord had not yet been revealed to Samuel? Similarly, the claim that the Lord revealed himself to Samuel by "the Word of the Lord" implies some distinction between the two. Perhaps other interpretations are possible that remove any distinction between the Lord and his "Word," but again, the text lends itself to an interpretation where the "Word of the Lord" is a distinct entity that acts as or on behalf of Israel's God.

Finally, Gieschen notes the narrative of Elijah on Mount Horeb as another example where one can perceive a distinction between the Lord and his Word.[4] In 1 Kings 19:9, we are told "the word of the LORD came to him saying, 'What are you doing here Elijah?'" After Elijah's response, "the word of the Lord" clearly replies and says, "Go out and stand on the mountain before the LORD, for the LORD is about to pass by." On the surface of this text a clear distinction exists between "the Word of the Lord" and the Lord himself. Again, other interpretations might exist that would minimize or reduce the distinction between the Lord and his Word, but as with the previous two examples, it is evident that this text provides the reader with the possibility of concluding that the Lord and the Word of the Lord are distinct.[5]

To be clear, the present argument is not that any of these texts, in their original context, seek to communicate a clear distinction between the Lord and the Word of the Lord or even reflect a known tradition of such distinction. While they may in fact do so, their possible intent is far beyond the pale of this project. The present argument is that texts existed in Hebrew scriptures that could easily be read as creating a distinction between the Lord and his Word, and that such texts could be used to establish or undergird a belief within the Second Temple period that "the Word of the Lord" was a distinct entity. Analysis of other Second Temple literature is necessary in order to determine whether any Jews of this period did in fact understand God's Word in this way.

THE WORD OF GOD IN SECOND TEMPLE RELIGIOUS TEXTS

The concept of God's Word is also quite prevalent in the religious literature of the Second Temple period. At times, it is simply used to convey divine communication, much like in the scriptures. But as in the scriptures, there are also times in which God's Word seems to take on a distinct identity. In this regard, there is certainly continuity between the scriptures and these later religious texts of the Second Temple period, but there is also clear development.

In the scriptures, the Word of God could be understood as an agent that engages God's servants (e.g., Abraham, Samuel, Elijah, etc.), and in Second Temple literature, God's "Word" could be understood to be acting in the same capacity, such as when the Word of God comes to and speaks to Enoch and Baruch (1 En. 67:1; 2 Bar. 1:1; 10:1). But this body of literature seems to present the Word of God as more than simply an agent by which God engages human servants or messengers.

While God's Word is associated with creation in the Hebrew scriptures (e.g., Ps 33:6), this function becomes more pronounced and explicit in later Second Temple literature. The Wisdom of Solomon claims that God made all things by his "[W]ord" (9:1). Similarly, the book of Jubilees 12:4 claims that God created everything by his Word (cf. Sib. Or. 3:20).[6] 4 Ezra 6:38 reads, "I said, 'O Lord, you spoke at the beginning of creation, and said on the first day, "Let heaven and earth be made," and your [W]ord accomplished the work.'"[7] And after describing the work of the third day, 4 Ezra 6:42 claims "For your [W]ord went forth, and at once the work was done." Similarly, 2 Baruch says that God's Word fixed the firmament of the world (21:4; see also 56:4).[8]

In addition to creating, God's Word is also depicted as a means through which God accomplishes various divine works and purposes in both heaven and on earth. Sirach claims that it is by God's Word (λόγος) that the sun accomplishes its task and that the universe is held together (43:5, 26). In Sirach's descriptions of the powerful deeds of Elijah, it is by God's Word that the rains of heaven were held back and by which the dead were raised (48:3, 5). In 2 Baruch, God's Word holds back angels from making themselves known (51:11). 2 Baruch also present's God's Word as sovereign, as it is by that Word that God brings about future events and to that Word that "the beginning of the ages" is subservient (54:3). In the Wisdom of Solomon, God's "all powerful [W]ord" is depicted as a sword bearing warrior leaping from heaven, where it was presumably seated on God's throne (18:15–16). It travels to earth for the purpose of bringing judgment, and it is depicted as standing on earth but reaching into heaven (18:16). Finally, the Davidic Messiah of the Psalm of Solomon accomplishes his work of judgment and restoration by the Word of God (17:36).

Certainly, one could argue (and many have) that these traditions are creative literary personifications that intend to vividly describe the work and activity of God and that they do not intend to present God's Word as a distinct hypostasis. But given that the Jewish scriptures themselves could be read as depicting the Word of God as a distinct agent of God, such a reading is certainly plausible with these texts as well. In fact, it seems in these later Jewish traditions, the scope and nature of the agency of God's Word has expanded from what is seen in the scriptures. While there is certainly a link between God's Word/speech and creation in the scriptures, this role of the Word is more frequent and explicit in these later Jewish texts. The Word's role in exercising divine sovereignty over creation and particularly the depiction of the Word as a warrior leaping from God's throne to judge the world is more developed than any depiction of God's Word found in scripture.

Not only might these traditions be read by Second Temple Jews as presenting God's Word as a distinct divine agent, but they might actually reflect a growing Jewish tradition that recognized such a figure in the Jewish scriptures, one that pushed the tradition forward through creative interpretation. Based on the examples noted above, a clear case cannot be made either way, and thus we simply note the various ways in which such traditions could be understood. However, further examination of the Word of God tradition in other Second Temple literature may prove useful in verifying the existence of Jewish interpretive communities that identified God's Word as a distinct divine agent, and thus likely would have done so in the texts cited above.

THE WORD OF GOD IN PHILO

There is no body of Jewish literature in which the Word (λόγος) of God plays a more prominent role in its understanding of God than that of Philo. The Logos[9] appears over 1,400 times in the writings of Philo and is inseparable from his understanding of the God of Israel and the way in which that God engages his creation.[10] Therefore, a comprehensive account of Philo's view of the Logos is impossible in the present project,[11] and yet we can show how Philo understands the Logos as a distinct entity, one that would fit quite well within a two powers theology. To show this, we will first offer some general observations on Philo's descriptions for the Logos, and then we will review key examples of Philo's interpretations of biblical theophanies as Logophanies. Finally, we will then examine how Philo equates the Logos with the Angel of the Lord, and show how his commentaries on the relevant scriptures help to illustrate his understanding of the relationship between the Logos and God.

Philo's Understanding of the Logos

As far as describing the Logos, we must first note how Philo claims that the transcendent God of Israel cannot be named (*Somn.* 1.230), or rather that the best one can do in naming the "Father of the universe" is to call God, ὁ ὤν, or "the one who is" (*Abr.* 1.121).[12] Similarly, Philo claims that the Logos is the one who bears the names "beginning," "name of God," and even the title "God" (*Conf.* 146; *Somn.* 1.227–30; cf. *Conf.* 41), which are not names per se, but titles that somehow relate the Logos to God. Philo calls the Logos one of God's "powers," and, "So impossible to name indeed is the Existent that not even the Potencies [or Powers] who serve Him tell us a proper name (οὕτω μέντοι τὸ ὂν ἄρρητόν ἐστιν, ὥστ᾽ οὐδὲ αἱ ὑπηρετούμεναι δυνάμεις κύριον ὄνομα ἡμῖν λέγουσι)."[13]

Another such descriptor is the title of God's "first-born Son (πρωτόγονος υἱός)."[14] This even involves a sort of royal status for the Logos, in that as the Son he reigns over all of creation, including God's angels.[15] In his reign over the heavenly bodies, he is likened to a viceroy who rules on behalf of a great king.[16]

Because the Logos, God's Son, does divine acts, Philo is even willing to declare that the Logos is a δεύτερον θεόν, a "second God" (e.g., *QG* 2.62). This title, however, is not without nuance in his thought. When calling him this, the emphasis is on the "secondary" status: "For nothing mortal can be made in the likeness of the most high One and Father of the universe but (only) in that of the second God, who is His Logos."[17] Similarly, God's Logos is the one who gives divine gifts, but only in a secondary way. When explaining Jacob's statement from Genesis 48:15–16, Philo states, "He looks on God as feeding him, not His Word; but the Angel, who is the Word, as healer of ills. This is the language of a true philosopher. He thinks it meet and right that He that is should Himself in His own Person give the principal boons, while His Angels and Words give the secondary gifts; and secondary are such as involve riddance from ills."[18] In other words, the Logos is secondary to God in beneficence.

Although the Logos is second in relation to God, it is superior when it comes to all (other?) creation.[19] He explains:

> To His Word, His chief messenger, highest in age and honour, the Father of all has given the special prerogative, to stand on the border and separate the creature from the Creator. This same Word both pleads with the immortal as suppliant for afflicted mortality and acts as ambassador of the ruler to the subject. He glories in this prerogative and proudly describes it in these words "and I stood between the Lord and you" (Deut v. 5), that is neither uncreated as God, nor created as you, but midway between the two extremes, a surety to both sides.[20]

Therefore, God and the Logos are distinct and on different levels of existence.[21] This seems to require that the Logos be understood as a separate entity of some sort.[22] Even so, Philo insists on the unique proximity the Logos has to God, even to the point that they are inseparable and veritably indistinguishable.

Philo is deeply committed to the absolute transcendence of God and the inability of creation to access God or to even comprehend God.[23] Thus, for Philo, God is only accessible through his Logos.[24] In fact, God relates to all creation through the Logos because he created all things in and by his Logos.

When it comes to creation, Philo invokes the Pythagorean-Platonic explanation for the one and the many in a way that makes the Logos the key actor. Although God is eternal and therefore his actions are simple and simultaneous, one can speak of creation according to the scripture's language of six days because creation is ordered and temporal. Just as six both results from and consists of one, two, and three, so the world's creation originated from God's eternity and yet unfolded chronologically.[25] The Logos plays a key role, according to Philo, who uses the model of an architect. An architect has an idea for a city before it is built. So God had creation in his "divine Reason (τὸν θεῖον λόγον)" before the sensible world came to be.[26] Furthermore, the Logos is a "power (δύναμις)," who makes the world, not simply an abstract concept, or an attribute of God.[27]

Another important observation can be made here. Just as the first intelligent creature, man, was made in the Logos's image, so via an argument of composition, all creation is an image of the Logos.[28] For Philo's purposes, this claim simply supports his use of Platonic logic to explain the one and the many. Additionally, this demonstrates that when Philo thinks of "man" being made in the image of "God" he assumes that the God who is speaking and creating in Genesis is the Logos.[29]

Admittedly, as Philo explicates creation, he invokes Platonism and therefore leaves open the interpretation that the Logos for him is simply a way of speaking of God's activity, and not a distinct hypostasis. The Logos is the blueprint for and the "place (τόπος)" within which God creates.[30] This language preserves the uniqueness of God, for God is the one.[31] However, such an interpretation proves incorrect, or at least insufficient, since the Logos is not only the Image and Place of the world, but he is also the world's maker. This becomes even more apparent when compared with how Philo discusses the Logos's actions in the scriptures, including but not limited to the Logos's acts of creation. In the following theophanies, which turn out to be appearances of the Logos, the same tactic is employed where God is one and yet is many in terms of his "powers."

Philo's Interpretation of Theophanies

In addition to the various ways in which Philo describes the Logos, one can see his understanding of this hypostasis in the way he interprets scriptures. In Genesis 17:1 we read where "the LORD appeared to Abram" (cf. LXX = καὶ ὤφθη κύριος τῷ Αβραμ). Philo, however, insists that this was not God as "the Cause of all (τοῦ παντὸς αἰτίου)," but instead "the Lord (κύριος)" or "the Power (δυνάμεων)" of God appeared.[32] Philo defends this exegetically with the title used in the Septuagint: "And therefore the words are 'The Lord (not 'The Existent') was seen of him' (διὸ λέγεται 'ὤφθη' οὐ τὸ ὄν, ἀλλὰ κύριος)."[33] In other words, for Philo, God subsists in (at least)[34] two "Powers" which emanate from his Logos:[35] God and the Lord.[36] The Lord is the one who judges, while God is the one who is merciful, or as Philo puts it, "the Lord and Master of the bad, the God of those who are on the way to betterment (κύριος καὶ δεσπότης, τῶν δ᾽ ἐν προκοπαῖς καὶ βελτιώσεσι θεός)."[37] As evidence for this interpretation, Philo then refers to the scene where Jacob wrestled with a "man" (Gen 32:22–32, discussed further below), noting that the man (who, it turns out, is the Logos) refuses to be named, on which Philo comments, "His Word has no name of its own (ὁ λόγος αὐτοῦ κυρίῳ ὀνόματι οὐ ῥητὸς ἡμῖν)."[38] From this fact, Philo deduces that "the Lord's" appearance in Genesis 17:1 was not God, and (implicitly) not even the Logos, but one of the two powers that emanate from the Logos.[39] This view of God is further elaborated elsewhere, which brings us to the next time the Lord appears to Abraham.

In Genesis 18 Abraham offers hospitality to three "men," who in the biblical passage turn out to be a visitation from the Lord. Philo offers a complex explanation of this theophany to say, "the single object presents to it a triple vision, one representing the reality, the other two the shadows reflected from it (τριττὴν φαντασίαν ἑνὸς ὑποκειμένου καταλαμβάνει, τοῦ μὲν ὡς ὄντος, τῶν δ᾽ ἄλλων δυοῖν ὡς ἂν ἀπαυγαζομένων ἀπὸ τούτου σκιῶν)."[40] Philo then says the two shadows, side angels, are not God: "No one, however, should think that the shadows can be properly spoken of as God (μὴ μέντοι νομισάτω τις ἐπὶ θεοῦ τὰς σκιὰς κυριολογεῖσθαι)."[41] Instead, he finds that it is the Father in the middle, and God and Lord on the sides:

> the central place is held by the Father of the Universe, Who in the sacred scriptures is called He that is (ὁ ὤν) as His proper name, while on either side of Him are the senior potencies (δυνάμεις), the nearest to Him, the creative and the kingly. The title of the former is God, since it made and ordered the All; the title of the latter is Lord (κύριος), since it is the fundamental right of the maker to rule and control what he has brought into being.[42]

Philo continues to explain how the mind at its highest state of enlightenment sees God as one, but other times sees God as three, which is to envision God's essence and God's two powers, God the creator and the Lord King.[43] Here in the Oak of Mamre scene, Philo does not explicitly mention the Logos, which is unusual for him with theophanies in general, and which would be especially puzzling for this scene since he inserted claims about the Logos in the previous passage about two other theophanies.[44] As it turns out, the Logos is, in fact, in view, but this is not self-evident in this passage without comparing his comments to other places in his oeuvre since Philo returns to speaking of the divine "powers" to explain how God is one, and yet pluriform in some way. When explaining why only two went to Sodom (Gen. 19:1), and not three, Philo explains that it would be unfitting for God himself to go deliver condemnation. Instead he sent the other two, "This is the practice, I think, of kings also, who imitate the divine nature. They are their own agents in granting boons, but employ others to enforce punishment (οὗτό μοι δοκοῦσι καὶ τῶν βασιλέων οἱ μιμούμενοι τὴν θείαν φύσιν πράττειν, τὰς μὲν χάριτας δι' ἑαυτῶν προτείνοντες, τὰς δὲ τιμωρίας δι' ἑτέρων βεβαιοῦντες)."[45] In other words, these two "angels" (as the text calls them), are for Philo two Powers, named "God and the Lord," and they are distinct from the oneness of God and thus are other (ἑτέρων) in some way.

This form of a two powers paradigm is used again for the scene when "the Lord" appeared to Isaac (cf. Gen. 26:2). Philo questions why sometimes God is "the Lord God," but in this case only "the Lord" is named. The titles, he explains, correspond to God's "two powers (δυεῖν δυνάμεων)," which in turn correspond to God's "governance and kindness (ἡγεμονίας καὶ εὐεργεσίας)."[46]

Likewise, when explicating Jacob's dream, he once again uses a two powers paradigm. In Genesis 31:11–13 the Lord[47] speaks to Jacob in a dream, and references the place which Jacob called Bethel, or the House of God (cf. Gen. 28:11–22). Speaking of that house (or "place" /τόπος, as it is called in the Septuagint), God says, "I am the God who appeared to you in the place of God (ἐγώ εἰμι ὁ θεὸς ὁ ὀφθείς σοι ἐν τόπῳ θεοῦ)" (Gen. 31:13LXX), Philo asks if this reveals "two gods (δύο . . . θεοί),"[48] This translation does not capture well the fact that here and elsewhere Philo speaks of the Logos as the "Place."[49] It would probably be better to read this to say, "I am *the* God who appeared to you *through* the Τόπος [i.e., Logos] of God." Philo explains that the use of the article designates God proper (ὁ θεὸς), while the lack of an article in the second instance (ἐν τόπῳ θεοῦ) refers in this case to "the chief Word (τὸν πρεσβύτατον . . . λόγον)."[50] In other words, Philo believes the God who speaks to Jacob is distinct from the one whom Jacob saw at Bethel, the Place of god (lacking the article), the latter being the Logos. Philo will go on to discuss anthropomorphisms, including times when God appears "in the likeness of angels (ἐν σώματι ἀγγέλοις),"[51] which suggests that he understands the Logos to be one of them, God in the appearance of the warrior Angel of the Lord.[52] Thus, the Logos is not really a second god in a truly polytheistic (or at least ditheistic) understanding. One could, therefore, interpret Philo to say the Logos is nothing more than God's appearance, merely a Platonic emanation, an avatar of sorts, but not actually God himself. Such a conclusion once again proves inadequate, which is evident when we turn to other theophanies that Philo explains in terms of the tension between the one God and God's manifested "powers."

One of the most important theophanies for Philo, if not the Jewish tradition as a whole, is the scene in Exodus 3 where the Lord appears to Moses in the burning bush and reveals by what name God should be called.[53] The one who self-identifies as "He that is (ὁ ὤν)" in Exodus 3:14 is the Most High God, and yet God reveals this self-designation through the one who actually appeared and spoke these words to Moses, the Angel or Logos:

In the midst of the flame was a form of the fairest beauty, unlike any visible object, an image supremely divine in appearance, refulgent with a light brighter than the light of fire. It might be supposed that this was the image of Him that is (εἰκόνα τοῦ ὄντος εἶναι); but let us rather call it an angel or herald, since, with a silence that spoke more clearly than speech, it employed as it were the miracle of sight to herald future events.[54]

To be sure, the Logos who appeared in the burning bush is still distinct from "He that is (ὁ ὤν)."[55] Who was it, then, who appeared to Moses and claimed to be the "I Am"? It seems that God and his Logos act indistinguishably, except that God does not appear while his Logos does. God claims to be the "I Am" and Moses both sees and hears the Logos say these words.[56] This conclusion is further corroborated when God, speaking through his Angel, claims to be the God who had earlier appeared to Abraham, Isaac, and Jacob (Exod 3:15),[57] because Philo continues to see the Logos as the one who appeared to those earlier patriarchs.

The next significant theophany for our discussion involves any time when "the Lord" dwells in the tabernacle or temple, sitting on the ark of the covenant between the two cherubim. Philo equates these theophanies with the three "Men" who appeared to Abraham.[58] What is more, they represent a parallel way of speaking about the Logos. Commenting on Exodus 25:22,[59] Philo equates the two cherubim as God's two "powers" (*Cher.* 28; cf. 25). Then he somewhat ambiguously states, "while God is indeed one, His highest and chiefest powers are two, even goodness and sovereignty (κατὰ τὸν ἕνα ὄντως ὄντα θεὸν δύο τὰς ἀνωτάτω εἶναι καὶ πρώτας δυνάμεις ἀγαθότητα καὶ ἐξουσίαν)."[60] In other words, Philo believes that God sits invisibly between the two cherubim, or two powers. Those two are "God" the Power of goodness while the "Lord" is the power of sovereignty or kingship.[61] Here again, one must remember that both of these are either emanations from, or at least angels ruled by, the Logos, as can be seen when Philo describes the ark of the covenant.

When describing the ark of the covenant in detail, Philo makes it clear that it is the Logos, and not God per se, seated above "powers." In this case, there is, however, a third power: the two cherubim represent the powers of creativity and kingship (as in the prior example), while this time the lid represents the power of mercy.[62] Then in still another parallel case, where instead of the ark, a chariot is depicted (or, perhaps with the ark envisioned as God's chariot; cf. Ezekiel 1; cf. Psalm 104:3), Philo further explains how God is the One who speaks from the backseat, as it were, but it is explicitly the Logos seated above the other powers driving: "while the Word is the charioteer of the Powers, He Who talks is seated in the chariot, giving directions to the charioteer for the right wielding of the reins of the Universe (ἡνίοχον μὲν εἶναι τῶν δυνάμεων τὸν λόγον, ἔποχον δὲ τὸν λαλοῦντα, ἐπικελευόμενον τῷ ἡνιόχῳ τὰ πρὸς ὀρθὴν τοῦ παντὸς ἡνιόχησιν)."[63] Here the Logos has separate agency, but there is a close connection to God who directs it. This case is noteworthy because the Logos is not simply an aspect of God or a representation of God. Philo depicts him as a distinct figure holding the reigns while obeying God's directions.[64]

In sum, when referring to God's appearances as the Logos flanked by two powers, Philo varies to some extent in how he speaks of God, the Logos, and the Two (or more) Powers when expositing these biblical theophanies.[65] Even so, there is an underlying consistent rationale that would systematize Philo's thought.[66] This helps to establish that the Logos is in some sense distinct from God, an agent and not just an emanation.[67] While some scholars still insist that Philo's Logos is simply a personification of God's activity in the world,[68] too often the evidence is based on the general view that Philo's Jewish beliefs require him to hold to a strict monotheism, or oneness of Israel's God.[69] This, however, is to decide a priori what should be found in the evidence itself. Margaret Barker, for example, insists that the Logos is a distinct hypostasis, a second god, and this is especially noteworthy as something Philo could not have said, if it were not already present in his Jewish community.[70] Other scholars admit that even though Philo occasionally offers caveat's about God's oneness, the matter is still ambiguous in Philo since he so frequently speaks of the Logos as a separate entity.[71] Philo could simply be inconsistent and unsystematic.[72] Or, Philo could develop his ideas over time, and shift from a ditheistic or binitarian view of the Logos to a more strict monotheism—or vice versa.[73] We, however, think there is sufficient evidence to see a more consistent rationale behind Philo's view of the Logos. Sometime God and the Logos are so connected as to be left undifferentiated in Philo's discussion. Even so, the two lower powers of "God" and "Lord," often appearing as the two cherubim or flanking angels, are in a way a reflection of the God who always speaks and acts through his second power, the Logos. When speaking in Platonistic terms, Philo seems to say these are all simply emanations or refractions of the one God, which has allowed some scholars to continue to see the Logos as simply a personification in Philo. To see that Philo has something more in mind, let us briefly see how he identifies the Logos as the Angel of the Lord.[74]

Philo's Logos as Angel in Relation to the One (and the Many)

One special case of a theophany is when Philo speaks of the Logos as the Angel of the Lord.[75] We will further introduce the background of this concept from the scriptures themselves, below, in chapter 5. For now, let us focus on what Philo's treatment of this figure indicates about his view of the Logos, and the Logos's relationship to God. The Logos is God's chief or "eldest" Angel.[76] This makes the Logos-Angel a distinct entity sent by God and acting on God's behalf. We have already established how Philo reads the difference between the titles of "the Lord God" and "God" to say that there are "two powers (δυεῖν δυνάμεων)" in heaven.[77] Here, we can examine how Philo can conveniently, and with virtually no preliminary explanation, invoke the concept of two powers as a way of labelling the relationship of the Logos-Angel to the one God.[78]

To return to Philo's explanation of Jacob's dream (Gen. 31:11–13),[79] we noted how the Lord's statement, "I am the God who appeared to you in the place of God (ἐγώ εἰμι ὁ θεὸς ὁ ὀφθείς σοι ἐν τόπῳ θεοῦ)" (Gen. 31:13LXX)[80] prompted Philo to asks if there are "two gods (δύο . . . θεοί)."[81] Philo insists that there are not actually two gods because the use of the article designates God proper, while the lack of an article refers in this case to "the chief Word (τὸν πρεσβύτατον . . . λόγον)."[82] Here it must be remembered that in Genesis 31:11, it is "the Angel of God (הָאֱלֹהִים מַלְאַךְ/ὁ ἄγγελος τοῦ θεοῦ)" who is speaking to Jacob. This is important since Philo next discusses anthropomorphisms as God's accommodation for the weak-minded, not God's own form.[83] Such a caveat could suggest that he understands the Logos to be one of these anthropomorphisms, God in the appearance of the warrior Angel of the Lord, not really a second god.[84] However, it is not so simple, as seen when he further explains his view when he shifts to the scene where the Angel of the Lord appears to Hagar.

When God appears to Hagar as the Angel of the Lord (in Gen. 16:13), he must condescend to her epistemological level. Using ethnocentric logic, he explains that because Hagar is "Egyptian by descent she was not qualified to see the supreme Cause (οὐ γὰρ ἦν ἱκανὴ τὸ πρεσβύτατον ἰδεῖν αἴτιον, γένος οὖσα τῶν ἀπ᾽ Αἰγύπτου)."[85] In other words, some, like Hagar, mistake "the image of God, His [A]ngel the Word, as His very self (οὕτως καὶ τὴν τοῦ θεοῦ εἰκόνα, τὸν ἄγγελον αὐτοῦ λόγον)."[86] Notice once again that the Angel is the Logos, and yet not actually God as God really is. Instead, Philo further explains, the appearance of God as the Angel is like the sun's rays or the moon's halo.[87] This is an explanation Philo offers elsewhere.

In his *Questions and Answers on Genesis*, Philo again comments on Hagar's vision of the Angel of the Lord. As to her belief that the Angel was God, Philo elaborates:

> But it was not strange (for her) to believe that the angel was God. For those who are unable to see the first cause naturally suffer from an illusion; they believe that the second is the first. (They are like those) who have poor eyesight and

are not able to see the corporeal form which is in heaven, (namely) the sun, and believe that the rays which it sends to the earth are this itself.[88]

Here Philo makes a distinction between the Angel and God, and yet this may be because the Angel is a "power," like the sun's rays. This explanation is odd in that it does not seem to address the fact that the Angel seems to be an actual person or agent in the Genesis narrative, thus raising the possibility that the Angel is not actually a distinct agent. The simplest explanation for Philo's description is that his Platonism enables him to dismiss such anthropomorphisms and insist on God's ultimate oneness as the "first cause."[89] And yet, Philo offers more content to his claims.

It is interesting how his analogy of the sun and its rays shifts in the next lines. After restating how "the angel appeared like God," Philo offers another analogy. Instead of light he uses a water metaphor: "A well has two things, both depth and a source."[90] Both metaphors (sun-rays and font-pool) are used by later Christian writers to explain how the Father and Son relate as one and yet remain distinct.[91] For Philo's own context, however, these simply seem to enable to him to shift from the "one" to the "many" as needed when speaking of God and God's appearances. Much later, he returns to speaking of the Angel of the Lord as if he were a separate entity.

Commenting on Abraham's command to his servant to find a wife for Isaac, an act which he says will be guided by an angel (Gen. 24:7), Philo distinguishes between the prophetically "uttered word (προφορὰν λόγος)" of Abraham and the Angel himself, which is "another [W]ord (ἄλλον λόγον)."[92] Both are spoken forth by God, but while Abraham's word is an inspired speech, the Angel is a distinct agent. While Philo is clearly indebted to Platonism, one can still see his Jewish tradition guiding his accommodation, particularly when it comes to using the term *Logos* instead of *Nous*. This shift, according to Hannah, represents "a tradition in Alexandrian Judaism which was attributing a certain independence to God's Word."[93]

While the instances where Philo explains the Angel of the Lord as not truly a second god but as a second "power" appear to alleviate any tension in Philo, there are still other considerations.[94] For one thing, when Philo first addresses the dilemma of the angels and God, he invokes the Platonic solution to the one and the many, but in a way that has ramifications for more than just the Logos-Angel.[95] In fact, his logic applies to all intelligent entities, which is to say all angels and even all human souls.[96] This can be seen in the first instance when this issue arises in his *On Dreams*. When Philo outlines why in the highest form of knowledge humans perceive the one God but in lower forms of knowledge they perceive angels, he again uses the analogy of sun and sunrays: the lower rays are the "immortal 'words' which it is customary to call angels (ἀθανάτοις λόγοις, οὓς καλεῖν ἔθος ἀγγέλους)."[97] It should be noted that these are much more than extensions or representations of God.[98] They are distinct entities just as much as human souls are.[99] The difference is that the angels never veered from God in their desires. As such, they are:

> of perfect purity and excellence, gifted with a higher and diviner temper, that have never felt any craving after the things of earth, but are viceroys of the Ruler of the universe, ears and eyes, so to speak, of the great king, beholding and hearing all things. These are called "demons" by the other philosophers, but the sacred record is wont to call them "angels" or messengers, employing an apter title, for they both convey the biddings of the Father to His children and report the children's need to their Father.[100]

In other words, Philo's language about the higher and lower knowledge is his adaptation of Plato's solution to the problem of the "one and the many."[101] As such, the angels, including the Logos-Angel, is very much the "One" as known in lower emanations—as are human souls.[102] This claim does not take away from the fact that the Logos, other angels, and human souls are equally "the many" for Philo, and as such the Logos is as much a distinct entity as any other intelligent being.

Philo's Logos and the Heavenly Adam/Man

In Philo's exegesis of the creation accounts in Genesis and God's creation of the first man in particular, there are four points at which Philo distinguishes between the creation of two Adams rather than one.[103] One Adam is that which is indeed formed in the image of God.[104] This Adam is incorporeal, incorruptible, immortal, an idea, and not perceptible to the senses.[105] Philo refers to this Adam as the "heavenly man."[106] In contrast to this Adam/man is the Adam formed from the clay, who is perceptible to the senses, corporeal, a combination of body and soul, corruptible, and mortal.[107] In contrast to the "heavenly man," Philo refers to this Adam as the "earthly man."[108] While it has been argued that Philo is not always consistent with these distinctions and that he uses these concepts in different ways and for different purposes, it seems quite clear that in Philo there is a well-established concept of a "heavenly man/Adam" and an "earthly man/Adam"; the former of which is made in the image of God, is incorporeal, is imperceptible to the senses, and immortal, while the latter is not made in God's image (at least not fully or directly), is perceptible to the senses, and is mortal.[109]

Philo's Heavenly Man and the Logos: Distinct and Shared Identities

Philo's articulation of both a heavenly and earthly man has received significant attention from New Testament interpreters, as it has been proposed by many as a possible background for Paul's use of similar concepts in 1 Corinthians 15:45–49. Yet, relatively little attention has been given to the close connection that exists between the concept of Philo's heavenly Adam and the Logos. The connection can first be established through the concept of God's image. Philo refers to the Logos as God's image (*Fug.* 101; *Leg.* 3.96) and that "nothing mortal can be made in the likeness of the most High One and Father of the universe but (only) in that of the second God, who is His Logos" (*QG* 2.62). When such claims regarding the Logos are brought together with the claims that the "heavenly Adam" was made in God's image (*Opif.* 134; *Leg.* 1.31), a close bond between the two is established. Additional texts present the Logos as the archetype for the heavenly Adam. Consider the following:

> Bezalel means, then, "in the shadow of God"; but God's shadow is His Word, which he made use of like an instrument, and so made the world. But this shadow, and what we may describe as the representation, is the archetype for further creations. For just as God is the Pattern of the Image, to which the title of Shadow has just been given, even so the Image becomes the pattern of other beings, as the prophet made clear at the very outset of the Law-giving by saying, "And God made the man after the Image of God" implying that the Image had been made such as representing God, but that the man was made after the Image when it had acquired the force of a pattern.[110]

And additionally: "But the man made in accordance with (God's) form is intelligible and incorporeal and a likeness of the archetype, so far as this is visible. And he is a copy of the original seal. And this is the Logos of God, the first principle, the archetypal idea, the pre-measurer of all things" (*QG* 1.4) Here, the heavenly man is a copy of the "original seal," which Philo explicitly identifies as the Logos.

From this close connection between the heavenly Adam and the Logos, a four-level scale for creation of the first man is evident, one in which the Logos is the image of God, the heavenly Adam/man is the image of the Logos, and the earthly Adam/man is the image of the heavenly.[111] Such an understanding seems quite clear in the two texts presented here. Yet, there are times when Philo seems to present a three-level scale for the creation of the first man rather than a four-level scale. The following offers a good example: "for the Creator, we know, employed for its making no pattern taken from among created things, but solely, as I have said, His own Word. It is on this account that he says that man was made in the likeness and the imitation of the Word, when the Divine Breath was breathed into his face" (*Opif.* 139). In the text's larger context, it is quite clear that the man being described is the earthly man not the heavenly man, and thus, in this text the earthly man is patterned after the Logos. Thus, the three-level scale is God-Logos-Earthly Man. A similar three-level scale may be present just five verses earlier:

> By this also he shows very clearly that there is a vast difference between the man thus formed (the earthly man) and the man (the heavenly man) that came into existence earlier after the image of God: for the man so formed is an object of sense-perception, partaking already of such or such quality, consisting of body and soul, man or woman, by nature mortal; while he that was after the (Divine) image was an idea or type or seal, an object of thought (only), incorporeal, neither male nor female, by nature incorruptible.[112]

Here, the three levels appear to be God-Heavenly Man-Earthly Man. It is possible that the reference to the "image of God" may be for Philo a reference to the Logos, and if so, a four-level schema is present. Yet, this is uncertain. If the three-level reading is correct, then an interesting parallel emerges between this text and the three-level model noted above. That parallel could naturally leave the reader with the conclusion that the Logos and the heavenly man are one in the same rather than two distinct entities, as both seem to occupy the same middle place in the respective three-level scales.

Yet, additional texts in Philo more firmly support a shared identity between the Logos and the heavenly man. There are three texts of particular importance, all of which come from the same work of Philo, *On the Confusion of Languages*.[113] Here we will work through them in the order they appear.

In discussing the origins of the sons of Jacob (Gen 42:11), Philo says the following:

> And therefore when I hear those who say "We are all sons of one man, we are peaceful," I am filled with admiration for the harmonious concert which their words reveal. "Ah! my friends," I would say, "how should you not hate war and love peace, you have enrolled yourselves as children of the one and the same Father, who is not mortal but immortal—God's Man (ἄνθρωπον θεοῦ; man of God), who being the Word (Logos) of the Eternal must needs himself be imperishable."[114]

In this text, Philo speaks of a "man of God," who he specifically identifies as the Logos, from whom the sons of Jacob are descended. While the immediate context may lead one to conclude that the "man of God" is Jacob/Israel (as the sons of Jacob are indeed all descended from him), such an identification is uncommon in Philo.[115] Also, while at times human/earthly figures in Israel's scripture function like the Logos, (i.e., little logoi), they are not identified as ὁ λόγος τοῦ θεοῦ (the Word of God). Instead, a reference to Adam seems possible here, as Adam would indeed be regarded as the father of the sons of Jacob. The descriptor of "immortal" would also fit better with the heavenly Adam as conceived by Philo than it would Jacob or any other human within the Philonic corpus. If this identification is correct, then the heavenly Adam would here be explicitly identified as the Logos by Philo. At this point, we grant that while an Adam interpretation has much in its favor, it remains uncertain. What cannot be denied is that here Philo equates a "man of God" with the Logos, with the question remaining, who is that man? The subsequent passages, within the same text, present a similar equation and do so in an explicit Adamic context. Thus, such texts strengthen the Adamic interpretation of the "man of God" proposed here. The next relevant text contains Philo's analysis of a man described in Zechariah 6:12:

> "Behold a man whose name is rising," strangest of titles, surely, if you suppose that the being composed of soul and body is here described. But if you suppose that it is that Incorporeal one, who differs not a whit from the divine image, you will agree that the name of "rising" assigned to him quite truly describes him. For that man is the eldest son, whom the Father of all raised up, and elsewhere calls him His first-born, and indeed the Son thus begotten followed the ways of his Father, and shaped the different kinds, looking to the archetypal patterns which that Father supplied.[116]

Here, Philo's description of this man clearly draws on the earthly man and heavenly man dichotomy that he has outlined elsewhere (see passages noted above). The earthly man is that composed of both soul and body (*Opif.* 134) while the heavenly man is incorporeal (*Opif.* 134). The man of Zechariah 6:12 is, according to Philo, clearly the heavenly man. While Philo's subsequent description of this man does not explicitly reference the Logos, he uses descriptors that he uses elsewhere to describe the Logos. Thus, these descriptors seem to strongly suggest that here Philo is identifying the heavenly man as the Logos. At many points, Philo refers to the father/son relationship of God and his Logos, and he specifically refers to the Logos both as God's eldest and first-born.[117] Philo also claims this man does not differ in any way from the "image of God," a concept that Philo regularly equates to the Logos itself.[118] In addition to these common descriptors that are used for the Logos, the heavenly man also shares functions attributed by Philo to the Logos. Here this heavenly man is said to have "shaped the different kinds" and done so by using the archetypal patterns given by God. This function seems to be none other than serving as an active agent of God in creation, a role that Philo frequently attributes to the Logos.[119] In light of this evidence, it seems an unavoidable conclusion that, although Philo does not explicitly identify this heavenly man with the Logos, he certainly intends just such an identification. In the next text, Philo offers an explicit description of the Logos:

> But if there be any as yet unfit to be called a Son of God, let him press to take his place under God's First-born, the Word (Logos), who holds the eldership among the angels, their ruler as it were. And many names are his, for he is called, "the Beginning," the Name of God, and His Word, and the Man after His image.[120]

It is noteworthy that in the previous passage (*Conf.* 62), Philo referred to the heavenly man as God's first-born, and here he uses the same identification for the Logos, even further supporting the case for their shared identity. Also noteworthy is this passage's identification of the Logos as "the Man after his image (ὁ κατ' εἰκόνα ἄνθροπος)." The reference to a man after/according to an image, presumably God's own image, is surely an Adamic reference, namely, Philo's heavenly Adam. Thus, it seems in this text that Philo is claiming that the Logos is rightly called (and so identified as) the heavenly man. When read in concert with the previously analyzed texts (*Conf.* 41 and 62–63), the accumulative case that Philo, in *On the Confusion of Languages*, equates the Logos with the heavenly man is quite strong.[121]

Objections to a Shared Identity between the Heavenly Man and Logos

What then is to be made of the places where Philo appears to differentiate between the Logos and the heavenly man (e.g., *QG* 1.4)? Do such instances preclude the analysis offered here? In his classic treatment of Philo's "heavenly man," A. J. M Wedderburn believes that they do preclude such a conclusion. Even after considering the same texts analyzed here and in many instances coming to similar results, Wedderburn contends that because Philo elsewhere presents the heavenly man as being made in the image of the Logos, it cannot be that Philo understands the two entities to be one in the same.[122] Contra Wedderburn, we contend the existence of texts in which Philo makes a clear distinction between the heavenly man and Logos need not make null and void texts in which the two are understood to have a shared identity. Inconsistencies in Philo are quite common and widely recognized. They can exist for a variety of reasons: change in Philo's own thought (early vs. late Philo), change in Philo's exegetical approach (e.g., literal vs. allegorical or allegorical vs. ethical), change in Philo's audience, or perhaps simply a misunderstanding on the part of Philo's modern readers (i.e., only an apparent inconsistency). Here, a change in Philo's own thinking could be evident. While both the four-level scale (God-Logos-Heavenly Man-Earthly

Man) and the three-level scale (God-Logos/Heavenly Man-Earthly Man) reflect Platonic thought, the former appears to be more thoroughgoing in that thought than the latter. This may suggest that the four-level scale developed from the three-level scale, development that resulted from a more rigorous application of Platonic thought to a previously held position. Disentangling the identities of the Logos and Heavenly Man seems to be the more natural Platonic movement than collapsing their distinction. Thus, it is quite possible that Philo began with a tradition in which the two entities shared an identity, but as a result of Platonic influence, Philo came to see them as distinct. Yet, development in thought is not the only explanation. It is also possible that Philo's intended audience might offer an explanation. Philo might collapse the identities of the Logos and heavenly man for readers who are familiar with a tradition in which the two share an identity, or he might split the two into separate entities for an audience that would have difficulty comprehending their unity. For the purposes of the present study, the specific explanation of the two different Heavenly Man/Logos schema's is not ultimately important. What is important is that the existence of a four-level scale in Philo need not lead to the conclusion that a three-level scale could not be communicated by Philo.

Wedderburn also objects to equating the Logos and heavenly man on the basis that the former is often depicted in Philo as a cosmic entity that is God's agent through which God brings about the cosmos itself while the latter lacks such cosmic dimensions and functions.[123] To solve the problem, Wedderburn proposes that in these passages, Philo is not using Logos in the sense of the cosmic agent of God that brings about the created order, but rather the Logos which is equated with immanent reason. Yet, the very texts being analyzed resist the conclusion that Philo is speaking of Logos that is immanent reason rather than the cosmic entity that is God's agent in creation. It is the cosmic Logos that Philo identifies as his first-born and the "image of God," and it is that Logos to which Philo equates the heavenly man (in *Conf.* 1.62–63). In the same text, the heavenly man appears to be engaged in the very act of creation using God's archetypal patterns, a function of none other than the cosmic Logos. In the same text in which Philo explicitly equates the Logos with "the man according to God's image," he also equates the Logos to the very name of God and identifies him as the one who has eldership over God's angels. Such identifications surely belong to the cosmic Logos and not merely the logos as immanent reason. In our estimation, the arguments offered by Wedderburn against equating the Logos with the heavenly man in *On the Confusion of Language* are easily surmountable, and thus the most natural and defensible reading of Philo in these texts is one that equates the Logos with the heavenly man. This shared identity between the Logos and a heavenly man in Philo has significant implications for later figures we will consider, particularly figures like the Son of Man and Melchizedek. If Philo can understand the Logos in terms of a human figure, it sets an important point of comparison regarding what is possible for other Second Temple authors.

CONCLUSIONS ON PHILO'S LOGOS

In conclusion, Philo treats the Logos as an independent agent acting on behalf of God and yet one who at times appears to be God.[124] When the question arises as to whether this is a "second god," the complex answer is that the Logos is divine and so a δεύτερος θεός, and yet it is preferable to speak of the Logos as a second "power." Thus, Philo can easily accommodate a Platonic explanation of the one and the many wherein the Logos is one of the many manifestations of the One. Even so, this does little to alleviate that tension when considering the Logos as the Angel of the Lord, since throughout Philo's oeuvre he speaks of this Angel as if he were an independent entity, as he does of every other angelic and human being. For Philo, the Logos is as much a distinct entity as any angel or soul, and yet this figure has a special status in that he acts as God himself and is even, at times, interchangeable with God in Philo's commentaries. It is likely that some form of a two powers paradigm may be present in his day that enables him to place the Logos both within the One God and yet see him as distinct, an agent of God. Regardless, the Logos is more than just a personification of God. He is a distinct person or agent, who acts as a second divine power. Additionally, we noted that Philo also connects this second divine power with a human identity by equating the Logos with the notion of a heavenly Adam/man. Such a connection between the Logos and the image of a human finds continuity in the connection Philo sees between the Logos and the Angel of the Lord, who often appears in the Hebrew scriptures as a human. While it is tempting to assume that Philo is an outlier in Second Temple Judaism (given the influence of Platonism, among other things), we will see that Philo is, in fact, not at all alone in speaking of God's Word in these ways.

THE WORD OF GOD IN THE TARGUMS

The Aramaic Targums are Aramaic paraphrases of the Hebrew Bible. They are the product of paraphrasing the Hebrew scriptures, when read in the synagogues, into the common language of Palestine, Aramaic. This practice may date back to the Persian period, but the traditions that emerged from this practice were not written down until much later.[125] The practice seems to have begun in Palestine, and was initially oral in nature.[126] Though the date at which a written Targum emerged is uncertain, many place this event within the first century CE.[127] At some point, a version of this Targum became prominent in Babylonian Judaism. It was standardized, authorized, and became an official text for many Jews. These official Aramaic paraphrases are recorded in Targum Onkelos, which paraphrases the entire Torah, and Targum Jonathan, which paraphrases the Prophets. The language of these texts reflects Aramaic that seems to predate 135 CE, and their official use within Judaism was established by the third century C.E..[128] While these official Targums were being used in Babylon, it seems the targumaic tradition was much less fixed in Palestine, with Palestinian targumaic traditions that were distinct from the official Targum Onkelos circulating and developing.[129] These traditions fall under the category known as Palestinian Targum, and they are preserved in Pseudo-Jonathan, Fragmentary Targum, the Cairo Geniza Fragments, and Neofiti 1. Of these four witnesses to the Palestinian Targum, only Pseudo-Jonathan and Neofiti 1 are complete texts. While there is certainly commonality between these texts, they often diverge significantly, both from each other and from the established tradition of Onkelos. Estimations of the dates of these various expressions of the Palestinian Targum vary widely. Pseudo-Jonathan, for example, has been dated by some to the seventh century and by others to the fourth—it is regarded by some to contain both the earliest and latest targumaic readings.[130] Of the Palestinian Targum texts, most regard Neofiti 1 as the earliest, with some dating it as early as the first century CE and others dating as late as the fourth century. But regardless of the date at which these written traditions were composed, most agree that the origins of at least some of the traditions in these texts could be, and likely are, much earlier. Thus, most interpreters of these targumaic traditions would agree that they include traditions that find their origin in the Second Temple period, even though there is little agreement as to which traditions find such early origins and as to how to determine a tradition's date of origin.

In light of this information, using the targumaic tradition to assess conceptions of God's Word in the Second Temple period presents difficulties. For the moment, we will leave these difficulties aside and simply consider significant depictions of God's Word in the targumaic tradition. At a later point, we will consider the relevance of these depictions for understanding the ways in which God's Word could be understood in the Second Temple period.[131]

According to Targumaic scholar Martin McNamara, "the Word of the Lord" (or *memra* of the Lord in Aramaic)[132] is "the designation for God most characteristic of all the Targums."[133] The phrase is found a significant 178 times in the official Babylonian Targum Onkelos, but in the Palestinian Targums its frequency almost doubles.[134] In Pseudo-Jonathan, the phrase is found 322 times, often used to paraphrase references to YHWH in the Hebrew text.[135] It functions similarly in Neofiti 1, where it appears 312 times, but in the marginal notes retained in the text of Neofiti 1 the phrase appears a staggering 636 times.[136] These marginal notes are almost exclusively commenting on places in the text where the original paraphrase has maintained the reading of YHWH from the Hebrew text, and thus the notes seem to be directing the reader to either understand or at least read these paraphrases as "the Memra" of YHWH rather than YHWH. It is the presentation of the the Memra of the Lord in Neofiti 1, likely the earliest Palestinian targumaic tradition, that we will consider below.

Throughout the Palestinian Targum Neofiti 1, "the Memra of the LORD" is the primary agent of divine action. In Genesis 1, it is almost exclusively "the Memra" and not YHWH that creates the world. "The Memra of the LORD" speaks creation into existence and the text regularly claims that the events of creation occur according to decree of "his Memra." In the few occasions in which the paraphrased text maintains the Hebrew reading of the divine name, the marginal notes of Neofiti 1 direct the reader to read the text as "the Memra of the LORD" instead. Later, the tradition of God's Memra creating is found in the story of Melchizedek, where both Melchizedek and Abraham claim that the "Most High God" created the world by "his Memra." Human interactions with God in the Hebrew text are almost always described, either in the paraphrase itself or the marginal notes, as interactions with "the Memra of the LORD" or "the name of the Memra of the LORD." In Genesis 3:8, Adam and Eve hear the "Memra of the LORD" walking in the Garden of Eden. In the establishment of the Noahic covenant, YHWH makes the covenant between his Memra and creation, rather than between himself and creation (Gen 9). In the Abrahamic visitations from "the LORD," it is "the Memra of the LORD" that appears to Abraham rather than YHWH. Whereas YHWH speaks directly to Moses from the burning bush in the Hebrew text of Exodus 3,[137] in the Aramaic paraphrase, it is "the Memra of the LORD" that speaks.[138] Instead of YHWH himself accompanying Moses on his return to Egypt, God tells Moses he will be with him by means of "his Memra." God's Memra is depicted as dwelling in the land with God's people and protecting them from plague (Exod 8:18). Whereas in the Hebrew text God appears to Moses on mount Sinai in a cloud, in the paraphrase, it is God's Memra rather than God himself that is revealed (Exod 19:9). Additionally, God's Memra seems to be the object of worship, as altars are built and prayers are offered to "the Memra of the LORD" or "the name of the Memra of the LORD," whereas in the Hebrew text such worship is offered to YHWH himself (Gen 8:20; 12:8; 13:4, 18).

These examples, which are only a small representative sample, seem to depict God's Word as the primary way in which—if not an entity through whom—the one God of Israel both creates and interacts with his creation. A distinction between God and his Memra (or the "name of his Memra") is clearly intentional in the text of the Palestinian Targum as expressed in Neofiti 1, but the nature and significance of that distinction is debated. Does such distinction simply reflect a translation device dealing with anthropomorphic depictions of God or does it carry more theological weight, and depict God's Word as a distinct hypostasis?[139] We will return to this debate in the next chapter.

IDENTIFYING COMMONALITY IN JEWISH TRADITIONS REGARDING GOD'S WORD

In all of the traditions examined above, God's Word is depicted as a means of divine agency, though the nature and scope of this agency varies throughout these traditions. Throughout most of these traditions, one finds a connection between God's Word and the act of creation, though this connection experiences development from the God who speaks creation into existence in Genesis 1 to the divine Logos in Philo, which is both the pattern for creation and the agent which brings it about. God's Word is also depicted as a means by which God engages human messengers, though again, such depictions seem to experience significant development.

In the Hebrew Bible there are places in which God's Word could be interpreted as a distinct entity that comes to human beings (Abraham, Elijah, etc.) and speaks to them on behalf of God, though these examples coexist with numerous examples of God directly engaging these messengers without any indication of a mediator. Compare such diverse presentations of divine and human engagement with the works of Philo and the Palestinian Targum Neofiti 1, all of which present God's Word as a virtually exclusive mediator between humanity and the transcendent God of Israel.

At various points in the scriptures, God's Word is depicted as a means of God's sovereignty over the world as well as God's powerful actions within the world. Such depictions continue to appear in Second Temple literature, but they are more frequent, graphic, and explicit in describing the sovereignty and power of God's Word. Clearly, the traditions from the scriptures in which the Word of God is presented as a divine mediator have not only been noted by some in the Second Temple period, but they have also been expanded and developed. The question we have repeatedly asked to this point is whether or not these diverse "Word of God" traditions went so far as to understand God's Word as a distinct divine entity or second power. It is to this question that we turn in the following chapter.

NOTES

1. Following the common practice in English Bible translations, we have kept the NRSV's use of all capital letters for the Tetragrammaton when quoting scripture passages. Otherwise, we try to avoid all capitals when referring to the "Lord" of Israel.

2. See Gieschen, *Angelomorphic Christology*, 103–4.

3. Gieschen, *Angelomorphic Christology*, 104.

4. Gieschen, *Angelomorphic Christology*, 105.

5. Gieschen, *Angelomorphic Christology*, 105, uses this text in an attempt to equate in some way the Word of the Lord with the Angel of the Lord.

6. This book is variously dated to the first half of the second century BCE; see bibliography in Daniel M. Gurnter, *Introducing the Pseudepigrapha of Second Temple Judaism* (Grand Rapids, MI: Baker, 2020), 235–36; David J. Zucker, "A Jubilee (50) of Fascinating Facts about the Book of Jubilees," *Biblical Theology Bulletin* 50, no. 2 (2020): 92–96. Unless otherwise noted, all translations from the Pseudepigrapha are from James H. Charlesworth, *The Old Testament Pseudepigrapha,* 2 vols. (Peabody: Hendrickson, 2010).

7. Although 4 Ezra dates to the last decade of the first century CE, it was originally written in Hebrew and shows no signs of Christian influence. Therefore, most scholars utilize it as a strictly Jewish source that can offer insights into even earlier Second Temple Jewish thought; see Michael E. Stone and Frank Moore Cross, *Fourth Ezra: A Commentary on the Book of Fourth Ezra* (Hermeneia; Minneapolis: Fortress Press, 1990), 9–11; Stone and Matthias Henze, *4 Ezra and 2 Baruch: Translations, Introductions, and Notes* (Hermeneia; Minneapolis: Fortress Press, 2013), 2–3; and Gurtner, *Introducing the Pseudepigraph*, 93–95.

8. Like 4 Ezra, 2 Baruch is likely written in the late first century CE or early second century CE, but it reflects a Jewish milieu; see Stone and Matthias Henze, *4 Ezra and 2 Baruch*, 9–11; and Gurtner, *Introducing the Pseudepigrapha*, 107–9.

9. While discussing Philo, we will refer to the "word" as Logos, as such is both common in Philonic studies and it communicates the significance that Philo gives to the Greek word λόγος over and against ῥῆμα (both of which can be translated "word").

10. See G. Mayer, logos, *Index Philoneus* (Berlin: De Gruyter, 1974).

11. For bibliography on the Logos in Philo, see Scott D. Mackie, "Seeing God in Philo of Alexandria: The Logos, the Powers, or the Existent One?" *Studia Philonica* 21 (2009): 25–47, at 29 n.11; and Carl Judson Davis, *The Name and Way of the Lord: Old Testament Themes, New Testament Christology* (London: Bloomsbury Publishing, 1996), 54–55.

12. All citations from Philo are from the LCL, unless otherwise noted.

13. *Mut.* 2.14.

14. E.g., *Agr.* 51; *Conf.* 63; 146; *Somn.* 1.215.

15. E.g., *Agr.* 51; *Conf.* 146; *Cher.* 36.

16. E.g., *Agr.* 51; *Mut.* 15–16; and *Abr.* 122. Other examples where the "kingly" belongs more to the "Lord"/Logos instead of "God" will be discussed further below.

17. *QG* 2.62.

18. *Leg.* 3.177: τροφέα τὸν θεόν, οὐχὶ λόγον, ἡγεῖται, τὸν δὲ ἄγγελον, ὅς ἐστι λόγος, ὥσπερ ἰατρὸν κακῶν· φυσικώτατα· ἀρέσκει γὰρ αὐτῷ τὰ μὲν προηγούμενα ἀγαθὰ αὐτοπροσώπως αὐτὸν τὸν ὄντα διδόναι, τὰ δεύτερα δὲ τοὺς ἀγγέλους καὶ λόγους αὐτοῦ· δεύτερα δ᾽ ἐστὶν ὅσα περιέχει κακῶν ἀπαλλαγήν. Parallel statements from *Abr.* 122 are cited below for Gen 18. Abbreviated versions of this same commentary are in *Conf.* 180–82 and *Fug.* 67.

19. See Philo's clear statement on how everything but the "unoriginate (τὸ ἀγένητον)" God is subject to change and therefore less than God in *Opif.* 12.

20. *Her.* 205–6: τῷ δὲ ἀρχαγγέλῳ καὶ πρεσβυτάτῳ λόγῳ δωρεὰν ἔδωκεν ἐξαίρετον ὁ τὰ ὅλα γεννήσας πατήρ, ἵνα μεθόριος στὰς τὸ γενόμενον διακρίνῃ τοῦ πεποιηκότος. ὁ δ᾽ αὐτὸς ἱκέτης μέν ἐστι τοῦ θνητοῦ κηραίνοντος αἰεὶ πρὸς τὸ ἄφθαρτον, πρεσβευτὴς δὲ τοῦ ἡγεμόνος πρὸς τὸ ὑπήκοον. ἀγάλλεται δὲ ἐπὶ τῇ δωρεᾷ καὶ σεμνυνόμενος αὐτὴν ἐκδιηγεῖται φάσκων· "κἀγὼ εἱστήκειν ἀνὰ μέσον κυρίου καὶ ὑμῶν," οὔτε ἀγένητος ὡς ὁ θεὸς ὢν οὔτε γενητὸς ὡς ὑμεῖς, ἀλλὰ μέσος τῶν ἄκρων, ἀμφοτέροις ὁμηρεύων.

21. It should be noted that the Logos's created status is somewhat unclear in Philo. There are two places where the Logos may be described as uncreated in Philo's oeuvre. The first is in *Leg.* 3.100, where Philo insists that the mind cannot use ordinary sight, "but lifting its eyes above and beyond creation a clear vision of the uncreated One, so as from Him to apprehend both Himself and His shadow. To apprehend that was, we saw, to apprehend both the Word and this world (ἀλλ᾽ ὑπερκύψας τὸ γενητὸν ἔμφασιν ἐναργῆ τοῦ ἀγενήτου λαμβάνει, ὡς ἀπ᾽ αὐτοῦ αὐτὸν καταλαμβάνειν καὶ τὴν σκιὰν αὐτοῦ, ὅπερ ἦν τόν τε λόγον καὶ τόνδε τὸν κόσμον)." At first, it appears that "the uncreated One . . . and his shadow" correspond to the Logos and the world. However, this set of phrases here are more likely successive and not appositive so that the Logos and the world are both the shadow of the uncreated One; see Mackie, "Seeing God in Philo of Alexandria: The Logos," 35. The other occasion is in *Cher.* 87, where Philo describes all creation as an image of "the Archetype, which is truly good and beautiful, even the uncreate, the blessed, the imperishable (ἀρχέτυπον τὸ πρὸς ἀλήθειαν καλὸν τὸ ἀγένητον καὶ μακάριον καὶ ἄφθαρτον ἀπεικονισθέντα)." The "archetype" is a term almost always used to describe the Logos in Philo. However, in this passage, the Logos is nowhere explicitly mentioned. Instead, Philo is describing how "God alone (μόνος ὁ θεὸς)" stands distinct from creation (*Cher.* 86). Therefore, it would appear that here Philo is not primarily thinking in terms of the Logos as the archetype, and how the Logos fits within the salient conception of the creator/ creature distinction is left unanswered. Elsewhere, Philo speaks of "the Divine Word (λόγος θεῖος)" as the Image of God: "He is Himself the Image of God, chiefest of all Beings intellectually perceived, placed nearest, with no intervening distance, to the Alone truly existent One (αὐτὸς εἰκὼν ὑπάρχων θεοῦ, τῶν νοητῶν ἅπαξ ἀπάντων ὁ πρεσβύτατος, ὁ ἐγγυτάτω, μηδενὸς ὄντος μεθορίου διαστήματος, τοῦ μόνου, ὃ ἔστιν ἀψευδῶς, ἀφιδρυμένος)" (*Fug.* 101). It is, therefore, telling that when Philo speaks of created beings, he differentiates them from the Logos (who appeared as the Angel of the Lord in Gen. 16): "[things] which are hidden from created beings, [the Angel] knows with certainty (ἅπερ ἄδηλα γενέσει, σαφῶς οἶδεν ἐν οἷς φησιν)" (*Fug.* 204).

22. For further discussion on the philosophical commitments in Philo that require this distinctness for the Logos, see Ronald Cox, *By This* Same Word: *Creation and Salvation in Hellenistic Judaism and Early Christianity* (BZNW 145; Berlin: de Gruyter, 2007), 96–130.

23. E.g., *Det.* 86–87; *Leg.* 1.38; *Post.* 15, 168–69; *Deus* 62; *Somn.* 1.65–67. See discussion in Scott D. Mackie, "Seeing God: The Logos," 25–47; and Mackie, "Seeing God in Philo of Alexandria: Means, Methods, and Mysticism," *Journal for the Study of Judaism* 43, no. 2 (2012): 150–58.

24. Philo claims that the divine Logos is the image of God himself and that which is "placed nearest, with no intervening distance to the alone truly existent one" (*Fug.* 101). For Philo, only the Logos can traverse the space that separates God from his creation: "To his word (Logos) . . . the Father of all has given the special prerogative, to stand on the border and separate creature from Creator. This same Logos both pleads with the immortal suppliant for afflicted mortality and acts as ambassador of the ruler to the subject" (*Her.* 205). And elsewhere Philo claims, "The incorporeal world is set off and separated from the visible one by the mediating Logos as by a veil" (*QE* 2.94). Subsequently, the Logos is the means by which the transcendent God both creates and engages creation: "that same [Logos], by which he made the universe, is that by which he draws the perfect man from things earthly to himself" (*Sac.* 8).

25. *Opif.* 17–20.

26. Cf. Plato, *Timeaus* 29e.

27. *Opif.* 21. Baudouin S. Decharneux, "Divine Powers in Philo of Alexandria's De opificio mundi," in Divine Powers in Late Antiquity, ed. Anna Marmodoro, and Irini-Fotini Viltanioti (Oxford: Oxford University Press, 2017), 133, remarks on this passage to say, "The divine *Logos* is then an intelligible power (or *the* intelligible power par excellence) and the intelligible city is a thought of the *Logos*—divine architect." Similarly, David T. Runia. *On the Creation of the Cosmos according to Moses* (Philo of Alexandria Commentary Series, 5.1; Atlanta: Society of Biblical Literature Press, 2005), 144, also comments, "The part of Philo's elaborate doctrine that is most relevant here is his presentation of two chief powers, each associated with a divine name: the creative power as indicated by the name *theos*, the kingly or sovereign power by the name *kurios.*"

28. E.g., in *Opif.* 25 and 139.

29. Gen 1:27 is cited in *Opif.* 25.

30. *Opif.* 20.

31. *Opif.* 23.

32. *Mut.* 15–16, "And so the words 'The Lord was seen of Abraham' (Gen. xvii. 1) must not be understood in the sense that the Cause of all shone upon him and appeared to him, for what human mind could contain the vastness of that vision? Rather we must think of it as the manifestation of one of the Potencies which attend him, the Potency of kingship, for the title Lord betokens sovereignty and kingship (ὥστε τὸ 'ὤφθη κύριος τῷ Ἀβραὰμ' λέγεσθαι ὑπονοητέον οὐχ ὡς ἐπιλάμποντος καὶ ἐπιφαινομένου τοῦ παντὸς αἰτίου—τίς γὰρ ἀνθρώπειος νοῦς τὸ μέγεθος τῆς φαντασίας ἱκανός ἐστι χωρῆσαι;—ἀλλ᾽ ὡς μιᾶς τῶν περὶ αὐτὸ δυνάμεων, τῆς βασιλικῆς, προφαινομένης· ἡ γὰρ κύριος πρόσρησις ἀρχῆς καὶ βασιλείας ἐστί)." See also *Abr.* 122, where God

himself appears, while sending his "two powers" as royal ambassadors: "This is the practice, I think, of kings also, who imitate the divine nature. They are their own agents in granting boons, but employ others to enforce punishment (οὗτό μοι δοκοῦσι καὶ τῶν βασιλέων οἱ μιμούμενοι τὴν θείαν φύσιν πράττειν, τὰς μὲν χάριτας δι᾽ ἑαυτῶν προτείνοντες, τὰς δὲ τιμωρίας δι᾽ ἑτέρων βεβαιοῦντες)."

33. *Mut.* 17. The challenge for Philo's interpretation is that in the original Hebrew it is "the Existing One" or YHWH (יְהֹוָה) that appears, but the Tetragrammaton is glossed with *Kurios* in the Septuagint—a point Philo seems to not know or does not remember. H. A. Wolfson, *Philo: Foundations of Religious Philosophy in Judaism, Christianity and Islam* (Cambridge, MA: Harvard University Press, 1947), 1:88, claimed Philo did know Hebrew, but more recent scholars disagree; e.g., David T. Runia, *Exegesis and Philosophy: Studies on Philo of Alexandra* (Hampshire: Aldershot, 1990), I:13; and David Winston, "Philo Judaeus," in *The Encyclopedia of Religion*, 2nd ed., ed. L. Jones (2005), 10:7106. It is possible that Philo's Greek copy of the scriptures retained the Tetragrammaton in Hebrew, Aramaic, or transliterated form, but this is highly debatable; see James R. Royse, "Philo, Κύριος, and the Tetragrammaton," *The Studia Philonica Annual* 3 (1991), 167–83.

34. More "powers" will be enumerated below. Furthermore, Philo sees all things as "powers" in a sense, but only God has "active power" while all creatures have "passive power" which responds to God's activity. See further discussion in Decharneux, "Divine Powers in Philo," 127–39.

35. For the two lower powers ("God" and "Lord"), being united in and emanating from the Logos (who is the higher second power to God), see *Cher.* 27–30 and *QE.* 2.68.

36. See further discussion in Nils A. Dahl and Alan F. Segal, "Philo and the Rabbis on the Names of God," *Journal for the Study of Judaism in the Persian, Hellenistic and Roman Period* 9, no. 1 (1978):1–28.

37. *Mut.* 19. This may also be indicated in Philo's explanation of God's creative activity: in his *Opif.* he can frequently refer to God's "power" and "powers" in creation in a way that may correspond to the two-fold nature of God's activity (e.g., *Opif.* 7, "powers as Maker and Father (τὰς δυνάμεις ὡς ποιητοῦ καὶ πατρὸς)"; later in this same paragraph God as creator is described as "Father and Maker . . . a father . . . and an artificer (τὸν πατέρα καὶ ποιητὴν . . . πατὴρ . . . δημιουργὸς)"; and *Opif.* 20, where one speaks of "the Divine Reason, which was the author of this ordered frame (τὸν θεῖον λόγον τον ταῦτα διακοσμήσαντα)," followed (*Opif.* 21) by a description of this same "power (δύναμις)" as both "Father and Maker (τὸν πατέρα καὶ ποιητήν)."

38. *Mut.* 15.

39. Mackie offers a helpful discussion of the two powers "God" and "Lord" in the writings of Philo ("Seeing God: The Logos," 29–30). Both powers are divine intermediaries, with "God" being associated with goodness and creative capacity and "Lord" being identified with sovereignty and judgment (Mackie, "Seeing God: The Logos," 29 n.14). Both however are united in the Logos (*Cher.* 27–30) and emanate from the Logos (*QE.* 2.68). See also, John Dillon, *The Middle Platonists, 80 B.C. to A.D. 220*, rev. ed. (Ithaca, NY: Cornell University Press, 1996), 161–63; Segal, *Two Powers in Heaven*, 175; Fred Strickert, "On the Cherubim," *SPhA* 8 (1996): 40–57.

40. *Abr.* 119.

41. *Abr.* 120.

42. *Abr.* 121–22: ἔστιν . . . πατὴρ μὲν τῶν ὅλων ὁ μέσος, ὃς ἐν ταῖς ἱεραῖς γραφαῖς κυρίῳ ὀνόματι καλεῖται ὁ ὤν, αἱ δὲ παρ' ἑκάτερα αἱ πρεσβύταται καὶ ἐγγυτάτω τοῦ ὄντος δυνάμεις, ἡ μὲν ποιητική, ἡ δ' αὖ βασιλική· προσαγορεύεται δὲ ἡ μὲν ποιητικὴ θεός, ταύτῃ γὰρ ἔθηκέ τε καὶ διεκόσμησε τὸ πᾶν, ἡ δὲ βασιλικὴ κύριος, θέμις γὰρ ἄρχειν καὶ κρατεῖν τὸ πεποιηκὸς τοῦ γενομένου.

43. *Abr.* 122. See similar explanations in *Sacr.* 59 and *QG* 4.2.

44. I.e., Gen 16; and 26 in *Mut.* 15–16 discussed in the previous paragraphs.

45. *Abr.* 144.

46. *Somn.* 1.162.

47. In Gen 31:13 it is in fact "the Angel of the Lord" who speaks (cf. Gen 31:11). Philo does not address this, but only quotes what "God" says in the first person. More will be said about the Logos as the Angel of the Lord (below) and in chapter 5 we will further discuss the relationship of this Angel to God.

48. *Somn.* 1.228. Similarly, in his allegorical treatment of Moses, Aaron, Nadab, Abihu, and the seventy elders of Israel encountering God on Mount Sinai (Exod 24:9–11, a text that in Hebrew claims that these men saw God), Philo, following the Septuagint, claims that they saw the "place" where God stood (rather than God himself), and he identifies this Τόπος as the Logos: *Conf.* 95–97, "the place which in fact is the Word (τὸν μὲν τόπον, ὃς δὴ λόγος ἐστί)."

49. *Opif.* 20.

50. *Somn.* 1.230.

51. *Somn.* 1.232.

52. See further discussion in chapter 5 of this book.

53. Ultimately, God cannot be named according to Philo (*Somn.* 1.230), so this is not God's name technically speaking, but the name by which Moses and others should call on God.

54. *Mos.* 1.66.

55. See a few lines later in *Mos.* 1.66, where it is not God ("he who is [εἰκόνα τοῦ ὄντος εἶναι]"), but "the [A]ngel [who] was a symbol of God's providence (ὁ δὲ ἄγγελος προνοίας τῆς ἐκ θεοῦ)."

56. Segal, *Two Powers*, 163, "It is by virtue of the revelation of the divine name to Moses that the *logos* comes to be equated with the name of God."

57. *Mos.* 1.76.

58. Cf. Philo, *Deo*, which is only extant as an Armenian fragment, where he identifies the "Lord" and two Seraphim of Is 6:1–3 with the "three men" of Gen 18. See discussion of Philo and other interpretations in Bogdan G. Bucur, "'I Saw the Lord': Observations on the Christian Reception History of Isaiah 6," *Pro Ecclesia* 23, no. 3 (2014): 309–30, esp. 313. For the text of *Deo*, see Folker Siegert, "The Philonian Fragment *De Deo*: First English Translation," *Studia Philonica* 10 (1998): 1–33.

59. "There I will meet with you, and from above the mercy seat, from between the two cherubim that are on the ark of the covenant, I will deliver to you all my commands for the Israelites" (NRSV; LXX: καὶ γνωσθήσομαί σοι ἐκεῖθεν καὶ λαλήσω σοι

ἄνωθεν τοῦ ἱλαστηρίου ἀνὰ μέσον τῶν δύο χερουβιμ τῶν ὄντων ἐπὶ τῆς κιβωτοῦ τοῦ μαρτυρίου καὶ κατὰ πάντα ὅσα ἂν ἐντείλωμαί σοι πρὸς τοὺς υἱοὺς Ἰσραηλ).

60. *Cher.* 27. For discussion of the complexity of this and similar passages in Philo, see Francesca Calabi, *God's Acting, Man's Acting: Tradition and Philosophy in Philo of Alexandria* (*SPhA* 4; Leiden: Brill, 2008), 87–90.

61. E.g., *Her.* 166 and *Fug.* 100.

62. *Fug.* 100–101: "the lid of the ark, which he calls the Mercy-seat, representing the gracious power; while the creative and kingly powers are represented by the winged Cherubim that rest upon it. The Divine Word, Who is high above all these, has not been visibly portrayed, being like to no one of the objects of sense (τὸ ἐπίθημα τῆς κιβωτοῦ—καλεῖ δὲ αὐτὸ ἱλαστήριον,—ποιητικῆς δὲ καὶ βασιλικῆς τὰ ὑπόπτερα καὶ ἐφιδρυμένα Χερουβίμ· ὁ δ᾽ ὑπεράνω τούτων λόγος θεῖος εἰς ὁρατὴν οὐκ ἦλθεν ἰδέαν, ἅτε μηδενὶ τῶν κατ᾽ αἴσθησιν ἐμφερὴς ὤν)"

63. *Fug.* 101.

64. Although Philo may not have a Roman chariot from a triumph in mind, there is a remarkable parallel description of the event in the later Christian writer, Tertullian. In *Apol.* 33.4, he describes how behind the lord who holds the reins of the chariot a "voice" reminds him that he is not God.

65. At one point (*Fug.* 94–95), Philo can even speak of God, the Logos and five powers, when expounding on the cities of refuge so that each corresponds to attributes of God. This results in there being the Logos and Five Powers, the Creative Power, the Royal Power, the Gracious Power, the prescriptive Legislative Power, and the prohibitive Legislative Power. See Robert Radice, "Philo's Theology and Theory of Creation," in *Cambridge Companion to Philo*, ed. Adam Kamesar (Cambridge: Cambridge University Press, 2009), 140–41.

66. Contra Segal, *Two Powers in Heaven*, 175, "How these powers relate to the *logos* is ambiguous. . . . Basically, he uses whatever exegesis makes most sense in the allegorical context."

67. Cox, *By the Same Word*, 139, concludes, "the Logos is an entity between God and matter, an intermediary."

68. E.g., David Winston, *Logos and Mystical Theology in Philo of Alexandria* (Cincinnati: Hebrew Union College Press, 1985), 15–25, who equates "personification" with "hypostatization"; Segal, *Two Powers,* 164, who concludes that Philo's Logos is often described as a second god, but "who nevertheless is only the visible emanation of the High, ever-existing God"; Thomas H. Tobin, "Logos," in *The Anchor Bible Dictionary* 4 (New York: 1992), 351, who concludes that Philo's Logos is "not a straightforward description of a being other than God. It was a real aspect of the divine reality through which God was related, although indirectly, to the universe"; Runia, *Philo in Early Christian Literature: A Survey* (Assen, MN: Fortress, 1993), 41, who describes the Logos as "that aspect of God which is turned towards creation."

69. E.g., Camilla Hélena von Heijne, *The Messenger of the Lord in Early Interpretations of Genesis* (BZAW 412; Berlin, De Gruyter, 2010), 234, concludes that Philo must be speaking of the Logos as God's angelmorphic emanation, because "It therefore seems to be an over-interpretation to claim that Philo and his fellow hellensitic Jews should have literally believed in a second God." Another such passage that could

be considered is *Opif.* 26, where Philo seems to indicate that there is none other than God before creation: "who was there beside him? (τίς γὰρ ἦν ἕτερος)." However, in the same paragraph (*Opif.* 24), Philo can speak of the Logos as an independent creative agent: "the Word of God when He was already engaged in the act of creation (εἶναι ἢ θεοῦ λόγον ἤδη κοσμοποιοῦντος)."

70. Margaret Barker, *The Great Angel: A Study of Israel's Second God* (Louisville, KY: Westminster John Knox Press, 1992), 131–32.

71. For example, Runia, *Philo*, 41, initially concludes, "The question rises as to whether it is separable from God himself. Philo appears to vacillate on whether he should regard it as a separate hypostasis or not. Most often (but not always) he considers the Logos at the most conceptually separate from God." Ruinia's comments are understandable, but it is worth noting that in explaining Philo's view of God, he can be more certain about the "personal" nature of God: "God is the Supreme being. He is not, however, (just) a principle, but 'someone' (we would say a 'person') to whom one can relate." (*Philo*, 39). This may explain why he appears less certain in his later study: Runia, "Logos," in *Dictionary of Deities and Demons in the Bible*, 2nd ed., eds. Karel van der Toorn, Bob Becking, Pieter W. vad der Horst (Leiden and Grand Rapids, MI: Brill and Eerdmans, 1999), 528, "Philo personifies the Logos . . . In many texts the Logos represents God's presence or activity in the world, so that the distinction between God and Logos is more conceptual than real. There are other texts, however, in which the Logos is presented as an hypostasis separate from and ontologically inferior to God himself." Similarly, Mackie, "Seeing God," 37, concludes, "there is some ambiguity as to whether the Powers and the Logos are autonomous ontological realities (i.e., hypostases), or merely theophanic manifestations," and he finds three instances where the Logos operates as an independent agent in Philo (*Migr.* 168–75; *Leg.* 3.169–78; *Sacr.* 8).

72. Von Heijne, *The Messanger*, 232, concludes, "Philo was not a systematic theologian by modern standards, and there are certain inconsistencies in his works, for example, the depiction of the 'Logos' varies."

73. See Maren R. Niehoff, *Philo of Alexandria: An Intellectual Biography* (New Haven, CT; London: Yale University Press, 2018), 209–24, who finds the Platonistic Logos to be an early version of his thought. For additional secondary literature on these options, see Chester, "Jewish Messianic Expectations and Pauline Christology," in *Paulus und das antike Judentum*, eds. M. Hengel and U. Heckel (Tübingen: Mohr Siebeck, 1992), 48 n.76.

74. To be consistent, we have elected to capitalize "Angel" when speaking of the Angel of the Lord in particular, just as Philo scholars capitalize the Logos or "Word."

75. Von Heijne, *The Messenger,* 201, "the angel of the Lord appears to be identified as the 'Logos' in many of Philo's interpretations of our pericopes."

76. E.g., *Conf.* 146, "Son of God . . . God's First-born, the Word, who holds the eldership among the angels, their ruler as it were. And many names are his, for he is called, 'the Beginning,' and the Name of God, and His Word (υἱὸς θεοῦ . . . τὸν πρωτόγονον αὐτοῦ λόγον, τὸν ἀγγέλων πρεσβύτατον, ὡς ἂν ἀρχάγγελον, πολυώνυμον ὑπάρχοντα· καὶ γὰρ ἀρχὴ καὶ ὄνομα θεοῦ καὶ λόγος)." Cf. *Her.* 205.

77. *Somn.* 1.162.

78. Discussed above. Also, see von Heijne, *The Messenger,* 202, "although the human mind cannot comprehend the essence of God, His activities or δυνάμεις/'powers' can be known. . . . The two main 'powers' are expressed in God's creative activity and in His governing and sustaining of the world."

79. Discussed above.

80. *Somn.* 1.228–30.

81. *Somn.* 1.228.

82. *Somn.* 1.230.

83. *Somn.* 1.231–37.

84. von Heijne, *The Messenger,* 204, "God in his essence remains unfathomable but, through his 'Logos,' 'He who IS' reaches down to and makes himself know to humankind. The 'Logos' is god in his knowability."

85. *Somn.* 1.41.240.

86. *Somn.* 1.41.240.

87. *Somn.* 1.41.239.

88. *QG* 3.34.

89. Tuschling, *Angels and Orthodoxy*, 95, offers a nuanced view of Philo's indebtedness to Middle Platonism, following the study by Chester, "Jewish Messianic Expectations," 48–52. Philo certainly credits Greek philosophy for his understanding of the angels in general (e.g., *Gig.* 2.6).

90. *QG* 3.35.

91. This translation of the Armenian text is almost certainly a cognate to the metaphor found in early Christian writers; (e.g., *Epistle of Barnabas* 5; Justin Martyr, *Dialogue with Trypho* 128; Irenaeus, *Against Heresies* 2.13.5; Ps.-Hippolytus, *Against Noetus* 11.1, Origen, *On First Principles* 4.28; Tertullian, *Against Praxeas* 8.5–7; Athanasius, *Defense of the Nicene Definition* 25). Cf. Plato, *Rep.* 6.e, on the analogy of Truth and Knowledge as lower forms of Goodness, much like light rays are emanations of the sun.

92. *QG* 4.90.

93. Darrell D. Hannah, *Michael and Christ: Michael Traditions and Angel Christology in Early Christianity* (WUNT 2.109; Tübingen: Mohr Siebeck, 1999), 80–81.

94. Michael F. Bird, *Jesus among the Gods: Early Christology in the Greco-Roman World* (Waco, TX: Baylor University Press, 2022), 93, "Philo's Logos is a hypostatic representation of God spliced with angelic creatureliness to become a genuine in-between entity."

95. In *Opif.* 13–14, Philo, following Plato's *Timeaus*, invokes a Pythagorean explanation for all creation: just as 6 consists of 1, 2, and 3, so God made all things at once from eternity, and yet creation unfolded in an ordered way temporally.

96. Radice, "Philo's Theology," 140–41, notes how angels can represent the Logos.

97. *Somn.* 1.115.

98. Peter Frick, *Divine Providence in Philo of Alexandria* (Tübingen: Mohr Siebeck, 1999), 55, who shows that Philo sees angels as pure intellect, not matter, "however, it often happens that they [angels] imitate the forms of men . . . they have a hypostatized mode of existence."

99. *Somn.* 1.140.

100. *Somn.* 1.140–41: καθαρώταται καὶ ἄρισται, μειζόνων φρονημάτων καὶ θειοτέρων ἐπιλαχοῦσαι, μηδενὸς μὲν τῶν περιγείων ποτὲ ὀρεχθεῖσαι τὸ παράπαν, ὕπαρχοι δὲ τοῦ πανηγεμόνος, ὥσπερ μεγάλου βασιλέως ἀκοαὶ καὶ ὄψεις, ἐφορῶσαι πάντα καὶ ἀκούουσαι. ταύτας δαίμονας μὲν οἱ ἄλλοι φιλόσοφοι, ὁ δὲ ἱερὸς λόγος ἀγγέλους εἴωθε καλεῖν προσφυεστέρῳ χρώμενος ὀνόματι· καὶ γὰρ τὰς τοῦ πατρὸς ἐπικελεύσεις τοῖς ἐγγόνοις καὶ τὰς 142τῶν ἐγγόνων χρείας τῷ πατρὶ διαγγέλλουσι.

101. John Dillon, "Philo's Doctrine of Angels," in *Two Treatises of Philo of Alexandria: A Commentary on "De Gigantibus" and "Quod Deus Sit Immutabilis,"* eds. David Winston and John M. Dillon (Chico, CA: Scholars Press, 1983), 197, "Philo's doctrine will therefore concord very largely with whatever else we know of Middle Platonic daemonology."

102. Cf. *Gig.* 3.12. This makes Barker's conclusion (*The Great Angel*, 131, "Philo shows beyond any doubt that the Judaism of the first Christian century acknowledged a second God") too simplistic. The Logos for Philo is God's first emanation among many. Even so, Philo seems to utilize the language of his day ("Second God" and "Two Powers") to explain this complicated and mysterious understanding of God as entailing a plurality.

103. *Opif.* 134–36; *Leg.* 1.31; 2.4; *QG* 1.4. It has been noted by a number of interpreters that *Leg.* 1.31 and 2.4 seem to focus not on two distinct men, such as a heavenly Adam and an earthly Adam, but rather between two types of men, those that are like the heavenly and those that are like the earthly. While such a distinction seems accurate, what seemingly lies behind these two categories of men, is Philo's belief in the existence of an original heavenly man who is incorporeal and immortal, and an earthly man who is corporeal and mortal. It is on the basis of the existence of such entities that Philo builds his ethical understanding of two types of men. As such, these passages are taken here as, at the very least, indirect evidence for Philo's understanding of both a heavenly and earthly man. For discussion, see A. J. M. Wedderburn, "Philo's 'Heavenly Man,'" *NovT* 15, no. 4 (1973): 311; Stephen Hultgren, "The Origins of Paul's Doctrine of the Two Adams in 1 Corinthians 15:45–49," *JSNT* 25, no. 3 (2003): 344–57.

104. *Opif.* 134; *Leg.* 1.31; 2.4

105. *Opif.* 134–36; *Leg.* 1.31; 2.4; *QG* 1.4

106. *Leg.* 1.31

107. *Opif.* 134; *Leg.* 1.31; 2.4; *QG* 1.4

108. *Leg.* 1.31. Philo can also use the language of "first man" and "second man," with the "first man" being equated with the "heavenly man" and the "second man" being equated with the "earthly man" (see *Opif.* 134 and *Leg.* 2.5). However, there are other instances in which the man created from clay, or the "earthly man" can be referred to as the "first man" as well (*Opif.* 136).

109. For discussion of Philo's inconsistencies and the different ways Philo uses these concepts, see Hultgren, "The Origins," 344–57; Tobin, *The Creation of Man: Philo and the History of Interpretation* (CBQMS 14; Washington: The Catholic Biblical Association of America, 1983), 25–27; Gerhard Sellin, *Der Streit um die Auferstehung der Toten; Eine religionsgeschichtliche und exegetische Untersuchung von 1 Korinther 15* (FRLANT 138; Göttingen: Vandenhoeck & Ruprecht, 1986).

110. *Leg.* 3.96.

111. For such a reading, see Wedderburn, "Heavenly Man," 312; D. T. Runia, "God and Man in Philo of Alexandria," *JTS* 39, no. 1 (1988): 67; J. M. Creed, "The Heavenly Man," *JTS* 26, no. 102 (1925): 133.

112. *Opif.* 134.

113. *Conf.* 42, 62–63, 146.

114. *Conf.* 42.

115. See Wedderburn, "Heavenly Man," 315.

116. *Conf.* 62–63k.

117. For God as father, see *Fug.* 109; for eldest, see *Det.* 82; *Her.* 205; *Somn.* 1.230; for first-born, see *Agr.* 51; *Conf.* 1.146; *Somn.* 1.215.

118. *Fug.* 101; *Leg* 3.96; *Spec.* 1.81.

119. *Cher.* 1.127; *Sac.* 8; *Somn.* 2.45; *Spec.* 1.81.

120. *Conf.* 146.

121. For similar conclusions, see, for example, Peter Schäfer, *The Jewish Jesus: How Judaism and Christianity Shaped Each Other* (Princeton: Princeton University Press, 2012), 208–9; C. H. Dodd, *The Interpretation of the Fourth Gospel* (Cambridge: Cambridge University Press, 1953), 70–71; J. C. O'Neil, "If God Created Adam in His Own Image, in the Image of God Created He Him, How is Christ the Image of God?," *Irish Biblical Studies* 21 (1999): 79–87, makes a cursory case for connection between the Logos and Adam in early Jewish Messianic hope. Though it seems Steenburg misreads *QG* 1.4, one of two texts on which he makes his judgment, he too equates the Logos with the heavenly man in Philo; see D. Steenburg, "The Worship of Adam and Christ as the Image of God," *JSNT* 39 (1990): 104. Much earlier, Egon Brandenburger made a case for a connection between the identification of Philo's heavenly Adam and Logos, arguing that their shared identity is evidence of a gnostic redeemer figure (*Adam und Christus: exegetisch-religionsgeschichtliche Untersuchung zum Röm. 5, 12–21 (1. Kor. 15)* [WMANT 7; Neukirchen: Neukirchener, 1962], 68–157.)

122. Wedderburn, "Heavenly Man," 323.

123. Wedderburn, "Heavenly Man," 323–24.

124. Von Heijne, *The Messenger*, 232, concludes, "Basically, it seems that if the biblical ambivalence between God and His angel, who Philo also called 'Logos,' is maintained in Philo's theological system. Just as the identity of the angel and God is merged in our pericopes, so is that of God and His 'Logos' in Philo's teaching. However, Philo was not a systematic theologian by modern standards, and there are certain inconsistencies in his works, for example, the depiction of the 'Logos' varies."

125. See Martin McNamara, *Targum and New Testament* (WUNT; Tübingen: Mohr Siebeck, 2011), 213.

126. See McNamara, *Targum and New Testament*, 213–15; Philip S. Alexander, "Jewish Aramaic Translation of Hebrew Scriptures" in *Mikra: Text, Translation, Reading & Interpretation of the Hebrew Bible in Ancient Judaism & Early Christianity*, ed. Martin Jan Mulder (Peabody: Hendrickson, 2004), 242–43.

127. See McNamara, *Targum and New Testament*, 214; S. A. Kaufman, "Dating the Language of the Palestinian Targums and their Use in the Study of First

Century ce Texts," in *The Aramaic Bible: Targums in Their Historical Context*, eds. D. R. G. Beattie and Martin McNamara (JSOTSup 166; Sheffield: Sheffield, 1994), 130; E. Y. Kutscher, "The Language of the Genesis Apocryphon," in *Aspects of the Dead Sea Scrolls*, eds. Ch. Rabin and Y. Yadin (Scripta Hierosolymitana 4; Jerusalem: Magnes Press, 1958), 10.

128. See McNamara, *Targum and New Testament*, 98–99.

129. See McNamara, *Targum and New Testament*, 213–15. It is uncertain whether Targum Onkelos abbreviated existing Palestinian Targums or whether the subsequent Palestinian Targum's expanded what is represented in Targum Onkelos. It is quite possible that Onkelos was one of many existing Targumaic traditions.

130. Alexander, "Aramaic Translation," 219–20.

131. For further bibliography and discussion on this concept in the Targums, see von Heijne, *The Messenger of the Lord*, 39–40.

132. Similar to our use of the word Logos when discussing Philo, we will use "Memra" when discussing God's word in targumaic literature. Such usage is consistent with targumaic studies and will help distinguish the concept represented by "Memra" from other similar concepts related to divine communication.

133. McNamara, *The Aramaic Bible: Targum Neofiti 1 Genesis* (Collegeville: Liturgical Press, 1992), 37.

134. McNamara, *The Aramaic Bible*, 37–38.

135. McNamara, *The Aramaic Bible*, 37–38.

136. McNamara, *The Aramaic Bible*, 37–38.

137. Although it is the "angel of the LORD" who appears in Exod 3:2, the LORD/God speaks directly to Moses in 3:3–7 (not the "Word" as in Targum Neofiti 1).

138. As do other sources from this time period; e.g., Philo, *Mos.* 1.66 and *Ezekiel the Tragedian* 99 (*OTP* 2:813), where the Angel in the burning bush is called "God's Word."

139. For an overview of the history of this debate, see McNamara, *Targum and Testament Revisited: Aramaic Paraphrases of the Hebrew Bible*, 2nd ed. (Grand Rapids, MI: Eerdmans, 2010), 155–61; and Heijne, *The Messanger of the Lord*, 39–40.

Chapter 3

God's Word's as a Second Power in Heaven

In the previous chapter, we repeatedly asked how the depictions of God's Word in Second Temple literature should be understood. While we argued that for Philo the Logos was a distinct entity, here we pull all the evidence together from the previous chapter and assess whether God's Word is best understood as a distinct entity within the Second Temple period and, if so, whether that entity should be understood as a second power in heaven. Before continuing, it is important to articulate the basic interpretive options when considering the literary depictions of God's Word outlined above. The first interpretive option is that these depictions of God's Word are vivid literary depictions of an attribute or function of the one God of Israel, or perhaps even an idiomatic way of referencing God himself, and thus the Word is not a distinct entity.[1] The second interpretive option is that these depictions are more than the result of creative literary artistry, but they present God's Word as a distinct entity.[2] Here we will consider arguments for and against God's Word as a distinct entity. After making a case that God's Word is best understood as a distinct entity within the thought world of the Second Temple period, we will consider the nature of this entity by applying to it the criteria outlined in chapter 1.

ARGUMENTS AGAINST GOD'S WORD AS A DISTINCT ENTITY

There are three distinct arguments made against seeing the Word as a distinct entity in Second Temple Jewish texts. In this section we will briefly relay all three, followed by a rebuttal of these arguments.

Argument 1: God's Word as an Idiomatic Reference to God Himself

Regarding depictions of God's Word in the scriptures, depictions in which God's Word comes to, and appears to, God's prophets, and accomplishes God's task, it is argued that these traditions simply express the tradition that Israel's God expressed his will "immediately and directly to his people through prophetic inspiration and vision."[3] Relatedly, the concept of God's Word is also a way of expressing God's will brought to effect in the world, similar to the ancient concept of a king's command bringing about the reality of that command.[4] While at times there may seem to be a distinction between Israel's God and the Word that God speaks, it is argued that this is best explained by the "accident of idiom" rather than by the hypostatization of God's Word.[5] Thus, to speak of God's Word doing something was simply an idiomatic way to speak of God himself doing something.

The same logic is applied to similar examples found in later Second Temple religious texts. Though the descriptions and actions of God's Word might be expanded and more vividly described in these texts, these developments are explained in terms of development in idiomatic expression rather than development in the actual identity and function of God's Word as a distinct entity or being.[6] Again, God's Word is understood as simply another way of describing the activity of God in the world. It is acknowledged that God's Word is the means by which Judaism can express the immanence of God without violating a strong commitment to God's transcendence.[7] James Dunn sums up this position in the following way: "In short, *all three expressions* (God's word, wisdom, and spirit) *are simply alternative ways of speaking about the effective power of God in his active relationship with his world and its inhabitants.*"[8]

Argument 2: God's Word as a Theological Device Used to Explain Divine Immanence

For those who reject God's Word as a distinct entity, Philo's depiction of God's Logos is a more significant challenge. In Philo, the Logos is clearly established as an entity that is distinct from God, though also properly identified as at the very least a god. As seen above, this concept is well thought out and carefully articulated by Philo, and merely reducing the distinct being of the Logos in Philo to an accident of idiom is simply impossible. Thus, in addressing Philo's use of the Logos, Dunn carefully engages Philo's understanding of the Logos in order to ascertain what this concept truly means for the Jewish philosopher. Through his analysis, Dunn argues that for Philo, the Logos is the divine thought of God coming into expression in the world, expression that includes creation and divine manifestation.[9] In essence, Dunn concludes that for Philo, the Logos is not truly a distinct being or entity but simply God himself as he is knowable to humanity.[10] Thus, Philo's understanding of the Logos is not that much different than the way Dunn understands the "word" in other Second Temple religious literature, namely the Logos is merely a way of speaking of the immanence of a God that is understood to be utterly transcendent—Philo's understanding of this concept is simply more developed and subject to greater philosophic influence.

Regarding the use and depiction of "the Memra of the LORD" in the Palestinian Targums, it is widely recognized that the replacement of the LORD with "the Memra of the LORD" was clearly an intentional move within the targumaic tradition, one that was almost certainly made for a theological purpose. However, the majority of targumaic and rabbinic scholars conclude that this evidence does not indicate a belief in God's Memra as a distinct divine being. Instead, it is argued that, that God's Memra is simply used as a "buffer word," one that both replaces embarrassing anthropomorphisms and also allows avoidance of direct interaction between God and his creation.[11] Thus, while God's Memra might appear to be a distinct divine entity in the Palestinian targumaic tradition, it is actually a concept created and invoked in order to protect God's transcendence. If such a conclusion is accepted, then the Memra of God in the Palestinian Targum Neofiti 1 is functioning quite similarly to the way in which the concept is explained in the scriptures, Philo, and Second Temple religious literature.

Argument 3: The Absence of Any Cult or Worship Related to Divine Wisdom

The hypostatization of divine attributes or virtues was actually quite common in ancient pagan religion. Studies in the history of religion offer many examples, including the hypostatization of *Maat* (a trait of Egyptian deities that brought about order in the universe), *Iustitia* (a divine virtue of Roman gods that ensured justice), and *Felicitas* (a divine virtue of Roman gods that brought favor and fortune).[12] Such hypostatization resulted in these divine attributes/virtues becoming independent gods and goddesses in their own right, with priests, statues, and temples regularly devoted to facilitate their cultic worship. In light of such a development in the pagan world, it is theorized that if God's Word had, in fact, become a distinct being within Judaism, then we should expect to see cultic worship devoted to this divine attribute turned deity.[13] The fact that no such worship of God's Word exists in Second Temple Judaism is then taken as evidence it never made the transition from divine attribute to a distinct being, but simply remained the former.

ARGUMENTS FOR WORD AS DISTINCT FROM GOD

The basic starting point for virtually all interpreters who understand the above noted depictions of God's Word as a distinct being is the descriptions found in the Second Temple texts themselves.[14] The surface reading of many texts clearly depicts God Word as a distinct entity that performs distinct divine functions. As such, it seems the most natural way to understand God's Word is as a distinct entity. Clear evidence to the contrary is needed to reach a different conclusion. Thus, we turn to the arguments presented against God's Word as a distinct being above and consider their merit.

The first argument to address is the claim that the Word is best understood as an idiomatic way of referring to God himself or God's action in the world. Such arguments do indeed seem able to explain the hypostatic depictions of God's Word in some scriptures and Second Temple texts. In such texts, one can see how God's Word could often be an indirect way of referring to God himself. At times, the choice for the use of such an idiom is harder to explain, particularly instances in which a distinction between God and his Word are implied, (e.g., see the narrative of Elijah on mount Horeb in 1 Kgs), but even in such instances, an idiomatic explanation seems plausible. However, it must be noted that even if such a reading is plausible, there is nothing in the argument that demands it nor is there anything in the argument that precludes the possibility that Second Temple Jews could read these texts and perceive God's Word to be a distinct entity.[15] It must be allowed that the latter interpretive option could be available to Second Temple Jews. Thus, this argument offers a plausible interpretation of apparent hypostatic traditions regarding God's Word, but it does not establish this interpretation as the only plausible interpretation of such traditions.

As we have argued above, Philo offers a strong example of a Second Temple Jew that clearly understood God's Word as a distinct entity.[16] The argument against this conclusion was that Philo reflects a theological development in the idiomatic use of God's Word, a development that results from the perceived tension between God's transcendence and immanence. Given the deep commitment to God's transcendence, Philo relegates all expressions of God's immanence to God's Logos (or related realities such powers that emanate from God's Logos). Thus, God's Logos is not truly a distinct hypostatic being for Philo, but rather a theological necessity that creates a buffer between a transcendent God and his creation. Put differently, God's Logos is merely a linguistic way of explaining, philosophically, theologically, and exegetically, the immanence of a God that is utterly transcendent. It is argued that Logos is a mere theological construct for Philo (and perhaps for other Second Temple Jews as well). This same argument or one similar to it is also applied to the Palestinian Targum's depiction of God's Memra. While Targum Neofiti 1 seems to depict God's Word as a distinct divine agent and the means through which God creates and interacts with his creation, it is argued that these depictions merely function to either replace embarrassing anthropomorphisms (which they only occasionally do) or to create a buffer between the transcendent God and creation.

In terms of Philo specifically, we return to our argument above, that such an understanding of the Logos does not adequately account for Philo's complex treatment of it. While there are times in which Philo defaults to understanding the Logos in terms of "the one," an understanding that might justify these arguments that the Logos is none other than theological construct to protect God's transcendence, there are many times in which Philo explicates the Logos in terms of "the many." These latter examples greatly undermine the above offered arguments, as they demonstrate that Philo's Logos is as distinct an entity as any other angel or human soul. While all such entities can be understood as rightly being emanations from the one, they also can be rightly understood as distinct entities. In light of such an understanding of Philo, the Logos cannot be reduced to a mere theological construct, or personification of God's activity.

Daniel Boyarin has also answered those who see God's Word as a mere personification in Philo and the Memra theology of the Targums, noting that such logic ultimately collapses on itself.[17] Boyarin rightly asks if God's Word (Logos/Memra) is merely a theologically constructed circumlocutions for referring to God himself; circumlocutions functioning to maintain absolute divine transcendence, then who actually created the world; exercises sovereignty over it, or appears within it? Either the author/reader understands this figure to be God himself, in which case no real protection of divine transcendence has been accomplished other than through meaningless linguistic gymnastics, or God's Word is truly understood as distinct divine being through which the transcendent God can in fact be present.[18] In the end, this common theological explanation does not take seriously the commitment to divine transcendence that its proponents argue led to the developing conception of God's Word. According to Boyarin, this view of God's Word ascribes "only counterfeit coinage of linguistic simulation of a theology of transcendence of God without the theology itself."[19] If the commitment to the transcendence of God was taken seriously by the Jews who both read and produced the literature examined above, then God's Word ought to be understood as a distinct being. To understand it as anything else undercuts what seems to be a deep commitment to divine transcendence in Second Temple Judaism.

The final argument to address is the claim that the absence of any cultic devotion to God's Word, devotion that was granted to divine attributes and virtues turned deities in the pagan world, demonstrates that these concepts were not distinct beings but merely divine attributes or expressions of the God of Israel. While such an argument might be legitimate if one were addressing pagan polytheism, the argument is less convincing when applied to Jewish monotheism. There are two alternative explanations for the absence of a distinct cult to the distinct entity of God's Word. First, devotion to the God of Israel could be perceived as devotion to the totality of that God, including both a first power and second power. Parsing out distinct entities as objects of worship, if all such entities were understood as rightly identified as the God of Israel, could be redundant and an unnecessary development. In fact, it might be purposely avoided so as not to create the impression that Jews worshiped more than one God. Second, it is possible that Jews understood themselves to be worshipping the second power in any and all acts of religious devotion and that through the worship of the second power they also worshiped the first power. Such an explanation would fit with Philo's understanding of the Logos to sit on the ark of the covenant between the two powers, God and Lord. Thus, the Logos is understood as the YHWH that resided in Israel's Temple and that filled the tabernacle with the glory of God. Thus, it could be argued that Jews who affirmed a two powers theology understood their direct devotion in the Temple to go to the second power, through whom the first power also received worship. In light of these possible explanations, the fact that a distinct cult to God's Word did not exist in the Second Temple period, is not sound evidence that God's Word was merely a divine attribute in Second Temple Judaism rather than a distinct entity.[20]

Instead of denying hypostatic reality to the Logos in some Second Temple Jewish literature in the name of their theological service to a transcendence/ immanence tension, why not simply conclude that such a hypostatic identity was theologically constructed to address that very tension? Such a conclusion is a far more natural reading of Philo and the Targums, and one that does not gut these texts of any true protection of divine transcendence. Within a number of these arguments, there seems to be a deep commitment to the existence of a Second Temple orthodoxy regarding the singularity of God, one similar to that found in later rabbinic literature. Dunn betrays this very commitment when speaking of Wisdom as an equivalent for Logos:

> The seemingly attractive third alternative, Wisdom as a divine hypostasis, involves the importation of a concept whose appropriateness here is a consequence of the technical meaning it acquired in the much later Trinitarian controversies of the early church. It has not been demonstrated that Hebrew thought was already contemplating such within its talk of God.[21]

Here Dunn privileges his own position by claiming that the burden of proof lies with those who seek to demonstrate the existence of hypostatic thought in Second Temple conceptions of God. Dunn has essentially stacked the deck so that only his position can win. Any evidence related to Word (or Wisdom) being distinct divine beings cannot result in such a conclusion because of a predetermined assessment of what Jews must have believed about God. Thus, the very evidence that might undermine this predetermined assessment is rejected because of the predetermined assessment. But as we have argued in chapter 1, an alternative paradigm for understanding the God of Israel is available, namely a two powers paradigm. As we will argue below, this paradigm offers significant explanatory power for the data related to other hypostases or intermediaries.

THE LONELY VOICE OF PHILO AND THE VALUE OF TARGUMAIC EVIDENCE?

Of the various Second Temple witnesses to God's Word outlined above, Philo is clearly the most sophisticated and developed in his hypostatic depiction. Many have found it much harder to explain Philo's depictions in terms literary or linguistic creativity than hypostatic depictions of God's Word found in books like Wisdom of Solomon. As such, a common way forward is to conclude that Philo's depictions of God's Word represent a unique (or virtually so) development and expression within Second Temple Judaism.[22] Where one finds possible seeds of a hypostatic Word in Jewish scripture and other Second Temple literature, one finds full grown trees in Philo. Thus, one can argue that Philo's hypostatic conceptions of God's Word are not truly normative for Second Temple Judaism, but they are, in fact, aberrations unrecognizable to Second Temple Jews, who by and large were committed to the singularity of the one God of Israel. Thus, it is often concluded that while Philo's Judaism, heavily influenced by Platonism and Stoicism, might lead him to speak of the Logos as a second god, such an attribution would not be normative for most Second Temple Jews.

Such an assessment of Philo's witness to the Word in the Second Temple period is problematic for many reasons. First, while it must be noted that Philo's depictions of God's Word is more developed than what is found in Jewish scripture and other Second Temple literature, many functions and descriptions of the Word found in the former are also found in the latter. For example, Philo's depiction of God's Word as active in creation can also be found in Wisdom of Solomon, 4 Ezra, Jubilees, 2 Baruch, and throughout the Palestinian targums of Genesis. Philo depicts God's Word as sovereign over God's creation, and such depictions can also be found in 2 Baruch and Wisdom of Solomon. And Philo's depiction of the Word as the primary means by which God engages creation finds a striking parallel in the Palestinian targums. There is actually quite little in Philo's depiction of the function of God's Word that does not find a parallel in other Second Temple or targumaic literature.

While Philo's thinking on God's Word appears to be more developed than what is found in other Second Temple Jewish literature, one must ask whether such development is simply an accident of genre rather than evidence of more developed Philonic thinking. In other words, Philo produces philosophical and theological treatises that offer the opportunity (and expectation) for greater theological depth and articulation, whereas Wisdom of Solomon, for example, is Wisdom literature, a genre naturally limited in its theologically explanatory ability. For example, given the similarities between Philo and Wisdom of Solomon in the depiction of God's Word, we cannot rule out the possibility that the same sophisticated thought found in the former might not also undergird the depictions of that same Word found in the latter. Once this possibility is acknowledged, one can point to an even stronger indicator that this way of understanding the Word of God must have preceded Philo.

Philo is most often writing for a Jewish audience familiar with Jewish scriptures. It is striking then that Philo can frequently refer to God's Word, as well as its various functions, without any explanation or justification. It seems quite clear that Philo assumes his readers are familiar with these concepts and accept a certain basic understanding of God's Word that Philo can draw upon.[23] Philo never seems to have to defend his teaching on the Logos for his readers or explain how what he is saying is not in violation of Jewish monotheism, a conviction that Philo clearly holds. Such a lack of justification strongly indicates that Philo's teaching on God's Word shares common ground with his audience, and that they, like Philo, see no conflict in identifying the Logos as a distinct entity or even as a "second god."[24]

At the very least then, it seems we can say that Philo is representative of a normative Alexandrian Judaism, and not completely unique. And if this type of thinking existed among Alexandrian Jews, why would we conclude that it did not exist among other Hellenistic Jews? Other than an a priori commitment to a particular view of Jewish monotheism, there seems to be little reason. Even the degree to which Philo's treatment of the Logos was influenced by Platonism and Stoicism has come under scrutiny, with many interpreters arguing that Philo's presentation of the Logos is dependent on Jewish traditions rather than Greek.[25] Thus, there is good reason to believe that Philo's hypostatic depictions of God's Word were at home in his Hellenistic Jewish context and that Philo is no Second Temple aberration.

Daniel Boyarin has argued that the Logos theology evident in Philo, and that likely shared by other Hellenistic Jews (at least Alexandrian), was not solely of a "Hellenistic" provenance, but it was also prevalent in Palestinian Judaism as well.[26] Boyarin's evidence is certainly controversial, as he points to the Palestinian Targum's and their use of Memra to support his claim. He notes strong parallels between Philo's use of Logos and the use of Memra in the Palestinian Targum, particularly Neofiti 1 (e.g., the Memra of the Lord creates, the Memra of the Lord is that which interacts with human beings, the Memra of the Lord leads God's people as a pillar of cloud, etc.)[27] While Boyarin acknowledges that the Palestinian Targums could be quite late (even as late as the third or fourth century), this does not mean that they do not provide evidence for a Memra/Word theology in the Second Temple Judaism of Palestine; rather it demonstrates that such a theology persisted well into the rabbinic period that sought to stamp it out.[28] How plausible is it that later Palestinian Judaism of the second to fourth century developed a new and robust Memra theology a century after such a theology (Logos theology) was already manifest at least in some expressions of Hellenistic Judaism? Such development is particularly unlikely to have occurred in the climate of a rabbinic Judaism that we know resisted any sort of two powers expression.

A much more plausible theory is that a Memra/Word theology of the Palestinian Targums reflects a common theology within Palestinian Judaism in the Second Temple period, and that this theology of Palestinian Judaism was closely related to the Logos theology of Hellenistic Judaism—perhaps it was even the foundation for such expressions in Hellenistic Judaism. This Memra/Word theology, a theology that Boyarin argues was promulgated in the synagogues and not the rabbinic houses of study, then persisted into the rabbinic period, where it was frequently resisted because of its similarities with the growing Christian movement.[29] If Boyarin's reconstruction is correct, then Philo is by no means a lonely voice in the Second Temple period. In fact, Philo simply reflects a prominent Second Temple Jewish theology of God's Word, one that existed in both Hellenistic and Palestinian Judaism.

WHAT SORT OF DISTINCT ENTITY IS GOD'S WORD?

We have made the case that at least some Jews understood God's Word as a distinct entity rather than simply expressions of divine traits or divine action. But that raises the question of what sort of figure God's Word is. While some proponents of an exclusive Jewish monotheism work hard to reject any understanding of God's Word as a distinct entity (see Hurtado for example), Richard Bauckham allows that it could rightly share in the divine identity of Israel's God as a distinct entity.[30] Here we consider whether God's Word might be best explained in terms of a two powers theology and thus best identified as the second power. To this end, we will apply the criteria outlined in chapter 1 to God's Word.

Receiving Worship

Obviously, there is no distinct cult devoted to God's Word in the Second Temple period. Nevertheless, as noted above, Targum Neofiti 1 offers significant evidence of God's Word being the object of worship. In particular, Genesis depicts altars being built, animals being sacrificed, and prayers being offered to the Word (Memra) of the Lord (e.g., 8:20; 12:8; 13:4, 18). Additionally, as noted above, Philo envisions the Logos as the means by which the God of Israel is seated on the ark of the covenant. As such, it seems quite possible that Philo envisions the Logos as the object of worship in the cultic activity in the Temple. We contend that these interpretive traditions strongly indicate that Second Temple Jews could perceive the cult of the one God to, in some way, include the cultic worship of the Word, either with the worship of the immanent Word as the means through which the transcendent YHWH was worshipped or with Jewish cultic worship implying the worship of both the first and second power.

We contend, contra Hurtado, that these interpretive traditions strongly indicate that Second Temple Jews could perceive the cult of the one God to, in some way, include the cultic worship of the Word, either with the worship of the immanent Word as the means through which the transcendent YHWH was worshipped or with Jewish cultic worship implying the worship of both the first and second power.

Creating the Cosmos

As we saw above in our analysis of God's Word, it is regularly depicted as an entity through which creation came into being. This association between God's Word and the act of creating the cosmos is found in a wide variety of literary genres, including Wisdom literature, apocalyptic literature, hymnic literature, philosophical literature, as well as the targumaic traditions. In fact, perhaps no other activity is more frequently ascribed to God's Word than the action of creation itself. Thus, God's Word strongly meets this criterion.

Ruling over Creation

As we demonstrated above, God's Word is frequently depicted as reigning over the created order. Much like engaging in the act of creation, the depiction of the Word of God reigning over creation is present in a wide variety of literary genres. Of particular importance is the depiction of God's Word sitting on God's very thrown, an image that is closely tied to God's sovereignty and one that is rarely attributed to any being other than Israel's God.

Bearing the Name

Association between the Word and God's name is less common than the association between the Word and creation/sovereignty over creation. Yet, as noted above, there seems to be a clear association in Philo, where it is claimed that the Logos is rightly called "the name of God" (*Conf.* 146). Yet, this association with God's name is complicated by other texts in Philo. As noted above, Philo identifies the "Father of the universe" as "the one who is," and then in *On the Change of Names* states that the Logos is not "the one who is" but rather is the κύριος. This identification of the Logos as the κύριος is complicated by the fact that κύριος is the common term Philo used (or was used by Philo's Greek text) to translate the name YHWH when it appears in Israel's scriptures. Thus, there appears a tension, or even a confusion, in Philo, one in which the "Father of the universe" cannot rightly be named other than with the name "the one who is" (a reference to YHWH?), while the Logos is declared not to be "the one who is" yet is identified as "the name of God" and "Lord (Κύριος)"—that is, the replacement for YHWH in the LXX. Here Philo seems to present his modern interpreters with a sort of Gordian Knot, one in which the Logos is both rightly associated with the name of God but also in some way possibly distinct from it. Yet, the two powers theology outlined in chapter 1 might offer a way to cut said knot.

Taking the Role of YHWH

Both for having the name of YHWH and for playing the role of YHWH, it should be further noted that Philo has in a sense side-stepped the question of how to handle the Tetragrammaton. Instead of attempting to preserve the ineffable name via transliteration, he takes the name to its most abstract meaning ("who is"/to be) as referencing God as the source of all being. This, to him, obviously best suits the one he calls the "Father" of the Logos. And yet, the Logos, as God's only begotten Son, is the mirror image of the Father and functions as the "god" who creates, rules, and relates to the world. It must be remembered that, for Philo, the Logos is "the Lord" who appeared to Moses in the burning bush and spoke the ineffable name ("I AM that I AM"), and the Logos is the Lord who dwells in the Temple on the ark of the covenant. Of course for Philo's contemporary Jews these theophanies are appearances of YHWH. This explains the phenomenon reviewed above for Philo and the Targums, namely that the Word can simply replace the name YHWH in the scriptures. As we saw above in our analysis of God's Word, both Philo and Targum Neofiti 1 present numerous examples in which the Word (Logos/ Memra) replaces YHWH in both an interpretation or translation of the scripture. These texts offer us clear examples in which the Word is understood as the primary actor in texts that the Hebrew text ascribes to YHWH.

Holding Additional Titles

As with the last criterion, we cannot rigidly apply this test to the Word at this point because we have not yet fully reviewed the evidence. However, we have alluded to the fact that the Word is equated with the Angel of the Lord and the heavenly likeness of "Man" (= "one like a Son of Man"?), and in the chapters that follow, we will see examples where the Word also holds additional titles, such as Wisdom and the Son of Man. Therefore, this criterion will be better assessed in later chapters in comparison with other figures.

PRELIMINARY CONCLUSIONS ABOUT THE WORD AS THE SECOND POWER

Here we see in many Second Temple texs that like the God of Israel, God's Word rules over creation, is associated with the name of God, receives cultic worship, and is even read into Jewish scriptures where it is clearly YHWH acting in the Hebrew text. As seen in our discussion above, these features are attributed to God's Word in a wide variety of Second Temple literary traditions, including paraphrases of the scriptures in the Targums, Wisdom literature, apocalyptic literature, and philosophical literature. Thus, in light of these criteria, we contend that not only is God's Word often rightly identified as a distinct entity rather than the personification of divine actions, but also that it is often best identified as the second power in heaven. To be sure, such conclusions cannot be drawn for every reference to God's Word in this period. However, the strength of the arguments from both Philo and the Targums increase the likelihood that, even in the more ambiguous references, God's Word can be understood by some as both a distinct entity and the second power in heaven.

Clearly, the Word of God is a significant figure in Second Temple literature. By applying the six criteria set out in our first chapter, we have shown how there are numerous indicators that the Word was understood by some Second Temple Jews as a second power in heaven. At this point, however, our conclusions remain preliminary because (a) we have not assessed the evidence that describes the Word of God under other titles, such as Wisdom, and because (b) we have not compared how other figures, such as Adam and the high priest, may also appear to be second power figures and so require further reflection upon the Word's status. Therefore, we have carefully reviewed the evidence and applied our criteria to this figure, so that we can now turn to other such figures and have clear points with which to compare them. In our following chapter, we will see that the figure of Wisdom, primarily appearing in Wisdom literature, has much in common with the Word and thus can shed further light on our study.

NOTES

1. For those who hold to this position, see Dunn, *Christology in the Making*, 163–75, 215–30; S. F. Moore, "Intermediaries in Jewish Theology: Memra, Shekinah, Metatron," *HTR* 15 (1922): 41–85; Roland Edmund Murphy, *The Tree of Life: An Exploration of Biblical Wisdom Literature* (Grand Rapids, MI: Eerdmans, 2002), 133; idem, "Wisdom in the Old Testament," *Anchor Bible Dictionary* (1992): 4:926–27; Karen H. Jobes, "Sophia Christology: The Way of Wisdom?" in *The Way of Wisdom: Essays in Honor of Bruce K. Waltke*, eds. James I. Packer and Sven Soderlund (Grand Rapids, MI: Zondervan, 2000), 226, 237.

2. See Boyarin, *Border Lines*, 112–28; Schäfer, *Two Gods*, 62–65; Gieschen, *Angelomorphic Christology*, 103–13; Winn, "Identifying the Enochic Son of Man," 301–7.

3. Dunn, *Christology in the Making*, 217.

4. Dunn, *Christology in the Making*, 218

5. Dunn, *Christology in the Making*, 218.

6. Dunn, *Christology in the Making*, 219.

7. Dunn, *Christology in the Making*, 219.

8. Dunn, *Christology in the Making*, 219 (original emphasis).

9. Dunn, *Christology in the Making*, 224. For similar conclusions, see Moises Silva, "Logos," in *NIDNTTE*, vol. 3, 156–57.

10. Dunn, *Christology in the Making*, 226–28.

11. This position goes back to the Jewish Rabbi Maimonides (twelfth century), but was adopted by many interpreters during the twentieth century. The landmark work for this position seems to Moore, "Intermediaries." Moore is followed by many, including by H. L. Strack and P. Billerbeck, *Das Evangelium nach Matthäus erläutert aus Talmud und Midrash*, vol. 2 (München: Beck'sche, 1922), 333; F. C. Burkitt, "Memra, Shekinah, Metatron," *JTS* 24 (1923): 158–59; C.K. Barrett, *The Gospel according to John: An Introduction with Commentary and Notes on the Greek Text*, 2nd ed. (Philadelphia: Westminster, 1978), 128; Craig S. Keener, *The Gospel of John: A Commentary*, vol. 1 (Peabody, MA: Hendrickson, 2003), 349–50. W. E. Aufrecht, "Surrogates for the Divine Name in the Palestinian Targums to Exodus" (PhD dissertation, University of Toronto, 1979). A good review of scholarship on this issue can be found in McNamara, *Targum and Testament Revisited*, 154–61. McNamara, himself, previously held this understanding; see *The Aramaic Bible: Neofiti 1 Genesis*, 38; idem, *Targum and Testament, Aramaic Paraphrases of the Hebrew Bible: A Light on the New Testament* (Grand Rapids, MI: Eerdmans, 1972), 101–6, but in his revised edition of *Targum and Testament*, he is more open to the possibility of the Word of the Lord representing a hypostasis.

12. For discussion of *Maat*, see Ringgren, *Word and Wisdom*; Burton L. Mack, *Logos und Sophia: Untersuchungen zur Weisheitstheologie im hellenistischen Judentum* (Germany: Vandenhoeck & Ruprecht, 1973), 34–39; Dunn, *Christology in the Making*, 170. For discussions of deified Roman virtues, see Harold Mattingly, "The Roman Virtues," *HTR* 30, no. 2 (1937): 103–17.

13. See Larry W. Hurtado, *At the Origins of Christian Worship: The Context and Character of Earliest Christian Devotion* (Grand Rapids, MI: Eerdmans, 1999), 72–74; Dunn, *Christology in the Making*, 170–71.

14. See Gieschen, *Angelomorphic Christology*, 89–93; Winston, *Logos and Mystical Theology*, 9–25; Daniel Boyarin, *Border Lines: The Partition of Judeo-Christianity* (Philadelphia: University of Pennsylvania Press, 2004), 112–27.

15. Cf. Robert Hayward, *Divine Name and Presence: The Memra* (Totowa, NJ: Allanheld, Osmun, 1981), who, although he concluded that the targums in their final form present the Memra as a personification, and not a distinct hypostasis, also found that the earliest strata of the targums, in fact, do betray an older understanding of God's Word as a distinct agent.

16. Clearly, while not all agree, many do; see, for example, Gieschen, *Angelomorphic Christology*, 89–93; Winston, *Logos and Mystical Theology*, 9–25; Boyarin, *Border Lines*, 112–27; G. Schrenk, "lego" in *TDNT*, vol 4, 88–90; M. Hillar, "The Logos and Its Function in the Writing of Philo of Alexandria: Greek Interpretation of Hebrew Thought and Foundations of Christianity: Part Two," *JRR* 7 (1998): 36–53.

17. Boyarin, *Border Lines*, 117.

18. For this argument, see Boyarin, *Border Lines*, 117.

19. Boyarin, *Border Lines*, 117.

20. While here we offer this explanation for the worship of God's Word, it can also be applied to other entities that we conclude are recipients of cultic worship below. We would also note that such understandings of YHWH worship within a two powers paradigm also address Hurtado's claims regarding the presence of a pattern of devotion for the YHWH of Israel and the absence of such a pattern for devotion for other entities. We would argue that through the means noted here, the second power could naturally be understood to be included in the worship of YHWH and thus fully included in the pattern of YHWH devotion Hurtado has identified.

21. Dunn, *Christology in the Making*, 174. Seem similar thinking in Moore, "Intermediaries," 55.

22. Examples might include Erwin Goodenough, *An Introduction to Philo Judaeus* (New Haven, CT: Yale University Press, 1940); G. E. Sterling, "Philo" in *The Dictionary of New Testament Background* (eds. Craig A. Evans and Stanley E. Porter; Downers Grove, IL: IVP, 2000), 792. Following the Messina Colloquium, Herman C. Waetjen, "Logos προς τον θεον and Objectification of Truth in the Prologue of the Fourth Gospel," *CBQ* 63, no. 2 (2001), 383, concludes that Philo represents a pre-Gnostic stage in the development of Gnosticism proper. Also, cf. Ugo Bianchi, *Le Origini dello Gnosticismo Colloquio di Messina 13–18 Aprile 1966* (SHR 12; Leiden: Brill, 1967).

23. See Boyarin, *Border Lines*, 113; Winston, *Logos and Mystical Theology*, 11; Segal, *Two Powers*, 163.

24. Even when asked if the Logos entails belief in "two gods (δύο . . . θεοί)" (*Somn.* 1.228), Philo neglects to explain the Logos as a personification of God's actions, but instead insists that the Logos is differentiated from God in other ways, so that he can comfortably speak of "two powers (δυεῖν δυνάμεων)" (*Somn.* 1.162); discussed in chapter 2.

25. See Boyarin, *Border Lines*, 113–14; Hannah, *Michael and Christ*, 80–81. Also, see Niehoff, *Philo of Alexandria*, 209–24.

26. Boyarin, *Border Lines*, 116–20.

27. Boyarin, *Border Lines*, 119.

28. Boyarin, *Border Lines*, 118

29. Boyarin, *Border Lines*, 116–17. Also, Boyarin, *Border Lines*, 120–25, argues that such expressions of Judaism are to be included in the rabbinic polemics against the "two powers in heaven" heresy, a heresy that is frequently targeted in rabbinic literature. Boyarin rejects the common narrative that rabbinic Judaism quickly became normative for Jews of the post-temple era, and argues that rabbinic orthodoxy, an orthodoxy committed to the singularity of the God of Israel, had to be constructed over several centuries. Thus, the Palestinian Targums represent a dominant strand of Judaism that resisted rabbinic hegemony.

30. Bauckham, *Jesus and the God of Israel*, 16–17.

Chapter 4

God's Wisdom

In our previous chapters, we reviewed ways in which God's Word acts as distinct from God, and yet acts as God. We, therefore, concluded that many Jewish authors and audiences from the Second Temple period held to some form of a two powers paradigm wherein the Word of God was understood to be the second power in heaven.

In our present chapter we now turn to the figure of Wisdom. Beginning in Wisdom literature from the Hebrew scriptures, Wisdom seems to be a poetic way of describing God's activity, a personification perhaps. However, when turning to the later literature of the Second Temple, this figure takes on a life of her own.

WISDOM IN THE HEBREW SCRIPTURES

Throughout the Hebrew Bible, Wisdom is the possession of Israel's God (Ps 51:6; Job 12:13; 39:17), one that at times is bestowed upon individuals as a gift and at others seems obtainable through means such as proper fear of, or obedience to, God (Exod 35:31; 36:2; 1 Kings 4:29; Ps 110:10; Prov. 1:7; 2:6; 9:10; 15:33; Job 28:28).[1] Within the book of Proverbs, Wisdom seems to take on a distinct identity. Wisdom is depicted as crying out to God's people (1:20, 8:1), and she speaks warnings and judgments against those who do not listen to her. Wisdom laughs at those who ignore her (1:26). Wisdom places a crown on those who will listen to her (4:9). Wisdom loves those who love her (8:17). Wisdom builds a house, sacrifices animals, mixes wine, sets a table, and sends out maid-servants presumably to invite guests. All such descriptions of Wisdom seem like personifications of an abstract concept or divine attribute, and with such personifications the text vividly depicts the power and value of living in accordance with divine Wisdom. But one such depiction of Wisdom seems to stand out above the rest. In Proverbs 8, Wisdom speaks of being created by YHWH at the beginning of his work, before the beginning of the earth (vs. 22–23). Wisdom claims to be present with YHWH when the earth is created (vs. 24–30). Wisdom also claims to be "like a master worker" during the creation itself, a description that seems to indicate Wisdom's involvement in the act of creation. In addition to this depiction in Proverbs 8, Proverbs 3 claims that through Wisdom, God founded or established the earth—again, Wisdom is depicted as being involved in the act of creation. These depictions of Wisdom stand out among the personifications identified above, as Wisdom is described as a created entity before the creation of the earth. And while all previous actions performed by Wisdom are easily understood as conveying truths about the abstract concept or attribute of Wisdom, Wisdom's engagement in the act of creation itself is much harder to understand. For example, the depiction of Wisdom "calling out" clearly conveys the self-evidence of Wisdom that should be recognized by God's people. Wisdom, "loving those who love it," clearly conveys the reward that comes to those who live wisely. But it is much harder to understand what truth about wise thought and conduct is advanced through the depiction of Wisdom engaging in the act of creation itself. For all of these reasons, the depiction of Wisdom in Proverbs 8:22–31 and Proverbs 3:19 seem to do more than describe sapiential character and qualities. Instead they seem to be more theological in nature, functioning to reveal more about the God of Israel than the abstract concept of Wisdom (wise conduct/thought). This theological connection between God and Wisdom as an agent in creation seems to find expression in a handful of other passages of the Hebrew Bible. Psalm 104:23 claims that God made all things "by Wisdom." Similarly, Jeremiah 10:12 and 28:15 both claim that God has established the world "by his Wisdom." In light of this evidence, it seems possible that some of these depictions of Wisdom have moved past the simple literary device of personifying an abstract concept or divine attribute and move closer to descriptions of a distinct hypostasis.[2] After examining depictions of Wisdom in Second Temple literature, perhaps a clearer picture of Jewish understanding of Wisdom will emerge.

WISDOM IN SECOND TEMPLE RELIGIOUS TEXTS

Within the religious literature of the Second Temple period, Wisdom figures prominently in two books, Sirach (c. early second century BCE) and Wisdom of Solomon (c. first century CE). In Sirach, Wisdom is the property of Israel's God, which he grants to his people (e.g., 1:1, 7, 9–10).[3] Sirach also follows Proverbs in frequently personifying Wisdom. Wisdom walks with people (4:17), offers shelter (14:25–27), feeds and gives drink (15:3), teaches and gives help (4:11), torments, trusts, and tests (4:17). Like Proverbs, Sirach is adamant that God created Wisdom (1:4; 24:8–9), and that Wisdom preceded all other created things (1:4; 24:9). However, unlike Proverbs, there is no explicit claim that Wisdom participated in the act of creation.[4] In fact, Sirach repeatedly attributes the act of creation to Israel's God alone (15:14; 24:8; 43:33). Sirach's personifications of Wisdom primarily functions to vividly describe an abstract concept, much like the majority of personifications of Wisdom in Proverbs. However, Sirach 24 offers descriptions of Wisdom that seem to go beyond simple personification.

Like the descriptions found in Proverbs 8, these descriptions go beyond the use of vivid poetic language to convey general truths about an abstract concept or attribute and move toward descriptions of a distinct agent or being, one that is attributed theological significance. In Sirach 24, Wisdom is depicted as speaking. She declares heaven as its dwelling and even claims to sit on a throne that is a pillar of clouds (24:4). It also claims that it came forth from the "most high" and covered the earth like a mist (24:3). It is described as "encompassing the vault of heaven" and "traversing the depth of the abyss" (24:6). While Wisdom is not depicted as creating the earth, it claims to have power over the waves of the sea and all of the earth (24:6). Wisdom even ministers before Israel's God in the Holy of Holies (24:10–19). Sirach seems reluctant to depict this distinct being as one that is active in creation (a reluctance seemingly not found in Proverbs), but Sirach is perfectly comfortable depicting Wisdom as sitting on a throne in heaven, ministering before the God of Israel, and exercising sovereignty over the earth and sea.

In the Wisdom of Solomon, Wisdom again is depicted as the possession of God alone, a possession he bestows on those who seek it (6:13, 16; 7:17; 8:21; 9:6).[5] Like both Proverbs and Sirach, Wisdom is frequently personified. She appears to and meets those who seek her (6:16), her hands bring wealth (7:11), she is the mother of all good things (7:12), she labors by the side of the one who possesses her (9:10), and she protects and rescues those who serve her. As in both Proverbs and Sirach, these descriptions are easily understood as simple personifications functioning to vividly present an abstract concept or attribute. But like both Proverbs and Sirach (and perhaps more than both), Wisdom of Solomon offers descriptions of Wisdom that seem to transgress the boundaries of simple personification and depict Wisdom as a distinct entity.[6] Wisdom is described as the breath of the power of God and the "pure emanation" of God's glory (7:25). Wisdom is also described as the "reflection of eternal light," "a spotless mirror of the working of God," and "an image" of God's goodness (7:26).

Similar to the depiction of Wisdom's sovereignty over the world in Sirach, Wisdom of Solomon claims, "[Wisdom] reaches mightily from one end of the earth to the other, and she orders all things well" (8:1). While Wisdom of Solomon makes it clear that Wisdom dwells in heaven with God (8:3) and even sits beside the throne of God (9:4),[7] Wisdom clearly dwells with God's people and accompanies those who are faithful. Wisdom is even identified with the pillars of cloud and fire that guided Israel in the wilderness (10:17; compare with Sirach 24:4 and Song of Solomon 3:6) as well as an agent that was present with figures like Adam, Noah, Abraham, and Moses. Thus, Wisdom is depicted as an entity that is able to be present both in heaven and on earth at the same time. Wisdom of Solomon even claims: "Although [Wisdom] is but one, she can do all things, and while remaining in herself, she renews all things" (7:27). The purpose of this verse seems to be both the affirmation of Wisdom's "oneness" and her universal presence.

Where Sirach did not follow Proverbs in affirming Wisdom's role in the creation of the world, Wisdom of Solomon is adamant about this function of Wisdom. It claims that Wisdom "is the fashioner of all things" (7:22) and the "fashioner of what exists." (8:6). The author declares "God of my ancestors and Lord of mercy, who have made all things by your [W]ord, and by your [W]isdom have formed humankind to have dominion over the creatures you have made" (9:2). While it is clear in Wisdom of Solomon that God creates (1:14; 9:9; 11:17), it is also clear that Wisdom functions as an agent in that divine creative act. All of this language could easily lead a reader to conceive of Wisdom as a distinct entity that bears theological significance rather than simply an abstract concept or trait related to Israel's God.

While Wisdom features quite prominently in Sirach and Wisdom of Solomon, there are a handful of examples where similar descriptions of Wisdom can be found in other religious writings of the Second Temple period. A noteworthy example is found in 2 Enoch 30:8, where God claims that on the sixth day of creation, he commanded his "Wisdom" to create humanity out of seven different components.[8] In 1 Enoch 42, it is claimed that Wisdom could not find a place to dwell (presumably among the people of God on earth) and thus a place was found for Wisdom in heaven. Then it describes Wisdom again seeking a place among "the children of the people." After failing a second time, Wisdom returns to heaven and settles permanently with the angels. Interestingly, 1 Enoch 84:3 depicts Wisdom as dwelling on God's throne (compare with Wis. 9:4). These descriptions of Wisdom are clearly significant parallels of descriptions of Wisdom found in Sirach and Wisdom of Solomon. They are particularly significant because they illustrate that such conceptions of Wisdom were not limited to a particular literary world, such as Wisdom literature, but could transverse genres, even appearing in a radically different genre such as apocalyptic literature.

WISDOM IN PHILO

Wisdom also features quite prominently in the work of Philo of Alexandria.[9] Philo identifies Wisdom as one of four divine virtues, virtues that include wisdom, justice, courage, and self-control. These virtues seem to be part of God in some sense, but they are also realities created by God. For examples, Philo claims that "Wisdom" was the first thing that God quarried out of his own powers (*Leg.* 2.86) and that Wisdom is older than the creation of the universe (*Virt.* 62). Philo also claims a distinction between the virtues manifested in God's created world, namely, those found in human beings and the divine virtues. The former are only reflections of the latter that can be manifest in the world (*QG* 1.57). In other words, the Wisdom of God is distinct from earthly wisdom. Philo claims that the virtue of wisdom that exists in this world cannot be identified as God himself, but only the work of God (*QG* 1.11; see also *Leg.* 1.77). Such a claim seems to imply that the divine virtue of Wisdom, on which the earthly virtue of wisdom is patterned, could be identified with God, though it must be recognized as something that is in some way second to God (*Fug.* 50–52). Thus, for Philo, Wisdom is closely associated with God's identity and God is the fountain and source of all wisdom (*Fug.* 137; *Sacr.* 64; *Spec.* 1.277). Of the four divine virtues, wisdom seems preeminent. Philo claims that Wisdom is "the most divine and freehanded of all things" (*Prob.* 13). Wisdom is described as both brilliant and radiant (*Plant.* 40). It is both "radiance and light," and it is the archetypal model for the sun (*Migr.* 40; *QG* 1.7). According to Philo, Wisdom is holy and judges the earth (*Fug.* 195). With justice, it regulates all divine and human affairs (*Spec.* 2.231). It also functions to make human worship possible, as without Wisdom, it is impossible for the creation to worship the creator (*QG* 1.6). Philo also claims that Wisdom is the court and palace in which God dwells.

Philo also echoes Proverbs and other Jewish traditions in claiming that Wisdom is God's active agent in creation. Using biological imagery, Philo conceives of God as the Father of creation and Wisdom as the mother, with Wisdom receiving the seed of creation from God and then giving birth to it (*Ebr.* 30–31). Thus, Philo calls the world the only and beloved son of Wisdom, and Wisdom, the mother of the entire universe (*Ebr.* 31). At many other points, Philo identifies Wisdom as mother or mother of all things/creation (*Leg.* 2.49; *Fug.* 109; *Det.* 30, 54; *Conf.* 49.; *Her.* 53). Closely related to Wisdom's role in creation is Philo's identification of Eden (at times Paradise) with Wisdom. At times he seems to equate these two realities (*Leg.* 1.64–65, 77; *Somn.* 2.242; *QG* 1.6), but at one point clarifies that Eden is a symbol of

Wisdom (*QG* 1.8). Thus, it seems the mother of creation, Wisdom, is in some way reflected in her daughter, the perfect Eden.[10]

While Philo certainly offers a philosophical veneer to his understanding of Wisdom, he shares much in common with what we have seen in both the Hebrew Bible and other religious texts of the Second Temple period. These similarities include God as the source of Wisdom, Wisdom preceding creation, Wisdom as an agent through which God creates the universe, Wisdom as exercising sovereignty over the created order, and Wisdom closely associated with radiance and light. Philo's descriptions of Wisdom certainly seem to move past simple personification and appear much more like theologically ladened descriptions of a distinct entity.

COMMONALITIES IN THE JEWISH WISDOM TRADITIONS

In this survey of the theme of Wisdom in both the Hebrew Bible and Second Temple Jewish literature, a number of commonalities emerge. Each body of literature that we examined offers descriptions of Wisdom that seem to transgress the boundary of simple personification and present Wisdom as a distinct entity that is in some way an agent of God. Wisdom is consistently presented as created by God, though also consistently presented as being the first of all God's creation: Wisdom precedes the creation of the universe.[11] While Wisdom is a distinct agent of God, and while distinct from God, Wisdom also is depicted as divine. Although Wisdom is often depicted as a created being, she is also consistently presented as the agent through which God created the world (with Sirach being silent on the matter). It is noteworthy that while these descriptions of Wisdom are primarily found in the genre of Wisdom literature, they are not confined to this genre, and can be found, though less frequently, in prophetic, hymnic, apocalyptic, and philosophic literature. While there is significant commonality among the traditions we surveyed, there is also clear development. The depiction of Wisdom as an agent of God's sovereignty over creation is not found in the Hebrew Bible, but seems to emerge later, being evident in Sirach, Wisdom of Solomon, and Philo. The association of Wisdom with brilliance, radiance, and light, is only present in the relatively later works of Wisdom of Solomon and Philo. The same is true of connections between Wisdom and the divine nature, image of God, and divine reflection. This development suggests that as we move closer to the first century CE, at least some strands of Judaism depict Wisdom as a distinct being, that was active in the creation of the world, has grown in importance, and has taken on greater interpretive significance.

THE RELATIONSHIP BETWEEN
GOD'S WISDOM AND WORD

After considering both God's Wisdom and Word in the religious traditions of the Second Temple period, it has perhaps become clear to the reader that the depiction of these two concepts overlap significantly in many ways. Not only do both seem to be presented as distinct divine entities and agents through which the God of Israel accomplishes various tasks, but also, the tasks which they are depicted as accomplishing are strikingly similar. Both Word and Wisdom are depicted as divine agents through which God created the world. Both are depicted as exercising God's sovereignty over the world (e.g., ruling over the earth, holding the earth together, etc.). Word and Wisdom are often described with similar words or through similar concepts. Wisdom is identified as the first of God's creative acts, while God's Word is identified as his "first born son" and is associated with the beginning of creation. Both are associated with the throne of God, with Wisdom depicted as being next to the throne and the Word as springing forth from it. These similarities alone strongly suggest that these two concepts (or entities) are closely connected to each other. That such a connection was perceived by some in the Second Temple period is clearly seen in Wisdom 9:1–2, where synonymous parallelism is used to equate both Word and Wisdom: "O God of my ancestors and Lord of mercy, who have made all things by your *[W]ord*, and by your *[W]isdom* have formed humankind to have dominion over the creatures you have made" (emphasis added). While Philo does not directly equate Word and Wisdom, he indirectly does so by attributing to them the same functions. Nicola Denzey outlines the following similarities: both create the universe, both are identified as "eldest" and present at creation, both reflect the image of God, and both are models for primordial light.[12] Philo implicitly equates Wisdom and Word as James Dunn notes that the two seem to be equated through Philo's depiction of the manna given to Israel.[13] In *On the Change of Names,* manna is allegorized as "heavenly [W]isdom" (*Mut.* 259), whereas at many other points in Philo, manna is identified with the Logos (*Leg.* 3. 169f; *Sacr.* 86; *Det.* 118; *Fug.* 137). While Philo claims that the Logos flows from God's Wisdom, he also claims that the Logos is the source of that Wisdom. It seems the relationship between the two is very fluid for Philo, and that at times he is even able to use them synonymously.[14] In light of this evidence, we contend that for at least some (perhaps many) Second Temple Jews, Word and Wisdom were understood synonymously, and that whether they were understood as describing a distinct divine entity or merely as vivid poetic descriptions of divine attributes, or of God himself, they were often understood to be describing the same realities, rather than two distinct realities.

WISDOM AS A DISTINCT ENTITY

As we saw with the Word of God, some would contend that all Jewish literature describing God's Wisdom as a distinct entity are in fact poetic personifications. Initially, we could stipulate how Word and Wisdom are often equated, and since we have shown in previous chapters how God's Word is best understood in many texts to be a distinct hypostasis, it follows that Wisdom should be understood as such as well. However, rather than relying on simple deductions and comparisons, we will here review the arguments and evidence at play in this debate.

Argument 1: The Existence of Other Vivid and Poetic Personifications of Divine Attributes that are not Understood as Distinct Entities

It is often noted that there are many other divine attributes that are vividly personified in both the Hebrew Bible and Second Temple Jewish literature.[15] For example, in Psalm 85, faithfulness is describe as springing up from the ground, righteousness and peace will kiss each other, and righteousness will look down from the sky. In Psalm 43, the psalmist says "Oh send out your light and your truth, let them lead me." In Psalm 57:3, God is depicted as sending out his steadfast love and faithfulness. Wisdom of Solomon, a text particularly relevant to our discussion of Wisdom, says, "Your all powerful hand, which created the world out of formless matter" (11:17). In addition to these, James Dunn notes that the text often personifies negative realities as well. Job 11:14 says "and let not injustice dwell in your tent." Psalm 107:42 describes all wickedness as stopping its mouth. Dunn argues that though these realities experience personification in Jewish literature, it is clear that none of them are intended to be understood as distinct beings.[16] These, he argues, are best understood as the product of ancient literary device and idiom, rather than the hypostatization of abstract concepts or divine attributes. For Dunn, the so-called hypostatic depictions of Wisdom have far more in common with Jewish idiomatic practice than with the pagan hypostatization of divine attributes, and as such, he favors identifying Jewish depictions of Wisdom with the former rather than the latter.

Argument 2: The Fluidity of Wisdom as Depicted in the Hebrew Bible and Second Temple Literature

It is argued by some that the fluidity of the concept of Wisdom in the relevant literature suggests that it should not be conceived of as a distinct being.[17] Many such examples of such fluidity can be identified. In virtually all of the books considered above, Wisdom often appears as either an abstract concept or divine attribute rather than a distinct entity. Wisdom is equated with notions of knowledge and understanding (Prov 2:6), the fear of the Lord (Prov 9:10; 15:33; Ps 111:10; Sir 1:14), and the result of studying God's Law (Sir 39:1). Arguably, Wisdom does not appear in these sources as a distinct being but rather it appears as an abstract concept or attribute of God that is shared with and imparted to God's people. In light of such uses, it is argued that instances in which Wisdom does appear as a distinct entity should be simply understood as more vivid and creative poetic descriptions of what is clearly an attribute of God himself in other texts. Additionally, James Dunn argues that the so-called hypostatic depictions of Wisdom often appear alongside of affirmations of Jewish monotheism, with no suggestion that such depictions of Wisdom are in tension with that monotheism.[18] This lack of tension for Dunn supports the conclusion that such depictions of Wisdom do not describe a distinct divine entity but simply depict an attribute of the one God of Israel.

Argument 3: The Development of the Wisdom Tradition Shaped by Pagan Culture

As we noted in our analysis above, it does appear that there is development in Jewish Wisdom traditions as we move from texts like Proverbs to Wisdom of Solomon and Philo. Many interpreters have accounted for this development by theorizing influence from pagan culture and philosophy.[19] It is argued that the traditions in which Wisdom appears as a distinct divine being are the result of Judaism counteracting or accommodating pagan goddesses.[20] For example, the Egyptian goddess Isis was associated with creating the universe, and it is theorized that in response to this tradition, Jewish literature like Wisdom of Solomon associate creation with the feminine Sophia, God's Wisdom. Such a move would presumably make the Jewish faith more palatable or attractive to pagan neighbors. Thus, it is argued that such descriptions of Wisdom do not actually represent distinct divine beings, but represent realities expressed in pagan religions being Judaized and brought into the thought world of Jewish monotheism.

Assessing Wisdom's Status

In light of these arguments, Dunn and others conclude that what might appear to be hypostatic depictions of Wisdom are better understood as vivid personifications of either a divine attribute or function. Dunn is willing to allow that Wisdom might be a way in which Jews described the function of divine immanence, but he rejects the conclusion that she is a distinct being.

The first argument to address is the claim that depictions of Wisdom are best understood the same way as other personifications found in Jewish texts. Certainly there are occasions where the tasks and descriptions of Wisdom could be understood as simple personification used to give vibrancy to abstract concepts or divine attributes (e.g., Wisdom crying out to and warning God's people [Prov 1:20, 8:1] or Wisdom laughing at those who do not listen to her [Prov 1:26]). In this way, Wisdom might parallel similar personifications of attributes such as God's faithfulness, righteousness, and mercy. But many times, the manner in which Wisdom is described resists such an interpretation, and also sets it apart from the personification of concepts such as faithfulness and mercy. Wisdom is depicted as engaging in the very act of creation, functioning as a divine intermediary between God and creation, and exercising sovereignty over creation. Such tasks are not assigned to the divine attributes of faithfulness, mercy, or any other divine attribute. These depictions of Wisdom seem to move past vivid personification of abstract ideas/attributes and toward distinct and significant theological concepts. These examples raise the question as to why the author would assign such tasks to a concept like Wisdom, when such tasks are commonly the function of God himself. Such a move is hard to explain by literary device alone and begs for a more compelling theological answer.

The second argument is concerned with fluidity of the concepts of God's Wisdom. It is certainly true that at times Wisdom is not presented as a distinct being, but simply as an abstract concept or attribute of God himself. But does such fluidity deny the possibility that either author or reader could also conceive of Wisdom as a distinct being? It is not necessarily true that because Wisdom is at times described as an attribute of God or humans that it could also not be conceived as a distinct agent of God, perhaps an agent through which an attribute of God is manifest and shared with God's people. Philo certainly understands Wisdom in such a dualistic way. He distinguishes between the divine power of Wisdom, which is depicted as a distinct being and agent, and the manifestation of the characteristic of wisdom in God's creation, which Philo specifically states is not divine in the same manner as the heavenly power; the latter is merely a reflection of the former, and thus not depicted as a distinct divine being. In the Greco-Roman world, it was quite easy for people to speak of powers or "virtues" (in the Latin sense of the term) such as justice, faithfulness, good fortune, and wisdom as attributes of both gods and human beings, but at the same time conceive of all of them as distinct divine beings in and of themselves.[21] In light of such examples, it seems misguided to conclude that fluidity of the depictions of Wisdom in

Second Temple Jewish literature precludes Wisdom from being understood as a distinct divine entity.[22]

The third argument to address is related to the possible dependence of the Jewish Wisdom tradition and deities of the ancient Near East. It is argued that the hypostatic depictions of Wisdom are ways of either accommodating or counteracting pagan deities, by incorporating features of those deities into Jewish monotheism. In other words, these depictions of Wisdom are not truly hypostatic, but merely Jewish responses to pagan religion. It should first be noted that while such traditions are possible, they are far from certain, and the history of how such traditions developed is debated.[23] But regardless of whether dependence exists, it is hardly an argument against reading Jewish Wisdom traditions in terms of a second divine hypostasis. Such Jewish borrowing could indeed be the source of Jewish thinking for Wisdom as a divine hypostasis: the Egyptian goddess Isis that creates the world becomes the hypostatic Wisdom of the God of Israel through which that God creates the world. It is also possible that the similarities between pagan deities and Jewish Wisdom are the result of blending such pagan deities with a distinct hypostasis of Israel's God that already existed, perhaps something like Hellenistic philosophy's impact on Jewish depictions of God's Word. Concluding that dependence on pagan traditions somehow supports the position that seemingly hypostatic Wisdom traditions are indeed non-hypostatic, seems to be built on a presupposition of the singularity of the one God of Israel. But if one accepts that Second Temple Jews could understand their one God in terms of two powers in heaven, any evidence of pagan influence could be understood in terms of shaping Jewish depictions of such powers. As stated in our first chapter, we cannot privilege one view of Jewish monotheism over another as we approach the relevant evidence—the question of the nature of Jewish monotheism is currently an open one.

WISDOM AND THE PROPOSED CRITERIA

We are convinced that Wisdom is a distinct hypostasis in many Second Temple texts. This view is strengthened both by Wisdom's strong identification with the Word, which we have shown above, and by Wisdom's identity as the Angel of the Lord, which we will show in the following chapters. If we are right that Wisdom operates as an agent distinct from the Most High God, then it will prove helpful to review the criteria we set out in chapter 1 in order to see if Wisdom qualifies as a second power in heaven.

In our examination of Wisdom, we saw that she is regularly depicted as active in creating the cosmos. Such depictions can be found across a wide body of literature, including the Hebrew Bible, Philo, Wisdom of Solomon, and the Targums. Thus, this criterion supports the conclusion that Wisdom could often be identified in these texts as the second power in heaven.

We have also seen that Wisdom is also regularly depicted as reigning over the cosmos. Wisdom is even depicted as sitting on God's throne, a feature that is rarely attributed to anyone but God himself and is symbolic of cosmic rule. Thus, this criterion also supports the conclusion that Wisdom could be identified as the second power in heaven.

We have also demonstrated that for multiple Second Temple sources, Wisdom is equated with God's Word. Thus, the strength of the case set forward for establishing God's Word as a second power in heaven can be applied to God's Wisdom. Even if Wisdom is not supported as thoroughly by the criteria as God's Word, its shared identity with God's Word implies that the criteria that support the latter can also be applied to the former, at least in the works of Philo or the Wisdom of Solomon. Therefore, Wisdom's shared identity with God's Word greatly strengthens the case that Wisdom, like God's Word, is best understood as the second power in heaven.

CONCLUSIONS ABOUT WISDOM

As we saw with God's Word in our previous chapters, in this present chapter we have shown that Wisdom is not only a distinct entity, she fits several of the criteria for being identified as the second power in heaven. Furthermore, since Wisdom and Word are equated in many of these sources, we have come to the same conclusion for Wisdom that we did for God's Word: Wisdom was understood by some Jews in the Second Temple period to be the second power in heaven.

This conclusion will next be strengthened by turning to texts about the Angel of the Lord. We will assess this figure, using the same set of criteria outlined in chapter 1 to find this Angel to be the second power in heaven. What is more, the Angel will be shown to have been equated—at least in some sources—with God's Word and Wisdom.

NOTES

1. For studies on Wisdom in the Old Testament, see James L. Crenshaw, *Old Testament Wisdom: An Introduction*, 3rd ed. (Louisville, KY: Westminster/John Knox Press, 2010); Murphy, *The Tree of Life*; idem, "Wisdom in the Old Testament"; Leo G. Perdue, *Wisdom Literature: A Theological History* (Louisville, KY: Westminster/John Knox Press, 2007); Tremper Longman III, *The Fear of the Lord Is Wisdom: A Theological Introduction to Wisdom in Israel* (Grand Rapids, MI: Baker, 2017).

2. For our definition of "hypostasis," see the section on "Defining a Second Power" in chapter 1.

3. For commentary on Sirach, see Alexander A. Di Lella and Patrick W. Skehan, *The Wisdom of Ben Sira* (Anchor Bible 39; New Haven, CT: Yale University Press, 1987); Di Lella, "Wisdom of Ben-Sira" in *Anchor Bible Dictionary* vol. 4, 931–45; and John G. Snaith, *Ecclesiasticus or the Wisdom of Jesus, Son of Sirach* (CBCA; Cambridge: Cambridge University Press, 1974).

4. While some have argued that Wisdom is connected with creation in Sirach 24, this is far from explicit. See our critique of this position in our treatment of the High Priest in chapter 9.

5. For commentary on the Wisdom of Solomon, see David Winston, *The Wisdom of Solomon* (AB 43; New York: Double Day, 1979); idem, "Solomon, Wisdom of," in *Anchor Bible Dictionary* (1992), 4:120–27; Earnest G. Clark, *The Wisdom of Solomon* (CBCA; Cambridge: Cambridge University Press, 1974).

6. Bird, *Jesus among the Gods*, 175, concludes, "Wisdom becomes more than a poetic personification; it is a semi-independent entity."

7. Gieschen, *Angelomorphic Christology*, 94, translates 9:4 as Wisdom sitting on the thrown of God, rather than beside. Such a reading certainly enhances the estimation of Wisdom. However, it is our contention that the NRSV has provided the more probable translation of Wisdom sitting beside the throne rather than on the throne.

8. More on 2 Enoch's date and indebtedness to Second Temple tradition will be discussed below, in chapter 6.

9. For secondary literature on Philo, see our chapter 2.

10. Philo sees a similar relationship between the tabernacle and Wisdom, as he claims the tabernacle is an earthly imitation of divine Wisdom (*Her.* 112). One might conclude that Philo understood the tabernacle to be a means by which Israel could experience Eden in some sense.

11. While this theme is most prevalent in Wisdom literature, it is also found elsewhere. E.g., Tg.Neof. 1:1, "In the beginning, by means of [W]isdom the Son of God perfected the heaven and the earth" (for text, translation, and commentary, see Schäffer, *Two Gods*, 31).

12. Nicola Frances Denzey, "Genesis Traditions in Conflict? The Use of Some Exegetical Traditions in the '*Trimorphic Protennoia*' and the Johannine Prologue," *Vigiliae Christianae* 55, no. 1 (2001): 27–28.

13. Dunn, *Christology in the Making*, 171 n. 34.

14. For such a conclusion, see Denzey, "Genesis Traditions," 27–29; Boyarin, *Border*, 109–10; Sharon Lea Mattila, "Wisdom, Sense Perception, Nature, and Philo's Gender Gradient," *HTR* 89, no. 2 (1996): 109; E. R. Goodenough, *By Light, Light* (New Haven, CT: Yale University Press, 1935), 23 (here Goodenough claims that "Philo flatly identifies the Logos with Sophia"); Wolfson, *Philo*, 1:258–61; Mack, *Logos und Sophia*, 110 n. 10; Dunn, *Christology in the Making*, 171.

15. Dunn, *Christology in the Making*, 174–76. Similar arguments are also made by Ralph Marcus, "On Biblical Hypostases of Wisdom," *Hebrew Union College Annual* 23, no. 1 (1950): 164–67; Murphy, "Wisdom in the Old Testament," 926–27.

16. Dunn, *Christology in the Making*, 174–76.

17. Fluidity is a term Dunn uses in his argumentation (*Christology in the Making*, 171), but see similar lines of argumentation in R. Marcus, "On Biblical Hypostases of Wisdom," 164–67. See also Murphy, "Wisdom in the Old Testament," 926.

18. Dunn, *Christology in the Making*, 171.

19. See, for example, Ringgren, *Word and Wisdom*; H. Conzelmann, "The Mother of Wisdom," in *The Future of Our Religious Past: Essays in Honor of Rudolph Bultmann,* ed. James M. Robinson, trans. Charles E. Carlston and Robert P. Scharlemann (New York: Harper & Row, 1971), 232ff.; U. Wilckens, *Weisheit und Torheit: Eine exegetisch-religionsgeschichtliche Untersuchung zu 1. Kor und 2* (Tübingen: Mohr, 1959), 190–97; idem, "σοφία" in *TDNT*, vol. 7, 477–80; James M. Reese, *Hellenistic Influence on the Book of Wisdom and Its Consequences* (Analecta Biblica 41; Rome: Biblical Institute, 1970), 6–13; Murphy, "Wisdom in the Old Testament," 929; R. S. Hess, "Wisdom Sources" in *Dictionary of the Old Testament: Wisdom, Poetry and Writings*, eds. Tremper Longman and Peter Enns (Downers Grove, IL: IVP, 2008), 895–98.

20. Dunn, "Christology in the Making," 168–70; W. L. Knox, "The Divine Wisdom," *JTS* 38 (1937): 230–37.

21. See Mattingly, "Roman Virtues."

22. Tuschling, *Angels and Orthodoxy*, 99, finds that Wisdom is truly distinct from God, since she sits beside God (Wis. 9:4, cited above) "which reveals a higher degree of separation."

23. See the study by John S. Kloppenborg, "Isis and Sophia in the Book of Wisdom," *HTR* 75 (1982): 57–84; see also M. Fox, "World Order and Maʿat: A Crooked Parallel," *JANES* 23 (1995): 37–48.

Chapter 5

The Angel of the Lord

Angels, in general, loom large in Second Temple Jewish Literature.[1] In this era, they are understood as supernatural beings who occupy the space between the supreme God of Israel and humanity, and they aid the former in the administration of the cosmos. While "angel (ἄγγελος)" is the most common means for identifying these figures, they can also be identified as "gods," "powers," and "lords," among other names. While in most instances they are clearly distinct from the God of Israel and even bear distinct names, there are other instances in which the distinction between an angelic figure and the God of Israel appears blurred. At times, certain angelic figures might share in prerogatives that are generally reserved for the God of Israel alone. In other instances, certain angelic figures are closely associated with the name of God or seem to be easily and naturally interchanged with Israel's God in Second Temple interpretations of Jewish scripture. The most significant angelic figure to consider is that which is identified in the Hebrew Bible as the "Angel of the Lord": at times this angel seems to be a manifestation of God, while at other times it seems to be a separate entity doing God's bidding. As we saw in our discussion of God's Word above, Philo equated God's Logos with the Angel of the Lord. Our study of angels here builds on that previous discussion and begins by considering additional explicit treatments of this particular Angel (going forward we will capitalize in order to signify what appears to be uniqueness and theological significance for later texts). We will assess whether treatments of this Angel depict it similar to what is seen in Philo, namely this Angel as a distinct entity that could be understood as a "second power" in heaven. We will then consider other powerful angels, their possible relationship to and identification with the Angel of the Lord, and the role they might play in a two powers paradigm for Jewish monotheism.[2]

While a full survey of the references to the Angel of the Lord in the Hebrew scriptures cannot be offered here,[3] it is worth reviewing some of the key passages that shape later depictions of this entity in the Second Temple period, especially noting the distinct features of this Angel. We will then devote the bulk of our attention to exploring the understanding of this figure in Second Temple literature and assess how he is best understood during this period.

THE ANGEL OF THE LORD IN THE
HEBREW SCRIPTURES

Throughout the scriptures, a figure known as an/the Angel of the Lord appears, and while at times this individual is mysterious and not clearly identified, there is nevertheless a pattern that emerges wherein one particular Angel stands in as, or simply is, YHWH. This Angel appears to several individuals and is called both "the Angel of the Lord (מַלְאַךְ יהוה/ἄγγελος κυρίου)" and simply "the LORD (יהוה/κυρίος)."[4] Certain scripture passages simply describe this Angel's activity, usually as that of fighting Israel's enemies.[5] To be sure, caution must be used in interpreting any given passage, because other figures can also be described as an "angel of the Lord."[6] Even so, there are several examples where the designation is less clear, but the figure nevertheless appears to be this same distinct Angel.[7] Finally, there are a few instances where the text is in doubt, but likely refers to this distinct Angel.[8]

This Angel appears as a human, usually as a warrior, often with a sword.[9] He usually carries out God's judgment against Israel's enemies,[10] but at other times he stands against Israel for disobeying God.[11] As God's agent, this Angel is (at least at times) distinct from God,[12] but since he is also frequently addressed as "LORD (יהוה/κυρίος)"[13] and appears to be indistinguishable from God, or God per se,[14] there is debate about how best to interpret certain texts.[15] Yet, our interest is not in the way in which this figure was understood by the authors and original readers of the Hebrew scriptures. More relevant to the present project is the way in which this figure was understood in the Second Temple period. It is to this understanding, that we now turn our attention.

THE ANGEL OF THE LORD IN SECOND
TEMPLE RELIGIOUS TEXTS

The angelology of the Second Temple period is too vast to cover in full in the present chapter. Many texts speak of angels generally, and many also speak of one Angel as distinct. In this era, Jewish texts begin to name angels like Michael, Gabriel, and others. In these cases, some scholars have seen an adaptation of the earlier scriptures, while others find certain angels like Michael to still be distinct from and lower than the Angel of the Lord. Since these questions must be treated on a case by case basis, we will first review instances where Second Temple Jewish texts speak clearly about the Angel of the Lord as distinct from lower angels. Then, we will review texts where the case is more ambiguous. In both selections, we find various ways of describing the Angel, or at least an angel, as a power in heaven.

The Angel of the Lord in Philo

While the Angel of the Lord was discussed in our previous chapter as part of our treatment of God's Word in the writings and thought of Philo,[16] here we will briefly review some additional relevant data on Philo and the Angel of the Lord. Philo frequently speaks about angels in general.[17] Ontologically, angels are "incorporeal (ἀσωμάτους)" but appear in human form.[18] Functionally, they are God's agents or, to use his preferred terminology, "immortal 'words' which it is customary to call angels (ἀθανάτοις λόγοις, οὓς καλεῖν ἔθος ἀγγέλους)."[19] They are God's "'words' acting on our behalf as mediators (διαιτηταῖς λόγοις χρῆσθαι)" or legal-arbitrators.[20] As "words," their primary role is that of communication:

> These are called "demons" by the other philosophers, but the sacred record is wont to call them "angels" or messengers, employing an apter title, for they both convey the biddings of the Father to His children and report the children's need to their Father (ταύτας δαίμονας μὲν οἱ ἄλλοι φιλόσοφοι, ὁ δὲ ἱερὸς λόγος ἀγγέλους εἴωθε καλεῖν προσφυεστέρῳ χρώμενος ὀνόματι· καὶ γὰρ τὰς τοῦ πατρὸς ἐπικελεύσεις τοῖς ἐγγόνοις καὶ τὰς τῶν ἐγγόνων χρείας τῷ πατρὶ διαγγέλλουσι).[21]

In some sense they are "holy and divine (ἱεραὶ καὶ θεῖαι)," and yet they are clearly "servitors and lieutenants (ὑποδιάκονοι καὶ ὕπαρχοι)" of God.[22] Despite all he has to say about angels in general, Philo never gives a proper name to an angel. The one exceptional case is when Philo discusses the Angel of the Lord.[23]

As demonstrated above,[24] Philo clearly equates the Logos with the Angel of the Lord who appears frequently throughout the scriptures.[25] Philo claims that the Logos is God's chief or "eldest" Angel.[26] In this role as the Angel of the Lord, he is clearly a distinct hypostasis, and not simply a euphemistic way of speaking of God's actions. A clear instance of this is when Philo explains God's promise to send the Angel before the people in Exodus 23:20–21. For Philo, since God stipulates that "my name (ὄνομά μού)" is on this Angel, this Angel must be "the Divine Word (λόγῳ θείῳ)."[27] Even so, just as the Angel is distinct from God, the Angel is also distinct from everything else. He is a divine entity, even a "second god,"[28] and therefore the Angel of the Lord is for Philo, in some sense, distinct from "created beings (γενέσει)."[29]

As distinct from God and from all other creation, the Angel has a mediating role. Philo explains,

> To His Word, His chief [Angel], highest in age and honour, the Father of all has given the special prerogative, to stand on the border and separate the creature from the Creator. This same Word both pleads with the immortal as suppliant for afflicted mortality and acts as ambassador of the ruler to the subject. He glories in this prerogative and proudly describes it in these words "and I stood between the Lord and you" (Deut. v.5), that is neither uncreated as God, nor created as you, but midway between the two extremes, a surety to both sides.[30]

Furthermore, as the Archangel, this divine figure even sits in the place of God for Philo. For example, when commenting on Jacob's vision of the ladder to heaven, he explains, "The dream shewed the Ruler of the angels set fast upon the stairway, even the Lord (Ἐμήνυε δὲ τὸ ὄναρ ἐστηριγμένον ἐπὶ τῆς κλίμακος τὸν ἀρχάγγελον, κύριον)."[31] The significance of this claim is that in both the Masoretic text and the Septuagint, it is "the LORD (יְהוָֹה/κύριος), the God of your father Abraham" (Gen 28:13) who sits atop Jacob's ladder, but when Philo remembers this scene he inserts the Angel of the Lord.[32] This point is further illustrated when Philo does the opposite and speaks of the "Angel of the Lord" in the scene where Abraham was ready to sacrifice Isaac (*Abr.* 1.32). In the scripture itself it is simply "God" who commands Abraham to do this. It is not until the final moment that the Angel of the Lord calls for Abraham to stop (Gen. 22:11). God and the Angel of the Lord are distinct entities, and yet Philo speaks of them—at least at times—as so closely connected that they almost seem to be interchangeable.

We have already shown how Philo explicitly speaks of God in terms of "two powers." He speaks of the Angel of the Lord (who is divine and also called "the Lord") as the second power of heaven. The Angel, in other words, is another title or description of the Word, also known as the Wisdom of God. As we look to other bodies of literature, we consider whether this perspective of the Angel of the Lord is unique to Philo or whether other Second Temple literature presents the Angel of the Lord as the second power in heaven.

The Angel of the Lord in Wisdom Literature

When it comes to Wisdom literature of the Second Temple period, there is very little talk about the Angel of the Lord. Instead, as signaled in the scholarly label for this genre, any description of God's immanent activity in the world tends to speak of Wisdom herself, which we have discussed in chapter 4. Not only is the Angel of the Lord rarely mentioned in Wisdom literature, there are, in fact, relatively few references to angels, in general, within this body of texts. Yet, the references that we do find are significant. In Sirach 48:21 the Angel of the Lord guards against the Assyrians (cf. Ps 34:7/33:8LXX; 2 Kgs 6:17), but here it should be noted that there is no explicit comparison of this Angel with the Wisdom who acts so distinctly in Sirach 24. That being said, in Sirach 24:2 Wisdom is "in the assembly of the Most High" and "in the presence of God's host" and so very much is some kind of angel or is like the angels. Like the Angel of the Lord in Exodus 14:19, Wisdom can claim, "my throne is in a pillar of clouds (ὁ θρόνος μου ἐν στύλῳ νεφέλης)" (Sir 24:4). Moses is also said to acquire equality with the angels (45:1–5), and so for this author the angels likely consist of a scale of mediatorial roles between God and creation. Even so, Wisdom would be the highest (angel?) on this scale. Furthermore, if Wisdom is equal to or identified with the Angel of the Lord, then it explains how the Lord and the Angel of the Lord can stand in parallel in Sirach 48:21.[33]

In the Wisdom of Solomon, the case is similar. Explicit reference to angels is almost entirely absent.[34] However, a strong case can be made that Wisdom of Solomon identified Wisdom as the Angel of the Lord from the Hebrew scriptures: Wisdom "saved (ἐσώθησαν)" the people (9:18), which apparently refers to when she led the people out of Egypt (10:15–19, especially Wisdom as a pillar of fire in 10:17) and protected them in the wilderness (11:1–26). Similarly, it is Wisdom who helped Abraham and his son (10:5), which likely alludes to the Angel of the Lord staying Abraham's hand from sacrificing Isaac (Gen 22:11–12). Wisdom also helps Jacob against his brother (Wis 10:10–12), which alludes to Jacob's reunion with Esau before which the unnamed man (= angel?) wrestled with Jacob and thereby (the Angel of) the Lord blessed Jacob (Gen 32). All this leads von Heijne to conclude, "Thus, she plays the same role as the 'angel' of the Exodus-tradition."[35] Therefore, while the language about the "Angel" of the Lord has largely been replaced by the persona of Wisdom, the same motifs are explicit, and the audience can be expected to identify Wisdom as the Angel of the Lord from the Hebrew scriptures.

Thus, in two prominent pieces of Wisdom literature, we see something similar regarding the Angel of the Lord that we saw in Philo, namely the Angel of the Lord being equated with Wisdom. As we argued above, there is ample evidence to suggest that in the Second Temple period, Jews could have understood Wisdom to be a "second power." It is noteworthy, that Philo clearly equates the Logos with the Angel of the Lord, but elsewhere in Philo it is clear, that the Logos is synonymous with Wisdom.[36] Thus, in Philo, the Logos, Wisdom, and the Angel of the Lord are all understood to represent the same entity, an entity we contend should be understood as the second power. In Wisdom of Solomon, it appears we find the same triangulation of these three figures, as not only is Wisdom seemingly identified with the Angel of the Lord, but it is also identified with God's Word (Wis 9:1). That the same triangulation of Wisdom, Word, and the Angel of the Lord can be found in both Jewish Wisdom literature and Philo demonstrates a number of things. It further demonstrates that Philo is not unique in his thought regarding these entities, but instead these ideas are very much at home in the thought-world of Second Temple Judaism. It also further supports the notion that Second Temple Jews thought of Wisdom/Word as a distinct entity, as it is equated with the Angel of the Lord, who appears to be a distinct entity within Hebrew scriptures. Finally, it demonstrates that the same entity can be understood and described by different names, so that the "second power" could be identified by multiple titles.

The Angel of the Lord in the *Liber antiquitatum biblicarum*

The Angel of the Lord also appears in the *Liber antiquitatum biblicarum*, a Jewish text thought to have been originally written in Palestine in Hebrew sometime between 50 and 150 CE.[37] The text speaks of various angels, which it associates with power and strength, such as Zeruel, the *angelus qui preerat virtuti*, "angel who presides over power" in 27.10, and Zervihel, *angelum . . . super virtutem*, "the angel over power" in 61.5.[38] The text also references the "the Angel of the Lord" (61.9), but it is unclear if this angel is rightly identified with a previously named angel (e.g., Zervihel in 61:5). Yet, it is clear that the figure identified in the Hebrew Bible as "the Angel of the Lord" is in view at many points. The *Liber antiquitatum biblicarum* (hereafter, LAB) retells the story of Gideon and his encounter with the Angel of the Lord, a story in which the Hebrew Bible moves without explanation between the Lord and the Angel of the Lord (LAB 35; cf. Judg 6:11–24). That this Angel is understood by the LAB as the Angel of the Lord is made clear when it references the Angel that appeared to Baalam (LAB 18; cf. Num 22:21–35). Perhaps most importantly, the text depicts Baalam worshipping the Angel of the Lord,[39] which seems to be an interpretation of Baalam prostrating himself before the Angel of the Lord in Numbers 22:31. Here we find a Second Temple witness that seems to maintain the ambiguous relationship between the God and the Angel of the Lord that is found in the Hebrew Bible. No strong conclusions can be drawn from this text regarding whether the Angel of the Lord is understood to function as a "second power" (as seems the case in Philo and certain Jewish Wisdom literature). However, it does seem noteworthy that (1) the LAB interprets angels in relation to "power (*virtus*)" and (2) that the LAB seems to depict the Angel of the Lord as an appropriate object of worship. While not conclusive, both of these details would be consistent with the depiction of the Angel of the Lord as the second power in both Philo and Wisdom literature.

The Angel of the Lord in Josephus

Josephus rarely mentions angels.[40] Furthermore, he never names any angel. Instead, he often describes biblical texts about angels as the work of God, or he simply omits the passages about angels.[41] At times he does speak of angelic activity in a way that accommodates his audiences concepts, such as likening angelic inspiration to Greek δαίμονες.[42] Even when doing so, Josephus nevertheless portrays one figure as distinct from any other spiritual or supernatural being: he speaks of the Angel of the Lord in unique terms in relation to God.

It was once commonplace to speak of Josephus as holding to a strict monotheism, but this should be nuanced as it was at the outset of this study, allowing the one God of Israel reigning over all other gods, powers, and heavenly beings.[43] For example, Josephus has been shown to speak of "fate and God" in such a way that the God of Israel turns out to be "the highest deity" akin to Virgil's philosophical theism.[44] Similarly, Josephus's labelling of certain figures as "divine" is best understood in terms of the Jewish commitment to the heavens being densely populated with supernatural or "divine" figures.[45] This should not be surprising since Josephus explicitly spoke of other gods, when insisting they were beneath the Creator God: "[Abraham] was thus the first boldly to declare that God, the creator of the universe, is one, and that, if any other god contributed aught to man's welfare, each did so by His command and not in virtue of its own inherent power."[46]

Josephus's first mention of a single angel is in reference to Genesis 16 where Hagar meets "an angel of God" or "divine angel (ἄγγελος θεῖος)."[47] This identifier may simply place the angel within the category of "supernatural" beings, or as von Heijne claims, it simply notes the angel's divine role of communicating on behalf of God.[48] However, there may be more significance to the divine status of the angel for Josephus. For example, while it may be noteworthy that Josephus omits Genesis 16:13–14, where Hagar claims to have seen God as a result of seeing the Angel of the Lord, this scene may, in fact, shape his description of the Angel as "divine." This is further supported with other statements he makes about the Angel of the Lord in the Jewish scriptures.

Next, Josephus describes those who visited Abraham at the Oak of Mamre as "three angels (τρεῖς ἀγγέλους)" (*Ant.* 1.196), who were at first mistaken for men but who later declared themselves to be "messengers of God (ἀγγέλους τοῦ θεοῦ)" (1.198). The Genesis account famously becomes ambiguous at this point: two angels go to Sodom, but "the Lord" tells Abraham what he will do, which may indicate that one of the three visitors was in fact the Angel of the Lord (cf. Gen 18:16–19:1). Josephus simply relays how Abraham appealed "to God (τὸν θεὸν)" on behalf of the people of Sodom (*Ant.* 1.199). Josephus either reads the text to say that Abraham's conversation with the Lord was not, in fact, with any of the three visitors, or he equates one of the angels with God. There is, however, another explanation. Josephus may simply think of the angels as carrying out God's actions, and so anything they say or do may be credited to God. This may be the case when "God (Ὁ Θεὸς)," not the two angels (cf. Gen 19:11), blinded and then destroyed the men of Sodom (*Ant.* 1.202). Then again, this may be a summary statement about the whole scene, for in Genesis the two angels call on the Lord to destroy the city (cf. Gen 19:14, "the Lord will destroy this city"). If Josephus is not describing one of the three angels as "God," then it is curious that he does not explain why only two angels went on to Sodom.

The Angel of the Lord is also described in Genesis 22:11–12 as stopping Abraham from sacrificing Isaac and in Genesis 24:7, 40 as guiding Abraham's servant to Isaac's wife, Rebekah. However, Josephus simply speaks of "God" doing these actions (*Ant.* 1.233; 1.242–56). As mentioned above, sometimes Josephus replaces the mention of angelic actions in scripture by simply crediting God, which could explain these two scenes in his text.[49] However, such a reading does not explain why Josephus does speak of the Angel of the Lord intervening with Abraham and Isaac in the scenes that precede and follow these, and when he does so he calls the angel the "divine angel (θεῖον ἄγγελον)."[50] When describing Joseph's wrestling match in Genesis 32, Josephus first calls this "man" (cf. Gen 32:24) a "phantom (φαντάσματι)," but then he identifies this figure as "an angel of God (θεῖον ἄγγελον),"[51] or the "divine angel." It is significant that Josephus labels this figure an/the "angel" because nowhere in Genesis (cf. Hos 12:3–5) is he identified as such. Instead he is a "man" (Gen 32:24) that Jacob identifies as "God" and even "God Almighty" (Gen 32:30; 48:3). Thus, it seems Josephus has taken (or followed?) the interpretive step to identifying the man, whom Jacob identifies as God, as the Angel of the Lord.

Another telling example comes in the account of Balaam. According to Josephus, the false prophet is visited by "an angel of God (ἀγγέλου θείου)" also called "the divine spirit (τοῦ θείου πνεύματος)."[52] As in the biblical text, Josephus acknowledges that it is God who made the donkey speak: "she, so God willed, broke out in human speech (κατὰ βούλησιν θεοῦ φωνὴν ἀνθρωπίνην ἀφεῖσα)."[53] Josephus appears to differ from the scripture, however, when he narrates how "God (ὁ θεὸς)" insisted that Balaam continue his journey (4.111).[54] In Numbers it is the Angel of the Lord who does so. Perhaps, Josephus saw no difference between the two, or perhaps both are considered "God."

Two scenes from Judges also seem to conflate the Angel of the Lord with God in Josephus's telling.[55] Instead of the Angel of the Lord appearing to Gideon (Judg 6:11–12), Josephus has "a spectre in the form of a young man (φαντάσματος δὲ αὐτῷ παραστάντος νεανίσκου μορφῇ)."[56] This seems to be due to the fact that Gideon's response betrays no sense of awe. Nevertheless, Josephus next reports the conversation the Angel has with Gideon, only he credits the words of the Angel to God, so that "God himself (ὁ δὲ θεὸς αὐτὸς) promised to supply what he lacked and to grant the victory."[57] This may be due to the fact that at this point in Judges it is simply "the LORD"—and not the Angel? Or as the Angel?—who speaks (Judg 6:14–16). Similarly, instead of the Angel of the Lord, Josephus has "a spectre (φάντασμα)"[58] appear to Manoah's wife, but once again he proceeds to clarify that it is "the [A]ngel of God (ἄγγελος τοῦ θεοῦ)" when describing the rest of the encounter.[59] In other words, unlike his general pattern of omitting angels' actions and only speaking of God, Josephus retains the information about the Angel of the Lord in narrating key moments in Israel's ancient past.

The same phenomenon occurs in later scenes from Israel's history. For example, when Josephus recalls the scene where God sends a plague on Jerusalem through "the Angel of the Lord" (2 Sam 24:16/1 Chr 21:12). Josephus does not elaborate on the relation of "the [A]ngel (ὁ ἄγγελος)" to God, but simply credits him with the judgment of God's people (*Ant.* 7.327). Likewise, Josephus recounts how "God's angel (ἄγγελος τοῦ θεοῦ)" destroyed Sennacherib's army.[60] This refers to "the Angel of the Lord (יְהוָה מַלְאַךְ/ἄγγελος κυρίου)" named in 2 Kings 19:35.[61] Like the scriptures, Josephus sees this Angel as unique in carrying out divine judgment.

To conclude, we cannot claim much for Josephus when it comes to the Angel of the Lord in relation to God. Like the scriptures themselves, he sometimes describes the two as distinct, while at other times he seems to speak of the former as a representation of the latter. At least, he speaks of the former as "Lord" and "God." Perhaps, Josephus does not know how to parse the two figures, or perhaps he simply does not do so for his audience. Thus, Josephus does not offer evidence that supports the notion that the Angel of the Lord was understood as a "second power," but at the same time, he offers no evidence that would preclude such an understanding, as his treatment of the Angel of the Lord could be consistent with identifying this figure with such a second power.

The Angel of the Lord in the Targums

As discussed in chapter 2, the targums provide important points of comparison with other Second Temple literature. Even though they date to a later period (and are in fact very difficult to date precisely), they retain traces of earlier Jewish thought as well as display important developments in that thought. This is certainly the case with the subject of angels.[62] The targums vary in their treatment of angels, but there is a general trend to insert additional material about angels into the biblical texts, such as angels' names.[63] Furthermore, there is a general tendency to avoid anthropomorphic depictions of God by portraying the divine actions as if it were done by angels instead of God.[64] Above, we have already argued that in the targums we find strong evidence of a "Word/Memra" theology in which the Memra of the Lord is understood as a distinct entity and is best understood in terms of a second power. Later, we will also considered how concepts such as God's Name and Glory also function as just such a second power.[65] Thus, here we will focus on passages in which the Angel of the Lord is identified or equated with God's Memra, Name, Glory, and even God's very self.

We begin with the Angel of the Lord tradition in the Hagar narrative. The targumaic traditions for Hagar's encounter with the Angel in large part retains the ambiguous way in which he appears to be God, being able to move back and forth between references to the Angel and God.[66] Yet, it is noteworthy that in all of the extant targums for this verse,[67] Hagar prays in the name of the "Memra of the Lord" and it is added that the Memra was the one who spoke to Hagar.[68] In other words, the Angel of the Lord is equated with the Word of the Lord. This shared identity between the Angel and Word of the Lord is seen again in Targum Pseudo-Jonathan at Gen 21:17–20. Like the MT, the Angel of the Lord first speaks to Hagar about the Lord (21:17), and then God shows Hagar the well (21:19), but then, unlike the MT, which has "God (אֱלֹהִים)" help Ishmael (21:20), this targum has the Memra do this action, again indicating that the Angel of the Lord is the Memra.

The appearance of the three "men" to Abraham in Genesis 18 offers an example of a convergence of the Angel, Memra, and Glory of the Lord and the Lord himself. Targum Neofiti deviates from the MT text and makes the figure who speaks to Abraham an angel and not the Lord. This text speaks of "Three angels" and clarifies how "The three of them were sent for three things, because it is impossible for one angel from on high that he be sent for more than one thing."[69] The three tasks are (1) announcing the birth of Isaac, (2) rescuing Lot, and (3) destroying Sodom and Gomorrah. Even so, the first angel seems to be identified with the Glory of the Lord since Abraham begs him, "let not the Glory of your Shekinah go up from your servant,"[70] which seems to be indebted to Moses request in Exodus 33.[71] Yet, this Angel is also called the Lord's "Memra" through whom he spoke to Sarah.[72] The scene ends when this Angel departs: "And the Glory of the Shekinah of the Lord went up when it had finished speaking with Abraham."[73] Thus, here, what the MT identifies with the Lord is expressed as the Angel, Memra, and Glory of the Lord.

Another important example is the offering of Isaac in Genesis 22. In the Hebrew text, it is "God" who tempts Abraham (22:1), but the "Angel of the Lord" then stops him (22:11) and again speaks to him (22:15), saying, "By myself I have sworn, says the Lord" (22:16). The targums largely follow this pattern, only inserting the Angel's title as the Lord's "Memra." The reading goes as follows: It is "the Lord" who tempted Abraham,[74] except in Pseudo-Jonathan where it is "the Memra of the Lord." Then, it is "the Angel of the Lord" who stops Abraham in all the extant targums, but when this Angel speaks a second time, he has the Lord swear "by my Memra."[75] Targum Neofiti also describes how Abraham "worshiped and prayed in the name of the Memra of the Lord."[76] In this prayer Abraham foretells that his descendants will remember how "on this mountain the glory of the Shekinah of the Lord was revealed to him."[77] Therefore, again the Memra and Shekinah/Glory are ways of describing the Angel who interacts with Abraham.

A similar case is found with the text of Genesis 28. Instead of having YHWH atop Jacob's ladder, it is "the Glory of the Lord (יקרא דיי)" (28:13). Then, instead of God promising to preserve Jacob directly (as in the MT/LXX), in this Targum it is God's Memra that is promised to help (22:15). And yet, the one who speaks from this place still says, "I am the Lord, the God of your father Abraham" (28:13), and Jacob likewise still names the epiphany as one of the Lord himself (28:16). Then, whereas Genesis 28:22 has Jacob promise a sanctuary for "God (אֱלֹהִים)" (cf. LXX, θεοῦ), Targums Neofiti and Pseudo-Jonathan deem it a sanctuary for "the Name of the Lord." It should be noted that Targum Neofiti later refers back to this scene, rendering Genesis 35:1 as commanding Jacob to build an altar "to the name of the Memra of the Lord," instead of simply for God as in the MT and LXX.[78] Thus, again we see a convergence of Memra, Angel, Name, and Glory of the Lord into a single entity, an entity that seems to stand in the place of the Lord himself.

Numerous additional examples can be offered in which a convergence exists between some combination of the Angel of the Lord and the Lord's Memra, Glory, or Name: these identifiers describe the same entity in Exodus 3 (the account of the burning bush), Exodus 23:20–23 (the Angel of the Lord leading the Hebrews in the wilderness), Numbers 22–23 (Balaam), and Judges 6:21–23. Thus, we see in the targums what we saw in both Philo and Jewish Wisdom literature, namely an interpretive tradition that equates the Angel of the Lord with God's Word (closely associated with Wisdom), Name, and Glory. Again, this indicates what we have seen in Philo is not unique but actually prevalent in Jewish thought. Additionally, we would contend that this connection between the Angel of the Lord and the Memra of the Lord in the targums only further strengthens our previous argument that Memra of the targums is not simply a theologically constructed stand-in for the YHWH of Israel, but is rather best understood as a distinct entity, one that can be manifest in anthropomorphic-angelic form. As argued above, this distinct entity is best understood as a second power in heaven.

Furthermore, we contend that the very way the targums address these Angel of the Lord traditions further supports the notion that a robust two powers theology stands behind them. One of the functions of the targums is to offer interpretive clarity to the reader, particularly on passages where interpretive questions or confusion exists.[79] To accomplish this purpose, interpretive answers to confusing texts are often woven into the paraphrase of the texts themselves. In light of such a purpose of the Targums, it seems that one function of the interpretive traditions considered here is an effort to address the ambiguity of the Angel of the Lord traditions in which the Hebrew text moves quite seamlessly between what on the surface appears to be two distinct entities, the Angel of the Lord and the Lord of Israel. Yet, in such efforts, the targums neither flatten the distinction between the two, by claiming the Angel of the Lord is simply a circumlocution for the Lord (a common move of modern scholars), nor strictly divorcing them. Instead, the targums regularly identify the Angel of the Lord with concepts that (1) it presumes the reader is familiar with; and (2) is closely associated with the Lord himself (e.g., the Lord's Word, Name, and Glory). We contend that such an interpretive tradition only disambiguates these traditions if they are understood in terms of a two powers theology, with the Lord's Word (= Name, Glory, etc.) being understood as the second power in heaven. If the Lord's Word, Name, and Glory are, as some interpreters argue, merely buffer words that protect the transcendence of Israel's God, then they bring little clarity to the "Angel of the Lord" traditions and merely replace one ambiguous entity with others. But, if they are rightly understood by the reader as a second power, then the addition of these identifiers brings clarity to the Angel of the Lord traditions by identifying this figure as the "Lord" who appeared to Israel and by allowing the text to move seamlessly between this Angel and God. Thus, the very interpretive strategy the targum uses for explicating Angel of the Lord traditions seems to support an underlying two powers theology.

Assessing the Angel of the Lord's Status in Second Temple Judaism

When we apply our criteria for assessing whether an entity would be understood as a second power, there are several significant criteria that the Angel of the Lord does not meet. The Angel of the Lord is never depicted as participating in the creation of the world. The Angel of the Lord is rarely depicted as reigning over the cosmos or being seated in God's heavenly throne.[80] While there may be instances in which the Angel of the Lord is a recipient of worship, they are neither certain nor prevalent.[81] Yet, despite failing to meet these criteria, we contend the evidence that the Angel of the Lord was recognized as a second power is quite strong. First, we note Second Temple traditions that replace YHWH of the Hebrew text with the Angel of the Lord (see, for example, Philo's treatment of Jacob's ladder above). Yet, perhaps even more significant is the frequent identification of the Angel of the Lord with entities that we have already argued are best identified as the second power, particularly God's Word and Wisdom. Additionally, as we will see in the next chapter, the Angel is also often equated with God's Spirit and God's Face, and we will also show how God's name is in (or on) this Angel in a unique way. Thus, while the Angel of the Lord might not be depicted as an agent in creation, in Philo, Wisdom of Solomon, and the targums, the Angel is clearly identified as either God's Word or Wisdom in these texts, both of which are depicted as active in the creation of the cosmos. The same could be said with ruling over the cosmos. In light of this evidence, we contend that a significant strand within Second Temple Judaism interpreted the Angel of the Lord as a second power in heaven and that this interpretive tradition enabled an interpretation of Jewish scripture in which YHWH and the Angel of YHWH appear nearly interchangeable while remaining distinct.

ADDITIONAL ANGELIC FIGURES AS THE ANGEL OF THE LORD

Beyond the figure explicitly identified as "the Angel of the Lord," there are other significant angelic figures that require analysis. Some of these angels are given specific names, while others remain unnamed. Though these angels are never explicitly called "the Angel of the Lord," many interpreters have identified them as such. Here we consider such identifications and assess whether any of these angelic figures could rightly be identified as a "second power" in heaven. We begin with named angels and then consider those that are unnamed.

Yaoel in Apocalypse of Abraham

Though preserved in a Christian (Slavonic) translation,[82] the Apocalypse of Abraham is thought to have been written in the late first century CE, possibly in Hebrew.[83] In this text, a "voice" (9.1) speaks to Abraham, and then said voice sends "Yaoel of the same name, through the mediation of my (i.e., God's) ineffable name."[84] This Yaoel is an "angel . . . in the likeness of a man,"[85] and he is—somewhat ambiguously—described as dwelling in the seventh heaven as a "power through the medium of his [God's] ineffable name."[86] This is thought by some scholars to be a clear reference to the Angel of the Lord in Exodus 23:20–21, where God declares that his very name is in this Angel.[87] This angel's appearance is like the Ancient of Days in Daniel, with its hair white like snow (11.2–3). Yet it also seems to be depicted as a heavenly high priest, as it has a κίδαρις, or "headdress," like a rainbow on its head (11.2–3). In the LXX, the Greek κίδαρις (preserved here in the Slavonic) is used thirteen times, with eleven of those uses referring to the Aaronic priesthood.[88] He is also "with Michael" and so distinct from him (10.17). After instruction about sacrifice, Abraham and the angel kneel down and worship the Eternal One (17.2). When Abraham prays to the Eternal One, he recites numerous names for him, including "El, El, El, El, Yaoel . . . my protector."[89] Later, Abraham prays to the "Eternal One" who is "sanctified by your power."[90] In other words, Yaoel is the "power" of God, who shares God's very "name" (10.3). His name, Yaoel, derives from a combination of the Greek version of the Tetragrammaton (Ἰαώ) and the Hebrew word for God (אל).[91] Furthermore, he seems to rule the other angels: the other angels challenge each other (10.9; 18.9), but Yaoel teaches them "the song of peace which the Eternal One has in himself."[92] A final interesting detail is noteworthy. In chapter 19, the highest heaven is revealed to Abraham (seventh firmament). He sees a "host," or better, "power," "of the invisible glory," but then adds "I saw no one else there."[93] That God is presumably absent in this vision of the highest heaven is noteworthy. Rowland contends this is due to the fact that Yaoel, the visible manifestation of God, is no longer there because he is present with Abraham.[94] Thus, with the angel Yaoel, we have a number of important details that would be consistent with identifying it as the second power in heaven. First, he is depicted as sharing the divine name with the God of Israel. In fact, other Jewish texts attribute this name to the God of Israel (e.g., Apoc. Mos. 29.4; 33.5; LAE/Apoc. 33.5). That Yaoel declares that the divine name is within him, strongly suggests he should be understood as the Angel of the Lord, a figure that we have demonstrated is best understood as a second power in a number of Second Temple traditions. The physical description of Yaoel is also important. Not only does he share a resemblance with the Ancient of Days, but his description identifies him as a heavenly high priest. Yaoel is also presented as the ruler of God's angels, which would be consistent with Philo's depiction of the Logos as God's chief angel. Finally, the fact that God is nowhere to be found in Abraham's vision of the highest heaven, may indicate that Yaoel is rightly understood as the visible representation of God. Ultimately, Yaoel clearly meets two of our criteria, the close association with God's name, and being equated with other entities that have strong support for being identified as a second power. Yet, we contend that the relative strength of the evidence related to these criteria make a compelling case that Yaoel is best understood as a second power in heaven, and that such an identification is stronger than alternative explanations, such as seeing him as merely a principle or powerful angel.

The Angel Raphael in Tobit

Angelic figures feature prominently in the Book of Tobit.[95] Tobit is usually dated to the mid-third century BCE, and it was possibly written in Aramaic. Classifying its genre has proven difficult, but it is most often categorized as sapiential.[96] The story, set in Assyrian exile, offers guidance for its (diaspora?) audience. The wisdom offered for such living, however, is provided by the angel Raphael.

Tobit's son, Tobias, needs a guide for his journey, and he finds Raphael (5:4). Neither Tobit nor Tobias realize Raphael is an angel (or even "the angel of God [ἄγγελος τοῦ θεοῦ]" according to some versions).[97] Instead Raphael claims to be a distant "kinsman" named Azariah (5:13). Here, the irony of the name should be underscored: Raphael (רפאל) is a Hebrew name meaning "God heals," and yet this figure chooses a thinly veiled pseudonym, Azariah, which means "YHWH helps." Even though Tobit does not realize Azariah is the angel Raphael, he still prays and believes the "God in heaven" will protect Tobias on the journey by sending his angel (5:17; 5:22). The angel heals two of the main characters (12:3, 14), or rather he teaches Tobias how to perform healings: Tobias's future wife, Sarah, is exorcised of a demon (8:1–3); and Tobit's blindness is cured (11:10–13). In response, Tobit prays, "Blessed be God, and blessed be his great name, and blessed be all his holy angels" (11:14).[98] Raphael finally reveals himself to Tobit and Tobias as one of the seven[99] angels who enter into God's presence (12:15). The two men then thank God for "the angel of God (ἄγγελος θεοῦ)," or as some manuscripts read, "the Angel of the Lord (ὁ ἄγγελος κυρίου)."

The general consensus about Raphael in Tobit is that he is depicted as one of the archangels.[100] As such he is a creature of God, and clearly not in any way identified as God, as is the case with the Angel of the Lord in some other texts. This consensus, however, has recently been challenged.

Because Raphael appears in later Jewish lists of archangels, it is common to see this figure as one among many other angels. Other scholars, however, have claimed that Raphael as he first appears in Tobit is much more: taking this text on its own, some have claimed Raphael is in fact the Angel of the Lord.[101] The matter has been studied at length by Philip Muñoa who published a series of articles showing the similarities of Raphael in Tobit with the Angel of the Lord in the Hebrew scriptures. First, he argues that Tobit's depiction of Raphael represents an important development in Jewish angelology: Raphael is a preexistent heavenly figure who disguises himself as an Israelite, but who can also heal and cast out evil spirits.[102] Muñoa sees Tobit's

Raphael as precedent for early Christians understandings of Jesus.[103] More recently, Muñoa has gone beyond a general angelomorphic Christology, and reassesses Raphael's status.[104] Rather than being an angel, or even another mere archangel, Muñoa concludes, "There can be no doubt that Raphael is *the* angel of the Lord in Tobit."[105] If Muñoa and others are correct on this point, then this is the first time that a text names the Angel of the Lord. To return to the fact that Raphael in Hebrew means "The Lord Heals," so "Raphael's" healing work in Tobit support's Muñoa's claim: Raphael heals in the name of the Lord because he is the Angel of the Lord who in earlier texts shares the name of the Lord.[106]

At this point, we should acknowledge that Muñoa's case is contestable. He has failed to explain how Raphael is one among seven angels in Tobit 12:15 and is also the Angel of the Lord from earlier literature who is also simply known as the Lord.[107] At the least, Muñoa's case helps raise the question about additional archangels. Once Second Temple texts like Tobit begin enumerating archangels, it would seem that the Angel of the Lord must be seen as categorically distinct from God—that is, just another angel. The ambiguity between the Lord and the Angel of the Lord found in the scriptures, Philo, and the Targums would then disappear. This, however, is not necessarily the case when it comes to the Angel and other archangels. The highest ranking archangel may still be so close to God that he is the second power in heaven, outranking all other lower powers.[108] Of course, it is likely that different authors held to different views, and so this will be a matter to consider in all texts that enumerate a hierarchy of angels.

In short, the archangel Raphael in Tobit remains a possible candidate to be understood as the Angel of the Lord, but the doubt does not stem from the presence of other archangels. Instead, this figure seems to act the part of the Angel of the Lord from the earlier scriptures, but the fact is never made explicit by the text itself. Other examples provide similar case studies, such as a certain figure who appears in the *Book of Jubilees*.

The Angel of the Presence in Jubilees

The Book of Jubilees, usually dated to the second century BCE, is mostly narrated by the Angel of the Presence (= Phanuel or Penuel).[109] Because this angel is one of many who leads God's activity on earth,[110] some scholars think this angel is Michael.[111] The text, however, never names him as such and the evidence is in fact open to interpretation.[112] There are multiple "angels of presence" in this text in addition to other angels (Jub. 2.2; 2.18; 15.27).[113] Even so, the narrating Angel of Presence is distinct, according to von Heijne, because he claims to have spoken words that the scriptures attribute to God (Jub. 6.22; cf. Exod 23:16; 34:22; Deut 16:10; 12:22–24;

cf. Deut 12:1–3).[114] It should also be noted that the Angel of Presence is the one who went before the Hebrews in the wilderness (1.29; cf. Exod 14:19), and that this narrating Angel claims to be the one who stopped Abraham from killing Isaac (18.9–11; cf. Gen 22:11). A few lines later, unlike Genesis 22:15 where it is still the Angel, it is simply "the Lord" who called Abraham "a second time" (Jub. 18.14).

In other words, Jubilees sees the Angel of Presence as the "Lord" who appeared to the patriarchs and to Israel. Therefore, Jubilees often substitutes the Angel of Presence for God and vice versa, just as the scriptures themselves interchange the Angel of the Lord and the Lord. Also, as in the scriptures, God directly acts in history (such as creating, calling Abraham, giving the Law, etc.), and God does so without mention of an angelic intermediary. For example, "the Lord" appeared to Jacob and gave him the name Israel (Jub. 32.17–18; cf. Gen 32).

Even so, it is not clear that this text holds to a two powers paradigm; the evidence is ambiguous. On the one hand, the text opens by explaining that Moses received the law "by the word of the Lord." Similarly, the "glory of the Lord dwelt on Mount Sinai" and Moses sees "the appearance of the glory of the Lord" (1.2–3). On the other hand, the phrase "by the word of the Lord" is used frequently in the text in a way that does not necessarily suggest a distinct hypostasis, although it is possible that in these lines, the text imagines the Angel to be the Word and Glory of God (as we have seen previously in other Jewish traditions). Similarly, while this Angel of Presence is depicted as the Angel of the Lord from the scriptures (who is also simply called "the Lord"), the Angel tells Moses that "on the first day (the Lord God) created the heavens . . . and all of the spirits which minister before him: the angels of presence, the angels of sanctification . . . (etc.)."[115] All angels, therefore, including the Angel(s) of Presence, are created. This, however, does not rule out a two powers view, since Philo speaks of the Logos as both created in relation to God but uncreated in comparison to the rest of the world.[116] Jubilees seems to assume that there is a highest angel, and it places the Angel of Presence in the role of the Angel of the Lord from the scriptures. This further addresses the question raised above in Tobit: What is the relation between the Angel of the Lord and other angels? Perhaps in texts like Tobit and Jubilees, the Angel of the Lord (now named "Raphael" or "Presence") ranks as one among many archangels and angels. Or, perhaps, these texts still understand the Angel of the Lord to be the first and highest "power" besides God, and thus ranks higher than any other angel. If the Angel of Presence is equated with the Angel of the Lord from earlier scriptures, then it may be important that this Angel is the only one called "the Lord" and who acts as God in Israel's history, such as calling Abraham and giving the Law to Moses. We grant that this case is not as strong as previous instances, but what is seen in Jubilees coheres quite well with what we have seen in other Second Temple traditions in terms of presenting the Angel of the Lord as a second power in heaven.

The "Coming Angel/Messenger" in the Testament of Moses

The "Coming Angel/Messenger" in the Testament of Moses is worthy of consideration. The only extant copy of this text is in a fifth century Latin manuscript, but it is thought to be derived from an early first century CE Greek text.[117] A. M. Ceriani discovered it in the Ambrosian library in 1861, and he identified it with the Assumption of Moses mentioned by several ancient sources. This would be significant since that text is thought to be the source for the legend of Michael's contest with Satan over Moses's body.[118] However, no such contest is mentioned in this text, and it instead purports to be a "testament," or final speech, albeit it supernatural and prophetic in nature.[119] There are no apparent Christian interpolations, although it certainly was influential for some early Christians and so disentangling the extant Latin copy from its later Christian reception is admittedly dubious. As part of the text's foretelling of history, Moses prophesies of a coming angel or "messenger (*nuntius*)" who is from the highest heavens (*qui est in summo constitutes*).[120] Then, without explanation of a shift to a different character, the text reads, "For the Heavenly One will arise from his kingly throne. Yea, he will go forth from his holy habitation with indignation and wrath on behalf of his sons" (10.3). This is clearly using language from the scriptures about the Lord (cf. Deut 26:15; Isa 63:15; Jer 25:30; Mic 1:3), but in its context it seems to refer to the heavenly messenger the text just described. A few lines later, it reads, "For God Most High will surge forth, the Eternal One alone" (10.7). Thus, the text begins by describing a "coming angel" from the highest heaven, but without explanation segues into language that increasingly seems to describe the God of Israel. Although most readers find this angel to be distinct from the "heavenly One" on the throne, Barker sees the two titles as referring to the same figure because both sets of lines describe a warrior avenger who fights for Israel.[121] This is further supported by the fact that in Deuteronomy 32:43—Moses's farewell speech referenced at the beginning of this text (T.Mos. 1.2)—the same events are described of the Lord with no mention of an angel. The Testament of Moses ends with Joshua expressing concern that Israel cannot win without Moses (11.11–19), and then he falls at Moses's feet (12.10). Moses, however, rebukes Joshua, saying "Joshua, do not demean yourself" (12.3), which calls to mind the opening of the book of Joshua. There, the Lord calls on Joshua to be courageous (Josh 1:6–7; cf. 1:18), and he promises to fight on behalf of the people (Josh 1:5; 1:9; cf. 1:17). Then, before the first battle, the Angel of the Lord appears to Joshua, commanding him to remove his sandals (5:13–15; cf. Exod 3:4–5). In the lines that follow, the title "angel" is not mentioned, but it is simply YHWH who converses with Joshua on the battlefield, apparently as the Angel (Josh 6:1–5). In all likelihood, therefore, Testament of Moses has made the interpretive move of bringing together the Lord of Israel and the coming messenger in the same way that elsewhere in the Hebrew scriptures the Lord is seemingly equated with the Angel of the Lord. That is to say, the *Testament* understands the messenger to be none other than the Angel of the Lord. Such a move by the author of the Testament would find a natural explanation in the context of a two powers theology. Thus, while this text does not offer direct evidence of a two powers theology, such a theology would offer a very natural explanation for a text that is otherwise difficult to explain.

The Unnamed Angel "Lord" in Joseph and Aseneth

Joseph and Aseneth is an apocryphal account of Joseph and his wife (Gen 41:45).[122] Its date and origin are debated, with some arguing that the text is a later Christian text, dated around the second century CE and others arguing that it is a Jewish text that could date as early as first century BCE.[123] It is not our intention to engage in the debate over the book's date and origin here; yet, we move forward assuming the more widely held and traditional position, namely that the book is a product of Second Temple Judaism. The absence of explicit Christian content serves as our primary basis. Of particular interest for the present study is Aseneth's encounter with a heavenly figure. The episode begins after Aseneth has completed a long prayer to "the Lord," clearly a reference to the God of Israel. Once the prayer is complete, she sees "the morning star," which she interprets as "a messenger (ἄγγελος)."[124] Next, this star opened the heaven and "a man" came to Aseneth, whom she calls "Lord."[125] He introduces himself as "the chief of the house of the Lord and commander of the whole host of the Most High."[126] Aseneth looks at him to see that he was "in every respect similar to Joseph . . . except that his face was like lightning, and his eyes like sunshine, and the hairs of his head like a flame of fire of a burning torch."[127] This angel (or Angel) wrote Aseneth's name in the book of the living with his own finger (Jos. Asen. 15.4), an action which likely alludes to the same action as the God of Israel in (Exodus 31:18/ Deuteronomy 9:10; cf. Dan 5:5; John 8:6). This Angel, however, is not the Most High himself, which is stressed when Aseneth gives thanks that he was sent from the Most High (Jos. Asen. 15.12). Furthermore, the Angel himself refuses to tell her his name because his "name is in the heavens in the book of the Most high, written by the finger of God in the beginning of the book before all (the others)."[128] With no other name, Aseneth continues to call him "Lord" (e.g., *Jos. Asen.* 15.12; 15.13; 15.14; 16.4; 16.6; 16.11; 17.2; 17.4; 17.10). It is also noteworthy that Aseneth falls down and prostrates herself at the feet of this unnamed heavenly figure (15.11). While prostrate, she blesses the "Lord, God Most High," but she also declares to the heavenly figure, "blessed be your name forever." She also says that she will "praise and glorify" this figure forever and ever, an action that the figure does not discourage or declare inappropriate. Later, when Aseneth has no honeycomb to offer this heavenly figure (cf. Song 5:1; Luke 24:42), the Angel "spoke and it came into being. Surely this came out of your mouth, because its exhalation is like breath in your mouth."[129] When the figure departs, he does so on a chariot of fire pulled by four horses that appeared like lightning (Jos. Asen. 17.8), which alludes to the chariot of "the Lord" in various scriptures (cf. Ps 68:17; Isa 19:1; Ezek 1:15–17; 10:18–20; 11:22–23; Dan 7:9; Hab 3:8–9; 2 Kings 2:11–12; 6:17; 1 Chr 28:18). After he ascends to heaven in this chariot, Aseneth calls him "a god" or perhaps, "God," as textual witnesses varies, with some manuscripts including a definite article.[130] Thus, with this figure we see a collection of significant details. The figure is "chief of the house of the Lord and commander of the whole host of the Most High," a description that sounds quite similar to Philo's description of the Angel of the Lord/Logos. He engages in YHWH activity when he writes names in the book of life with his own finger. His name cannot be revealed and is identified as the first name to be written by God's finger in the book of life before all others.[131] That his name cannot be revealed would lead away from the conclusion that this figure is an exalted angel such as Michael, who is regularly named in Jewish tradition. He accepts what appears to be worship. He departs in a chariot that resembles the chariot of YHWH. And finally, Aseneth refers to this figure as either "God" or "a god." All of these details strongly suggest that this figure is best understood as the Angel of the Lord or the second power in heaven. Such an identification accounts for exalted attributions the figure receives, but also for the clear distinction between the figure and "the Lord, God Most High." We contend this scene from Joseph of Aseneth comes into greater clarity when read through the lens of a two powers paradigm.

Conclusions about Ambiguous Angelic Figures

Of the figures reviewed in this section, three seem to be rightly identified with the Angel of the Lord that appears in Hebrew scripture; Yaoel, the Angel of the Presence in Jubilees, and the unnamed Angel of Joseph and Aseneth. An identification with the Angel of the Lord would, based on our above discussion, suggest that such figures are best understood in terms of a "second power." Yet, beyond such an identification, several other factors meet our outlined criteria, including close association with the divine name, close association with YHWH texts and imagery, association with the ability to create, and being the object of worship and prayer. Thus, we contend that these figures are best identified as the second power. While the mysterious "coming angel" of the Testament of Moses cannot clearly be proven to be the Angel of the Lord, a two powers theology does carry explanatory power for a text that is otherwise quite baffling.[132] Raphael has been seen by some as the Angel of the Lord who belongs to a two powers paradigm, and the question remains as to whether Tobit or any given text imagines the highest ranking Angel to be a second divine hypostasis, the first of many angelic beings, or both.

CONCLUSIONS ABOUT THE ANGEL OF THE LORD

In our previous chapters we first saw how God's Word and then how God's Wisdom were depicted as a second power in heaven in various Second Temple texts. The Word and Wisdom of God acts as creator and sovereign ruler. This results in the Word or Wisdom sharing God's name, glory, and worship, and so appears to be divine. The case is so strong that many modern scholars, assuming an exclusive monotheistic model, found that the Word or Wisdom must not be a distinct hypostasis, but simply a personification of God's actions. We, however, attempted to show that the surviving texts in fact do depict a distinct entity at work under these titles.

In the current chapter, when we turn to the Angel of the Lord, there is no question that the Second Temple authors who described this figure understood him to be a distinct entity. The only question is whether this Angel is, in fact, divine, or whether he is God's agent who is given divine powers and roles. While the extant sources do not speak monolithically, there are numerous instances where the Angel of the Lord ranks above all other heavenly beings, even other angels and archangels with whom he is sometimes enumerated. Furthermore, the fact that the scriptures so often describe the Angel of the Lord as if he is God, it is no surprise that later texts wrestled (pun intended) with how best to articulate this Angel in relation to God. He is certainly distinct from God, but he may still be divine. For writers like Philo, this is easily explainable by seeing the Angel as the Word/Wisdom of God. For apocalyptic texts, often there are more esoteric ways of describing this heavenly figure. At times the Angel rules over creation, sits enthroned in heaven, appears theophanically to the patriarchs, shares the divine name, and is even enthroned in the temple. Therefore, given how many of the criteria we established in chapter 1 apply to this Angel, we conclude that many Jews from the Second Temple period assumed this Angel to be the second power of heaven. In some of our later chapters, we will see where other characters like the Son of Man and Melchizedek are sometimes depicted along the same lines as this Angel. But first it must be noted how this Angel also seems to be spoken of under other titles, such as God's Spirit, Name, and Face, and so it is to those other titles which we now turn.

NOTES

1. For general overview of angels in ancient Jewish texts, see Bousset and Gressmann, *Die Religion des Judentums*, 321–29; Mach, *Entwicklungsstadien des jüdischen Engelglaubens in vorrabbinischer Zeit* (Texte und Studien zum Antiken Judentum 34; Tübingen: Mohr Siebeck, 1992); Olyan, *A Thousand Thousands*; Kevin P. Sullivan, *Wrestling with Angels: A Study of the Relationship between Angels and Humans in Ancient Jewish Literature and the New Testament* (Leiden: Brill, 2004); and various essays in Friedrich V. Reiterer, Tobias Nicklas, and Karin Schöpflin (eds.), *Angels: The Concept of Celestial Beings—Origins, Development and Reception* (Berlin: Walter de Gruyter, 2007).

2. Tuschling, *Angels and Orthodoxy*, 5–11, reviews the importance of ancient Jewish angelology for two powers theology and early Christology.

3. For an overview, see Andrew S. Malone, "Distinguishing the Angel of the Lord," *Bulletin for Biblical Research* 21, no. 3 (2011): 297–314. Cf. von Heijne, *The Messenger of the Lord*, who offers a helpful study but is limited to passages in Genesis. For earlier bibliography on the Angel of the Lord, see Samuel A. Meier, "Angel of Yahweh," in *Dictionary of Deities and Demons in the Bible*, 2nd ed., eds. Karel van der Toorn, Bob Becking, and Pieter W. van der Horst (Grand Rapids, MI: Eerdmans, 1999), 95–108; and Aleksander R. Michalak, *Angels as Warriors in Late Second Temple Jewish Literature* (WUNT 2.330; Tübingen: Mohr Siebeck, 2012), 35 n.167.

4. E.g., Gen 16:7–14 to Hagar; Gen 22:11–15 to Abraham on Moriah; Exod 3:2–3, 20–23 (cf. Deut 33:1) to Moses; Exod 14:19–20 (cf. Exod 23:11, 33:1–3; Judg 2:1–5) to the Hebrews in the wilderness; Josh 5:13–15, 6:2 to Joshua; Judg 6:11–24 to Gideon; Judg 13:3–25 to Samson's parents; 2 Kgs 1:3, 15, to Elijah.

5. E.g., 2 Sam 24:15–25; 1 Chr 21:14–30 (cf. 2 Chr 3:1–2); 2 Kgs 19:35 (cf. 2 Chr 32:21); Ps 34:7/33:8LXX, 35:5–6/34:5–6LXX; Zech 1:7–17, 3:1–10, 12:8.

6. In Hag 1:13, Haggai is called "the angel of the LORD to the people (לְעָם . . . מַלְאַךְ יְהוָה/ὁ ἄγγελος κυρίου τῷ λαῷ)." Similarly, Mal 2:7, the priest is said to be "an angel of the LORD of hosts (מַלְאַךְ יְהוָה־צְבָאוֹת/ἄγγελος κυρίου παντοκράτωρ)."

7. Instances where the title "the Angel of the Lord" is either not used in full or used with some variation include Gen 18:1–16 to Abraham at Mamre; Gen 32 (cf. Gen 48:3; Hos 12:3–5) to Jacob; and Num 22 to Balaam. Even so, given the other elements provided about this figure, most interpreters accept this to be the Angel of the Lord himself. Similarly, given the clear echoes of the Sinai event in the opening theophany of Ezekiel, it is likely that the figure seated on the throne with the "appearance of a man" (Ezek 1:26) is referencing the Angel of the Lord. Likewise, in one Greek rendering of Dan 7:13, the Son of Man is not "like the Ancient of Days (ὡς παλαιὸς ἡμερῶν)," but instead, he was present "as the Ancient of days (ἕως τοῦ παλαιοῦ τῶν ἡμερῶν)." See C. Rowland, "The Vision of the Risen Christ in Rev. i.12ff.: The Debt of an Early Christology to an Aspect of Jewish Angelology," *JTS*

31, no. 1 (1980): 2–3, for the significance. This may even identify Michael (cf. Dan 10) as the Angel of the Lord who here comes as the Ancient of Days; according to Davis, *The Name*, 33, following J. Lust, "Daniel 7.13 and the Septuagint," *ETL* 54 (1978): 62–63.

8. E.g., Isa 9:6/9:5LXX, where the Messianic "Wonderful Counselor (יוֹעֵץ פֶּלֶא)" is changed to "Angel of Great Counsel (μεγάλης βουλῆς ἄγγελος)." Alternatively, in Isa 63:9, the "Angel of his presence (פָּנָיו וּמַלְאַךְ)" (cf. Exod 23:20–23; 33:14), is changed in the LXX so that it is not an angel but God himself: "not an ambassador, nor angel, but [God] himself saved them (οὐ πρέσβυς, οὐδὲ ἄγγελος, ἀλλ᾽αὐτὸς ἔσωσεν αὐτούς)." Another special case is Deut 32:8, where "the Most High (עֶלְיוֹן)" separates the nations according to the number of "the sons of Israel (יִשְׂרָאֵל בְּנֵי)." The LXX designates the number of "the angels of God (ἀγγέλων θεοῦ)." This translation relies on the older Hebrew construction of "sons of God," a fact now confirmed in three ways: a few variant LXX manuscripts have instead "sons of God (υἱῶν Θεοῦ)"; the Qumran version of this text has אל בני; and the Ugaritic text KTU 1.4 VI:46 provides an exact parallel of *Ēl* dividing the nations among his "seventy sons" (cf. Gen 10). For some scholars, this implies that YHWH was originally seen as one of the Sons of God and Israel was apportioned to him (a view championed by Otto Eissfeldt, *El im ugaritischen Pantheon* [Berichte über die Verhandlungen der Sächsischen Akademic der Wissenschaften zu Leipzig, Phil. His. Klasse 98.4; Berk: Akademie, 1951]; and more recently by Barker, *The Great Angel*, 21). For further details about the textual issues, see Michael S. Heiser, "Deuteronomy 32:8 and the Sons of God," *Bibliotheca Sacra* 158 (2001): 52–74, esp. 52–55; and for discussion on its implications, see Antti Laato, *The Origin of Israelite Zion Theology* (Library of Hebrew Bible/Old Testament Studies, 661; Edinburgh: T&T Clark, 2018), 119–21.

9. E.g., Num 22:3; 1 Chr 21:16. See full analysis in Michalak, *Angels as Warriors*, 2–4, and 35–50.

10. E.g., Exod 33:1–3; Josh 5:13–15; Judg 2:1–5; 2 Kgs 19:35; Ps 34:7/33:8LXX; 35:5–6/34:5–6LXX.

11. E.g., 2 Sam 24:15–25; 1 Chr 21:14–30. Alternatively in Zech 1:7–17; 3:1–10, it is the Angel who pleads with God on Israel's behalf.

12. See Exod 33:1–3, where God refuses to go with Moses but instead sends this Angel. According to Hannah, *Michael*, 21, this text demonstrates how the Angel of the Lord is not simply God's presence but has "a quasi-individual existence." Similarly, (if it is the same Angel and not *an* angel) in 1 Chr 21:15, the Lord stops the Angel from destroying Jerusalem. Barker, *The Great Angel*, 31, offers additional examples where the Angel is distinct from God (Zech 1:12; Gen 24:7; 1 Chr 21:27; Exod 23:20–23; 32:34; 33:2; Num 20:16; cf. Exod 23:21; 2 Sam 24; Gen 12:7; 26:23: 35:1).

13. In addition to the examples given above, see Exod 23:21, where God's "Name" is said to be in the Angel.

14. Barker, *The Great Angel*, 31, reviews instances where the Angel appears alone without reference to YHWH and, in fact, seems to be a manifestation of YHWH himself (32; ref. Ps 34:7; 35:5–6; 2 Kgs 1:3; 1:15; cf. Exod 12:12; Deut 32:35; Judg 2:2; Eccl 5:6; Iss 63:9), and then there are other texts in which YHWH and the Angel

seem to be interchangeable (33; ref. Zech 12:8; 3:1–7; Gen 48:15–16; Judg 5:23), and there are narratives where the Angel of the Lord seems to be YHWH himself (34; Gen 18:1–19:1; Judg 6:11–22; Judg 13:1–22; Gen 16:7–13; Exod 3:2–7; Gen 22:12; 2 Kgs 19:34–35; Isa 37:35–36), and finally the visions of various prophets testify to the identification of the Angel and YHWH (35–38; 1 Kgs 22:19–23; 1 Chr 28:18; Ezek 1:26; 8:2; 9:4; Dan 10:5–6; Isa 9:6).

15. For the full bibliography of older scholarship, see Frist Guggisberg, *Die Gestalt des Mal'ak Jahwe im AT* (Lyss: Dach Druck, 1979), 133–56. More recently, see discussion in Fossum, *The Name of God*; Barker, *The Great Angel*; Stephen L. White, "Angel of the Lord: Messenger or Euphemism?," *Tyndale Bulletin* 50 (1999): 299–305; and Malone, "Distinguishing the Angel of the Lord," 297–314. Additional debate has emerged in New Testament studies, in particular, regarding those who would see early Christian texts as using Angel Christology or Angelomorphic Christology; see Charles Talbert, *The Development of Christology during the First Hundred Years: And Other Essays on Early Christian Christology* (Supplements to Novum Testamentum 140; Leiden: Brill, 2011), 155–56 n.31, who discusses "an emerging consensus" in support of the two powers view, especially in reference to the role of the Angel of the Lord and Jesus. Similarly, see Bird, *Jesus among the Gods*, 190.

16. See chapter 2.

17. See overview in Dillon, "Philo's Doctrine of Angels," 197–205.

18. *Abr.* 23.118. Cf. *Somn.* 1.66, "the angels who are servitors to His powers, unbodied souls (τοὺς ὑποδιακόνους αὐτοῦ τῶν δυνάμεων ἀγγέλους, ἀσωμάτους ψυχάς)."

19. *Somn.* 1.115. Von Heijne, *The Messenger*, 205, "Philo also had a conception of angels as intermediaries between God and humankind. These angels are sometimes termed 'logoi' but are not to be confused with the supreme, divine 'Logos,' the totality of the 'powers.'"

20. *Somn.* 1.142. See Frick, *Divine Providence*, 54, on the angels as performing the function of God's "words."

21. *Somn.* 1.141. Cf. *Gig.* 2.6–7.

22. *Abr.* 23.115. Cf. *Abr.* 22.107, where the three "men" who appeared to Abraham are angelic and so have a "more divine nature (θειοτέρας ὄντες φύσεως)."

23. It should also be noted that although Philo never names Michael, some think he identifies Michael with the Angel of the Lord/Logos; see Hannah, *Michael*, 76 n.3, for bibliography.

24. See chapter 2.

25. Von Heijne, *The Messenger*, 201, "the angel of the Lord appears to be identified as the 'Logos' in many of Philo's interpretations of our pericopes."

26. E.g., *Conf.* 28.146: "Son of God . . . God's First-born, the Word, who holds the eldership among the angels, their ruler as it were. And many names are his, for he is called, 'the Beginning,' and the Name of God, and His Word (υἱὸς θεοῦ . . . τὸν πρωτόγονον αὐτοῦ λόγον, τὸν ἀγγέλων πρεσβύτατον, ὡς ἂν ἀρχάγγελον, πολυώνυμον ὑπάρχοντα· καὶ γὰρ ἀρχὴ καὶ ὄνομα θεοῦ καὶ λόγος)." Cf. *Her.* 205; and *Fug.* 101.

27. *Migr.* 31.174. Cf. Philo, *Agr.* 12.51, with ref. to Ps 23:1 and quoting Exod 23:20, where God shepherds creation by setting "His true Word and Firstborn Son

Who shall take upon Him its government like some viceroy of a great king; for it is said in a certain place: 'Behold I AM, I send My Angel before thy face to guard thee in the way' (προστησάμενος τὸν ὀρθὸν αὐτοῦ λόγον καὶ πρωτόγονον υἱόν, ὃς τὴν ἐπιμέλειαν τῆς ἱερᾶς ταύτης ἀγέλης οἷά τις μεγάλου βασιλέως ὕπαρχος διαδέξεται· καὶ γὰρ εἴρηταί που· Ἰδοὺ ἐγώ εἰμι, ἀποστέλλω ἄγγελόν μου εἰς πρόσωπόν σου τοῦ φυλάξαι σε ἐν τῇ ὁδῷ)." The Angel is "the divine Word (ὁ θεῖος λόγος)" in many of Philo's works: e.g., QG 3.28; Somn. 1.240; and Fug. 5.

28. QG 2.62. The Logos as a "second god" was discussed in chapter 2.

29. Fug. 204.

30. Her. 42.205–6: τῷ δὲ ἀρχαγγέλῳ καὶ πρεσβυτάτῳ λόγῳ δωρεὰν ἔδωκεν ἐξαίρετον ὁ τὰ ὅλα γεννήσας πατήρ, ἵνα μεθόριος στὰς τὸ γενόμενον διακρίνῃ τοῦ πεποιηκότος. ὁ δ᾽ αὐτὸς ἱκέτης μέν ἐστι τοῦ θνητοῦ κηραίνοντος αἰεὶ πρὸς τὸ ἄφθαρτον, πρεσβευτὴς δὲ τοῦ ἡγεμόνος πρὸς τὸ ὑπήκοον. ἀγάλλεται δὲ ἐπὶ τῇ δωρεᾷ καὶ σεμνυνόμενος αὐτὴν ἐκδιηγεῖται φάσκων· "κἀγὼ εἱστήκειν ἀνὰ μέσον κυρίου καὶ ὑμῶν," οὔτε ἀγένητος ὡς ὁ θεὸς ὢν οὔτε γενητὸς ὡς ὑμεῖς, ἀλλὰ μέσος τῶν ἄκρων, ἀμφοτέροις ὁμηρεύων.

31. Somn. 1.157–58.

32. Cf. other instances when it is the second power on the ladder, in Lad. Jac. 1.5–8; T. Jac. 2.14–16.

33. On the lack of traditional messianic language in this text, see Chester, "Jewish Messianic Expectations," 19–20.

34. Wis. 16:20, speaks generally about the "food of angels" (cf. Ps 78:25).

35. Von Heijne, The Messenger of the Lord, 142.

36. See chapter 4.

37. The dates proposed by scholars range considerably; see further bibliography in Howard Jacobson, A Commentary on Pseudo-Philo's Liber antiquitatum biblicarum (Leiden: Brill, 1996), 1:199–210, who suggests the text post-dates the Bar Kokhba revolt. Gurtner, Introducting the Pseudepigrapha, 259–60, reviews the feasible dates of 50–150 CE to find the matter inconclusive. The LAB is not cited by Christian writers and shows no signs of Christian influence.

38. LAB 61.5 (our trans.). Cf. Jacobson, A Commentary, 1:189, "the angel in charge of power." Most scholars think these are the same angel; see Jacobson, A Commentary, 2:1183.

39. LAB 18.9, "and he saw the angel and prostrated himself on the ground before him (et vidit angelum et adoravit eum in terra)" (text/trans. = Jacobson 25/119).

40. For a more complete treatment of Josephus's angelology, see Christopher Begg, "Angels in the Work of Flavius Josephus," Angels: The Concept of Celestial Beings—Origins, eds. Friedrich V. Teiterer, Tobias Niklas, and Karin Schöpfin (Deuterocanonical and Cognate Literature Yearbook; Berlin: De Gruyter, 2007), 525–36; and Michalak, Angels as Warriors, 211–21.

41. E.g., Ant. 1.51 on Gen 3:24. The one exception is the extraordinary case of the "angels" who corrupted the world before the flood in Gen 6:2 (see Ant. 1.74).

42. J. Levison, "Josephus' Interpretation of the Divine Spirit," Journal of Jewish Studies 46 (1996): 234–55.

43. E.g., James A. Montgomery, "The Religion of Flavius Josephus," *The Jewish Quarterly Review* 11, no. 3 (1921): 277–305, at 285.

44. Horbury, "Jewish and Christian Monotheism," 19.

45. See Fletcher-Louis, *Jesus Monotheism,* 145.

46. *Ant.* 1.155. We have altered the translation of the relative pronoun from "any other being (τι)" to "any other god" since, of course, Josephus is not referring to any "being" writ large, but to any gods other than the Creator by way of comparison to the theism of the Greek philosophers and in contrast to the polytheistic idolatry of all Gentiles. All other citations/translations are from the LCL, unless otherwise noted.

47. *Ant.* 1.189; cf. Gen 16:7LXX: ἄγγελος κυρίου. The same occurs at *Ant.* 1.219: "an angel of God (θεῖος ἄγγελος)."

48. Von Heijne, *The Messenger*, 245.

49. Von Heijne, *The Messenger,* 251, offers this explanation in commentary on these passages.

50. *Ant.* 1.189 (cited above) and 1.333.

51. *Ant.* 1.331. Jacob's new name, Israel, is also said to mean "opponent of an angel of God (τὸν ἀντιστάτην ἀγγέλῳ θεοῦ)" in *Ant.* 1.333.

52. *Ant.* 4.108.

53. *Ant.* 4.109. Cf. Num 22:28, "the Lord opened the mouth of the donkey."

54. Levison, "The Debut of the Divine Spirit in Josephus's *Antiquities*," *HTR* 87, no. 2 (1994): 123–38, finds Josephus to, in fact, distance God from direct action in this scene. But he does not address how the Angel of the Lord and God are equated in this line.

55. In his later book, there is another case as well. In *Ant.* 9.20, "the God of the Hebrews (ὁ τῷ Ἑβραίων θεὸς) appeared to the prophet Elijah." However, in 2 Kings 1:3 it is explicitly "the Angel of the Lord (מַלְאָךְ יְהוָה/ἄγγελος κυρίου)." Once again, Josephus could think of the Angel as a representative of God, as God himself, or as the second Power in heaven called Angel, Lord, and God.

56. *Ant.* 5.213.

57. *Ant.* 5.214.

58. *Ant.* 5.277.

59. *Ant.* 5.278–84.

60. *J.W.* 5.388.

61. Cf. 2 Chr 31:21, where he is simply "an angel (מַלְאָךְ/ἄγγελον)."

62. For angels in the targums, more generally, see David L. Everson, "A Brief Comparison of Targumic and Midrashic Angelological Traditions," *Aramaic Studies* 5, no. 1 (2007): 75–91; and idem, "Angels in the Targums: An Examination of Angels, Demons, and Giants in the Penteteuch Targums" (PhD Diss.; Hebrew Union College-Jewish Institute of Religion, 2009).

63. Yaacov Azuelos and Francesco Giosuè Voltaggio, "The 'Angel Sent from before the Lord' in 'Targum Joshua' 5,14," *Biblica* 96, no. 2 (2015): 166–67.

64. David L. Everson, "The Fish Grows Bigger: Angelic Insertions in Targums Neofiti and Pseudo-Jonathan," in *Aramaic in Postbiblical Judaism and Early Christianity*, eds. Eric M. Meyers and Paul V. M. Flesher (Duke Judaic Studies Series 3; Winona Lake, IN: Eisenbrauns, 2010), 236 and 238. Azuelos and Voltaggio, "The

'Angel Sent from before the Lord,'" 162, point out that there are a variety of concerns involved, including textual ones.

65. See our discussion in the following chapter 6. All translations from the targums that follow come from the series, *The Aramaic Bible* (= "AB"), edited by Martin McNamara, et al. (Wilmington, DE: Michael Glazier Press).

66. E.g., "angel of the Lord" in Tg.Neof. Gen 16:7, 9, 11 (AB 1A:99); Tg.Ps.-J. Gen 16:9, 10, 11 (AB 1B:63), and Tg.Onq. Gen 16:9,11 (AB 6:72).

67. Cf. Tg.Neof. Gen 16:13 (AB 1A:100); Tq.Onq. Gen 16:13 (AB 6:72); Tg.Ps.-J. Gen 16:13 (AB 1B:63). See further discussion in von Heijne, *The Messenger of the Lord*, 278–89.

68. See further discussion of the Memra in the previous chapters 2 and 3.

69. Tg.Neof. Gen 18:1 (AB 1A:103).

70. Tg.Neof. Gen 18:4 (AB 1A:104).

71. God agrees to go with Moses by sending his "presence" (Exod 33:14–15), and Moses next asks to see God's "glory" (33:18).

72. Tg.Neof. Gen 18:17 (AB 1A:105).

73. Tg.Neof. Gen 18:33 (AB 1A:106).

74. Tg.Neof. Gen 22:1 (AB 1A:116) and Tg.Onq. Gen 22:1 (AB 6:86).

75. Tg.Neof. Gen 22:16–18 (AB 1A:119); Tg.Ps.-J. Gen 22:16 (AB 1B:80); Tg.Onq. 22:16 (AB 6:86).

76. Tg.Neof. Gen 22:14 (AB 1A:118–19).

77. Tg.Neof. Gen 22:14 (AB 1A:119); cf. Tg.Ps.-J. Gen 22:14 (AB 1B:80), "the Shekinah of the Lord was revealed." A Genizah manuscript preserves a fragment of this passage, and on the ascent up Mount Moriah, Isaac sees "a pillar of cloud extending from heaven to earth" (Tosefta Gen 22:5 [Klein 1:34]), which is the sign to Abraham that Isaac is to be sacrificed.

78. Also, see Tg.Neof. Gen 35:3; and similar glosses for Gen 35:9 and 35:13 in Tg.Neof., Tg.Ps.-J., and Tg.Onq.

79. For such an assessment of a targum's purpose, see Alexander, "Jewish Aramaic Translations," 238–41.

80. Cf. T. Mos. 10.3; 1 En. 45:3; 51:3; 55:4; 61:8; 62:6; 69:29; 2 En 22–24; 4Q471b; and Philo, *Fug.* 100–101.

81. Cf. Num 22:31, 42; Judg 13:3–25; LAB 18.8; T. Jac. 2.14–16; LAE vita 14.2; Apoc. Ab. 33.5.

82. The text ends with a promise of a coming messiah who will free Abraham's descendants (from Rome?), but no further description of this messianic figure is given.

83. See details in Amy Paulsen-Reed, *The Apocalypse of Abraham in Its Ancient and Medieval Contexts* (Brill Reference Library of Judaism 69; Leiden: Brill, 2022).

84. Apoc. Ab. 10.3 Rec. Note that here and elsewhere, we have changed the spelling in the *OTP* from "Iaoel" to "Yaoel" for consistency and readability.

85. Apoc. Ab. 10.4.

86. Apoc. Ab. 10.7–8.

87. E.g., Fossum, *The Name of God*, 318; Hurtado, *One God,* 21, although he later (80–83) insists that this angel is not the divine Name embodied, but instead is indwelt

by it. This last point, however, does not seem to take seriously (a) the etymology of Yaoel nor (b) the fact that the Angel of the Lord is the one addressed as YHWH in many scripture passages.

88. See Bauckham, *Jesus and the God of Israel*, 225.

89. Apoc. Ab. 17.13. Cf. Apoc. Mos. 29.4 and 33.5, where God is addressed as Yaoel.

90. Apoc. Ab. 28.1.

91. See Quispel, "Gnosticism," in *Gnostica, Judaica, Catholica: Collected Essays of Gilles Quispel*, ed. J. van Oort; NHMS 55; (Leiden: Brill, 2008), 161, for further examples and discussion.

92. Apoc. Ab. 18.1.

93. Apoc. Ab. 19.4. Cf. 17.

94. "The Vision," 6–8.

95. See bibliography on Tobit in Joseph A. Fitzmyer, *Tobit* (Commentaries on Early Jewish Literature; Berlin: W. de Gruyter, 2003); and Stuart Weeks, Simon Gathercole, and Loren Stuckenbruck (eds.), *The Book of Tobit: Texts from the Principal Ancient and Medieval Traditions with Synopsis, Concordances, and Annotated Texts in Aramaic, Hebrew, Greek, Latin, and Syriac* (Berlin: De Gruyter, 2004).

96. Not least because of Tobit's explicit relation to Ahikar (see Tob. 1:21–22; 11:6–10; 11:18; and 14:10). Also, see the Wisdom instructions in Tob. 4, which represents the primary aim of the text according to Francis M. Macatangay, *The Wisdom Instruction in the Book of Tobit* (DCLS 12; Berlin: De Gruyter, 2011).

97. E.g., Tob. 12:22. For further details about Raphael, see Gieschen, *Angelomorphic Christology*, 135–36.

98. *Cod.Sin.* alters this slightly, adding another blessing of angels; see Stuckenbruck, *Angel Veneration*, 164–67, who concludes this as an instance of angel worship. Gieschen, *Angelmorphic Christology*, 136, agrees, only he thinks the worship is given only to the divine Name—Angel.

99. Cf. 1 En. 9.1; 1 QM 9.15; Apoc. Mos. 40.1, where he is one of four archangels.

100. E.g., Catherine Vialle, "Ange et Compagnon de Route: Le Personnage de Raphaël Dans Le Livre de Tobie (texte Court)," *Études théologiques et religieuses* 89, no. 2 (2014): 155, who concludes, "Un peu plus loin, Raphaël insiste sur le fait qu'il n'a pas agi de son propre chef mais qu'il a été envoyé par Dieu (12,18), ce qui tend à le présenter comme une créature proche de Dieu et, néanmoins, différente de lui."

101. Segal, *Two Powers in Heaven*, 190; and Gieschen, *Angelmorphic Christology*, 135–36.

102. Phillip Muñoa, "Raphael, Azariah and Jesus of Nazareth: Tobit's Significance for Early Christology," *JSP* 22, no. 1 (2012): 3–39.

103. Phillip Muñoa, "Before Mary and Jesus There was Raphael: An Antecedent to the Angelic 'Incarnations' of Jewish Christianity and Its Gospels," in *The Open Mind: Essays in Honour of Christopher Rowland*, eds. Jonathan Knight and Kevin Sullivan (London: T&T Clark, 2014), 165–82.

104. Phillip Muñoa, "Raphael the Savior: Tobit's Adaptation of the Angel of the Lord Tradition," *JSP* 25, no. 3 (2016): 228–43.

105. Muñoa, "Raphael the Savior," 232 (emph. added), referencing Tob 12:22. For further support, Munoa cites Joseph A. Fitzmyer, *Tobit* (CEJL; Berlin: De Gruyter, 2003), 299; and Carey A. Moore, *Tobit: A New Translation and Commentary* (AB 40A; New York: Doubleday, 1996), 274.

106. Muñoa, "Raphael the Savior," 235, also emphasizes that this is the first angel to disguise himself "as a Son of Man," which he sees as further precedent for early Christian interpretations of Jesus.

107. This could be supported by Herm.Sim. 9.6.1–2 (83.9.6.1–2), where six men supervise the building of the tower, but then in the middle of them appeared "a man of such lofty stature that he stood taller than the tower. And the six men who had supervised the building were walking with him on his right and on his left" (trans. Holmes 631). Later (90.9.12.7), the shepherd explains: "The glorious man . . . is the Son of God, and those six are the glorious angels who surround him on his right and on his left."

108. E.g., Philo calls the Logos an "archangel," and yet, he clearly thinks of the Logos as distinct from lower angels (e.g., *Conf.* 146; *Somn.* 1.25.157–58). Similarly, *Herm.Sim.* 9.6.1–2 (83.9.6.1–2), where six men supervise the building of the tower, but then in the middle of them appeared "a man of such lofty stature that he stood taller than the tower. And the six men who had supervised the building were walking with him on his right and on his left" (trans. Holmes 631). Later (90.9.12.7), the shepherd explains: "The glorious man . . . is the Son of God, and those six are the glorious angels who surround him on his right and on his left."

109. Literally "Angel of the Face" in Ethiopic. Cf. Isa 63:9; Tob 12:15; and 4Q216.

110. See Jacques V. Ruiten, "Angels and Demons in the Book of Jubilees," in *Angels: The Concept of Celestial Beings—Origins, Development and Reception*, eds. F. V. Reiterer, T. Nicklas, and K. Schöpflin (Deuterocanonical and Cognate Literature Yearbook; Berlin: Walter de Gruyter, 2007), 585–609.

111. E.g., Hannah, *Michael*, 50; for further bibliography, see Michalak, *Angels as Warriors*, 86.

112. Michalak, *Angels as Warriors*, 86, is undecided: "we lack concrete evidence to confirm it."

113. In Jub. 31.14, the sons of Levi who serve in the tabernacle are called "angels of presence." This shows how the earthly worship of God reflects the heavenly temple; see James VanderKam, "The Angel of the Presence in the Book of Jubiliees," *Dead Sea Discoveries* 7, no. 3 (2000): 378–93.

114. Von Heijne, *The Messenger of the Lord*, 151.

115. Jub. 2.2.

116. *Opif.* 2.12; discussed in chapter 2.

117. See Fiona Grierson, "The Testament of Moses," *Journal for the Study of the Pseudepigrapha* 17, no. 4 (2008): 265–80; and G. Anthony Keddie, "Judaean Apocalypticism and the Unmasking of Ideology: Foreign and National Rulers in the Testament of Moses," *Journal for the Study of Judaism in the Persian, Hellenistic and Roman Period* 44, no. 3 (2013), 301–38.

118. Cf. Jude 1:9.

119. Moses may even claim to have preexisted: "But he did design me, who was prepared from the beginning of the world, to be the mediator of his covenant" (T. Mos. 1.14).

120. Most scholars support this view, see Bühner, *Messianic High Christology*, 177 n.14. However, Fletcher-Louis, *All the Glory of Adam: Liturgical Anthropology in the Dead Sea Scrolls* (Leiden: Brill, 2002), 31–32, who sees this figure as a human priest who will be exalted based on the statement, "Then will be filled the hands of the messenger" (10.2). While this phrase may possibly signify sacerdotal connotations, the rest of the passage suggests something more along the lines of a messianic warrior figure (e.g., the next line in T. Mos. 10.2, "he will at once avenge them of their enemies"). To be sure, the two interpretations are not mutually exclusive; see the figure of Melchizedek in 11QMelch (discussed below and in chapter 8).

121. Barker, *The Great Angel*, 75.

122. The text of Joseph and Aseneth is primarily preserved in two recensions, a shorter recension published by Marc Philonenko (*Joseph et Aséneth* [SPB, 13; Leiden: Brill, 1968]) and a longer recension published by Christoph Burchard, (*Untersuchungen zu Joseph and Aseneth* [WUNT, 8; Tübingen: Mohr Siebeck, 1965]). Here we are following the longer recension of Burchard that is the basis for his translation in Charlesworth's *OTP*. The Charlesworth translation does provide the versification for the shorter recension in parenthesis.

123. For arguments in favor of a Christian origin, see Ross Shepard Kraemer, *When Aseneth Met Joseph: A Late Antique Tale of the Biblical Patriarch and His Egyptian Wife, Reconsidered* (Oxford: Oxford University Press, 1998), 225–44; and Rivka Nir, *Joseph and Aseneth: A Christian Book* (Sheffield: Sheffield University Press, 2012). Yet for arguments that the text is a product of Second Temple Judaism, see John J. Collins, "Joseph and Aseneth: Jewish or Christian" *JSP* 14, no. 2 (2005): 97–112; Stuckenbruck, "'Angels' and 'God'," 55–56; Jill Hicks-Keeton, "Aseneth between Judaism and Christianity: Reframing the Debate" *JSJ* 49 (2018): 189–222; Patricia D. Ahearne-Kroll, *Aseneth of Egypt: The Composition of a Jewish Narrative* (Atlanta: SBL Press, 2020).

124. Jos. Asen. 14.1–2.

125. Jos. Asen. 14.3 and 7.

126. Jos. Asen. 14.8.

127. Jos. Asen. 14.9. For this description in comparison with Daniel's Son of Man, see Christopher Rowland, "A Man Clothed in Linen: Daniel 10:6ff. and Jewish Angelology," *JSNT* 24 (1985): 100–110.

128. Jos. Asen. 15.12.

129. Jos. Asen. 16.11.

130. Jos. Asen. 17.9.

131. That God writes this figure's name in the book but that this figure writes others' names in the same book might suggest this figure plays a role in the creative act: i.e., this is a figure through whom God brings about life. That this figure creates honeycomb out of nothing only further corroborates such a conclusion.

132. Similarly, one could consider the texts from Qumran on Michael, Melchizedek, and the figure from the Self-Glorification Hymn. Those will be treated in chapter 8 of this book.

Chapter 6

Other Abstract Figures

At this point, we have reviewed evidence for God's Word, Wisdom, and Angel. These figures have been shown both to be divine and to have a unique relationship to the Most High God of Israel, which we argue can best be explained by understanding these titles as referring to the second power in many Second Temple Jewish texts. In the current chapter, we can turn to various titles for a heavenly figure so associated with God that scholars disagree as to the nature of said figure. Are references to God's Spirit simply a way of describing God's presence? When God's Name dwells in the temple is that a way of saying that God dwells there? Is God's Face a Hebraic way of talking about God's self-manifestation? While many modern scholars answer all of these questions in the affirmative, there is much evidence to the contrary. Therefore, in each case there are scholars who have come to see one or more of these figures as a distinct entity who acts on behalf of God, and who also is so closely associated with God to be spoken of as if it were the God of Israel.

As will be shown below, God's Spirit, Name, and Face, often need to be discussed in conjunction with one another, and thus we have elected to treat them together in one chapter. Because we are discussing several of these intermediary figures—or one intermediary figure known by an array of descriptors, we cannot provide as thorough of a review of all Second Temple Jewish literature for each figure or descriptor. Instead, in this chapter we will provide important examples where Spirit, Name, and Face (along with Word, Wisdom, and Angel) are depicted as a distinct divine entity. We will then assess all of these titles collectively to conclude that at least some Jewish literature in the Second Temple period use these titles (individually or collectively) for the second power in heaven.

THE SPIRIT OF GOD

Studying the term "spirit" in ancient Judaism is complicated by the way the term can refer to various concepts. For example, in the scriptures and in Second Temple Jewish literature the term (רוּחַ/πνευμα) can refer to a generic idea (e.g., "the spirit of fear"), a human spirit, an angel, or "the Spirit of the Lord."[1] It is this last reference on which we will focus, and yet the primary texts do not always allow for easy compartmentalization of these meanings.[2] One telling example is Isaiah 63, where the "Lord (יְהוָה/κυρίου)" (63:7) is called the people's "savior (לְמוֹשִׁיעַ/σωτηρίαν)" (63:8). Then the text explains how it was "the Angel of his presence (מַלְאַךְ פָּנָיו/ἄγγελος[3])" (63:9) who rescued Israel from Egypt, but the people responded by rebelling and thereby grieving "the holy Spirit (רוּחַ קָדְשׁוֹ/τὸ πνεῦμα τὸ ἅγιον)" (63:10).[4] In other words, since angels are spirits, the Angel of the Lord is "the holy Spirit," but the question remains as to whether this Spirit was in fact God's self-manifestation, or God's representative, or even a second power.[5]

When it comes to the Spirit of God, the scriptures and the Second Temple Jewish literature speaks in much the same way as has been seen above for the Word and Wisdom of the Lord. Often, "the Spirit" may be an expression used to describe God's activity and presence—that is, a personification. However, many texts speak as if the Spirit is a distinct agent, working on behalf of God—that is, a hypostasis. This becomes more frequent in the Second Temple period. For example, in Judith it reads, "Let all your creatures serve you, for you spoke, and they were made. You sent forth your spirit, and it formed them; there is none that can resist your voice" (16:14). In this case, the text may simply parallel God's S/spirit with God's act of speaking and God's "voice" and therefore the question of whether the Spirit is a distinct hypostasis in some ancient Jewish texts has been the focus of much secondary literature.[6]

All of this is helpfully illustrated in a recent study by Andrew W. Pitts and Seth Pollinger, who find that the Spirit, in fact, should be understood as a distinct entity.[7] Their conclusion is especially interesting, because they find that the Word and Wisdom of God are not distinct from God, but merely personifications of God's activity in the world.[8] Alternatively, they find that "sentient mediatorial agents" (i.e., angels and exalted humans) act on behalf of God, but are in no way divine.[9] The Spirit, they conclude, is the one exception to what they call "numerical monotheism" so that, "the Spirit seems both to participate within the exclusive activities of Yahweh and qualifies as (at the very least) a secondary expression of monotheistic deity."[10] The strength of this view is the numerous texts wherein the Spirit acts as Creator or at least God's agent in creation.[11] Although we agree with their conclusion regarding the

Spirit, we should note how their initial premise is somewhat undermined by the fact that numerous texts connect or even equate the Spirit with Wisdom, as they acknowledge.[12] Furthermore, their premise that no angel has divine status is likewise weakened when certain texts seem to equate the Spirit of God with the Angel of the Lord, as they also acknowledge.[13] Aside from their views of these other entities or concepts, their ultimate conclusion regarding the Spirit in ancient Judaism is worth quoting in full:

> The Spirit, then, seems to function as an agent, but not an agent independent of God since it shares in the divine identity with God. Yahweh, we might say, in Second Temple Jewish monotheism seems to be the first and principle instantiation of the divine identity—evidenced through his roles as creator, ruler, and redeemer—and the Spirit of Yahweh is the secondary instantiation of this identity by virtue of the Spirit's sharing in Yahweh's uniquely monotheistic functions.[14]

In general we agree with this conclusion, except we find the Spirit of the Lord to be one and the same as the Word and Wisdom of the Lord for many ancient Jewish authors. Therefore, although the term "spirit" is often used in other ways, the "Spirit of the Lord" can at times describe the second divine entity in a two powers framework.

One clear example where this is the case is a passage found in Philo.[15] First, it needs to be admitted that Philo can speak of "spirit" in the most general sense, much like his biblical sources. In this way, Philo interprets "the spirit of God" mentioned in Genesis 1:2 in the literal sense as "the air which flows up from the land."[16] And yet in the allegorical sense, Philo also says the Spirit is "knowledge in which every wise man naturally shares (ἐπιστήμη, ἧς πᾶς ὁ σοφὸς εἰκότως μετέχει)."[17] In this way, Philo explains how every prophet who is filled "with the divine spirit (πνεύματος θείου)" is filled with "wisdom, understanding, and knowledge (σοφίας, συνέσεως, ἐπιστήμης)."[18] Similarly, he elsewhere speaks of how Adam was made from clay, but "moulded . . . from the divine spirit."[19] Philo may merely speak of God's spirit and wisdom in an abstract sense here, and yet given his penchant for speaking of God's Wisdom and Logos as a distinct agent (and often agents of creation; see discussion above), it may be a false dichotomy to ask whether Philo understands the Spirit to be abstract and generic or distinct and hypostatic. This is especially clear in the case where Philo calls the Angel of the Lord who enabled Balaam to prophesy truly (Num 22–24) the "Spirit of God" (cf. Num 14:2, רוּחַ אֱלֹהִים/πνεῦμα θεοῦ).[20]

Philo's treatment of this scene from Numbers seems to have been a common one since Josephus also reads this passage the same way.[21] Josephus is a telling case, because he rarely speaks of any other entity than God as doing divine activity (as discussed above). And yet this is not the only instance where Josephus speaks this way of the Spirit. Josephus also has Solomon pray, "send some portion of Thy [S]pirit to dwell in the temple (μοῖράν τινα τοῦ σοῦ πνεύματος εἰς τὸν ναὸν ἀποικίσαι)."[22] This is an important example because in 1 Kings 8:29, Solomon prays that God's "Name" would dwell in the temple, since God transcends such localization, and since for many Second Temple Jews God's "Name" is another title for the second power (as shown below).[23] While we still cannot make too much of Josephus's statements, since there is little indication that he held to a two powers paradigm,[24] his ability to speak of the Spirit of God as the Angel of the Lord or the Name which resides in the temple likely reflects a common form of discourse in Palestine at his time.

Other earlier sources also further indicate that some Jews in the Second Temple period could speak of the Spirit as a distinct entity, such as some of the Wisdom literature. Wisdom, who was shown above to be an active hypostasis, is "a kindly spirit" in the Wisdom of Solomon (1:6), and she is "the Spirit of the Lord" who has filled the earth (1:7).[25] Later, this text describes Wisdom who formed humanity (9:2), and then she is called "God's Holy Spirit from on high (τὸ ἅγιόν σου πνεῦμα ἀπὸ ὑψίστων)" (9:17). Later, the text simply speaks of how God's "immortal Spirit (τὸ ἄφθαρτόν σου πνεῦμά) is in all things" (12:1). A similar view can be found in Sirach, where, the "[S]pirit" and "[W]isdom" are in poetic parallel (39:6). In the immediate context of the passage, there is nothing to indicate that these refer to a distinct hypostasis. However, ancient readers would likely think of this Wisdom-Spirit as a distinct entity since this is the way Wisdom was treated earlier in Sirach 24.[26] This would explain how Wisdom describes herself as coming from the "mouth of the Most High" so as to cover "the earth like a mist" (Sir 24:3): Wisdom is the Spirit or "Breath" from Genesis 1:2 who hovered over creation.

In apocalyptic texts from this time period, the Spirit's distinct role and activity is quite clear. In 2 Baruch, God is said to make the world "by the [S]pirit,"[27] and similarly God speaks to say "my [S]pirit creates the living."[28] In one of the Sibylline Oracles fragments,[29] "the Creator who has nourished all, who put a sweet [S]pirit in all and made it a guide for all mortals."[30] This statement is immediately followed by the assurance that "There is one God,"[31] as if to assure the reader that the Spirit's activity does not detract from the oneness of Israel's Lord. In 4 Ezra the prophet prays, "O Lord, you so spoke at the beginning of creation . . . and your [W]ord accomplished the work. And then the Spirit was hovering, and darkness and silence embraced everything."[32] One more example is found in the Apocalypse of Moses. The concluding doxology in one manuscript is to "God the Father . . . and to his eternal and life-giving Spirit," with no mention of anyone else (whereas most manuscripts are clearly Christianized so as to turn this statement into a Trinitarian blessing).[33]

Other sources to consider are those found at Qumran. Throughout the Dead Sea Scrolls, "spirit" has the same range of meanings found in the scriptures, including angels as "spirits."[34] In this sense, not only are humans called "spirits" in the Dead Sea scrolls, but the "gods" of each nation, including Israel's Lord, is a "S/spirit," and all of them answer to the God of gods.[35] Since this is the case, even when scrolls from Qumran refer to God's Spirit, there is a "lack of clarity" on whether any given reference is to "the" Spirit or "a" spirit.[36] One text, however, is unique, the Treatise on Two Spirits (1QS III, 13–IV, 26).[37]

This text survives as part of the Rule of the Community, and so it has a prominent place in the extant collection. At one point, God is said to place "two spirits" within "man," and these are "the spirits of truth (רוחות האמת) and deceit. . . . In the hand of the Prince of Lights is dominion over all the sons of justice; . . . And in the hand of the Angel of Darkness is total dominion over the sons of deceit."[38] A few lines down, the text adds, "the God of Israel and the [A]ngel of his truth (ומלאך אמתו) assist all the sons of light."[39] This text, like many from Qumran, uses "spirit" in various ways,[40] but there seems to be a close correspondence between, if not an equating of, the Angel of truth (מלאך אמת) and the Spirit of truth (רוח האמת).[41] If this text truly is an earlier treatise only surviving as redacted into the *Rule of the Community*,[42] then it is even more plausible that this reflects a remnant of an earlier two powers theology.[43] The same could be true for the numerous times where the Dead Sea scrolls equate the Spirit of God with Wisdom, especially when speaking of the Spirit's/Wisdom's actions in creation.[44]

In sum, it appears that the Spirit of God is sometimes described as a distinct agent, a hypostasis, in Second Temple Jewish literature. This becomes especially clear when the Spirit is another name for God's Wisdom and the Angel of the Lord. Given the fact that "spirit" is a very elastic term in ancient Hebrew and Greek, it is no surprise that this title is not as common or definitive as some of the other terms we have explored in this chapter. Even so, by looking to how the Spirit of God is depicted in many Jewish sources from this time period, we see further evidence that the "Spirit of God" is at times best understood as another name for the second power. This Spirit is an agent who is distinct from God and yet who is divine in so far as he creates, reigns over the world, and dwells in the Temple. It was mentioned above that the Spirit is also associated with the "Name" of the Lord, and so we now turn to that important discussion.[45]

THE NAME OF GOD

The proper name of the Lord, the Tetragrammaton,[46] is one of the most defining features of Israel's theology. In Exodus 3, when Moses asks for the divine name, God answers, "I AM WHO I AM" (3:14a). Moses is told that when his people ask who sent him, he should answer, "I AM has sent me to you" (3:14b). Next, in a curious repetition that has sparked centuries of debates,[47] God seems to alter the instructions slightly so as to say, "Thus you shall say to the Israelites, 'The LORD, the God of your ancestors . . . has sent me to you,'" adding "This is my name forever, and this my title for all generations" (3:15). In the original language, there is a shift from the first person to the third person, one letter's difference in the Hebrew: instead of referring to God as "I AM" (אהיה [AHWH]), Moses and "all generations" should call God "HE IS" (יוהי [YHWH]).

This Hebrew name, consisting almost entirely of aspirants and thereby practically ineffable, was not read aloud in the post-exilic period by at least some forms of Judaism—a practice which became normative in the rabbinic period.[48] Instead, the Hebrew word אדני/*Adonai* (= "Lord") was used as a substitute, apparently in order to avoid any hint of mispronunciation, insult, or blasphemy.[49] The same phenomenon occurred for Aramaic speaking Jews, who could use the word *Mar'* ("Lord") in place of the Tetragrammaton.[50] Likewise, texts like the Septuagint tended to substitute the term κύριος ("Lord") when translating the divine name, rather than giving a transliteration or an attempt at a more literal translation.

Although the simple substitution of "Lord" for the Tetragrammaton eventually became the most common method used in the Second Temple period, there were other options found in the surviving sources.[51] In some pre-Christian Greek manuscripts of Jewish scriptures the Greek text retains Hebrew characters for the divine name.[52] In other instances, Greek letters are used in an attempt to transliterate God's name, so that the text reads, ιαω.[53] Instead of a transliteration, some Jews attempted to translate the Tetragrammaton. Thus, Philo of Alexandria used the Greek phrase ὁ ὤν, which means "the One who is" to translate God's name.[54] In short, throughout the Second Temple period, Jews widely recognized the uniqueness and power of God's name.

For the purpose of this study, the importance of God's name is further seen in the way that the use of the term, "the name (שם/τὸ ὄνομα)," and not just the actual Tetragrammaton, comes to be a substitute for God in the scriptures.[55] In many biblical passages, the *Shem,* or "Name (שם/τὸ ὄνομα)," of God seems to replace, or represent God, or even act on behalf of God as a distinct hypostasis.[56] One passage even calls the divine "Name" God's "power (גְּבוּרָה/δυνάμει)."[57] Some modern scholars focus on what is known as "Name Theology," to say that the Hebrew scriptures originally depicted YHWH as present on earth, but later corrected this way of speaking of God. Instead of Israel's Lord acting in immanent terms, God remains transcendent in the heavens, leaving the Name of God to be worshipped in the temple.[58] In short, even if God is "in heaven" and does not actually reside in the temple, his Name does.

This "Name Theology," however, has been challenged.[59] The debate in part addresses the question of whether God's Name becomes a distinct hypostasis, or whether use of this term is a literary device that personifies God's presence without compromising God's transcendence. Robert Hamerton-Kelly, for example, concluded that the biblical material originally only entailed personification while later Jews interpreted the Name as a distinct hypostasis.[60] The matter was studied at length by Jarl E. Fossum, who concludes that in some biblical passages, "The Name must here be understood as a divine hypostasis."[61] More recently, however, Benjamin Sommer has claimed the biblical passages do "refer to a hypostasis, a quality or attribute of a particular being that becomes distinct," but then he adds more nuance, "[The Name is] never entirely independent . . . In many texts, God's Shem embodies but does not exhaust God's self, and it also maintains some degree of separate identity."[62] The Name's divine status and earthly actions have unsurprisingly sparked a number of studies interested in this figure as a precursor to Christian understandings of Christ's preexistence.[63]

In Second Temple Jewish texts there are several examples where texts refer to God's "name" being given to a certain figure, which seems to bestow divine status on that figure, while in other cases the "Name" itself acts as a distinct hypostasis. The latter kind can be found in Philo, who, in chapter 2, was shown to speak of the Logos as a second power in heaven, and describes the Logos in various ways. Among the many titles for the Logos, Philo includes "the Name of God (ὄνομα θεοῦ)."[64] The key biblical text informing Philo for this title is Exodus 3:14, where it is the Logos-Angel who appears to Moses and states that he should be called "I Am that I am" (Exod 3:14). Segal comments, "It is by virtue of the revelation of the divine name to Moses that the *logos* comes to be equated with the name of God."[65] This is why, whenever Philo finds the "Name" of God acting in the scriptures, he assumes this to be a distinct entity, not just a figure of speech.[66]

This way of reading is not unique to Philo. As shown in previous chapters, the targums likewise often inserted the term *Ha Shem*, or the Name, in the place of God.[67] For example, whereas Genesis 28:22 has Jacob promise a sanctuary for "God (אֱלֹהִים/θεοῦ)," Targums Neofiti and Pseudo-Jonathan deem it a sanctuary for "the Name of the Lord." It should be noted that Targum Neofiti later refers back to this scene, rendering Genesis 35:1 as commanding Jacob to build an altar "to the Name of the Memra of the Lord," instead of simply building the altar to "God" as in the MT and LXX.

Another notable passage is Exodus 23:20–23, which identifies the Angel of the Lord with God's "Name" and thereby this Angel even has the power to forgive sins.[68] Like the biblical text, God will "send an angel ahead" of Moses and the people.[69] Only in Targum Neofiti this figure is further specified. First, he is called "an angel of mercy."[70] Of course, Moses should "listen to his Memra . . . because his Memra is in My Name."[71] In the MT God tells Moses to listen to the Angel's "voice (בְּקֹלוֹ)" because "my name is in him (בְּקִרְבּוֹ שְׁמִי כִּי)."[72] Then, the relation of God's Name to the Angel's power to forgive sins is explained: "do not rebel against his words, for my holy name is invoked upon him, for he will not forgive or pardon your sins, for my holy name is invoked upon him."[73] The next verse then adds, "listen to the voice of my Memra,"[74] after which he is again called "my angel."[75] Since the forgiveness of sins is normally a divine act, in Targum Neofiti there is an apparent need to specify that the Angel of the Lord is simply an angel of mercy who has been delegated this role by the power of the divine name. This connection is important to mention because it shows that the targums do not only use the term "Name" as a literary device. At least at times, the targums depict this figure as an active agent, distinct from God and yet also called the "Lord" by the patriarchs and Israel. Furthermore, to return to the concept of God's Memra in the targums, this term has even been shown to be a way of describing God's self-designation, the Name which God placed in the Temple to be worshipped while God remained transcendent.[76]

This way of speaking of God's Name as an active agent can be found sporadically in other Second Temple texts. For example, according to Jubilees the Name created all things. In this text, Isaac makes his sons swear an oath "by the glorious and honored and great and splendid and amazing and mighty [N]ame which created heaven and earth and everything together."[77] Another example is found in the opening to the Prayer of Manasseh, a text that survives in Syriac but probably dates to the first or second century BCE,[78] God's Word and Name are synonymous and act in creation: "He who bound the sea and established it by the command of his [W]ord, he who closed the bottomless pit and sealed it by his powerful and glorious [N]ame."[79] In fact, the next line seems to label God's Word/Name as a "power": "He before whom all things fear and tremble; especially before your power."[80]

In some other Second Temple Jewish literature the Name of God does play a prominent role, but less as a distinct hypostasis and more as a way of linking God with God's agent acting in the world. Josephus, for instance, knows that God's proper name represents his power and so must not be spoken or revealed to outsiders.[81] In his retelling of the scene from Exodus 3 where

God reveals his name to Moses, Josephus says he is not allowed to tell this name to others: "of which I am forbidden to speak (περὶ ἧς οὔ μοι θεμιτὸν εἰπεῖν)."[82] Instead, Josephus speaks of "God" and for the most part shows no need to offer any additional substitute or intermediary persona in God's place. There is one interesting case reported by Josephus that illustrates God's Name as an intermediary for God—when Alexander the Great enters Jerusalem and encounters the Jewish high priest, dressed in his robe and wearing the divine "name" on his crown. All are surprised as Alexander bows down before the high priest and "prostrated himself before the Name (προσεκύνησε τὸ ὄνομα)."[83] When asked about this action, Alexander explained that he had not bowed down to the high priest, but to the Jewish "God (τὸν δὲ θεόν)."[84] This way of manifesting God's presence through his name and on a priest is also a connection found in various apocalyptic texts with figures that may be more than an exalted intermediary.[85]

Several apocalyptic sources link certain figures with the divine Name. In the Apocalypse of Abraham, a text surviving in a Christian Slavonic translation but thought to originate from a first century Jewish provenance,[86] there is a unique figure named Yaoel. This figure's name derives from the Greek rendition of the divine name "IAO" and the Hebrew word for God, "El." God sends this angel, "through the mediation of my [i.e., God's] ineffable name."[87] Furthermore, he is a "power through the medium of his [God's] ineffable name."[88] This almost certainly refers to Exodus 23:20–21, where God places the divine name in the Angel of the Lord. Therefore, Yaoel is not the "Name" per se,[89] but God's name serves as a link or designation that makes this figure unique from all others in this text.[90] This link between God and an angelic figure via the divine name is further reflected in the Enochic tradition, which we will address below.[91]

For now, suffice it to say, that the divine Name offered Second Temple Jewish writers a range of interpretive options, including seeing the Name itself,[92] or a heavenly figure with whom God shared the name, figures that we have argued are best identified with the second power.[93] The latter option tends[94] to be done with angelic figures, or even one angelic figure in particular,[95] as we have shown in our previous chapter. Here, we should note the parallel way in which the Tetragrammaton makes God's presence known through an intermediary, whether this is the high priest or the Angel of the Lord. Perhaps the claim in Exodus 23:20–21 that God's name is "in" the Angel is in fact a way of saying that God's name is placed "on" this Angel, just as the divine name was engraved on the high priest's crown. One is the highest "power" next to God, just as the other is the highest human on earth in terms of proximity to God. Both function as intermediaries on earth. The interpretation of these figures in the Second Temple period likely varies, with some seeing them both as exalted creatures, whereas others clearly viewed the Angel of the Lord, bearing the name of "the Lord," as something more.[96] In either case, the divine name functions to place God's presence "on" both and thereby before God's people. While few in this period understand the divine name as a distinct hypostatic, some examples can be found where the name is personified. In said cases, these rare examples likely refer to God's work in the world through an intermediary, perhaps even through the heavenly intermediary, arguably one thought to be the second power in heaven. Therefore, in a way, the Name theology of von Rad and others is correct: God's "Name" is said to dwell in the temple, which is to say that God's Word or "Angel" descends into the Holy of Holies, and the high priest functions as the human intermediary who can enter therein because he too has the divine name placed on him.[97] Passages about God's "Name" dwelling in the temple had to be reinterpreted in later rabbinic Judaism, wherein the name itself became ineffable and the concept of God's presence had to transcend one locale, meaning that "the name of the Lord" had to be interpreted simply as the Lord himself and not a distinct hypostasis.[98] It seems, however, such clarity was not universal in the earlier Second Temple period.

THE FACE OF GOD

In the scriptures it is clear that one cannot see God's "face (פָּנִים/πρόσωπον)" and live (Exod 33:20), and yet, there are exceptions.[99] Jacob expresses surprise to have lived after seeing God "face to face (פָּנִים אֶל־פָּנִים/πρόσωπον πρὸς πρόσωπον)," and so he names the site "Peniel (פְּנִיאֵל/Εἶδος θεοῦ)" (Gen 32:31). Other biblical figures express similar surprise at seeing God.[100] This textual background inspired later interpreters of the Second Temple period to sometimes speak of the "Face" of the Lord as if it were not just God's appearance, but a distinct hypostasis. For example, C. L. Seow explains, "In quite a number of biblical texts the *pānîm* of YHWH is YHWH's hypostatic presence. Thus it serves the same function as *Šēm* in the Deuteronomic theology, *Kābôd* [or] 'Glory' in the Priestly tradition, and *Shekinah* in later Jewish writings."[101]

The notion of the Face of the Lord as a second Power, distinct from God can be found in the Enochic tradition.[102] In 1 Enoch the distinction is not so clear. In his vision, Enoch sees the throne with God seated on it, and he then adds, "None of the angels was able to come in and see the face . . . the flaming fire was round about him (or 'it'?), and a great fire stood before him" (14:21–22). Enoch then hears God call, "Come near to me, Enoch, and to my holy Word" (13:24), which may be another name for God's "Face." This Word will be shown in our next chapter to be a distinct second power in (1 Enoch), since it is equated with the Son of Man. In 2 Enoch this Face appears again, with the same fiery appearance.[103] While 1 Enoch may be influenced by Christianity, and 2 Enoch certainly has, both texts also retain earlier pre-Christian content, and so this material on the Face of the Lord may come from the earliest Jewish strata in the text.[104]

This notion finds support from the pseudepigraphal Ladder of Jacob, written perhaps in the second century CE but reflecting an earlier Jewish strata.[105] The text contains the same description of God's fiery Face as a distinct entity, even though it is set in a different biblical context. The Ladder expands the account of Genesis 28:11–22, wherein Jacob sees a ladder to heaven. In the Genesis account, Jacob sees angels coming and going, but then "the Lord stood on it (יְהוָה נִצָּב עָלָיו/ὁ δὲ κύριος ἐπεστήρικτο ἐπ᾽ αὐτῆς)," and then next "the Lord God (יְהוָה אֱלֹהֵי/κύριος ὁ θεὸς)" spoke to Jacob (28:13). In the Ladder of Jacob the Lord and the Lord God seem to be understood as two distinct entities.[106] There are twenty-four angels on each side of the ladder, but "on the top of the ladder was the face as of a man, carved out of fire" (1.5), while "God was standing above its [the ladder's] highest face" and spoke to Jacob (1.8). In other words, Genesis 28:13 is interpreted so that this flaming Face seems to be the "Lord" who was "on" the ladder, while the "Lord God" who speaks from above him is distinct, which strongly suggests some form of a two powers paradigm at work.[107] Perhaps, the Face of flame is simply the highest angel, but—as was discussed in chapter 5—the Angel of the Lord figure is often depicted as "the Lord," the second power of heaven, including in 1 Enoch and in the Ladder of Jacob, and so this Face is likely equated with the Angel of the Lord (who is also the Lord). Other angels will often be associated with the Face of the Lord in some way, especially the one named Phanuel or Phaniel (= "Face of God"). He and others have been discussed further (in chapter 5), but suffice it to say that there are times where one figure stands above other angels.[108]

Another apocalyptic Jewish text that expands the scene from Genesis 28 is the Testament of Jacob. It survives in a late Coptic manuscript, but the text itself likely dates to the late first century or early second century CE.[109] Although it has definitive Christian elements, some of the core tenets of the text look to be pre-Christian. For example, the angel says to the patriarch, "Blessed are you also, O Jacob, for you have seen God face to face. You saw the angel of God—may he be exalted!—and you saw the ladder . . . Then you beheld the Lord siting at its top with a power which no one could describe" (2.14–16). Even if this is indebted to Christian thinking wherein Jesus is the second power, this portion of the text shows little signs of overt Christian language. If anything, this scene seems to rely on older categories. Similar material about God's Face is found in Joseph and Aseneth, an apocryphal account of Joseph and his wife (Gen 41:45) with no explicit Christian content.[110] In this account, the "man" who introduces himself as "the chief of the house of the Lord and commander of the whole host of the Most High"[111] has a unique face. This individual's face, however, is not like any other human; instead, he matches the description of the Face of God found in other apocalyptic texts: he was "in every respect similar to Joseph . . . except that his face was like lightning, and his eyes like sunshine, and the hairs of this head like a flame of fire of a burning torch."[112] The account then narrates several aspects of this heavenly figure that match descriptions of the Lord of Israel. Nevertheless, since he was clearly sent from the Most High God, when he departs, Aseneth calls him "a god."[113] In other words, the fiery Face of God, which is called a "power" in other apocalyptic Jewish texts, seems to have been accommodated by the author of Joseph and Aseneth and imagined to have been an angelic figure who could descend and act as the Lord of Israel. This kind of thinking is easily explained by a two powers paradigm, which further substantiates our conclusion in our previous chapter.

Another text where the Face of God is mentioned is the Prayer of Joseph. This text only survives in fragments, and may stem from the first century of the Common Era. Origen knows of its use "among the Hebrews."[114] The text claims to reveal Jacob's true identity: although he seemed to have forgotten his preexistent state while on earth as a human, Jacob is, in fact, the highest heavenly being next to God.[115] The patriarch states, "I, Jacob, who is speaking to you, am also Israel, an angel of God and a ruling spirit. . . . I am the firstborn of every living thing to whom God gives life."[116] Israel then claims he was wrestling with Uriel, the eighth angel in rank who was jealous of Israel. Even as a preexistent angel, however, it is clear that Jacob himself is not the second Power of God, but the text may reference such a second Power in terms of the "Face" of God.[117] When reminded of his rightful place, Israel calls himself, "the archangel of power of the Lord and the chief captain among the sons of God . . . the first minister before the face of God."[118] Elsewhere, Jacob-Israel is "chief captain of the power of the Lord."[119] This concept of a "power," along with the descriptions of Israel's rank and role, has close parallels with Wisdom, especially as accommodated in Philo's Logos.[120]

The concept of the Face of the Lord in all likelihood originated as a euphemism for speaking of God's presence or appearance. And yet, in the Second Temple period, there are many instances where the concept seems to have developed.[121] Either the "Face" of the Lord has shifted to being a cipher or to being a name for the second power.

CONCLUSIONS ABOUT GOD'S
SPIRIT, NAME, AND FACE

In the present chapter we have only offered a preliminary overview of these various figures. This is because much of our discussion necessarily becomes repetitive in our cross-references to our earlier chapters on God's Word, Wisdom, and Angel. Nonetheless, in light of our earlier in-depth study of these figures, we have shown how many Second Temple Jewish sources spoke of God's Spirit, Name, and Face as a distinct, divine entity, and yet uniquely associated the figure(s) with God in a way that is unlike other lower heavenly beings.

As was also referenced sporadically in this chapter, there are other titles which potentially offer additional insights into how some Jewish writers from this period understood the second power in heaven. These include concepts like God's Glory and Shekinah. However, in the interest of focusing on those instances which provide the clearest examples, we have limited ourselves to the titles listed above.

At this point, we can turn to another figure who has often been understood as a heavenly or even divine individual: the Son of Man. With him, we easily avoid any concerns of him being a mere personification, for he, like the Angel of the Lord, is a distinct agent in the scriptures and in the Second Temple literature. Moreover, in our review of the material devoted to the Son of Man we can return to a more thorough treatment of one figure, since he is depicted in various ways across a variety of sources.

NOTES

1. The standard study is that of Daniel Lys, *"Ruach": Le souffle dans l'Ancien Testament* (Paris: Presses universitaires de France, 1962).

2. For other important facets of the Spirit's role from this period, see John R. Levison, *The Spirit in First-Century Judaism* (Leiden: Brill, 1997); and Max Turner, *Power from on High: The Spirit in Israel's Restoration and Witness in Luke-Acts* (Journal of Pentecostal Theology Supplement Series 9; Sheffield: Academic Press, 1996), 101–37.

3. The LXX does not use the "presence" or "face"; cf. Vulg., *angelus faciei*.

4. Cf. Hag 2:5, where God's "Word (דָּבָר/[missing in LXX])" made a covenant with the people when they came out of Egypt, and God's "Spirit (רוּחִי/τὸ πνεῦμά)" remains with them.

5. The same ambiguity is found in the targums; see Pere Casanellas, "The Use of the Expressions 'Prophetic Spirit' and 'Holy Spirit' in the Targum and the Dating of the Targums," *Aramaic Studies* 11, no. 2 (2013): 167–86.

6. See discussion in Jörg Frey, "How did the Holy Spirit Become a Person?," in *The Holy Spirit, Inspiration, and the Cultures of Antiquity: Multidisciplinary Perspectives*, eds. Jörg Frey, John R. Levison, and Andrew Bowden (Ekstasis 5; Berlin: De Gruyter, 2014), 348–51.

7. Andrew W. Pitts and Seth Pollinger, "The Spirit in Second Temple Jewish Monotheism and the Origins of Early Christology," in *Christian Origins and Hellenistic Judaism: Social and Literary Concerns for the New Testament*, eds. Stanley Porter and Andrew W. Pitts (Early Christianity in its Hellenistic Context 2; Leiden, The Netherlands: Brill, 2013), 135–76.

8. Pitts and Pollinger, "The Spirit," 153, following Dunn, *Christology in the Making*, 176; and Hurtado, *One God, One Lord*, 46–47. For their disagreement with Dunn on the Spirit (*Christology in the Making*, 134–36), see Pitts and Pollinger, "The Spirit," 161.

9. Pitts and Pollinger, "The Spirit," 153.

10. Pitts and Pollinger, "The Spirit," 154.

11. Second Temple texts include 4 Ezra 6:38–39, "O Lord, you spoke at the beginning of creation . . . and your [W]ord accomplished the work. And then the Spirit was hovering . . . so that your works might appear"; 2 Baruch 21:4, "the one who fixed the firmament by the [W]ord and fastened the height of heaven by the [S]pirit"; 23.5, "For my [S]pirit creates the living"; cf. Philo, *Leg.* 1.33; *Opif.* 30–31.

12. Pitts and Pollinger, "The Spirit," 154–56.

13. Pitts and Pollinger, "The Spirit," 163. They later (p. 176) add, "unlike angel-morphic (sic) mediatorial figures, still shares in the divine identity." We disagree with this interpretation of the Angel of the Lord, who often appears to be the Lord himself; see our discussion in the previous chapter 5.

14. Pitts and Pollinger, "The Spirit," 160.

15. For further discussion and bibliography, see Levison, "The Prophetic Spirit as an Angel according to Philo," *Harvard Theological Review* 88 (2 1995), 189–207; and Levison, *The Spirit*.

16. *Gig.* 1.22; cf. *QG* 4.5, for a different interpretation.

17. *Gig.* 1.23.

18. *Gig.* 1.23; with ref. to Exod 31:2–3.

19. *QG* 1.51.

20. *Mos.* 1.274–77. Josephus, *Ant.* 4.108 and 118 treats this passage the same way.

21. *Ant.* 4.108 and 118. For further discussion of the Spirit in Josephus, see Levison, *The Spirit*.

22. *Ant.* 8.114.

23. See further discussion below.

24. See Segal, *Two Powers in Heaven*, 13.

25. Cf. Wis. 7:22, where in Wisdom is the "spirit" of good things.

26. See chapter 4.

27. 2 Bar. 21:4.

28. 2 Bar. 23:5.

29. These fragments have no Christian content, and so are generally thought to represent a late Second Temple Jewish context, perhaps dating as early as the second

century BCE. See John J. Collins, "Sibylline Oracles," in *Old Testament Pseudepigrapha*, ed. James H. Charlesworth (Peabody, MA: Hendrickson, 1983), 1:360 and 469; and Ashley L. Bacchi, *Uncovering Jewish Creativity in Book III of the Sibylline Oracles: Gender, Intertextuality, and Politics* (Leiden: Brill, 2020), 13–20 and 54–55. For further bibliography and discussion, see Rieuwerd Buitenwerf, *Book III of the Sibylline Oracles and its Social Setting* (Studia in Veteris Testament Pseudepigrapha; Leiden: Brill, 2003), 72–75.

30. Sib. Or., frag. 1:5–6.

31. Sib. Or., frag. 1:7.

32. 4 Ezra 6:38–39.

33. Apoc. Mos. 43.5.

34. Jörg Frey, "Paul's View of the Spirit in the Light of Qumran," in *The Dead Sea Scrolls and Pauline Literature*, ed. Jean-Sébastien Rey (Studies on the Texts of the Desert of Judah 102; Leiden: Brill, 2014), 237–60, 249. For a more in-depth survey, see Arthur E. Sekki, *The Meaning of Ruaḥ at Qumran* (Atlanta: Scholars Press, 1989).

35. See Reinhard G. Kratz, "Deity and Divine in the Hebrew Bible and the Dead Sea Scrolls," in *Sibyls, Scriptures, and Scrolls: John Collins at Seventy*, eds. Joel S. Baden, Hindy Najman, and Eibert J. C. Tigchelaar (JSJSup 175.1; Leiden: Brill, 2017), 636–54.

36. Frey, "Paul's View of the Spirit in the Light of Qumran," 256–57.

37. The following citations of this text and its translation are from F. García Martínez and E. Tigchelaar (eds.), *The Dead Sea Scrolls Study Edition,* 2 vols.; Leiden: Brill, 1997), 74–79.

38. 1QS III, 17–21.

39. 1QS III, 24–25.

40. E.g., in 1QS IV, 3–4 and 21, "spirit" is used in a general sense to talk of the "spirit of meekness, of patience, general compassion" (etc.), and of how God will cleanse humans "with a spirit of holiness . . . he will sprinkle over him the spirit of truth like lustral water."

41. Frey, "Paul's View of the Spirit," 251, surveys the secondary literature to conclude, "there can be little doubt that contemporary readers saw an angelic reality behind the two spirits."

42. See discussion in Peter Porzig, "The Place of the 'Treatise of the Two Spirits' (1QS 3:13–4:26) within the Literary Development of the Community Rule," in *Law, Literature, and Society in Legal Texts from Qumran*, eds. Jutta Jokiranta and Molly Zahn (Studies on the Texts of the Desert of Judah 128; Leiden: Brill, 2019), 127–52.

43. At the least, this paradigm avoids the problematic concept of "dualism" that has been much debated for this and other texts from Qumran. See the essays in Géza G. Xeravits (ed.), *Dualism in Qumran* (London: T&T Clark, 2010).

44. See examples in Pitts and Pollinger, "The Spirit," 158.

45. A similar comparison is found in the Babylonian Talmud, which tends to replace references to God's Spirit with the term "Shekinah"; see Casanellas, "The Use of the Expressions 'Prophetic Spirit,'" 171. That discussion, however, takes us beyond the period of view in our current study, and so must be left to the side.

46. Meaning "four letters," i.e., יהוה/YHWH.

47. See Wilkinson, *Tetragrammaton*.

48. On the dates and evidence for when this substitution occurred, see Wilkinson, *Tetragrammaton*, 61–64 and 79–83.

49. Cf. Lev 24:16, esp. in the LXX. Also, see Origen, *In Psalmus* 2 (PG 12:1104), for testimony about how Jews refused to say God's proper name (which he writes with the Greek letters Ἰαὴ); because the divine name is ineffable (τετραγράμματον ἀνεκφώνητον), Hebrew-speaking Jews say Ἀδοναῖ, while Greek-speaking Jews say Κύριος.

50. An important point for New Testament studies where this Aramaic term is applied to Jesus. E.g., 1 Cor 16:22; cf. Rev 22:20.

51. For further debate on Jewish use of κύριος for the divine name, see Joseph A. Fitzmyer, *A Wandering Aramean: Collected Aramaic Essays* (Chico, CA: Scholars Press, 1979), 115–42 (= "The Semitic Background of the *Kyrios*-Title"). It is worth noting the example of George Howard who claimed that Christians would have originally wanted to keep the God of the Hebrew Bible and Jesus distinct. This assumption led him to argue that the original Jewish versions of the LXX would not have used κύριος as a substitute of the divine name and that Christian scribes of the LXX only conflated the two later and then substituted the name; see Howard, "The Tetragram and the New Testament," *Journal of Biblical Literature* 96 (1977): 63–68. Howard's claims for LXX texts not using κύριος have been rejected by the consensus of scholars because his theory introduces further problems (see Wilkinson, *Tetragrammaton*, 92–94). Our argument in this project—that even some NT authors understood Jesus to be the κύριος of the LXX—would show Howard's premise as flawed from the outset.

52. E.g., 8HevXIIgr (see Emanuel Tov, R. A. Kraft, and P. J. Parsons, *The Greek Minor Prophets Scroll from Nahal Hever (8HevXIIgr)* [Oxford: Oxford University Press, 1990], 12 for discussion, and see instances on 29–77); and PFouad 266 (see Zaki Aly and Ludwig Koenen, *Three Rolls of the Early Septuagint: Genesis and Deuteronomy* [Bonn: Rudolf Habelt, 1980], 37–127 for instances).

53. E.g., pap4QLXXLeviticus, frg.1 line 3, frg.2 line 1, frgs. 20–21 line 4; cf. frgs.6–7 line 12 (see Patrick W. Skehan, Eugene Ulrich, Judith E. Sanderson, and P. J. Parsons, *Qumran Cave 4: IV, Palaeo-Hebrew and Greek Biblical Manuscripts* [Oxford: Clarendon Press, 1992], 169–74). Also, see Diodorus Siculus (*Bibliotheca historica* 1.94), who reports how the Jews believe Moses received the law from "Iao (Ἰαὼ)"; cf. Origen, *Commentary on John* 2.7.

54. E.g., *Mos.* 1.75–76, "God replied: "First tell them that I am He Who is, that they may learn the difference between what is and what is not, and also the further lesson that no name at all can properly be used of Me, to Whom alone existence belongs (ὁ δὲ "τὸ μὲν πρῶτον λέγε" φησίν "αὐτοῖς, ὅτι ἐγώ εἰμι ὁ ὤν, ἵνα μαθόντες διαφορὰν ὄντος τε καὶ μὴ ὄντος προσαναδιδαχθῶσιν, ὡς οὐδὲν ὄνομα τὸ παράπαν ἐπ᾽ ἐμοῦ κυριολογεῖται, ᾧ μόνῳ πρόσεστι τὸ εἶναι)." Cf. Exod 3:14LXX: ἐγώ εἰμι ὁ ὤν.

55. E.g., Lev 18:21; Deut 12:2–5, 11; 2 Sam 7:13; 1 Kgs 8:16; 2 Kgs 21:7; Jer 7:10–12; Ps 20:2LXX; Isa 30:27; 60:9; Amos 2:7; Tob 11:14.

56. According to Andrei A. Orlov, *Embodiment of Divine Knowledge in Early Judaism*, (London ; New York: Routledge, 2021), 112, the Name tends to be used for audial, rather than visual, revelations of God.

57. Ps 54:3/53:3LXX (53:1 ET).

58. Championed by Gerhard von Rad, *Deuteronomium-Studien* (Göttingen: Vandenhoeck & Ruprecht, 1947) (cf. ET = *Studies in Deuteronomy* [London: SCM Press, 1953]).

59. For the secondary literature, see Sandra L. Richter, *The Deuteronomistic History and the Name Theology: Leshakken Shemo Sham in the Bible and the Ancient Near East* (Berlin: De Gruyter, 2014), 26–36.

60. Robert Hamerton-Kelly, *Pre-Existence, Wisdom, and the Son of Man: A Study of the Idea of Pre-Existence in the New Testament* (SNTSMS 21; Cambridge: Cambridge University Press, 1973), 15–21. Orlov, *Yahoel and Metatron: Aural Apocalypticism and the Origins of Early Jewish Mysticism* (Texts and Studies in Ancient Judaism 169; Tübingen: Mohr Siebeck, 2017), 16, concludes something similar: while Moses and other exalted intermediaries can embody or represent the divine Name, sometimes the Name itself is "personified."

61. Fossum, *The Name*, 85, esp. for Isa 30:27.

62. *The Bodies of God*, 59.

63. See Jean Daniélou, *The Theology of Jewish Christianity*, trans./ed. John A. Baker (Philadelphia: Westminster Press, 1978), 147ff.; Richard Longenecker, "Some Distinctive Early Christological Motifs," *NTS* 14 (1968): 526–45, esp. 533–36; and Davis, *The Name*. For Samaritan and early "Gnostic" sources, see Fossum, *The Name of God*.

64. *Conf.* 28.146.

65. Segal, *Two Powers*, 163.

66. See further in Orlov, *Yahoel and Metatron*, 50–53.

67. Also, see T. Neof. Gen 35:3; and similar glosses for Gen 35:9 and 35:13 in T. Neof., T. Onq., and T. Ps.-J.

68. This passage was also influential for many Second Temple texts in terms of linking the Angel of the Lord with God's "Name." See Orlov, *Yahoel and Metatron*, 17–21.

69. Tg.Onq. Exod 23:20; Tg.Ps.-J Exod 23:20.

70. Tg.Neof. Exod 23:20.

71. Tg.Onq. Exod 23:21; Tg.Ps.-J Exod 22:23.

72. The LXX is similar: τὸ γὰρ ὄνομά μού ἐστιν ἐπ' αὐτῷ.

73. Tg.Neof. Exod 23:21.

74. Tg.Neof. Exod 23:22.

75. Tg.Neof. Exod 23:23.

76. Hayward, *Divine Name and Presence*, 148.

77. Jub. 36.7.

78. According to J. H. Charlesworth, *OTP* 2:625–27.

79. Pr.Man. 3.

80. Pr.Man. 4.

81. For full discussion, see Nathanael J. Andrade, "The Jewish Tetragrammaton: Secrecy, Community, and Prestige among Greek-Writing Jews of the Early Roman Empire," *Journal for the Study of Judaism in the Persian, Hellenistic and Roman Period* 46, no. 2 (2015): 198–223.

82. *Ant.* 2.276.

83. *Ant.* 11.331. For additional sources about the high priest's crown bearing the Tetragrammaton, see Josephus, *J.W.* 4:164; 5.5.7; and Philo, *Mos.* 2.23.114; 2.26.132.

84. *Ant.* 11.334.

85. For further discussion of the high priest bearing the divine name and acting as a (divine?) intermediary, see our chapter 9.

86. The Christian interpolations are clear in section 7, but do not pertain to the passage addressed here. See full discussion in Orlov, "Praxis of the Voice: The Divine Name Tradition in the Apocalypse of Abraham," *Journal of Biblical Literature* 127, no. 1 (2008): 53–70.

87. Apoc. Ab. 10.3 Rec.

88. Apoc. Ab. 10.7–8.

89. Hurtado, *One God, One Lord*, 80.

90. As discussed in chapter 5.

91. Cf. 1 En. 48:2; 3 En. 12:1, 12:5. See further discussion in our chapter 8.

92. Gieschen, *Angelomorphic Christology*, 77, "the Divine Name—could be hypostatized as an angel."

93. See further discussion in Orlov, *Yahoel and Metatron*, 47–50.

94. Orlov, *Yahoel and Metatron*, 16, sees numerous intermediaries like Moses "personify" the Name, and so can speak of the unique ways in which the Angel of the Lord or Yahoel are indwelt by and clothed with the Name. These will be addressed further in our chapter 9.

95. The Tetragrammaton itself can be associated with angelic "hosts" or "powers," and therefore many texts lend themselves to being interpreted such that YHWH (or at least the Angel of the Lord, see the previous chapter 5) is ranked among, and as the leader of, these powers. In other words the second power may be one among many others for ancient Jews (cf. our discussion of Philo in chapter 2). For instance, the title "Lord of Hosts" is often translated in the LXX as "Lord Almighty (κύριος παντοκράτωρ)": e.g., 2 Sam 7:8; 7:27; 1 Chr 17:24; Mic 4:4; Nah 2:14; 3:5; Hab 2:13; Zech 2:12–13; 3:7; 3:9–10; 4:6; 4:9; 5:4; 6:12; 6:15; 7:3; 7:9; 7:12–13; 8:1–4; 8:6–7; 8:9; 8:11; 8:14; 8:18–20; 8:22–23; 9:15; 10:3; 12:5; 13:7; 14:16–17; 14:21; Mal 1:4; 1:6; 1:8; 1:9–11; 1:13; 1:14; 2:2; 2:4; 2:7–8; 2:12; 2:16; 3:1; 3:5; 3:7; 3:10–12; 3:14; 3:17; 3:19; 3:21. However, it can also be translated as "Lord of the powers (κύριος τῶν δυνάμεων)": e.g., 2 Sam 6:2, for "the LORD of hosts who is enthroned on the cherubim"; 2 Sam 6:18; 1 Kgs 18:15; 2 Kgs 3:14; 19:31; Pss 23:10; 45:8; 45:12; 47:9; 83:2; 83:4; 83:13; Zeph 2:9; 2:10; Hag 1:2; 1:5; 1:9; 1:14; 2:4; 2:6–9; 2:11; 2:23; Zech 1:3–4; 1:6; 1:12; 1:14; 1:16–17; 7:4. (Alternatives include where the title is transliterated [e.g., 1 Sam 15:2; 17:45; and almost all instances in Isaiah; cf. Rom 9:29; Jas 5:4], and in Jeremiah where "hosts" is usually dropped from the "Lord's" description.) For YHWH as one of the various angelic hierarchies in Second Temple Jewish literature, see Michalak, *Angels as Warriors*, 56–69.

96. Discussed in chapter 5.

97. Cf. Deut 12:5; 12:11; 12:21; 14:23–24; 16:2; 16:6; 16:11; 26:2; and Jer 7:10–14.

98. Samuel S. Cohon, "The Name of God: A Study in Rabbinic Theology," *Hebrew Union College Annual* 23, no. 1 (1950), 589–90.

99. See discussion in Simeon Chavel, "The Face of God and the Etiquette of Eye-Contact: Visitation, Pilgrimage, and Prophetic Vision in Ancient Israelite and Early Jewish Imagination," *Jewish Studies Quarterly* 19, no. 1 (2012): 1–55.

100. Cf. Hagar in Gen 16:13 with the Angel of the Lord, but there is no mention of God's "face"; the same is true for Gideon's parents in Judg 13:20–21. Gideon sees the Angel of the Lord "face to face" and fears for his life (Judg 6:22; cf. Moses's habit of speaking with "God, face to face" in Exod 33:11).

101. "Face," in *Dictionary of Deities and Demons in the Bible*, eds. K. van der Toorn, B. Becking, and P. W. van der Horst (Leiden: Brill, 1995), 322–25, at 322. The Angel of the Lord was also known as the "Glory" of the Lord in Samaritan literature; e.g., Ben Hayyim, *Tibat Marqe* 3:56–57, "Let us now be frightened by . . . the Glory (כבודה) . . . It was as though the Glory (כבודה) was saying: 'I have might; I cannot stand men's guilt—this is what I taught you in every place. There is no deed (too) mighty for me.'" Text/trans. from Abraham Tal (ed.), *Tibåt Mårqe/The Ark of Marqe: Edition, Translation, Commentary* (Studia Samaritana 9; Berlin: De Gruyter, 2019), 274–77.

102. See Andrei Orlov, "Ex 33 on God's Face: A Lesson from the Enochic Tradition," *Scrinium* 3, no. 1 (2007): 323–36.

103. *2 En.* 22.1 [J], describes the "face of the Lord, like iron made burning hot in a fire and brought out, and it emits sparks and is incandescent." Similarly, *2 En.* 22.1A, has Enoch see "the face of the Lord, strong and very terrible" (*OTP* 1:137). Cf. *2 En.* 39.5[J]/39:3–4[A].

104. For further discussion of the date and original context, see Orvlov, "The Sacerdotal Traditions of 2 Enoch and the Date of the Text," *New Perspectives on 2 Enoch: No Longer Slavonic Only*, eds. Andrei Orvlov, Gabriele Boccaccini, and Jason Zurawski (Studia Judaeoslavica 4; Leiden: Brill, 2012), 103–16; and Timothy A. Gabrielson, "An Early Reader of James? Ethical Parallels between the Epistle and 2 Enoch," *JSNT* 43, no. 2 (2020): 226–47.

105. The text survives in a Christian form, but the Christian expansions are easily identifiable, leaving the original Jewish apocalyptic (Lad. Jac. 1.1–4.36) from the first century apparent for readers. See Alexander Kulik, "On Traditions Shared by Rabbinic Literature and Slavonic Pseudepigrapha," *Journal for the Study of the Pseudepigrapha* 28 (1 2018): 45–67; Christfried Böttrich, "A New Approach to the Apocryphal Ladder of Jacob," *Journal for the Study of the Pseudepigrapha* 28 (3 2019): 171–81.

106. Cf. Philo, *Somn.* 1.157–58, who says Jacob saw not God, but "the Ruler of the Angels, the Lord (τὸν ἀρχάγγελον, κύριον)" on the ladder (discussed in chapter 2).

107. Orlov, "The Face as the Heavenly Counterpart of the Visionary in the Slavonic Ladder of Jacob," in *Of Scribes and Sages: Early Jewish Interpretations and Transmission of Scripture*, vol. 2, ed. Craig A. Evans (London: Bloomsbury/T&T Clark, 2004), 61–62.

108. April D. DeConick, "Heavenly Temple Traditions and Valentinian Worship: A Case for First-Century Christology in the Second Century," in *Historical Origins of the Worship of Jesus Conference Volume, St. Andrews, Scotland 1998*, eds. J. Davila and C. Newman (Supplements to JSJ; Leiden: Brill, 1998), 308–41 at 329; and David

J. Halperin, *The Faces of the Chariot: Early Jewish Responses to Ezekiel's Vision* (Texte und Studien zum Antiken Judentum 16; Tübingen: Mohr Siebeck, 1988), 425.

109. Malka Z. Simkovich, "Echoes of Universalist Testament Literature in Christian and Rabbinic Texts," *Harvard Theological Review* 109, no. 1 (2016): 1–32, at 1–2.

110. See discussion in previous chapter 5.

111. Jos. Asen. 14.8.

112. Jos. Asen. 14.9. For this description in comparison with Daniel's Son of Man, see Rowland, "A Man Clothed in Linen," 100–110.

113. Jos. Asen. 17.9.

114. Origen, *Comm. Io.* 2.25 (ANF 9:341).

115. Chester, "Jewish Messianic Expectations," 53, "This succession of epithets shows that Jacob-Israel is not only pre-existent, but is also supreme, apart from God, in the heavenly realm, set above all other angels; his earthly manifestation in the form of Jacob is merely temporary."

116. Pr. Jos. frag. A.

117. Schäfer, *Two Gods*, 60–61, observes, "Thus the angel Jacob/Israel moves very close to God. He is not God, but remains an angel; he is, however, the only living being with God before creation, the sole servant before the face of God."

118. Schäfer, *Two Gods*, 60–61.

119. Pr. Jos., frag. C.

120. Chester, "Jewish Messianic Expectations," 53. Cf. Philo, *Conf.* 146; and see Heijne, *The Messenger*, 226–28, for the parallels and further discussion.

121. For more examples, see Olyan, *A Thousand Thousands*, 105–9. In most cases, Olyan finds the "hypostasis" (a term he avoids) to be only a "special figurative treatment" (i.e., a personification), but in the case of the Angel of Presence, or the Face of God, he concludes that this entity is, in fact, a "divinization" (i.e., a hypostasis). See Olyan, *A Thousand Thousands*, 91 and 105.

Chapter 7

The Son of Man

A figure identified as the (or a) Son of Man appears in three different Jewish textual traditions from the Second Temple period, the book of Daniel, 4 Ezra, and 1 Enoch.[1] The Daniel tradition seems to be the first of these three and the one on which 4 Ezra and 1 Enoch are expanding. Here we consider each of these traditions and how to assess the Son of Man figure therein and his relationship to the God of Israel.

THE SON OF MAN IN DANIEL

In the visions of Daniel 7, Daniel sees one like a "Son of Man" who comes on the clouds of heaven and appears before the "Ancient of Days," a clear reference to the God of Israel. This "Son of Man" is given an eternal kingship over the entire world (Dan 7:13–14). The identity of this seemingly human "Son of Man" figure is unclear. In the subsequent explanation of Daniel's vision, he is told that the last and final kingdom, that given to the Son of Man figure, is a kingdom that is given to the holy ones of Israel and that these holy ones will possess the kingdom forever. From this explanation, many interpreters have concluded that the "Son of Man" is merely a symbol for the people of Israel, to whom God will grant the eschatological kingdom.[2] Such a conclusion comes from a natural reading of the text and is entirely plausible. However, the description of the Son of Man figure has led others to differing conclusions about his identity. This figure rides on the clouds, an act that is closely associated with divine beings, including the God of Israel.[3] Such a heavenly origin has led some to question whether this figure is rightly equated with the people of Israel and instead contend that he represents a heavenly agent to whom God grants everlasting kingship.[4] The connection to Israel that is made in verses 18, 22, and 27 is then understood in terms of the Son of Man figure as a heavenly ruler, possibly even a messianic figure, that represents, but is not rightly equated, with the people of Israel.

155

Regardless of the intention of the original author, it is clear that many readers of Daniel in the Second Temple period understood this Son of Man as an actual figure or being and not simply as a symbol for Israel. As we will see below, both the author of 4 Ezra and the *Parables of Enoch* understand this Danielic Son of Man as a heavenly and messianic figure, with both expanding greatly this Danielic tradition.

Yet, if the Danielic Son of Man is understood as an actual figure rather than a symbol, how should his relationship to the God of Israel be understood? As noted above, riding on clouds is suggestive of a divine identity. But there is little else in Daniel's description of this figure to conclude he should be equated with Israel's God, from whom he is clearly distinct. Thus, regarding Daniel 7:13 and a two powers theology, the best one could say is that it could fit such a theological framework, but nothing in the text demands one.

However, there is a translation of Daniel 7:13 that is at least suggestive of a two powers interpretation. The Old Greek version of Daniel 7:13 states that the Son of Man comes in the clouds "as the Ancient of Days" rather than "before the Ancient of Days."[5] While some have argued that this text is ultimately the result of a copyist error, Loren Stuckenbruck has made a significant case that this divergent reading might best be explained at the level of translation and the theological commitments of the translator: the translator understood the Son of Man to be a divine being that was closely associated with the Ancient of Days.[6] Benjamin Reynolds notes a number of features that suggest just such an association. First, is the Son of Man's coming on the clouds. Not only is association with clouds closely associated with divinity in the ancient near east, but it is particularly associated with Israel's God.[7] Thus, the Son of Man coming in the clouds creates a strong similarity to the God of Israel. Second, the Son of Man seems to receive worship in the Old Greek translation, worship that parallels the worship given to Israel's God. In verse 14, the word λατρεύω is used to describe the actions of the nations of the earth toward the Son of Man. In the LXX, the word is frequently used to convey the offering of service to the God of Israel within the context of cultic worship.[8] In fact, in Daniel, it is used three times to describe cultic worship offered to Nebuchadnezzar (3:12, 14, 18) and three times to describe the worship of Israel's God (3:28; 6:16, 20). That the Son of Man figure might receive the same sort of cultic service offered to Israel's God closely associates the two, especially given the fact that worshipping Nebuchadnezzar is denounced in Daniel. Finally, both the Ancient of Days and the Son of Man are described as being approached in a similar manner by "the standing ones (οἱ παρεστηκότες)." In Daniel 7:10, a great multitude of people are standing (παρειστήκεισαν) before the Ancient of Days, and in 7:13 "the standing ones," presumably those who were also standing before the Ancient of Days in 7:10, are also present before the Son of Man. As recipients of the same action, the Son of Man and the Ancient of Days are closely associated with each other.

This Greek translation of Daniel 7:13 is indeed more suggestive of a two powers theology than the Aramaic text. The Son of Man actually appears as the Ancient of Days (and as in the Aramaic, comes in the clouds of heaven, a feature closely associated with divinity). Additionally, both are approached by multitudes in a similar way, and the Son of Man seems to receive worship like the God of Israel. Ultimately, the Son of Man of this Greek translation only meets one of our proposed criteria, making a case that he represents the second power possible but still inconclusive. The direction taken by subsequent interpreters of the Danielic Son of Man will be helpful in further assessing the Son of Man figure.

THE SON OF MAN IN 4 EZRA

In 4 Ezra 13, Ezra has a vision (the sixth vision) in which he sees a "Son of Man" figure rising up out of the sea and flying on the clouds of heaven. This seems to be a clear reference to the Danielic Son of Man figure. In the vision, the Son of Man goes on to destroy a multitude that opposes him, not with weapons, but with the fire that comes from his mouth. After this destruction he gathers a peaceful multitude to himself. In the explanation of this vision, it is clear that this Son of Man is an eschatological judge and once God declares him to be his own son.

While the Son of Man is never explicitly called the Messiah in the sixth vision, such identity seems clearly implied as this figure does things and is described in ways that are attributed to God's Messiah in previous visions. He is the one God has hidden for many ages, he will deliver God's creation through judging and destroying the wicked, and he will reign over God's people after his judgment is complete.[9] It is quite clear that 4 Ezra understands the Danielic Son of Man to be a distinct figure (not a symbol for Israel) who is rightly identified as God's Messiah and eschatological judge. This figure is widely recognized as a heavenly messianic figure, though most interpreters do not conclude the figure should in any way be identified as Israel's God. Yet, interestingly, 4 Ezra's description of this Son of Man does seem to apply a YHWH text to this figure. In 4 Ezra 13:12–13, the Son of Man figure comes down from a mountain and calls a multitude of people to him. Later, this detail is explained as the lost tribes of Israel being brought to the Son of Man figure. Daniel Boyarin points out the parallel between this passage and Isaiah 66:20, "They shall bring all your kindred from all the nations as an offering to the LORD, on horses, and in chariots, and in litters, and on mules, and on dromedaries, to my holy mountain Jerusalem, says the LORD, just as the Israelites bring a grain offering in a clean vessel to the house of the LORD."[10] This text describes the lost tribes being brought to YHWH, who is on his holy mountain, while the text of 4 Ezra describes the same group being brought to the Son of Man, who comes down from the mountain to receive them. The application of this YHWH text to the Son of Man seems undeniable. Boyarin agrees with most scholars that throughout the sixth vision, the presentation of Son of Man "seems to fall more towards the pole of the human Davidic Messiah tradition than the Second Divinity."[11] As such, Boyarin concludes that 13:12–13 represents a strand of Son of Man tradition like that we will see in 1 Enoch, but that the tradition has been suppressed by another strand of tradition.[12] We question whether such a bifurcation is necessary. Could Jews not hold in tension both a heavenly divine Messiah and a Davidic one? The Christian movement will do this very thing. Why deny to Second Temple Judaism the creativity of the Christian movement birthed from it? Regardless, we see in 4 Ezra one of our criteria being met, the application of YHWH texts to the Son of Man figure. This evidence is highly suggestive in terms of this Son of Man figure representing a second power, and in fact, it has lead Peter Schäffer to conclude, "The Messiah in 4 Ezra is truly a son of God, a younger God alongside his father, the older god."[13] We learn more about Second Temple views of this figure in our next text, 1 Enoch.

THE SON OF MAN IN THE PARABLES OF ENOCH

Of much greater relevance is the Son of Man tradition in the Parables of Enoch (or Similitudes). The Parables of Enoch constitute chapters 37–71 of the extant Ethiopic text of Enoch or 1 Enoch. Yet, before considering the Parables's significance, we must first assess the issue of their date of composition.

The relevance of the Parables for reconstructing the context of the New Testament and the development of the Christology found therein is debated, with much of the debate centering on the Parables date of composition. While for much of the twentieth century, the Parables were recognized as a product of the late first century BCE or early first century CE, their absence on the Enochic material at Qumran raised doubts regarding such a dating. The absence of the Parables in the Qumran library played a significant role in J. T. Milik's theory that the Parables were quite late, perhaps as late as 270 CE.[14] And while many rejected Milik's extremely late date, his conclusion that the Parables post-date the Qumran community had the greater impact, particularly among New Testament scholars. Perhaps most noteworthy is James Dunn, who in his highly influential work *Christology in the Making*, concludes that the Parables are most likely post-Christian and may even be a response to the Christian movement.[15] As a result of such conclusions, the Parables have played a relatively minor role in reconstructing the Christology of the early Jesus movement. But within the last two decades, there has been a significant push among Enochic interpreters to establish the Parables as a product of Second Temple Judaism and to date the Parables prior to the destruction of Jerusalem and perhaps as early as 40 BCE.

The case for dating the Parables between 40 BCE and 70 CE begins by assessing the absence of the Parables in the Enoch literature at Qumran. Despite the claims of Milik and others, there are many plausible explanations for the absence of the Parables in the Qumran literature. First, it cannot be ruled out that the Parables were present at Qumran but simply did not survive the past two thousand years. But even if one could definitively conclude the Parables were not a part of the Qumran library, this absence need not lead one to conclude that the Parables were not yet written. There are a number of books that are firmly dated prior to 70 CE that are not found in the literature at Qumran, including Esther, the Assumption of Moses, and the Psalms of Solomon. The reasons for this absence could simply be that the Parables were composed in the early to mid-first century, outside the Qumran community, and thus were never known by that community. There are also aspects of the Parables that would have been unacceptable to the Qumran community and thus rejected by them—the equality of the sun and moon (1 Enoch 41) would be a prime example. In light of this evidence the majority of Enochic interpreters reject the Parables's absence in the DSS as necessitating a post 70 CE date of composition.

Once one dispenses with the necessity of a post 70 CE date, a number of factors can be considered that place the Parables in the last century of the Second Temple period. First, there is no indication in the Parables that the Temple in Jerusalem has been destroyed, and in fact, 1 Enoch 56:7 seems to imply that the walls of Jerusalem are still surrounding the city. Second, there is a reference in 1 Enoch 56 to an invasion of the Parthians and the Medes, an invasion that seems best identified with the invasion of 40 BCE.[16] Third, the Parables critique and predicted judgment of landlords reflects the reign of Herod the Great, during which significant amounts of land passed from Jewish to Gentile ownership and left many Jews as tenant farmers on land they once owned.[17] Fourth, 1 Enoch 67:5–13 makes references to hot water springs in which kings and mighty ones will bathe for the healing of their bodies. This passage is best understood as reference to Herod the Great's attempt to find healing in the famous hot springs of Kallirrhoë, an attempt that would prove unable to save the life of the client king.[18] It is in light of this evidence that the majority of Enochic interpreters today conclude that the Parables are a product of the last century of the Second Temple period, and perhaps as early as 40 BCE.[19] Though still not a fully resolved issue, we move forward with this majority position.

Two figures feature prominently in the Parables. The first is best identified with the God of Israel. Throughout the Parables, he is generally identified as "The Lord of Spirits," a title that seemingly reflects the title "Lord of Hosts" that is frequently found in the Hebrew Bible.[20] Though less frequent than "Lord of Spirits," the title "Head of Days," is also used to describe the God of Israel. This title is likely dependent on the title "Ancient of Days" found in Daniel 7. This connection to Daniel 7 is made virtually certain by the physical description of the "Head of Days" as one with a head covered in white wool, a description also given to the "Ancient of Days" in Daniel 7:9.

A variety of titles are used to identify the second figure, the primary subject of this study. These include the "Righteous One," "Chosen one," "Messiah," and "Son of Man." He is regularly presented as being in the presence of the Lord of Spirits and is even depicted as dwelling under the wings of the Lord of Spirits (39:6). He is closely associated with both righteousness (46:3; 48:4, 7), wisdom (48:7; 49:3; 51:3), and possibly even the name of God (48:2–3). His primary role is that of both judge and ruler over the entire creation (41:9; 46:4–5; 48:4; 49:3; 52:4; 55:4; 61:8–9; 62:6). Closely associated with these roles is the frequent and striking depiction of this figure seated on what seems to be God's glorious and heavenly throne (45:3; 51:3; 55:4; 61:8; 62:6; 69:29). In addition to being seated on God's throne, he is frequently depicted as an object of what appears to be human worship (46:5; 48:5; 62:6, 9). Finally, it also appears that this Son of Man figure is preexistent (48:3–4, 6; 62:7), and in fact, as will be discussed more fully below, is linked to the action of creation itself (69).

This Son of Man figure has been the object of significant debate. He is particularly problematic for those proponents of an exclusive monotheism (discussed in chapter 1), as he seems to transgress what these proponents contend are absolute boundary markers between God and all other entities (e.g., the reception of cultic worship, sitting on God's thrown, and engaging in the act of creation). As such, proponents of exclusive monotheism have sought to explain away these problematic details, arguing, for example, that the Enochic Son of Man (from here on, ESM) does not receive true worship, but rather than he merely receives honorific obeisance. In our application of our criteria to the ESM, we will consider the merits of these debates and the degree to which this figure might be understood in terms of a two powers theology. In the following subsections, we will return to our criteria set out in the opening chapter, but in the order that best suits the evidence for the Son of Man.

Receiving Worship

As noted above, the ESM is frequently depicted as the object of human worship (46:5; 48:5; 61:7; 62:6, 9). Larry Hurtado has long been a leading voice in rejecting the conclusion that the ESM is truly a recipient of divine worship.[21] Yet, quite recently, Richard Bauckham, who once accepted that the ESM was worshipped and sat on the divine throne, has joined Hurtado's position in rejecting both conclusions.[22] Both Hurtado and Bauckham claim that the ESM, as God's appointed eschatological agent, receives mere obeisance and not true worship. For Hurtado and Bauckham, this obeisance is no different than that which Isaiah prophesied regarding the Servant of the Lord (Isa 45:14; 49:7, 23; 60:14), an argument strengthened by the Parables's presumed dependence on the Isaianic Servant Song.[23] Additionally, Hurtado and Bauckham both mitigate what some have seen as evidence for the cultic worship of the ESM by claiming that he is not worshiped while sitting on a divine heavenly throne, but that he is only shown obeisance while he sits on an earthly throne.[24] In this way, the ESM is merely an agent of God that receives appropriate reverence rather than a second divine figure that receives cultic worship. Yet, these arguments from Hurtado and Bauckham require closer examination.

Four passages are of particular importance in assessing whether the ESM is the object of cultic worship in the Parables. These passages can be divided into two groups. The first two passages attribute to the ESM language used to describe the worship of the Lord of Spirits. In Parables 46:5, in discussing the ESM, it states, "For they do not extol and glorify him and neither do they obey him, the source of their kingship." Then later in 62:6, again in discussing the ESM, it states, "Kings, governors, and all the landlords shall bless, glorify, and extol him who rules over everything, him who has been concealed." These passages become striking when compared to passages that attribute the same language to Lord of Spirits: "For they do not extol the name of the Lord of Spirits" (46:7); "And with one voice, they shall supplicate and pray—glorifying, praising, and blessing the Lord of Spirits" (47:2); "they shall glorify, bless, and sing the name of the Lord of Spirits" (48:5); "then they shall all speak with one voice, blessing, glorifying, and extoling, sanctifying the Lord of Spirits" (61:9). In this last example, the order of the words describing the worship of the Lord of Spirits parallels exactly the words describing actions given to ESM in Parables 62:6.[25]

Despite these strong parallels in cultic language being applied to both the Lord of Spirits and the ESM, Bauckham rejects these as examples of the latter receiving cultic worship. In a mere footnote, Bauckham dismisses 46:5 as an example of cultic worship granted to the ESM because he sees the text as informed by Daniel 5:20–21, in which Nebuchadnezzar is deposed of his kingly throne by God, and as such he claims, the ones whom the kings of 46:5 do not extol and glorify is God and not the ESM.[26] Yet, such an argument fails for two reasons. First, in the context of the Parables, it is indisputably the ESM who is the subject of the passage and the object of both "extoling" and "glorifying." That Bauckham so quickly dismisses such a glaring piece of contextual evidence with virtually no explanation is surprising. Second, to read "God" into the place of the ESM based on God doing something similar in Daniel 5 not only lacks a sufficient basis to override the explicit context of the Parables, but it also a priori excludes the possibility that the Parables understand the ESM as a second power who acted in the narrative of Daniel 5. In this move, Bauckham presumes the truth of his own position over that of the position he is arguing against. In our assessment, Bauckham's attempt to dismiss this text as an example of the ESM receiving the same cultic activity as the God of Israel fails, and thus, 46:5 remains a strong example of the former receiving cultic worship.

Regarding Parables 62:6, Bauckham seeks to dismiss this text as an example of worship given to the ESM by trying to remove the ESM as its object.[27] First, he argues that "him who rules over all" is more likely a reference to God than to the ESM, as the ESM is never depicted as ruling throughout the entirety of the Parables. Second, he argues that the phrase, "who was hidden," a phrase that makes it clear that the Son of Man is the object of the cultic activity, is a later Christian gloss. Both of these arguments have significant weaknesses. First, Bauckham's claim that the ESM never rules but only judges, is highly questionable. The fact that the ESM is repeatedly depicted as seated on a throne, strongly suggests some sort of reign or rule. Also, the very act of judging from a throne seems to be inextricably linked to the role of a king or ruler. Bauckham's bifurcation of these two roles is artificial and strained. It should also be noted that in 46:5, the ESM is described to be the source of the kingship of the kings of the earth. Such a role of appointing kings seems to go beyond the actions of a mere judge and describes the "king making" power of a greater ruler. Additionally, the primary source of origin for ESM is Daniel 7, in which the Son of Man is given eternal kingship and dominion over the entire world. That the author of the Parables and its readers would somehow divorce the ESM from the kingly role the Son of Man is granted in Daniel 7 seems highly implausible. And perhaps the most important piece of evidence is the very verse in question, where the Son of Man is described as "ruling over all." That the Son of Man is in view, and not the Lord of Spirits, is strongly supported by the immediate context, as the 62:6 is immediately preceded by an explicit reference to the Son of Man: "And pain shall seize them when they see the Son of Man sitting on the throne of his glory." Such immediate context makes it clear that the antecedent for the pronoun in 62:6 ("him") is the Son of Man, and not the Lord of Spirits. It is odd then that Bauckham claims that the ESM is never depicted in the Parables as ruling to explain away a text in which the ESM seems to be clearly depicted as ruling. In light of this evidence, Bauchkam's move to claim that the phrase "who was hidden" is a later Christian gloss lacks merit, as the phrase fits perfectly within the verse's context: it rightly applies to the Son of Man who is described as hidden in 48:6 and 62:7. In light of these arguments, we contend Bauckham's efforts to preclude these two texts as evidence of the ESM receiving the very same cultic activity received by the Lord of Spirits fail under close scrutiny.

Consideration of two additional texts is required. In Parables 48:5, the ESM is described in the following way: "All who dwell upon the earth shall fall and worship before him." This language is repeated, though in a more dramatic way in Parables 62:9: "On that day, all the kings, the governors, the high officials and those who rule the earth shall fall down before him on their faces and worship and raise their hopes in the Son of Man, they shall beg and plead at his feet for mercy." Again, there are striking parallels between this language and the language used to describe the Lord of Spirits in two instances bookending this passage:

The all shall *fall down and worship* the Lord of Spirits (57:3, emphasis added):

> In those days, the governors and kings who possess the land shall plead that he may give them a little breathing spell from the angels of his punishment to whom they have been delivered; so they shall *fall and worship* before the Lord of Spirits, and confess their sins before him (63:1, emphasis added).

Clearly the language of "fall and worship" that is used for both the ESM and the Lord of Spirits is significant, but the additional parallels between 62:9 and 63:1 are even more striking. In both passages, it is the kings and governors who "fall and worship," and in both passages, these figures are seeking mercy from the one they fall down before and worship. It is as if the two passages have been intentionally constructed to parallel each other for the purpose of depicting the ESM like the Lord of Spirits.

Both Bauckham and Hurtado claim that despite the parallel language used for both the ESM and the Lord of the Spirits in these texts, the actions of falling down and worshipping the former should be understood as mere obeisance, while when the same activity is given to the latter, it is clearly cultic worship.[28] Two primary arguments are used to this end. The first argument is that this activity is given to the ESM while he is on earth and not in heaven, and thus it is best understood as obeisance. Yet, we see two weaknesses to this argument. First, the ESM's location in these passages is at best ambiguous, with many concluding that the ESM sits not only on a heavenly throne but God's very throne (a case we will consider below).[29] If the throne is in heaven, the Parables could be depicting humanity and the kings of the earth bowing down before the ESM seated on a heavenly throne. Such a location of the throne would strongly confirm that the actions of falling down and worshipping are cultic worship and not mere obeisance.

Second, we also contend that the importance of the location of these actions has been exaggerated by both Hurtado and Bauckham. There is no reason that cultic worship cannot be granted to the ESM while in an earthly location. We would note that both Bauckham and Hurtado understand Jesus to receive worship while still on earth, with both citing Matthew 28:17 as an example of worship rather than mere obeisance.[30] We contend that given that the language used to describe the cultic worship of the Lord of Spirits is used to describe the ESM, the location of that worship (i.e., heaven or earth) is of little importance to assessing the nature of what the language describes.

In fairness to both Bauckham and Hurtado, their argument is not based solely on the location of the ESM when receiving prostration. As noted above, they also see these texts drawing directly on texts from Isaiah in which people are described as prostrating themselves before God's servant. The most relevant text is Isaiah 49:7, which describes actions given to God's chosen servant in the following way: "Kings shall see and stand up, princes, and they shall prostrate themselves, because of the LORD, who is faithful, the Holy one of Israel, who has chosen you." But would dependence on such a text dictate that the worship of the ESM in the Parables must also be understood as mere obeisance? While the Parables dependence on Isaiah at this point is widely recognized, it must be acknowledged that at other points the Parables not only use imagery from the Servant Song, but also push beyond the strictures of the borrowed text, developing it in significant ways.[31] Fletcher-Louis notes that while in Isaiah, the suffering servant is "known," "called," and "remembered" while in his mother's womb, the ESM is "chosen," "named," and "hidden" before the creation of the of the world.[32] If the Parables take such a significant leap forward in Isaiah's depiction of God's servant at this point, certainly a development in Isaiah's depiction of the obeisance this figure receives is also possible. In fact, who is to say that the author of the Parables, perhaps as a proponent of a two powers theology, does not interpret Isaiah 49:7 in terms of worship? Thus, one cannot strictly deny the possibility of cultic or divine worship of the ESM in this passage simply on the basis of its Isaianic intertextuality.[33]

In fact, we contend that two pieces of evidence suggest that the Parables have developed this Isaianic tradition from one in which mere obeisance takes place to one in which worship is granted. First, we point to the fact established above, namely that the same cultic language of "blessing," "extoling," and "glorifying" is intentionally used for both the Lord of Spirits and the ESM. This shared language demonstrates that the author of the Parables views the ESM as a legitimate object of worship. Second, we point to the fact that the act of falling down and worshipping is granted both to the Lord of Spirits and the Son of Man, with one example having them receive these actions from the same group of people, and those people requesting mercy from both figures. It seems from this evidence that an intentional parallel is being created between the Lord of Spirits and the ESM, and thus, the prostration and worship before one should be understood in the same way as that given before the other. When the language that is used to describe the worship of the God of Israel is, in the same context, being used to describe the worship of the ESM, it seems to be special pleading to conclude one is true divine worship and the other is mere obeisance.

In addition to this careful analysis of each example, we also believe there is value in looking at the totality of the Parables and how they would be perceived by a first century reader. In the Parables, the reader is introduced to a heavenly figure, one who is identified as God's Messiah and clearly understood as the same figure that rides on clouds and appears before Israel's God in Daniel 7. The figure also is seemingly described as being preexistent, as he is "given a name in the presence of the Lord of Sprits . . . before the creation of the sun and moon . . . before the creation of the stars" (48:3), and "concealed in the presence of the Lord of Spirits prior to creation and for eternity" (48:6), and "concealed from the beginning, and the Most High One preserved him in the presence of his power" (62:7).[34] This preexistent figure is then depicted as sitting on a heavenly throne (the nature of which will be discussed below). This heavenly preexistent figure, who sits on a heavenly throne, then receives the cultic activity of blessing, extoling and glorifying in the same manner as the Lord of Spirits. In addition, all of humanity prostrate themselves before him and later the kings of the earth are described as doing the same thing. When all of these factors are taken together, are we to believe that a first century Jewish reader would most naturally arrive at the conclusion that this exalted figure was only receiving mere obeisance rather than true cultic worship? Would they really engage in the painstaking detailed analysis offered by Bauckham to arrive at the conclusion that indeed no, true cultic worship is not being offered? To us, this seems highly unlikely. Yet, for those who would defend such a position, it seems they must at least admit that the author of the Parables was not particularly careful in his or her efforts to preclude the reader from perceiving the ESM as an object of cultic worship. Such lack of care raises the question of what degree the author believed such protection was even important.

When all this evidence is taken together, we contend that it strongly supports the conclusion that ESM receives cultic worship and not mere obeisance. In fact, he receives the very divine worship that is granted to Lord of

Spirits, the God of Israel. As such, the ESM strongly meets this proposed criterion.

Creating the Cosmos

Few interpreters have sought to make a connection between the ESM as an agent of creating the cosmos, but we contend that careful attention to the narrative of the Parables results in just such a conclusion. In 1 Enoch 64–69:25, it addresses the Noahic flood, as well as the evil for which this flood was a judgment, evil in which fallen angels played a significant role. In 1 Enoch 69:2–25, it seemingly offers the conclusion to this section in its description of fallen angels. In verses 13–14, verses fraught with interpretive challenges, the notions of a chief oath and a secret name are introduced to the reader. It seems the content of the oath is first controlled or protected by a soon-to-be fallen angel named Kasbe'el, who desires to reveal the oath to humankind. This angel also seeks knowledge of a secret name from the angel Michael, a name that seems closely related to the oath. Kasbe'el wants to reveal this secret name to humankind along with the oath. Whether Kasbe'el is able to convince Michael to give him the name is unclear, as is whether Kasbe'el ever revealed the name to the inhabitants of the earth. What seems clear is that in verse 15 the angel Michael has control of the oath and presumably the secret name associated with it.[35] Then, in verse 16, the secret content of the oath is revealed to the reader, namely that the oath was responsible not only for the act of creation itself but also that the oath sustains and orders the creation.[36] Yet, immediately after the secret of this oath is revealed, an unspecified "they" rejoice, give praise, blessing, and exaltation because the name of the ESM has been revealed to them, that is, the mysterious oath and the name of the ESM are one and the same. Most Enochic interpreters conclude that these verses are misplaced and thus determine that they cannot be describing what has immediately preceded them in verses 2–25.[37] But such an assessment cannot rule out whether that redactional activity took place within the Second Temple period. In fact, the redaction bears no clear Christian fingerprints and seems very much in line with Second Temple Jewish thinking. These factors would suggest that this redaction took place within the Jewish matrix of the Second Temple period, and as such would reflect a Second Temple perspective on the ESM. There seems to be no reason to preclude the present and final form of chapter 69 from the matrix of Second Temple Judaism. If one is following the final form of the third parable's narrative, what has been immediately revealed to the reader, and thus the most reasonable cause for rejoicing, is the oath and its role in creation. Thus, when considering the narrative flow of the passage, the most logical conclusion is that the mysterious oath that created the cosmos is rightly equated with the ESM.

Such a conclusion fits well with other pieces of the Parables's narrative. First, the oath is closely linked to a secret name in verses 13–14, which suggests that the revealing of the oath is in some way a revealing of this secret name. Second, the ESM has also been associated with a name that existed prior to the sun and the constellations (48:2–3) and which, in the narrative of the Parables, has not yet been revealed to the reader and so remains secret. Thus, one might conclude quite naturally that with verses 13–29 the third parable culminates in the revealing of the name of the ESM, a name that the reader has already been told was given before the creation of the heavenly luminaries. In short, the ESM is the powerful divine oath that both created and sustains not only those very heavenly luminaries, but the entire cosmos.

Ruling Over Creation

While many have concluded that the ESM is depicted as a sovereign figure, and one who rules over the cosmos, this position has recently been challenged.[38] As noted above, Bauckham has argued that the ESM is strictly depicted as a judge and is decidedly not depicted as a ruler. Above, we rejected this unique assessment of the ESM, noting many factors support the conclusion that the ESM is one who rules, including, he is regularly depicted on a throne which is a symbol of ruling, the act of judging the world is closely associated with the role of one who rules over it, the ESM is depicted as one who appoints kings, which seems to fall under the scope of a ruler, the ESM is understood as the figure form Daniel 7, whose primary task is dominion and kingship, and finally Parable 62:6 explicitly states that the ESM rules over everything. This evidence strongly connections the ESM with ruling. Yet, the question of the scope of his reign remains. Does he reign over the cosmos or merely over the earth? We contend that many factors support the former.

Perhaps the most important issue related to this debate is the nature of the throne on which the ESM sits. On numerous occasions, the ESM is said to sit on "the throne of glory/his glory" (45:3; 51:3; 55:4; 61:8; 62:5; 69:27, 29). This very phrase is also used to describe the throne of the Lord of Spirits (47:3; 60:2; 62:2–3). Two questions emerge from this data. First, is the reader intended to envision one throne or two? Second, is the ESM being depicted on a divine throne or perhaps God's very throne. While most interpreters conclude that there is only one throne, the divine throne, on which the Lord of Spirits and the ESM are depicted as sitting, Matthew Black, followed by Bauckham, argues that the Parables envision two thrones, one for the Lord of Spirits, the divine throne, and one for the ESM.[39] The basis for this argument is that in the same Parables, both the Lord of Spirits and the ESM are depicted as sitting on "the throne of *his* glory." With the assumption that "his" would imply the unique possession of the throne, the text is understood to be

describing two entities sitting on two distinct thrones as opposed to two entities sitting on one throne. Yet, two figures on one throne seems to be what
we see in the New Testament, as the ascended Jesus sits at God's right hand
on his throne. To this possibility, Bauckham states, "While we could envisage the Messianic Figure sitting with God on God's throne (as the ascended
Jesus does in the New Testament), it is not plausible that God's throne could
be called the Messianic Figure's own throne, however exalted we might
imagine this figure to be."[40] But here again, Bauckham precludes a priori
the possibility of a two powers theology, in which both the Lord of Spirits
and the ESM are rightly identified as YHWH. In such a framework, the two
could sit on the single divine throne that would be for both rightly identified
as "his throne." That the majority are right, and that the Parables envision one
single divine throne that is shared by both the Lord of Spirits and the Son of
Man finds strong support in 51:3: "In those days, the Elect One shall sit on
my throne, and from the conscience of his mouth shall come out all secrets
of wisdom, for the Lord of Spirits has given them to him and glorified him."
Here the Lord of Spirits declares that the Elect One (ESM) "will sit on my
throne," making it explicit that the throne on which he sits is the very throne
of God.[41] While there is a textual variant for this verse that reads "his throne"
rather than "my throne," the older and generally more reliable manuscript
tradition provides the latter reading.[42] We would note that such a claim would
be consistent with second power figures we have considered previously.
Wisdom of Solomon depicts God's "all-powerful [W]ord" as a sword bearing
warrior leaping from God's throne (18:15–16). Philo also depicts the same
Word sitting on God's throne, the ark of the covenant (*Fug.* 100–101). Below,
we will make a thorough case for identifying the ESM with this very Word.
We believe this tips the scales in favor of the conclusion that the Parables do
indeed depict the ESM sitting on God's very throne.

Yet here we offer an alternative and perhaps mediating possibility. The
vision of Daniel 7:9 describes *thrones* being put in place, and then God
taking his seat on his throne. It is possible that the author of the Parables is
influenced by this plural reference to heavenly thrones, and that he envisions
two heavenly thrones, one for the Lord of Spirits and one for the ESM. If this
is indeed the case, we would contend that it need not be concluded that the
heavenly throne of the ESM is any less divine than that of the Lord of Spirits.
Behind such a conception of two thrones could be the very two powers theology we are proposing. As such, both thrones would be divine. Additionally,
the description of Parable 51:3 in which he, Lord of Spirits, claims the ESM
sits on "my throne," could make sense in this context, as both divine thrones
would be the proper possession of the Lord of Spirits. In this way, both
thrones would be understood as belonging to the one God of Israel.

Regardless of whether one heavenly throne is envisioned or two, we contend that the depiction of the ESM sitting on such a thrown would convey sovereignty over the cosmos. A number of other details support just such a conclusion. In Parable 55, the ESM is depicted as judging Azaz'el and the entire company of rebellious supernatural forces. That the scope of the ESM's judgment includes not only those living on earth but the supernatural forces that occupy the heavens strongly suggests that the scope of his reign is cosmic and not limited to the earth alone. Additionally, as noted above, Parable 62:6 specifically describes the ESM as "him who rules over everything." When this descriptor is combined with the ESM sitting on a heavenly throne, it seems to support a reign that is cosmic in scope rather than earthly. In light of this evidence, we contend that the evidence strongly supports the conclusion that the ESM is depicted as sovereign over the entire cosmos. If this conclusion is correct, then the ESM rules over all other heavenly or supernatural beings, making him unique in his relationship to God.

Bearing the Name

It is also possible that the Parables intend to link the ESM with the name of Israel's God. In 1 Enoch 48:2–3, it twice declares that before creation, the ESM was "named by the name" in the presence of the Lord of Spirits. While the text never explicitly says this name is the personal name of God, it does often reference the "name of the Lord of Spirits," which may indicate it is that very name that is given to the ESM. It is also noteworthy, that the secret oath of 1 Enoch 69 is closely associated (or identified) with a secret name, and it is this secret name, that is revealed to be the name of the ESM. Because this oath brings about the creation of the cosmos, there is reason to believe this name is the personal name of Israel's God, YHWH.[43] As discussed above, other Second Temple Jewish texts describe the "Name" of the Lord as the second power.[44]

Taking the Role of YHWH

At a number of points, the Parables attribute YHWH texts of Hebrew scriptures to the ESM.[45] In 1 Enoch 52:6 and 53:7, it describes mountains melting like wax before the "Chosen One," the very imagery that is used in certain theophanic texts to describe YHWH (Mic 1:3–4; Ps 97:4–5).[46] Similarly, 1 Enoch 46:4 depicts the ESM breaking the teeth of the wicked, an action attributed to YHWH in Psalm 3:7 and 58:6. The Parables also seemingly transform the "day of YHWH" into the "day of the Chosen One." Thus, the ESM meets this proposed criterion.

The Son of Man as Enoch

It must be acknowledged that in 1 Enoch 71, Enoch, the character that up to this point has been conveying the numerous visions of the book, may be identified with the ESM. This possible identification with a known and created human being has led some to conclude that the ESM cannot be understood as divine but rather as an exalted human figure.[47] Before specifically addressing the relevant criterion, an important caveat is necessary. Many interpreters of the Parables recognize chapter 71 as an addition by a later redactor, a position supported by the fact that up to this point in the Parables, Enoch and the Son of Man figure are clearly distinct.[48] Yet, even if chapter 71 is original to the Parables, it is not entirely clear that Enoch is being equated with the Son of Man figure that dominates the Parables. In this chapter, Enoch is certainly brought into the highest realm of heaven and encounters the God of Israel. He claims his body is "mollified" his "spirit is transformed." In this heavenly place, an angel comes to Enoch and says, "You, Son of Man, who art born in righteousness and upon whom righteousness has dwelt, the righteousness of the Antecedent of Time will not forsake you" (71:14). The angel goes on to tell Enoch that all to come will follow his path (that of righteousness) and that they will dwell together with him. The final verse of the chapter states, "So there shall be length of days with that Son of Man, and peace to the righteous ones; his path is upright for the righteous, in the name of the Lord of Spirits forever and ever" (71:17). While many have concluded on the basis of 71:14 that Enoch is being identified with the Son of Man figure that is described throughout the Parables and that thus, the Son of Man references in the last verse should also be understood as Enoch, another interpretation is possible, and perhaps preferable. It is possible that the angel's reference to Enoch as Son of Man in 71:14 is best understood in terms of a "human one," like the numerous such references given to Ezekiel. Thus, he is simply to be addressed as a human being and not be identified with the heavenly Son of Man of the Parables or the last verse of chapter 71. In favor of such a position is that the word used for "man" when the Son of Man is applied to Enoch is different than the word present in all other uses of the Son of Man in the Parables.[49] The fact that throughout the Parables, Enoch has seen the glorious Son of Man and is clearly distinct from him also supports this interpretation. Additionally, Enoch has already been addressed in exactly this way in Parables 60:10, where the angel says to him, "You, son of man, according (to the degree) to which it will be permitted, you will know hidden things." No interpreter understands this to be an attempt to equate Enoch with the Son of Man who is also the Messiah or Elect One. That Enoch can be identified as "son of man" in this way within the Parables, strongly supports the conclusion that in 71:14, he is being addressed in the same way. If such a reading were adopted, chapter 71 would be describing Enoch as a human forerunner, who will be followed and modeled by all future righteous ones. Together with these righteous ones, Enoch will live under the glorious reign of the Son of Man described throughout the Parables. This reading would solve the long-noted problem of Enoch being clearly differentiated from the ESM throughout the Parables only to find in the final chapter he is that Son of Man.[50]

However, even if identifying Enoch with the glorious Son of Man was the original intent of the Parables, a divine identity should not necessarily be precluded. While Enoch does appear in the antediluvian genealogies of Genesis, he is a mysterious figure of whom it is uniquely said he "walked with God; then he was no more, because God took him" (Gen 5:24). That such a description could lead to speculation about Enoch's identity, particularly in the theological climate of the Second Temple, is highly plausible. Such speculation might include the possibility that Enoch was an earthly manifestation of the second power or that the human Enoch experienced a form of theosis and was in some way mapped on to or merged with the second power, the Son of Man.[51] Thus, we contend that the possible connection between Son of Man and Enoch, a questionable connection indeed, does not disqualify the former from being understood as a second power in heaven.

Holding Additional Titles

In the Parables's construction of the ESM figure, a number of strands of Hebrew scripture and thought have been woven together. Most interpreters of the Parables recognize that the author is weaving together imagery and concepts from Daniel 7, the Deutero-Isaianic Servant of the Lord, Davidic traditions, as well as the Wisdom tradition.[52] While many have recognized the Wisdom tradition of Proverbs 8 as giving some shape to the Parables's depiction of the ESM, few are willing to identify this wisdom with the ESM.[53] Here we contend that the relationship between the ESM and the twin tradition of God's Word and Wisdom is far greater than most interpreters have acknowledged, and that the ESM is best identified as the apocalyptic embodiment of God's Word and Wisdom.

The similarities between the traditions of God's Word/Wisdom and the ESM are numerous. Both preexist creation, and if our arguments regarding the ESM above are accepted, both are connected to the very act of creating the cosmos. Both exercise sovereignty over the cosmos. Both sit on heavenly thrones, and arguably, God's very throne. Both are depicted as recipients of cultic worship. These features are rarely applied to anyone but Israel's God, thus the fact that they are attributed to both the ESM and Word/Wisdom is significant, and we contend, strongly suggest a common identification. For Jews familiar with traditions of God's Word/Wisdom being preexistent, closely associated with God's throne, and the object of divine worship, it would not be a significant leap of the imagination to see the ESM as an embodiment of God's Word/Wisdom. Such an imaginative leap would seem particularly at home in apocalyptic literature, where embodiments of abstract and spiritual realities were common. The fact that we have seen elsewhere both Word and Wisdom associated with a human form in the Angel of the Lord or a Heavenly Adam/Man only further supports the conclusion that the ESM shares the same relationship with these twin concepts. In fact, we have seen the targums equate God's Memra with the Angel of the Lord, Philo equates the Logos with both the Angel of the Lord and a Heavenly Adam/Man, and Wisdom literature equates Wisdom with the Angel of Lord. Identifying the ESM as God's Word and Wisdom should not only be unsurprising, but it might actually be expected.

While the strong similarities between the ESM and God's Word/Wisdom might lead readers to make the imaginative leap noted above, the connection between these two concepts within the Parables themselves only strengthens a mutual identification. Wisdom is a prominent motif throughout the entire Book of Enoch in general, and the Parables are no exception. In 1 Enoch 42, before the ESM is first directly identified, Wisdom is portrayed as seeking a place to dwell, and after failing to find such a place among humans, it takes up its residence in heaven among the angels. Here there is no direct link to the ESM or Chosen One, but with this story, the Parables depict Wisdom as a distinct entity, one that dwells in heaven in the presence of God's angels. The Parables are clearly familiar with and favorable to a conception of Wisdom as a distinct and personified entity. Though not proof of mutual identification, it is noteworthy that both the Lord of Spirits and the ESM dwell in the presence of angels, as Wisdom is also depicted as doing. In addition, connections are made between the ESM/Chosen One and Wisdom. In 1 Enoch 48:1, the naming of the ESM is immediately preceded by a description of a spring of righteousness which is surrounded by springs of wisdom, from which the thirsty drink and are filled. The proximity of these springs of righteousness and wisdom with the naming of the ESM, who will bring both wisdom and righteousness, may tie these two realities together. A connection between the ESM and Wisdom is strengthened only by a handful of verses later where the text claims that the Wisdom of the Lord of Spirits reveals the ESM to the holy and righteous (48:7). Such a depiction would be consistent with Wisdom revealing herself to the holy and righteous (Prov 1:23; 8:1–20; 9:1–6; Wis 6:12–16; 7:24–28; 10:1–21; Sir 1:16–19; 4:17–18; 15:1–5) and/ or both God's Wisdom being a source of God's Word (and vice versa) in Philo (*Fug.* 97; *Somn.* 2.242, 245). In 49:3, the reader is told that the ESM is filled with the spirit of Wisdom, and later in 51:3, the text claims that secrets of Wisdom will go forth from the mouth of the Chosen One. Thus, the ESM is revealed by wisdom, but also reveals wisdom. If the ESM was identified with God's Word, then in being both revealed by wisdom and the revealer of wisdom, he would be quite similar to the Logos as depicted in Philo (*Fug.* 97; *Somn.* 2.242, 245). When taken all together, these verses tie the ESM closely together with the hypostasis of Wisdom.

Perhaps the strongest and boldest means by which the ESM is identified with God's Word/Wisdom might be found in chapter 69, the conclusion of the third and final parable.[54] As discussed above, chapter 69 depicts the revealing of a powerful oath that is depicted as that which creates and sustains the cosmos. The revealing of this oath is then equated with the revealing of the ESM, thus identifying the former with the latter. The meaning and significance of this oath is debated. Some have sought for explanations in the notions of laws or covenants related to luminaries in the Hebrew Bible and other Jewish texts.[55] Some have looked at the notion of oaths or the role of God's name in the act of creation in both hekhalot and rabbinic literature.[56] While influence from the former seems likely, the late date of the latter may undermine its value. A more plausible way forward, and one noted by surprisingly few interpreters, is to identify this oath with God's Word and Wisdom, particularly since there is such a well-established tradition in Second Temple Judaism that attributes not only creation but the governance of the created order to that Word/Wisdom.[57] That this Enochic oath does the very thing that God's Word/Wisdom is widely known to do, strongly suggests the two are one and the same. The case becomes even stronger in light of evidence that God's words were often equated to oaths. Such a belief is seen in Philo's interlocutor whose position regarding God and oaths is described in the following way: "Moreover, the very words of God are oaths and laws of God and most sacred ordinances" (*Leg.* 3.204). While Philo disagrees with this as an argument against God's need to swear by his own being, he does seem to agree with the equating of anything spoken by God to an oath: "But God is trustworthy in His speech as elsewhere, so that His words in certitude and assurance differ not a whit from oaths" (*Sacr.* 1.93). Thus, given such an understanding of God's very words, that they themselves are certain and eternal oaths, it seems natural that a divine "oath" might be used in apocalyptic texts as a symbol for God's preexistent Word, a Word that in a prominent strand of Second Temple Jewish thought brought about, ordered, and sustained God's creation.

When this reading of the Parables is combined with identifying the "divine oath" as the preexistent Word/Wisdom of God, the reader is only left to conclude that the ESM himself is properly identified with God's preexistent Word/Wisdom, the oath that created and sustains the universe. Such an identification with God's Word and Wisdom, two entities we have previously established as being understood as the second power in heaven, only strengthens the conclusion that the ESM should be understood in the same way.

CONCLUSIONS: THE SON OF MAN
AS THE SECOND POWER

The ESM meets a large number of the proposed criteria, and thus, we would contend there exists a strong case that this figure is rightly identified as the YHWH of Israel and not simply an angelic figure or exalted human that shares in divine prerogatives. The distinction between the Son of Man and the Lord of Spirits finds an easy explanation in a two powers paradigm. In addition to the ESM of the Parables, we noted two additional traditions, the Old Greek version of Daniel and 4 Ezra, which also provide evidence, though to a lesser degree, that the "Son of Man" of the Aramaic Danielic tradition was understood as a second power in heaven. Such evidence demonstrates that a noteworthy number of Second Temple interpreters of Daniel accepted the apocalyptic Son of Man figure therein as a second power in heaven, one who would usher in God's will in the eschaton.[58]

To be sure, other figures could also be used to explain this Son of Man figure, such as Melchizedek and other so-called exalted humans. Therefore, in the following chapters we will review the sources for these individuals to see how they align with the material covered so far. Although the sources are fewer for these figures, there are still important details that emerge which help us further understand how a human figure could possibly be understood as the second power in heaven.

NOTES

1. We have set aside the use of the phrase "son of man," in Ezek. Likewise, per our methodology in this present volume, we bracket out all Christian uses of this phrase, such as in the Gospels.

2. For discussion of such a position, see Kirk, *A Man Attested by God*, 142–47.

3. J. A. Emerton, "The Origin of the Son of Man Imagery," *Journal of Theological Studies* 9 (1958): 225–42, at 231–32, famously concluded, "the act of coming with clouds suggests a theophany of Yahwe himself. If Dan. vii.13 does not refer to a divine being, then it is the only exception out of about seventy passages in the OT."

4. Matthew Black, "The Throne-Theophany, Prophetic Commission, and the 'Son of Man,'" in *Jews, Greeks, and Christians: Religious Cultures in Late Antiquity*, eds. Robert G. Hamerton-Kelley and Robin Scroggs (Leiden: Brill, 1976), 61, comments, "This, in effect, means that Dan. 7 knows of two divinities, the Head of Days and the Son of Man."

5. Here is the original Greek text: ἐθεώρουν ἐν ὁράματι τῆς νυκτός, καὶ ἰδοὺ ἐπὶ τῶν νεφελῶν τοῦ οὐρανοῦ ἤρχετο ὡς υἱὸς ἀνθρώπου, καί ὡς παλαιὸς ἡμερῶν παρῆν. This is often translated: "I was watching in the night vision and behold! One came on the clouds as a son of man; and he was present as an/the Ancient of Days." In this translation, the figure that comes on the clouds is one and the same as the figure that appears as the Ancient of Days, a striking develop in the interpretation of Daniel 7. In his recent study of the "Son of Man," Richard Bauckham has argued that this common translation is misguided, and that a preferable translation would be: "I was watching in the night visions and behold! On the clouds of heaven came one like a son of man, and one like an ancient of days was present" (*Son of Man*, 169). In this translation, the one who comes on the clouds of heaven is distinct from the ancient of days. Yet, this translation seems to violate the natural flow and logic of the language. For there to be a change in the subject within this sentence, a marker of such a change would be expected, though none can be found. Additionally, such a translation seems to violate the intended synonymous parallelism that is intended, i.e., "the one who comes in the clouds as a son of man" is intentionally paralleled and further described as "one who is present as an/the ancient of days."

6. See Stuckenbruck, "'One Like a Son of Man' in the Old Greek Recension of Daniel 7:13: Scribal Error or Theological Translation," in *Son of Man Problem: Critical Readings*, ed. B. Reynolds (London: T & T Clark, 2015), 276.

7. For discussion, see Benjamin Reynolds, "The 'One Like the Son of Man' according to the Old Greek of Daniel 7,13–14," in *Son of Man Problem: Critical Readings*, B. Reynolds (London: T & T Clark, 2015), 74–75.

8. See Exod 3:12; 4.23; 7:16, 26; 8:16; 9:1, 13; 10:3, 7, 24, 26; Deut 4:19, 28; 6:13; 7:4, 16; 8:19; 11:13, 16, etc.

9. Markus Bockmuehl, *Revelation and Mystery in Ancient Judaism and Pauline Christianity* (Tübingen: Mohr Siebeck, 1990), 37–38, notes that both the Son of Man in 4 Ezra and the Enochic Son of Man (to be discussed later in this chapter) are hidden with God in heaven before being sent to earth.

10. See Boyarin, "Enoch, Ezra, and the Jewishness of 'High Christology,'" in *Fourth Ezra and Second Baruch: Reconstruction after the Fall*, eds. Matthias Henze and Gabriele Boccaccini (JSJSup; Leiden: Brill, 2013), 351.

11. Boyarin, "Enoch, Ezra," 351–52.

12. Boyarin, "Enoch, Ezra," 351–52.

13. Schäfer, *Two Gods*, 58.

14. See J. T. Milik, *The Book of Enoch: Aramaic Fragments of Qumran Cave 4* (Oxford: Clarendon, 1976), 89–100.

15. See Dunn, *Christology in the Making*, 77–82. Hurtado, *Lord Jesus Christ*, 296, follows Dunn in questioning both the dating of the Parables and their relevance. See also Tilling, *Paul's Divine Christology*, 214–15.

16. For discussion, Luca Arcari, "A Symbolic Transfiguration of a Historical Event: The Parthian Invasion in Josephus and the Parables of Enoch," in *Enoch and the Messiah Son of Man: Revisiting the Book of Parables*, ed. Gabriel Boccaccini (Grand Rapids, MI: Eerdmans, 2007), 478–86; James H. Charlesworth, "The Date and Provenience of the Parables of Enoch," in *Parables of Enoch: A Paradigm Shift*,

eds. Darrell L. Bock and James H. Charlesworth (JCTCRS 11; London: T & T Clark/ Bloomsbury, 2013), 47. Note that G. Bampfylde argued that the battles related to this invasion began 51–50 BCE, and that the Parables might be better understood to be referring to the battles of these early attacks; Bampfylde, "The Similitudes of Enoch: Historical Allusions," *JSJ* 15 (1984): 9–31.

17. See Charlesworth, "Date and Provenience," 48–53.

18. For what is, in our estimation, the most compelling argument for this position, see Darrell D. Hannah, "The Book of Noah, the Death of Herod the Great, and the Date of the Parables of Enoch," in *Enoch and the Messiah Son of Man: Revisiting the Book of Parables*, ed. Gabriel Boccaccini (Grand Rapids, MI: Eerdmans, 2007), 469–77.

19. See, for example, S. Uhlig, *Das äthiopische Henochbuch* (JSHRZ 5.6; Gütersloh: Gütersloher Verlagshaus, 1984); Bampfylde, "Similitudes," 9–31; Matthew Black, *The Book of Enoch or I Enoch: A New English Edition* (SVTP 7; Leiden: Brill, 1985), 181–88, 221–22; John J. Collins, *The Scepter and the Star: The Messiahs of the Dead Sea Scrolls and Other Ancient Literature* (ABRL; New York: Doubleday, 1995), 177–82; Gabriele Boccaccini, "Finding a Place for the Parables of Enoch within Second Temple Jewish Literature" in Gabriel Boccaccini, in *Enoch and the Messiah Son of Man: Revisiting the Book of Parables*, ed. Gabriel Boccaccini (Grand Rapids, MI: Eerdmans, 2007), 263–89; Hannah, "Date of the Parables," 469–77; Pierluigi Piovanelli, "'A Testimony for the Kings and the Might Who Possess the Earth': The Thirst for Justice and Peace in the Parables of Enoch," in *Enoch and the Messiah Son of Man: Revisiting the Book of Parables*, ed. Gabriel Boccaccini (Grand Rapids, MI: Eerdmans, 2007), 363–79; Daniel Boyarin, "Was the Book of Parables a Sectarian Document," in *Enoch and the Messiah Son of Man: Revisiting the Book of Parables*, ed. Gabriel Boccaccini (Grand Rapids, MI: Eerdmans, 2007), 380–85; George W. E. Nickelsburg and James C. VanderKam, *1 Enoch* (Hermeneia; Minneapolis: Fortress, 2012), 58–66; Charlesworth, "The Date and Provenience," 37–57; Arcari; "Symbolic Transfiguration," 478–86; Darrell L. Bock, "Dating the Parables of Enoch: A Forschungsbericht," in *Parables of Enoch: A Paradigm Shift*, eds. Darrell L. Bock and James H. Charlesworth (JCTCRS 11; London: T & T Clark/Bloomsbury, 2013), 58–113.

20. In 1 En. 39:12–40:1, the Parables seem to draw on Isaiah 6:3, but this text renders the Isaianic divine epithet "Lord of Hosts" as "Lord of Spirits." For discussion, see Nickelsburg and VanderKam, *1 Enoch*, 41.

21. Hurtado, *Lord Jesus Christ*, 38–39.

22. Bauckham, *Son of Man*, 40–100.

23. See Hurtado, *Lord Jesus Christ*, 38–39; and Bauckham, *Son of Man*, 93–100; For a similar position, see Kirk, *Man Attested*, 152–53.

24. Hurtado, *Lord Jesus Christ*, 39, n.38; Bauckahm, *Son of Man*, 93–101.

25. This phenomenon is astutely pointed out by James Waddell, *The Messiah: A Comparative Study of the Enochic Son of Man and the Pauline Kyrios* (JCTCRS 10; London: Bloomsbury, 2011), 92, 96–100.

26. Bauckham, *Son of Man*, 94–95, n. 48.

27. Bauckham, *Son of Man*, 97–99.

28. Bauckham, *Son of Man*, 99–101; Hurtado, *Lord Jesus Christ*, 38–39.

29. Note that even Bauckham acknowledges that at least in some instances in the Parables, the Son of Man's throne is heavenly (*Son of Man*, 45).

30. See Bauckham, *Jesus and the God of Israel*, 25; and Hurtado, *Lord Jesus Christ*, 338.

31. Fletcher-Louis, *Jesus Monotheism*, 179.

32. Fletcher-Louis, *Jesus Monotheism*, 179.

33. Fletcher-Louis, *Jesus Monotheism*, 180.

34. A number of interpreters challenge whether the ESM is indeed preexistent, claiming that it is only his name and identity that are being addressed, rather than figure himself. See, for example, James VanderKam, "Righteous One, Messiah, Chosen One, and Son of Man in 1 Enoch 37–71," in *The Messiah: Developments in Earliest Judaism and Christianity*, ed. James H. Charlesworth (Minneapolis: Fortress, 1992), 179–82; Kirk, *Man Attested*, 153–54; Bauckham, *Son of Man*, 71–76. While such an explanation can work well with 48:3–4, and perhaps be dependent on a text like Ps 72:17 (see Kirk, *Man Attested*, 2016), the case is harder to make in 48:6, where the figure himself is described as "concealed in the presence (Lord of Spirits) before the creation of the world for eternity" and in 62:7 where the ESM himself is "concealed from the beginning" and "preserved" by the presence of the power of the Most High. VanderKam acknowledges that 62:7 is difficult to explain in terms of the mere concealment of the ESM's name, and as such must argue that "beginning" does not refer to a time prior to creation ("Righteous One," 180–81). Yet, such an argument sounds like special pleading when earlier references to the ESM's concealment clearly make reference to the event preceding creation. In light of such previous texts, the most natural way of understanding "beginning" is the beginning of creation. Bauckham has sought to separate the text of chapter 48 from that of chapter 62, arguing that the former refers to the naming of the ESM prior to creation, while the latter refers to the mere hiddenness of the ESM from the rulers of the world, while having no connection to preexistence (*Son of Man*, 72–73). Here he must rely on what he claims is a Christian gloss in 48:6 "concealed in the presence," a claim for which no clear evidence exists (*Son of Man*, 73). He also must, like VanderKam, understand "from the beginning" in 62:7 to be referring to something other than the beginning of creation, a move that becomes easier when he bifurcates the purposes of 48:3–4, 6 from 62:7. We contend that these moves to separate the ESM from preexistence are strained and unconvincing, and that the most natural readings of these texts present a preexistent figure. For a similar conclusion, see Markus Bockmuehl, *Revelation and Mystery*, 37–38.

35. For discussion of this complicated text, see Nickelsburg and VanderKam, *1 Enoch*, 305–7. See also David Winston Suter, *Traditions and Composition in the Parables of Enoch* (SBLDS 47; Missoula: Scholars Press, 1979), 19–23; and Jonathan Ben-Dov and Eshbal Ratzon, "The Oath and the Name in 1 Enoch 69," *JSS* 60, no. 1 (2015): 19–51.

36. Suter, *Traditions and Composition*, 22–23, claims that the oath itself is never revealed, but only that its powers are revealed. But this claim seems inconsistent with the declaration of verse 16, "And these are the secrets of the oath." It seems clear to

us that what is being provided in verses 16–25 are the identity and contents of the oath that have long been kept a secret. Here, the apocalyptic Parables reveal this long-held secret to the reader, a common feature of the genre. For discussion of the oath's participation in creation, see Nickelsburg and VanderKam, *1 Enoch*, 307–9.

37. See Black, *Enoch*, 249; and Nickelsburg and VanderKam, *1 Enoch*, 313–14, for discussion of such a conclusion. Note Bauckham who follows this position in his assessment of the ESM (*Son of Man*, 89). In 1 En. 65–69:1, it is widely recognized as an interpolation (see Nickelsburg and VanderKam, *1 Enoch*, 294–96). In the rest of chapter 69, a number of distinct sections have been identified. Nickelsburg separates 69:2–12 and 69:26–29 from 69:13–25. The former he argues could be a part of the original parables, while the latter he regards as an interpolation (Nickelsburg and VanderKam, *1 Enoch*, 297–314; for additional discussion, see Ben-Dov and Ratzon, "The Oath," 19–51; and Suter, *Traditions and Composition*,19–23. Despite this interpolation, there is little reason to believe that the text in its current form did not exist in the first century CE, and as such, is representative of Jewish thought at this time.

38. Bauckham, *Son of Man*, 29–30.

39. Black, *Book of Enoch*, 214, 220; Bauckham, *Son of Man*, 40–47.

40. Bauckham, *Son of Man*, 41.

41. The most natural understanding of this declaration would be God's heavenly throne, though one might argue that it refers to an earthly throne that is established by God, i.e., the throne of Israel's king is ultimately God's throne. The problem with such a reading is that there is little precedent in either the Hebrew Bible or other Second Temple literature where the throne of Israel's king is identified as God's throne. In 1 Chr 29:23, the throne of Israel's king is described as the "throne of the Lord," but this descriptor is lacking in the LXX. A similar reference is found in 2 Chr 9:8. However, there is no instance in which God directly refers to his own throne where the referent is the earthly throne of Israel's king. In fact, in all instances in which God uses the phrase "my throne," it is never used to describe the throne of an earthly king (see Isa 66:1; Jer 49:38; Ezek 43:7).

42. Bauckham, *Son of Man*, 42; For those who favor the reading "my throne," see Nickelsburg and VanderKam, 1 *Enoch*; and Daniel C. Olson, *Enoch: A New Translation* (North Richland Hills, TX: BIBAL Press, 2004). For those who favor the reading "his throne," see Black, *The Book of Enoch*, 214; Michael A. Knibb, *The Ethiopic Book of Enoch: A New Edition in Light of the Aramaic Dead Sea Fragments* (Oxford: Clarendon, 1978), 2:135.

43. For a more thorough discussion, see Gieschen, "The Divine Name," 65–69.

44. See chapter 6.

45. For those who note that the Parables attribute YHWH texts to the ESM, see Bauckham, *Jesus and the God of Israel*, 228–32; Fletcher-Louis, *Jesus Monotheism*, 182.

46. For similar analysis, see Bauckham, *Jesus and the God of Israel*, 228–32; Fletcher-Louis, *Jesus Monotheism*, 182.

47. See, for example, Kirk, *A Man Attested by God*, 151–55. For a rebuttal to Kirk's arguments regarding a human rather than divine identity for the Enochic Son of Man, see Winn, "Identifying the Enochic Son of Man," 295–300.

48. For discussion, see Collins, *The Scepter and the Star*, 178–81; Knibb, "The Structure and Composition of the Parables of Enoch," in *Enoch and the Messiah Son of Man: Revisiting the Book of Parables*, ed. G. Boccaccini (Grand Rapids, MI: Eerdmans, 2007), 62–63; Nickelsburg, "Discerning the Structure(s) of the Enochic Book of Parables," in *Enoch and the Messiah Son of Man: Revisiting the Book of Parables*, ed. Gabriel Boccaccini (Grand Rapids, MI: Eerdmans, 2007), 42–43.

49. The parables use either the word *sab'e*, "people" or *eg^wula- "emma heyyāw*, 'mother of the living,' while the word in the phrase applied to Enoch is *be'esi* "a masculine person." See the note in translation offered by Ephraim Isaac in Charlesworth, *OTP*, 1:50. This is why R. H. Charles, *The Apocrypha and Pseudepigrapha of the Old Testament* (Oxford: Clarendon Press, 1913), 2:237, corrected the text from "Thou art" the Son of Man to "This is . . . "

50. We will address the later texts which intentionally equate Enoch with the Son of Man; see chapter 8.

51. For the latter option, see Helge S. Kvanvig, "The Son of Man in the Parables of Enoch," in *Revisiting the Book of Parables*, ed. G. Boccaccini (Grand Rapids, MI: Eerdmans, 2007), 200–210; and Schäfer, *Two Gods*, 45–53.

52. For recognition and discussion of these strands, see Black, *Enoch*, 145–168; VanderKam, "Righteous One," 169–91; Helge Kvanvig, "The Son of Man in the Parables of Enoch," 179–215; and Boccaccini, "Finding a Place," 363–79.

53. For example, see Dunn, *Christology in the Making*, 73, 76; and Boccaccini, "Finding a Place," 276–77, Nickelsburg, "Son of Man," 140.

54. See discussion before this note regarding the ESM's role in creation.

55. See Ben-Dov and Ratzon, "The Oath," 42–43; Ben-Dov, "Exegetical Notes on the Cosmology in the Parables of Enoch," in *Enoch and the Messiah Son of Man: Revisiting the Book of Parables*, ed. Gabriel Boccaccini (Grand Rapids, MI: Eerdmans, 2007), 149; Suter, *Traditions and Composition*, 19–20.

56. See Ben-Dov and Ratzon, "The Oath," 44–46; Ben-Dov, "Exegetical Notes on the Cosmology," 149; Suter, *Traditions and Composition*, 22–23; Olson, *Enoch*, 271; Orlov, *Yahoel and Metatron*, 38–40.

57. Nickelsburg and VanderKam draw a comparison between this divine oath and personified wisdom of Proverbs 8 (*1 Enoch*, 307); see also Knibb, *The Ethiopic Book of Enoch*, 2:162.

58. Cf. the fragment of Daniel from Qumran (4Q246), which according to Schäffer, *Two Gods*, 41 and 44, portrays the Son of Man as "an angelic, second divine figure next to the Most High God" who beyond any other angel has "unprecedented proximity to God."

Chapter 8

Melchizedek and Enoch

Within the Hebrew Bible there are two figures that might be regarded as equal in terms of the mystery that surrounds them, Enoch and Melchizedek. Enoch is listed among Adam's descendants. He is the sixth generation after Adam, born to Jared, and father of Methuselah. He is unique in that, unlike all of the other named descendants, he is said to have—like Adam—walked with God. But perhaps even more intriguing is the claim that Enoch "walked with God, and he was no more, because God took him" (Gen 5:24). Enoch is thus the only descendant whom the text does not describe with the phrase, "and he died." This description of Enoch is provocative and led to significant speculation in the Second Temple period.

Melchizedek appears in Genesis 14 where he is described as both the king of Salem and the priest of "God most High." After Abram's defeat of Chedorlaomer and his conspirators, he is met by Melchizedek with both bread and wine. After Melchizedek gives Abram a blessing, Abram gives to Melchizedek a tithe from the spoils of war. Melchizedek is then not heard of again in the Hebrew Bible until he is mentioned in Psalm 110, when God declares that the figure at the heart of the hymn will be "a priest forever in the order of Melchizedek" (110:4). Like the mysterious description of Enoch, this description of Melchizedek captured the minds of certain Second Temple Jews, resulting in speculation about his identity. Here we consider both of these mysterious figures and how they might be understood to relate to the God of Israel and the concept of a second power in heaven.

MELCHIZEDEK

The mysterious priest-king of Salem, Melchizedek, who appears twice in the Hebrew Bible (Gen 14 and Ps 110) is not a particularly prominent figure in Second Temple literature, but he is at times the object of interpretive interests.[1] Of particular relevance to the present investigation is the depiction

of Melchizedek in the Dead Sea Scrolls. While scrolls scholars have specu-
lated that Melchizedek may be in view in the *Vision of Amram* (4Q543–547,
548–49) and possibly in *Songs of the Sabbath Sacrifice* (4Q401 and 11Q17),
the only clear and certain references to Melchizedek comes in 1QapGen XXII
(*Genesis Apocryphon*) and 11 QMelch. The treatment of Melchizedek in the
Genesis Apocryphon is of little note, as it primarily recounts the episode
found in Genesis 14, adding only minor interpretive glosses. Yet, 11QMelch
is far more significant. This text is a depiction of eschatological events,
including the liberation and ingathering of God's people, the celebration of
various jubilees, the atonement of sin, and the defeat and judgment of God's
enemies. What is striking about this text is the central role given to the figure
of Melchizedek in these events, and, in particular, that he regularly seems to
stand in the place of Israel's God. The text claims that Melchizedek himself
will bring about the return of God's people, a role that is attributed to YHWH
throughout the Hebrew Bible.[2] It is seemingly Melchizedek who brings about
the blessings of Jubilee and the day of atonement for the "sons of light." It
is also Melchizedek who will function as God's eschatological and cosmic
judge, as he defeats and exacts God's judgment on "Belial and the spirits of
his lot." Yet, more significant than the role Melchizedek plays is the manner
in which the scroll describes his activity.

In three instances, the scrolls either replace or identify a reference to the
God of Israel with Melchizedek. The first example is found in the scroll's
paraphrase of Isaiah 61:2, where instead of saying "the year of the LORD's
favor (שנת־רצון ליהוה)" the scroll says, "the year of Melchizedek's favor (לשנת
הרצון למלכי)."[3] Here the figure of Melchizedek replaces the Tetragrammaton.
The second instance follows in the immediate line where the scroll contains
a unique reading of Psalm 82:1. The psalm originally, states, "God (אלהים)
has taken his place in the divine council (בעדת־אל); in the midst of the gods
(אלהים) he holds judgment." However, in 11QMelch the first mention of
"God (אלהים)," which is clearly the Most High God of Israel in the psalm, is
said to be about Melchizedek: "Melchizedek . . . as is written about him in
the songs of David, who said 'Elohim will stand in the divine council, in the
midst of the gods he judges.'" Then, in the third example, which immediately
follows the identification of Melchizedek with the "Elohim" of Psalm 82:1,
Melchizedek is also identified as the YHWH of Psalm 7:8–9: "And about him
(i.e., Melchizedek) he said: 'And above it to the heights return: God (אל) will
judge the peoples.'" While the text of the scrolls reads "God (אל)," the psalm
originally reads "the LORD (יהוה)." On its own, this would not be noteworthy since it was a common scribal practice to replace the Tetragrammaton
with the word אל. However, what is remarkable is that the reference itself to
יהוה/ אל is said to be about Melchizedek. Thus, again, it seems Melchizedek
is again understood to be replacing, or thought to be, the Lord of Israel. What

conclusions can be drawn about Melchizedek's identity from 11QMelch? Here we consider the various theories that have been proposed regarding this mysterious figure's identity.

Melchizedek as Either an Angel or Messiah

Since the publication of the scrolls, the earliest interpreters argued that Melchizedek should be understood as an angelic figure, most commonly the angel Michael.[4] Initial reasons for such an identification include: (1) Melchizedek being identified with "Elohim," which can be used to identify angelic beings; (2) Melchizedek's undertaking functions that Michael takes in other Qumran and Second Temple texts; and (3) speculation in Second Temple literature about the heavenly priesthood of Michael might provide both a background and link to Melchizedek in 11QMelch. Later, some scrolls scholars suggested that Melchizedek might have been present in other scrolls, but because of the fragmentary nature of the scrolls his name was lost. The most noteworthy example is found in the *Vision of Amram*, where one finds a figure named Melchiresha, a name that means "king of evil." It has been suggested that he is the counterpart to Melchizedek, whose name means "king of righteousness." Additionally, in the *Vision of Amram*, Melchiresha is pitted against Michael. These two data points are then combined to make a case that Michael is rightly equated with Melchizedek.

But an identification with Michael is not without problems. First, 11QMelch never mentions Michael or gives any indication that such an identification is intended. Second, there is nowhere else in Jewish literature where Melchizedek is identified as an angel, including the Hebrew Bible, the DSS, or any other Second Temple text. Third, the argument that uses Mechiresha and his conflict with Michael to connect the latter to Melchizedek is highly speculative, as Melchizedek's name does not appear in any scroll that also depicts Mechiresha. Finally, no other Jewish tradition applies YHWH texts to the angel Michael in the way that the scrolls apply such texts to Melchizedek.

Another noteworthy identification of Melchizedek, though it has fewer proponents than an identification with Michael, is that of Israel's Messiah.[5] Perhaps the most thorough and comprehensive case for such an identity is made by Paul Rainbow. Rainbow notes that the functions of Melchizedek in the DSS are all functions that are, in other traditions, performed by Israel's Messiah. He notes that the identification of Melchizedek with "Elohim" is similar to such an identification being given to Israel's kings, and as such could be explained by Melchizedek's role as Messiah. But Rainbow's case largely rests on the texts of Hebrew scriptures that are the exegetical focus of 11QMelch; Leviticus 25:8–13, Isaiah 52:7, Isaiah 61:1–2, and Daniel 9:24–25. Rainbow demonstrates how three of these four texts (Isa

52:7; 61:1–2; and Dan 9:24–25) were widely interpreted messianically in the Second Temple period. The only exception is Leviticus 25:8–13, but the concept of a Jubilee year that is found in this text certainly featured in Jewish eschatological hope. That Melchizedek features prominently in the exegesis of such messianically oriented texts, in Rainbow's assessment, tips the scales to a messianic identity for Melchizedek, over and against an identification with an angelic identity in general, and the archangel Michael in particular.

Melchizedek as the YHWH of Israel

In addition to these two possible identifications of Melchizedek, a third option has emerged, though its adherents are small in number. This option contends that Melchizedek should be identified with the God of Israel, or put another way, that Melchizedek is simply another divine title for YHWH.[6] The argument is primarily based on the evidence provided above, namely texts in which Melchizedek replaces YHWH or is identified as YHWH in the scroll's treatment of at least three texts from Hebrew scriptures. It is contended that the most natural way to read these texts is to simply equate Melchizedek with YHWH himself. While angels and human kings could bear the attribution "Elohim," the Elohim that Melchizedek is seemingly identified with in Psalm 82:1, is none other than YHWH of Israel. Even more compelling is the scroll's transformation of "the year of YWHW's favor" to "the year of Melchizedek's favor." Here the eschatological blessing which clearly belongs to and is established by YHWH is attributed to Melchizedek. Three different lines of argumentation have been taken to refute such a conclusion: (1) contending that in texts cited above, Melchizedek does not actually take the place of YHWH; (2) noting that both Melchizedek and the God of Israel are two distinct entities in the scrolls and thus the former cannot be identified as the latter; and (3) Melchizedek is a human priest in Genesis 14 and thus he cannot be identified as the God of Israel. Here we will consider and respond to each of these objections.

YHWH Texts Attributed to Melchizedek

Richard Bauckham has argued that 11QMelch does not, in fact, identify Melchizedek as the God of Israel. He notes that in Psalm 82:1, the text contains three references to divine figures: Elohim (figure one) stands in the assembly of El (figure two), and judges Elohim (collectively figure three).[7] Bauckham argues that the exegete authoring the scroll understands the two uses of Elohim in the passage to be referring to two different entities, with the first referring to a singular entity and the second multiple "divine/heavenly" entities. He then notes that the interpreter likely understands the reference to El as a reference to YHWH. From these two pieces of information, Bauckham argues that the exegete cannot identify the first Elohim with YHWH, thus this first reference can be identified with Melchizedek, who Bauckham understands as a heavenly angelic figure.

While such a proposal is possible, it is not without problems. The use of El in this context could be understood to describe the nature of the assembly that Elohim (YHWH) stands within, namely a divine assembly, and not the assembly of YHWH proper. Interestingly, the LXX seems to go in this direction, as it translates "El" with the plural θεῶν. As such, the LXX interprets the passage to depict the God of Israel standing in the assembly of the gods, where he judges the gods. It is quite possible that the scrolls interpret the passage in the same manner, and thus, identify Melchizedek as the God of Israel in this text from Hebrew scripture.[8]

Regarding the scroll's use of Psalm 7:8b–9a, Bauckham argues that the first part of the citation, "And above [it] (the assembly) to the heights return," is the reference to Melchizedek, while the latter part of the citation, "God will judge the peoples" is a reference to YHWH and not Melchizedek.[9] He argues that the exegete is linking this passage to Psalm 82:1 for two reasons: (1) both refer to a heavenly council in the context of judgment; and (2) both refer to an exalted heavenly figure taking its place in the council who is not YHWH. But this second reason is suspect. As we have argued above, it is quite possible that Psalm 82:1 refers to only one figure, YHWH, and not two. If that is indeed the case, then it is likely that the citation of Psalm 7:8a–9b also only envisions one figure. The figure who returns to the heavenly assembly (7:8b) is none other than the figure who judges the people in 7:9a. If that is the case, then the exegete composing the scrolls is indeed identifying Melchizedek with the YHWH of the Hebrew Bible. Further supporting such a reading of the scrolls is found two lines later, where the scrolls clearly claim, "But, Melchizedek will carry out the vengeance of God's judgements." Here it seems quite clear that the author of the scroll envisions Melchizedek to be performing the action ascribed to YHWH in Psalm 7:9.[10]

Interestingly, Bauckham does not address the scroll's identification of Melchizedek with YHWH in its paraphrase of Isaiah 61:2. We would contend that the ease with which the author of the scroll is able to replace YHWH with Melchizedek in this text of the Hebrew Bible only increases the likelihood that the author is doing so in the exegesis of both Psalm 7 and 82.

Melchizedek as a Distinct Entity from YHWH

The scroll does seem to depict both Melchizedek and the God of Israel as distinct entities. Line thirteen says, "But, Melchizedek will carry out the vengeance of God's judgement." Not only do God and Melchizedek appear to be distinct, but Melchizedek clearly seems to be functioning as an agent of God.[11] For many interpreters, this would naturally preclude an identification of Melchizedek with Israel's God. However, it is at this point where a two powers paradigm offers an easy and natural way forward. If Melchizedek is understood as the second power, and the figure identified as God, for whom Melchizedek is an agent, is understood as the first power, the problem of the text depicting two distinct entities disappears.[12] If both entities are rightly identified as the YHWH of Israel, then it would be quite natural for the scrolls to ascribe YHWH passages to the figure of Melchizedek, yet at the same time present Melchizedek in terms of divine agency.

Melchizedek as a Human High Priest in Genesis

To some degree, all these Melchizedek traditions find their origin in the story of Genesis 14, in which Abram encounters Melchizedek, the king of Salem (Jerusalem) and priest of God Most High.[13] A natural objection to identifying Melchizedek as the God of Israel would be his identification as a human being in this episode of Genesis. In response to such an objection, such a human identification has not stopped the majority of interpreters from associating this figure with an exalted angel, even Michael himself. We think it is safe to say that however Melchizedek was supposed to be understood in the story of Genesis 14, he is understood as being more than a mere human figure in 11QMelch. In fact, given 11QMelch as well as the references to Melchizedek in the Christian book of Hebrews, it seems that Melchizedek was the object of significant interpretive speculation in at least some strands of Second Temple Judaism. If the human priest Melchizedek could in some way be transferred from human priest to angel by the Qumran community, it is certainly plausible that he could in fact be elevated more highly than that, namely to the position of the second power. The origin of such an interpretive move is not difficult to find. In Genesis 14:20, Abram, after receiving a blessing from Melchizedek, gives to him a tithe of all that he had won in the preceding battle. Such a detail is highly provocative, as a tithe is what is to be given to the God of Israel (see, for example, Gen 28:22; Lev 27:30–33; Num 18:21–26; Mal 3:8). It seems that such a gift to a human being was indeed seen as troublesome to some Jews, as the retelling of this episode in Jubilees completely removes any mention of Melchizedek. Instead of Abram giving a tithe to Melchizedek, he gives the tithe to the God of Israel. One could contend that the Qumran exegetes saw a similar problem, but rather than remove Melchizedek, they understood him in terms of a second power, the Lord of Israel to whom tithe is properly given.

When we consider similarities between Melchizedek and previous depictions of the second power in Judaism, the case for such an interpretive move grows stronger. In Genesis 14, Melchizedek is a mysterious priest and king in Jerusalem who receives a tithe from Abram. We have already seen in Philo where the Logos, which we have argued is best understood as the second power, is presented as both a king that rules from God's throne and a priest that serves before God. What we did not note was that Philo also seems to establish a connection between Melchizedek and the Logos, where the former is in some way identified as a human representative of the latter.[14] The Enochic Son of Man, whom we have likewise argued is best understood as the second power, also rules from God's throne and seems to play a priestly role in forgiving sins. If these ideas were in any way representative of, or comparable to, Jewish thinking about a second power, such a combination of roles together with the great patriarch Abram giving this figure a tithe, could plausibly lead to the creative interpretive conclusion that Melchizedek was the second power in human form—a conclusion that finds a possible parallel in Philo. In fact, we would argue that it is more plausible that this constellation of details would lead to the conclusion that Melchizedek was, in fact, the second power or immanent YHWH than it would lead to the conclusion that Melchizedek was a mere angel.[15] Angels are not given tithes, but YHWH is. Nowhere else are YHWH texts applied to ordinary angels, but YHWH texts are applied to Melchizedek. Thus, if the author of 11QMelch has engaged in an interpretive practice that has transferred the seemingly human priest of Genesis 14 into something greater, which clearly seems to be the case, we contend that there is a stronger case that the greater identity is not that of an ordinary angel but rather that of the second power, namely the immanent YHWH.

Conclusions about Melchizedek

In our examination of Melchizedek in 11QMelch, we see that he only meets one of our criteria for establishing a figure as the second power in heaven. Melchizedek clearly replaces YHWH in at least one, and likely three, YHWH texts of the Hebrew Bible. Yet, in addition to meeting this criterion, other considerations should be made. First, the Melchizedek figure of 11QMelch demands explanation of some sort. He is clearly a figure of tremendous significance and is understood by the author of the scroll to be more than he appears to be in Genesis 14. Relatively few options are then available, and they include an angelic figure, Israel's Messiah, some other exalted human closely connected to eschatological events, or the YHWH of Israel. We have made the case above that if one allows for a two powers theology, an identification with the YHWH of Israel seems the stronger conclusion. Yet, what about identifying Melchizedek with the Messiah of Israel or another exalted human? In Jewish tradition, other human figures were seemingly associated with eschatological events, including Moses, Elijah, and perhaps Enoch, depending on the originality of his association with the Enochic Son of Man.[16] Setting Enoch aside for now, the actions attributed to Melchizedek in the eschaton seem far greater than any ascribed to Moses or Elijah. Additionally, there are no examples of Moses or Elijah replacing YHWH in YHWH texts as Melchizedek does here. Both these features work against the conclusion that Melchizedek is merely a non-messianic exalted human agent of God during the eschaton—his function and the means by which he is described seems to supersede such an identity.

But what of an identification as Messiah? Here we would contend that a messianic identification is entirely possible, but also that such an identity does not in any way preclude identifying Melchizedek as the second power. We saw in the Parables of Enoch that the Son of Man figure, whom we argued was best understood as the second power, was also clearly identified as the Messiah. There is then precedent for bringing together messianic thought and two powers theology into a coherent whole. That is to say, the Messiah of Israel was understood by some as the embodiment of the second power. Thus, one could conclude that the Melchizedek of 11QMelch is rightly identified both as the Messiah and as the second power.

Such a dual identification then brings us to an interesting parallel with Enoch as the Son of Man. Regardless of whether the Parables intended to identity Enoch as the Son of Man, at the very least, some redactor of the parable did. And while some might contend that such an identification might weaken identifying the Enochic Son of Man as the second power, in light of what we see in 11QMelch, it, in fact, might not. If our argument is correct, and the author of the scroll is indeed presenting the figure of Melchizedek as both the second power and possibly the Messiah, then the parallels with the Parables of Enoch are striking. Both in the Parables and 11QMelch, there is significant interpretive development regarding a mysterious figure from the book of Genesis, Enoch, who walked with God for three hundred years and then was mysteriously taken by God so that he "was no more"; and Melchizedek, a mysterious figure who was king of Jerusalem, priest to God Most High, to whom Abraham offered a tithe, and then never appears again. Both play a significant role in administering eschatological judgment. Both stand in the place of YHWH in distinct YHWH texts. The Son of Man (perhaps identified as Enoch) is identified as Messiah and Melchizedek, both engage in actions closely associated with messianic ideas and are closely associated with messianic texts of the Hebrew Bible. A striking constellation of details is shared by both the Enochic Son of Man and Melchizedek of 11QMelch. And yet one more relevant piece of information needs to be considered.

As noted above, the Parables of Enoch, though likely dated to the Herodian period, do not appear in the copies of 1 Enoch found at Qumran. This noteworthy absence may find its explanation in the similarities between the Son of Man of the Parables and the Melchizedek of the scrolls. If the community at Qumran and the community that produced the Parables both held a two powers theology and found an expression of the second power in their exegesis of a mysterious figure from the Hebrew Bible, though disagreed on the identity of that figure, it would not be surprising to see the exegetical tradition of one absent in the writings of the other and vice versa.

Therefore, our case for understanding Melchizedek as the second power includes one important criterion that he meets, but it moves beyond them to additional considerations. In our estimation, the case for identifying him as the second power is stronger than the case for identifying him as either an ordinary angel or a non-messianic exalted human. Additionally, the messianic signals connected to Melchizedek in the scrolls are not at odds, but rather cohere, with identifying Melchizedek as the second power, just as the Enochic Son of Man is connected to messianic identities and texts. Finally, in a number of ways the Melchizedek of the scrolls shares a number of striking similarities with a figure for which we have already made a strong case and is rightly understood as an expression of the second power, namely the Enochic Son of Man. These similarities strengthen the conclusion that the Melchizedek of the scrolls also represents an expression of the second power. Such a conclusion also offers a plausible explanation for why the Parables of Enoch, that feature the Enochic Son of Man as the second power, are missing from the versions of 1 Enoch at Qumran. The Qumran community had their embodiment of the second power in the figure of Melchizedek and had no room for another.

ENOCH AND METATRON

The figure of Enoch captured the exegetical imagination of Second Temple Jews as well as those of the rabbinic period. In what has come to be known as 1 Enoch, a variety of "Enochic" traditions have been brought together into one singular text. These texts are held together by the common feature of Enoch revealing heavenly mysteries to the reader. In our discussion of the Son of Man above, we have already examined a portion of this text, what has been identified as the Parables (or Similitudes) of Enoch (1 Enoch 37–71). All of the material that comprises 1 Enoch can be dated to the Second Temple period, with a majority of it predating 100 BCE. Additional Enochic traditions can be found in 2 Enoch, a text in which Enoch again is a revelator of heavenly visions. The date of this text is highly uncertain, with people dating it anywhere between the Second Temple period and the late Middle Ages. The earliest extant manuscripts have clearly experienced Christian redaction, though it is recognized by many that some traditions therein likely find their origins in a pre-Christian text. Of equally uncertain date and origin is the writing known as 3 Enoch.[17] Unlike 1 and 2 Enoch, Enoch is not the revelator of heavenly visions in 3 Enoch. Instead, 3 Enoch describes the heavenly ascent of Rabbi Ishmael (a well-known rabbi of the early second century CE), who was guided on his heavenly vision by the angelic figure Metatron. The reason for the title 3 Enoch is the identification of the angelic figure Metatron with the exalted human figure Enoch. While some traditions in 3 Enoch may be quite early, the text and most of the traditions therein likely date to the fifth or sixth century CE, with some redactional activity occurring even later. Here we consider the depiction of Enoch in each of these traditions and consider his relevance for the reconstruction of Second Temple Jewish monotheism.

In 1 Enoch, Enoch is a human figure who is uniquely brought into heaven and given access to heavenly secrets. Additionally, there is a scene in the Parables of Enoch in which Enoch seems to be transformed in some way. In Parables 71:11, Enoch claims "I fell on my face, my whole bodied mollified and my spirit transformed." However, the nature of this transformation is uncertain. An angel says to Enoch, "You, son of man, who art born in righteousness and upon whom righteousness has dwelt, the righteousness of the Antecedent of Time will not forsake you" (71:14). In our analysis of the Enochic Son of Man above, we noted that some argue Enoch is being identified with the Son of Man/Messiah who has played a prominent role in the Parables. Yet, as we argued above, this conclusion is far from certain. It is quite possible, and we believe likely, that Enoch is simply being address as a human being (cf. Ezekiel), and not being identified as the messianic and heavenly figure of the Parables.[18] If Enoch is not being identified with the Son of Man, then his transformation could be understood either in terms of him becoming an angel (see 2 Enoch) or the transformation of his human bodying into a spiritual one, that is, some sort of exalted/immortal body. We contend that while Enoch is clearly an exalted and important human figure in the 1 Enoch tradition, perhaps one who even joins the ranks of the angels, he likely falls short of being identified as a second power in heaven.[19]

In 2 Enoch, it seems to expand on the tradition we just analyzed in 1 Enoch (the Parables). While Enoch is again a revelator of heavenly visions, he describes his own transformation into an angelic figure. The Lord declares that Enoch will stand in front of his face forever, and then instructs Michael to remove his earthly clothes and replace them. Enoch then describes looking at himself, and declaring, "I had become like one of the glorious ones" (21:10). Enoch is then depicted as sitting to God's left with (or perhaps even closer than) the angel Gabriel (22:5). It seems that 2 Enoch has interpreted the above described episode from 1 Enoch 71 in terms of Enoch's transformation from a human being to an angelic being. Yet, this seems to be the extent of Enoch's transformation, namely to the height of an angelic figure. He does not meet any of the criteria we have outlined above, and thus, should not be regarded, even in this later Jewish/Christian influenced text as a second power in heaven.

In 3 Enoch, it further develops the Enoch traditions found in both 1 and 2 Enoch.[20] Here, Enoch, on his ascension, is transformed into the angel Metatron.[21] Metatron is described as "more exalted than all the angels" (4:1). God calls him the "lesser YHWH" (12:5), and he is the one of whom it is written, "My name is in him"—clearly a reference to the Angel of the Lord in Exodus 23:21.[22] He is also consistently referred to as "the Prince of the Divine Presence" throughout 3 Enoch. God gives to him a crown and seats him on a heavenly throne, both of which convey his sovereignty over the cosmos. Yet, this scene of Enoch/Metatron's exaltation comes to an abrupt halt when a certain Aher enters the seventh heaven.[23] Aher sees Metatron and his exalted status, and being filled with fear, he declares, "There are indeed two powers in heaven!" (16:3). This declaration is responded to swiftly by God who declares Aher an apostate (16:4). Metatron is then taken from his throne and struck with sixty lashes of fire.

Here Metatron seems to meet a number of our criteria. He bears the divine name. He sits on a divine throne and exercises sovereignty over the cosmos. And he is closely identified with the Angel of the Lord, a figure we have previously identified as a second power in heaven. Yet, the text of 3 Enoch dates to the later rabbinic or early Medieval period, and thus is not a reliable resource for reconstructing Second Temple Jewish monotheism. What value then does it have for our project and why have we addressed it here? While 3 Enoch is not a witness to Second Temple Jewish convictions, it is an important witness to the awareness of a two powers theology within the rabbinic period. In 3 Enoch, it allows for the human Enoch to be highly exalted to the great height of the angel Metatron and, as such, to even bear many of the identity markers we proposed. Yet, at even such heights, the text clearly rejects the belief in two powers in heaven, and even has the divine voice calling God's people to abandon a two powers apostasy.

In 3 Enoch, it is not the only place in which a heresy connected to Metatron is found; in fact, it appears to be a later development of an earlier rabbinic tradition.[24] The earliest reference[25] to Metatron is when R. Nachman (d. late 3rd cent.) gave advice on how to answer the "heretics (מינים)" (= those who believe in "two powers"?). He cites an earlier, otherwise unknown, R. Idit, who responded to a "heretic (מין)" who asked why in Exodus 24:1 God said "come up to the LORD (ייי)" instead of "come up to me." R. Idit answered, "This is Metatron (מטתרון), whose name is like the name of his master, as it is written: 'for my name is in him' (23:21)." The heretic next declares, "But if so, you should worship him!"[26] This, of course, is unacceptable to R. Nachman, who then attempts to define Metatron as God's angelic ambassador, not a second deity. In other words, the early rabbinic material knows of those who interpret the Angel of the Lord as a second deity, but deems such teaching heretical. While this scene does not denounce "two powers" explicitly, it does not need to do so. Such an understanding of the Angel of the Lord as a second divine entity is clearly in view and rejected.

Another significant Talmudic reference[27] to Metatron, and one much closer to that found in 3 Enoch, makes the two powers heresy explicit. Like the account in 3 Enoch, a certain Aher sees Metatron enthroned in heaven, and exclaims that there are "two powers."[28] For this "heresy," Aher is banished from heaven forever. Metatron, the text explains, is not divine, but only sits on the throne occasionally as a scribe,[29] which is obviously a polemic against those "heretics" who thought his enthronement signified something more. Against those who link Enoch's scribal role with Metatron, Paz explains, "Metatron does not actually receive the title 'scribe' in the story and the (part-time) scribal office attributed to him seems secondary, mainly introduced in order to give an excuse for the fact that Metatron could be found sitting, without assuming he is truly enthroned." Metatron, in other rabbinic literature already had a role that placed him (nearly?) in the place of God.[30] For example, he is the Angel of the Lord who appeared to Moses in the burning bush, according to Hekhalot Zutrati.[31]

In these rabbinic sources, Metatron is not only depicted as the Angel of the Lord, he is said to be the Son of Man. Yet, he is not connected with Enoch in any way. Thus, it seems 3 Enoch represents a development in this tradition, one that brings this rabbinic tradition of Metatron together with the traditions found in 1 and 2 Enoch. The exalted human turned angel Enoch of 1 and 2 Enoch becomes the figure of Metatron described in this rabbinic tradition. From this development of the Enoch tradition, we can conclude a number of relevant things. First, we can conclude that in the Second Temple period, there is little evidence, if any, that Enoch was understood as a second power figure.[32] Only if one concludes that Enoch is identified as the Son of Man in Parable 71, would one need to consider such a possibility. Second, and perhaps more importantly, this tradition betrays an ongoing belief in two powers in heaven held by some within the rabbinic period and beyond, one which both 3 Enoch and the related rabbinic texts reject as heresy.

As a corrective, this text explains that Metatron is, in fact, Enoch who was elevated to angelic status and given this unique name and role.[33] This belief likely involved the perception of a second power, perhaps named Metatron and identified with the Angel of the Lord, who was understood as a lesser YHWH. Such a second power figure is strikingly similar to what we have been reconstructing in the Second Temple period, and thus, a case for continuity has significant ramifications for our proposal.

As we stated in our introduction, our interests in studying all of this literature is primarily to discern the larger context of the early Christian practice of seeing Jesus as the one who appeared in the theophanies of scripture while still seeing him as distinct from the God he called Father. To be sure, the connections between the two powers heresy attacked by the rabbinic literature and early Christian practice of identifying Jesus as the divine Son of God is complex. We are not making claims here about direct dependence in either direction. Instead, we see the rabbinic material about two powers as further confirmation that there was still an active tradition in the common era that understood a second divine figure to be manifested in Israel's scriptures, known under various titles. Peter Schäfer offers a thorough review of this material and concludes, "There can be little doubt that pre-Christian Judaism developed ideas that helped pave the way to a 'binitarian' theology—cases in point are speculations about Logos and Wisdom, certain angelic figures, Adam as the original *makro-anthropos*, and other exalted human figures—of which the early New Testament speculations about the Logos Jesus are but one particularly prominent example."[34] Schäfer's confidence may not be shared by all, and so we will review the argument for dating second power theology to the pre-rabbinic period in our concluding chapter. For now, suffice it to say that the Metatron figure illustrates how a two power paradigm was active in the rabbinic period, and since these sources match well with what we have seen in various ways in earlier Second Temple sources, the material about Metatron sheds some light on earlier instantiations of this way of understanding Israel's Lord.

CONCLUSIONS ABOUT "EXALTED HUMANS" LIKE MELCHIZEDEK AND ENOCH

In this chapter we have focused on two human figures as they appear in two different sources, namely, Melchizedek in 11QMelch and Enoch in 3 Enoch,[35] respectively. The two cases offer very different results, and yet both point to a two powers paradigm. In 11QMelch, Melchizedek seems to be equated with YHWH through the use of Hebrew scripture, and yet he also remains distinct from the Most High God. In 3 Enoch the earlier rabbinic tradition depictions of Metatron are, as it were, clarified so that Metatron turns out not to be a divine figure but Enoch who has been exalted. This is so because some, deemed "heretics," think Metatron is the second power in heaven and worship him as such.

Here we see divergent interpretive traditions related to ambiguous and shadowy figures in the Hebrew Bible. The first is Melchizedek, of whom we have a tradition from the DSS in which he is clearly more than a mere human and as we have argued above, best understood as a second power in heaven. With Enoch, however, even though the mysterious circumstances regarding the end of his life (see Gen 5:24) inspired later imaginative accounts of his exaltation, Enoch nevertheless remained decidedly human and not a second power figure. This is probably because, in Genesis, Enoch is an unambiguous character whose lineage is explicit—a stark contrast with Melchizedek (cf. Heb 7:3). Therefore, Enoch's unambiguous identity removes him from being a candidate for the second power, while Melchizedek's ambiguous identity allows him to be such a candidate. Nevertheless, in 11QMelch it is probable, and in 3 Enoch it is certain, that some held a two powers view. The only difference being that the former text seems to affirm it, while the latter unreservedly rejects it.

In our next chapter, we will review additional figures who are often described by scholars as exalted humans. While none of our criteria are decisive on their own, they each do play a part in helping to understand if any given figure was understood in the Second Temple period to be a second power in heaven. Some of the so-called exalted humans may be depicted in ways that would meet a few of our criteria, and yet we will see again how those with an unambiguous human identity do not appear as a second power. Alternatively, one figure, whose identity remains elusive, may be understood as such. We can now turn to other supposedly exalted humans to assess the evidence.

NOTES

1. For references to Melchizedek in Second Temple literature, see Jubilees 13.25–27, Hebrews 5–7; the *Genesis Apocryphon* (1QapGen XXII) and 11QMelch, Josephus, *Ant.* 1.180–82 and *J.W.* 6:438, and Philo, *Leg.* 3.79–82. Also, see the later Christian text (formerly thought to be by Hippolytus), *Refutatio omnium haeresium* 10.24.1, for a group who believed that Melchizedek was a "a power (δύναμίν)," claiming that he is "the Power above all (ὑπὲρ πᾶσαν δύναμιν)" (text/trans. from M. David Litwa, *Refutation of All Heresies* [Writings from the Greco-Roman World 40; Atlanta: SBL Press, 2016], 734–35). This case is especially interesting since it is listed along with other groups thought to be "Jewish Christian" groups, such as the Ebionites (10.22) and the Elkasaites (10.29), and it is followed by a genealogy and chronology of Israel (10.30.1–7).

2. See Deut 30:3; Ps 53:7; 126:1; 146:7; Jer 23:3; Ezek 34:13. For this argument see Rick Van de Water, "Michael or Yhwh? Toward Identifying Melchizedek in 11Q13," *JSP* 16, no. 1 (2006): 79.

3. For the text and a translation, see Florentino García Martínez and Eibert J. C. Tichelaar, *The Dead Sea Scrolls Study Edition* (Leiden: Brill, 1998), 2:1206–9. We have altered the translations slightly to match the NRSV.

4. For the earliest arguments to such an identification, see A. S. van der Woude, "Melchisedech als himmlische Erlösergestalt in den neugefundenen eschatologischen Midraschim aus Qumran Höle XI" *Oudtestamentische studiën* 14 (1965): 354–73, and J. T. Milik, "*Melkî-Ṣedeq et Melkî-Reša'* dans les anciens éscrits juifs et chrétiens (I)," *Journal of Jewish Studies* 23 (1972): 95–144. For those who have followed such a position, see F. Garcia Martínez, *Qumran and Apocalyptic* (Leiden: Brill, 1992), 176; VanderKam, *The Dead Sea Scrolls Today* (Grand Rapids, MI: Eerdmans,1994), 171.

5. For a more thorough treatments of this position, see Paul Rainbow, "Melchizedek as a Messiah at Qumran," *BBR* 7 (1997): 179–94; Michael Flowers, "The Two Messiahs and Melchizedek in 11QMelchizedek," *JAJ* 7 (2 2016): 194–227. For others who offer similar conclusions, see Jean Carmignac, "Le document de Qumran sur Melchisédeq," *Revue de Qumran* 7 (1970): 343–78; Anders Hultgård, "The Ideal 'Levite,' the Davidic Messiah, the Savior Priest in the Testament of the Twelve Patriarchs," in *Ideal Figures in Ancient Judaism*, eds. John J. Collins and George W. E. Nickelsburg (SBLSCS 12; Chico, CA: Scholars Press, 1980), 93–110; David Flusser, "Melchizedek and the Son of Man," in *Judaism and the Origins of Christianity* (Jerusalem: Magnes Press, Hebrew University, 1988), 186–92.

6. See Franco Manzi, *Melchisedek e l'angelologia nell'epistola agli Ebrei e a Qumran* (Analecta Biblica, 136; Rome: Pontifical Biblical Institute, 1997), 63–96; Van de Water comes to a similar conclusion but modifies Manzi's position by understanding Melchizedek in light of a two powers theology ("Michael or Yhwh?," 75–86).

7. See Bauckham, *Jesus and the God of Israel*, 222, for the following argument regarding Psalm 82:1 in 11QMelch.

8. Loren Stuckenbruck supports just such an interpretation of this text in the 11QMelch; see Stuckenbruck, "Melchizedek in Jewish Apocalyptic Literature," *JSNT* 41, no. 1 (2018): 132. Here, we would note that if Bauckham is correct, a two powers theology could explain the exegesis he offers. The first Elohim that is identified as Melchizedek could be understood as the immanent YHWH, with El being understood as the transcendent YHWH. Thus the text states that the "immanent YHWH" stands in the assembly of the "transcendent YHWH" and judges the angels.

9. See Bauckham, *Jesus and the God of Israel*, 223–24 for Bauckham's argument on Psalm 7:8–9 in 11QMelch.

10. See Stuckenbruck, "Melchizedek," 132, for such a reading of the scroll.

11. Such a distinction leaves Manzi open to the possibility that Melchizedek is indeed a divine agent rather than YHWH. See Manzi, *Melchisedek*, 91–92.

12. This is the solution offered by Van de Water, "Michael or Yhwh."

13. Virtually every Second Temple and rabbinic interpretive tradition regarding Melchizedek equate Salem with Jerusalem.

14. In Philo's allegorical reading of the Melchizedek episode, he seems to understand Melchizedek as either an allegorical representation of the Logos or possibly identifies him as the Logos. In *Leg.* 3.82 Melchizedek is described as a priest that gives to Philo's readers divine wine that ironically brings to them true sobriety. Such

a claim is odd if Melchizedek is understood as merely a historical priestly king of Salem. Yet, this oddity is solved as Philo quickly identifies the Logos as a priest, noting his unique access to magnificent ideas about God. It seems here that the priest Melchizedek who provides people with divine wine is none other than the Logos. This connection is strengthened as the descriptor for Melchizedek from Genesis 14:18, "his own high priest," is applied to both Melchizedek and the Logos (compare *Leg.* 3.79 with 3.82). On such a reading of Philo and a possible parallel between Philo and the exegesis of 11QMelch, see Van de Water, "Michael or Yhwh," 86. For others who see Philo identifying Melchizedek in some way with the Logos, see Jutta Leonhardt-Balzer, *Jewish Worship in Philo of Alexandria* (TSAJ 84; Tübingen: Mohr Siebeck, 2001), 216–17.

15. Here we note a distinction between the Angel of the Lord and all other angels, archangels or otherwise, as we have already made the case that the Angel of the Lord is best understood as a means of identifying a "second power." See chapter 5 of this book.

16. The tradition that Elijah would play a role in the unfolding of eschatological events finds its origins in Malachi 3:23–24/3:22–23LXX (ET = 4:5–6). All the New Testament Gospels seem to bear witness to such a tradition, as do the DSS (4QVision[b]ar 4–5). For a thorough treatment of Elijah in Jewish eschatological traditions, see Ernst Lohmeyer, "Die Verklärung Jesu nach dem Markus-Evangelium," *ZNW* 21 (1922): 188–89, and more recently, Anthony Ferguson, "The Elijah Forerunner Concept as an Authentic Jewish Expectation" *JBL* 137, no. 1 (2018): 127–45. Though the expectation of Moses as an eschatological figure in Second Temple Jewish thought is not as well established as that of Elijah, there is evidence that such an expectation existed. For discussion, see Adela Yarbro Collins, *Mark: A Commentary* (Hermeneia; Minneapolis: Fortress, 2007), 425–26. See also, John C. Poirier, "The Endtime Return of Elijah and Moses at Qumran," *DSD* 10, no. 2 (2003): 221–42.

17. See further discussion in Annette Yoshiko Reed, "From Asael and Šemiḥazah to Uzzah, Azzah, and Azael: 3 Enoch 5 (§§ 7–8) and Jewish Reception-History of 1 Enoch," *Jewish Studies Quarterly* 8, no. 2 (2001): 107–10.

18. For arguments in support of this conclusion, see our discussion in chapter 7 regarding the Enochic Son of Man.

19. As acknowledged above, it is possible that Enoch is rightly identified with the heavenly Son of Man in the Parables, but we find this identification unlikely.

20. For the text, see Peter Schäfer, *Synopse zur Hekhalot-Literatur* (Tübingen: Mohr-Siebeck, 2020), 4–39 (§1–§79). For the debates on the origins of the Metatron tradition, see Boyarin, "Is Metatron a Converted Christian?," *Judaïsme Ancien* 1 (2013): 13–62; and Boyarin, "The Quest of the Historical Metatron: Enoch or Jesus," in *A Question of Identity: Social, Political, and Historical Aspects of Identity Dynamics in Jewish and Other Contexts,* eds. Dikla Rivlin Katz, Noah Hacham, Geoffrey Herman, and Lilach Sagiv (Berlin: de Gruyter, 2019), 153–62; and Schäfer, *Two Gods*, 99–133.

21. For full discussion, see Orlov, *The Enoch-Metatron Tradition* (Texts and Studies in Ancient Judaism 107; Tübingen: Mohr Siebeck, 2005).

22. Fossum, *The Name of God*, 321.

23. The name Aher means "Other" and is a pseudonym for Elisha ben Abuya, who allegedly taught antinomianism in the early second century CE. See Segal, *Two Powers*, 9; and for further discussion of this figure, see Alon Goshen-Gottstein, *The Sinner and the Amnesiac: The Rabbinic Invention of Elisha ben Abuya and Eleazar ben Arach* (Stanford, CA: Stanford University Press, 2000).

24. For a lengthier discussion and secondary literature, see Orlov, *Yahoel and Metatron*.

25. *b. Sanh.* 38b. The text and translation is from Yakir Paz, "Metatron is not Enoch: Reevaluating the Evolution of an Archangel," *Journal for the Study of Judaism* 50 (2019): 55–56.

26. Schäffer, *Jewish Jesus,* 107, reviews the debated passages in Exodus to conclude, "the point is not only that the heretic has a strong argument for his interpretation but also that his argument supports the plain meaning of the biblical text against the rabbi's exegesis."

27. An unrelated theme is how Metatron teaches children; e.g., b. ʿAbod. Zar. 3b (cited in Paz, "Metatron is not Enoch," 65).

28. *b. Ḥag.* 15a (cited in Paz, "Metatron," 73). For further discussion, see Schäfer, *Jewish Jesus*, 127–29.

29. However, see the important correction regarding Metatron's lack of scribal status elsewhere made by Paz, "Metatron," 74–75.

30. Daniel Johansson, "'Who Can Forgive Sins but God Alone?': Human and Angelic Agents, and Divine Forgiveness in Early Judaism," *Journal for the Study of the New Testament* 33 (4 2011), 351–74. After reviewing the possibilities in Second Temple literature, Johansson finds that the only other person who can forgive sins is the Angel of the Lord (cf. Exod 23:21; Zech 3:4). A telling example for Johansson is *b. Sanh.* 38b and *Exod. R.* 32.4, where the rabbis fear that some use this as an excuse to worship this Angel.

31. Hekhalot Zutrati 1: ובה עשה משה את האותות והמופתים שעשה במכרים. ובו הכה את המצרי האש אשר בסנה. ונגלה עליו מטטרון שר סגי יהוה שר צבא יהא. ואמר משה משה (text from Schäfer, *Synopse*, 144 §341).

32. Paz, "Metatron," 52–100, shows that Metatron is not equated with Enoch until 3 Enoch and *b. Ḥag.* 15a, a common tradition which equated the two in order to claim that Metratron is not a second power, but an exalted human. In other words, Enoch was assumed by all to be human and not divine, and thereby a safe identity for Metatron.

33. For full discussion, see Orlov, *The Enoch-Metatron Tradition*.

34. Schäffer, *Jewish Jesus*, 141.

35. We have focused on 3 Enoch for the sake of convenience, but the same applies to the parallel passage in *b. Ḥag.* 15a. We make no claims about the relationship between these texts, other than to assume that they share a common tradition.

Chapter 9

Exalted Humans

When considering a possible boundary between the one God of Israel and all other reality, exalted human figures is a category that requires consideration. Many proponents of an inclusive monotheism will point to exalted human beings that seem to share in an activity or trait that exclusive monotheists claim is a sole prerogative of Israel's God. Furthermore, some proponents of a two powers paradigm have put forward such exalted humans as an example of a second power in heaven. Here we consider such figures and how they might best be assessed in terms of their relationship to the God of Israel and Jewish monotheism.

ADAM

Second Temple literature has numerous examples in which the protoplast Adam is an exalted figure.[1] Much of this exaltation is related to Adam's role as God's first appointed ruler or king over the earth. In this role, Adam, who is made in the image of God, functions as "god" over earth where God has placed him.[2] The pre-fallen Adam may also be associated with the concept of divinely granted glory, and in this way becomes a model for the future glory that will characterize the eschatological people of God.[3] In most of these traditions, Adam is clearly no more than an idealized and exalted human figure, one that exemplifies the ideal human identity prior to the expulsion from Eden and of the eschatological future. Yet, in one unique tradition, Adam's exaltation might push beyond such a mere human identity and actually broach what exclusive monotheists like Hurtado claim to be a strictly divine prerogative. This tradition is found in most extant versions of the Life of Adam and Eve (LAE from this point forward).[4]

The basic narrative of LAE recounts Satan relaying to Adam the reason he was expelled from heaven.[5] In Satan's account, he describes Adam's creation, noting that Adam's "countenance and likeness were made in the image of God" (13.2).[6] In fact, Satan claims that God himself declared to Adam, "I have made you in our image and likeness" (13.2). Satan then recounts how the angel Michael called all of the angels and commanded them to "Worship the image of the Lord God, as the Lord God has commanded" (14.1). Michael is the first angel to worship Adam, and he continues to command the other angels to do the same. Satan refuses to worship Adam, claiming that he was made before Adam, and that it would be more proper for Adam to worship Satan. Some angels follow Satan in refusing to worship, while others follow Michael's instruction. For refusing to worship, Satan is cast out of the presence of God, and for this reason set about to harm Adam through tempting his wife Eve. Thus, in the *LAE* we have an account, relayed by Satan, where the protoplast Adam appears to receive worship from angelic figures, worship that is commanded by the God of Israel.

This tradition has featured prominently in the work of Crispin Fletcher-Louis, who argues that it offers a clear example of a human figure being included in the worship of the God of Israel.[7] Andre Orlov uses the tradition to argue in another direction, namely that the Adam of the *LAE* is depicted as a second power in heaven.[8] Either approach would seem to undermine the paradigm of exclusive monotheism significantly. Here we take a close look at this tradition and consider its significance for assessing the nature of Second Temple Jewish monotheism.

While this tradition is certainly intriguing in the ways it may support certain reconstructions of Jewish monotheism (i.e., either the inclusive or two powers paradigm), there are significant questions regarding its relevance for such reconstructions. Both Larry Hurtado and Richard Bauckham have pointed to the uncertain date and nature of the *LAE* and contend that it could both post-date the Second Temple period and be the product of post-apostolic Christianity rather than Judaism.[9] Obviously, if either were the case, the *LAE* would be largely irrelevant as evidence for Jewish conceptions of the God of Israel during the Second Temple period. In Richard Bauckham's dismissal of the relevance of the *LAE* for reconstructing the matrix of Second Temple Judaism, he cites the work of Marinus de Jonge and Johannes Tromp, who, on what they admittedly recognize as scant evidence (largely a reference to the Acherusian Lake, for which no known Jewish parallel can be found), favor a Christian rather than Jewish origin for the *LAE* tradition.[10] In a later work, de Jonge, again arguing for a Christian rather than Jewish origin, points to the similarity between the description of God's mercy toward Adam and Eve in both the *LAE* and the works of Irenaeus, Tertullian, and Theophilus of Antioch.[11]

Yet, others have argued that the tradition indeed has Jewish origins and should be identified as a product of Second Temple Judaism. Like de Jonge and Tromp, Jean-Daniel Kaestli previously argued for a Christian origin, though on the basis of the parallels between the fall of Satan tradition in the *LAE* and other Christian traditions.[12] However, through the influence of Jan Dochhorn, Kaestli has recently changed his mind. Dochhorn has sought to demonstrate that the *LAE* reflects significant exegetical engagement with the Hebrew Bible rather than the LXX.[13] In a more recent work, Dochhorn has gone as far as to argue that the narrative form of the *LAE* may even date as early as the time of Archelaus.[14]

Thus, while many of the extant versions of the *LAE* certainly bear Christian influence and interpolation, it remains far from certain that the *LAE*'s ultimate origins are Christian rather than Jewish. In fact, the more recent arguments from Dochhorn that favor a Jewish origin and Second Temple provenance will require significant attention from those who have previously championed a Christian origin. It is then not enough for proponents of an exclusive mono-theism merely to dismiss the tradition's relevance for the Second Temple period on the grounds of the tradition's origins. Because it is a possible wit-ness to Second Temple Judaism, the tradition must be seriously considered.

To this end, Bauckham has also argued that the tradition does not depict true cultic worship but rather mere veneration. He is likely right in his argument that the word behind the Latin *adorare* ("worship") is the Greek προσκυνέω, which can convey the act of cultic worship but can also convey the act of adoration/veneration of one who is superior.[15] Bauckham opts for the latter, claiming that the angels merely offer veneration to a superior and not cultic worship.[16] However, Fletcher-Louis offers a strong rebuttal. He notes that the object of *adorare* is not Adam per se, but rather the "image and likeness" of God that in some way resides in or is closely associated with Adam. It is noteworthy that the command given by Michael, first to all the angels and then twice to Satan directly, is "Worship the image of the Lord God" (14.1; see also 14.2 and 15.2), and never "worship Adam." It is actually Satan and not Michael who says, "I do not have it in me to worship Adam" (14.3), explicitly stating that Adam is the object of worship. Fletcher-Louis argues that since the object of worship is explicitly identified as the image and likeness of God, then true worship and not mere veneration is indeed intended.[17] This argument is quite strong, and as such, the claim that the text only intends to portray veneration rather than worship appears weak and unable to resolve the tension between the worship of Adam seen in the *LAE* and an exclusive monotheistic understanding of Jewish religious devotion and practice.

While excluding this tradition on the basis of its questionable origins and the nature of the devotion it depicts fails, a third option remains, one yet to be considered. Surprisingly, analysis of the worship of Adam tradition has never, to our knowledge, considered the source of the tradition within the actual narrative of the *LAE* or the implications of that source for the narratival reliability of the tradition. In the narrative, the source of the account of Adam receiving worship is Satan, a detail that should raise the question of whether he is best understood as a truthful and reliable narrator. Here we consider the possibility that the *LAE* is depicting Satan as a deceptive narrator and that as such, the reader is meant to understand his testimony about Adam receiving worship deceitful and inaccurate.[18]

Perhaps the first important consideration is the reputation that a figure such as Satan would have in the minds of the *LAE*'s audience. While assessments of Satan in the Second Temple period are difficult due to the lack of a coherent narrative regarding him and the variety of names given to powerful demonic opponents of Israel, it is not difficult to conclude that as a powerful demonic figure he would have a reputation for deception.[19] Whether rightly identified with the figure of Satan or not, the Second Temple period contains numerous traditions in which powerful demonic figures function to deceive God's people. In 1 Enoch 69:6, it presents such a figure, one named Gadreel leading Eve astray. The Damascus Document presents Belial as a deceiver of Israel (CD 4.12–19) and leading God's people into apostasy (CD 12.2–3). In the War Scroll, an "Angel of Darkness" leads astray the "sons of deceit" (1QS III, 20–22). The New Testament frequently notes the deception of Satan. In Revelation 12:9, the serpent is identified with Satan (and the Devil), and is described as the "deceiver of the whole world." In John 8:44, the Devil is regarded as the "father of lies," "a liar," and one "in whom there is no truth." And Paul claims that "Satan disguises himself as an angel of the light," a claim that implies a deceptive intent (2 Cor 11:14). While these New Testament texts are decidedly Christian and some may technically postdate the Second Temple period, it seems most probable that these ideas are not Christian inventions, but rather draw on the body of tradition in which powerful demonic figures, Satan or otherwise, are known for deceiving God's people. These traditions demonstrate that Second Temple readers would perceive powerful demonic figures as deceptive, and thus, be cautious in accepting the testimony of a figure like Satan.

Yet, in addition to what was likely a built-in cautiousness regarding the testimony of powerful supernatural figures among Second Temple readers, the text of the *LAE* itself is clearly familiar with the serpent of Genesis 3 being connected to Satan, as this tradition is explicitly referenced in chapter 33. The text describes Satan trying to convince the serpent to aid him in deceiving Eve. After the serpent first resists, Satan says, "Be my dwelling place, and through your mouth I will speak what needs to be spoken."[20] Additionally, in chapter 10, the text implies the readers familiarity with Satan's deception of Eve through the serpent: "But when Adam saw her and the devil with her, he cried out with tears and said, 'O Eve, Eve, where is the work of your penitence? How have you again been seduced by our enemy by whom we have been deprived of our dwelling in Paradise and of spiritual joy?'" (*LAE* 10.3–4).[21] Both of these texts strongly suggest that readers are expected to be familiar with Satan's role in the initial deception of Eve that resulted in the expulsion from the garden, a familiarity that would lead them to associate Satan with deception in general.

The *LAE* text itself contains many indicators that the readers should not trust Satan's testimony. Immediately before the episode in which Satan recounts Adam's worship by angels, there is an account of Satan deceiving Eve a second time. As a result of their expulsion from the garden, Adam and Eve are without food and in danger of dying from starvation (*LAE* 2–4). They decide to engage in acts of penance in order that God might provide for their hunger (*LAE* 5.1–3). While Eve is engaged in her act of penance (standing up to her neck in the Tigris river), Satan comes disguised as an angel of God. He pretends to weep with her and tells her a series of lies; (1) that God has heard her and accepted her penance; (2) that all the angels of heaven have interceded before God on her behalf; and (3) that God sent him to end her penance and to give her the food from Paradise that she had before (*LAE* 9.1–5). Eve believes these lies and after coming out of the water is led by Satan to Adam. Adam, who is not deceived, bemoans Satan's second deception of Eve (see the reference to *LAE* 10 above).[22]

It is noteworthy that this episode, in which Satan lies to Eve about God's instructions comes immediately before the episode in which Satan tells Adam of God's command that angels should worship Adam. Readers already reluctant to trust the testimony of Satan would no doubt be even more so in the pericope in which Satan describes the worship of Adam, particularly when that testimony is preceded by Satan lying to Eve about God's instruction regarding her penance. One might argue that the arrangement of these two pericopes functions to signal to the reader that Satan's testimony regarding God's command that angels worship Adam is, like his testimony to Eve, deceptive and unreliable.

Additional narrative clues that suggest Satan's testimony is unreliable are found in the very pericope containing that testimony. The first clue is that Adam is completely unaware of being an object of worship even though Satan claims it was to Adam that the angels purportedly bowed down and worshipped. This detail would be consistent with the conclusion that the event never occurred and Satan has invented it. The second and perhaps more important clue is found in Adam's response to Satan's story: "Hearing this, Adam cried out with a great shout because of the Devil, and said: 'O Lord, my God, in your hands is my life. Make this adversary of mine be far from me, who seeks to ruin my soul'" (*LAE* 17.1). Both the Armenian and Georgian versions read "who desires to lead me astray" in place of "who seeks to ruin my soul." Regardless of the precise wording, it seems that a stable part of the tradition has Adam communicating to God that he perceives in Satan's testimony regarding himself as an object of worship as an effort to mislead or ruin him in some way. If the story relayed by Satan was truthful, it is hard to understand how it would serve to destroy Adam's soul. Yet, if the story is false, the statement makes perfect sense, as Satan's actions can be understood as yet another attempt to lead Adam to perceive and grasp for himself an identity that is greater than what he actually possesses: a divine identity. Thus, Adam's response to Satan's testimony seems to be a strong narrative clue that the very testimony is yet one more intentional deception that seeks to bring God's newly created humanity to destruction.

In light of this analysis, even if this episode, is a Second Temple tradition and the worship described therein is cultic rather than mere veneration, there is still the strong possibility that what the episode describes is meant to be understood as yet another deception from Satan. The reader would conclude that God never actually commanded angels to worship Adam. The fact that no other Second Temple tradition exists in which Adam is rightly depicted as an object of angelic worship only increases the likelihood that Second Temple readers would perceive Satan's narration as deceptive and unreliable.[23]

If the testimony of Satan is understood as deceitful, the tradition is no longer evidence that supports an inclusive understanding of Jewish monotheism. It would also eliminate Adam as an example of a two powers paradigm for Jewish monotheism. Perhaps it could be argued that the tradition reflects the worship of a heavenly Adam figure, one that might be equated with God's Word (see discussion above), and thus this figure could be understood as a second power. However, the text of the LAE seems to make no distinction between a heavenly and earthly Adam, and it is clearly the earthly Adam that Satan claims was worshipped by the angels. Thus, there is little reason to conclude that the LAE is presenting a heavenly Adam/Word figure as an object of worship.

MOSES

Like Adam, the figure of Moses is often revered and exalted in Second Temple literature. Philo, for example, depicts Moses as one to whom God has granted sovereignty over the entire world, so that even the basic elements of the world obey him (*Mos.* 1.155–156). He makes much of the biblical tradition in which God tells Moses that he will be "god" to both Aaron and Pharaoh (Exod 4:16 and 7:1). Philo even claims that God made Moses both "god and king" over the entire nation of Israel (*Mos.* 1.158). For Philo, Moses is exalted above other human beings, as he is raised up by God's Logos to the honor of the world itself (*Sacr.* 8). He surpasses all other humans in virtue and knowledge of God (*Sacr.* 8). Despite such an exalted view of Moses and the fact that, in Philo's assessment, he is unmatched by any other human figure, he is decidedly human and not God.[24]

Yet, there is a Moses tradition that some perceive as pushing against the claims of an exclusive monotheism. One case is often put forward as evidence for an inclusive or even two powers monotheism: Moses as he is depicted in the Exagogue of Ezekiel the Tragedian.[25] The Exagogue is a dramatic narration of the events of Exodus. In the second act, Moses reports the content of a dream. In this dream, Moses sees a giant throne that sits on Mt. Sinai and "touched the clouds of heaven."[26] A "man," noble in appearance, is sitting on the throne wearing a crown and holding a scepter (70–71). Moses is called to the throne, where he is asked to sit upon it. The man also gives Moses both the crown and the scepter (74–76). The man then departs from the throne, leaving Moses sitting alone on the throne. While seated on the throne, Moses is able to gaze upon the entire earth, as well as below and above it (77–78). Then, a multitude of stars prostrate themselves before him (79–80). After waking from "the dream," Moses's father-in-law then interprets this dream as a sign that Moses himself will cause a throne to rise and that he will rule over humans himself.[27]

This episode is noteworthy for two particular reasons. One, Moses is depicted as sitting on what might be regarded as God's heavenly throne, an action closely associated with sovereignty over the cosmos.[28] Two, Moses is possibly depicted as the recipient of worship from heavenly agents, that is, the stars—worship that is generally reserved for the God of Israel alone. Thus, Moses is depicted as engaging in what are often regarded as the prerogatives of Israel's God. Much debate surrounds the interpretation of this episode, including debate over the significance of Moses sitting on what appears to be a divine throne and debate over the significance of the stars prostrating themselves before Moses (Is this worship or simply obeisance in recognition of a superior?). For proponents of an exclusive monotheism, this episode merely presents a dream that communicates Moses as God's earthly viceroy and progenitor of the future kingdom of Israel.[29] Such a dream finds strong parallels to the dreams of Joseph (Gen 37:5–11). Yet, for proponents of an inclusive monotheism, it is a powerful example of God sharing what exclusive monotheists claim he cannot and does not share, namely God's throne, the sovereignty over creation that throne communicates, and cultic worship. Here we consider these debates and assess the Moses of the Exagogue.[30]

The first question to address is whether Moses sits on God's throne or another exalted throne. The vast majority of interpreters conclude that this throne is none other than God's throne.[31] The details that lead to this conclusion include the fact that the throne reaches up into heaven from Mt. Sinai, that a divine figure may be depicted as seated on the throne, and that from the throne Moses is able to see the entire earth, as well as, both below the earth and above the heavens. While such details could be indicating the throne belongs to God, for a number of reasons it seems that such a conclusion is not a certain one.

Perhaps the most important detail that favors the throne as God's very own is that of a seemingly heavenly or divine figure seated on the throne. That the figure is wearing a crown and holding a scepter strongly suggests sovereignty, a detail that fits with the identity of Israel's God. R. G. Robertson notes that the image is likely drawn from texts like Ezekiel 1, in which God is depicted as a man, as well as Daniel 7 in which both one like a "Son of Man" and the "Ancient of Days" are depicted.[32] It is also possible that the figure represents an angelic figure such as Michael, who is at times identified as Israel's protector and patron angel (see Dan 10:21, 12:1; 1 QM 17:6–8). Regardless of a specific identity, it might be noted that all of these figures are "heavenly," and as such, they would point to the conclusion that the throne itself is heavenly not earthly. Yet, such a conclusion fails to acknowledge an important tradition in Hebrew scriptures, namely God granting human reign over the earth in general, and Israel in particular. God, who is clearly the sovereign king of all his creation, hands kingship over the earth to Adam and Eve in the creation account. Similarly, though God is frequently depicted as Israel's King (e.g., 1 Sam 8:7; Ps 93:1–2; Isa 43:15; 44:6), he relents to Israel's request for a human king. In this way, God, in a real way, hands over the kingship of Israel to a human representative. Thus, even while we might conclude that the figure on the throne in Moses's vision is Israel's God, the significance and identity of the throne that this figure is granting Moses remains unclear. While it could be God's heavenly throne, one that represents sovereignty over the entire cosmos, it could also merely represent earthly sovereignty or sovereignty over Israel, which God is handing over to Moses. The preferred choice between these options must rely on additional details, and cannot be made on the identity of the enthroned figure alone.

One such detail is the described location of the throne. It is described as sitting on Mt. Sinai. This location is decidedly earthly rather than heavenly, and as such would seem to support that the throne represents earthly rather than cosmic rule. However, the throne does indeed reach all the way to heaven, allowing the one seated upon it to see both below the earth and above the heavens. Such details might suggest the throne represents cosmic rather than merely earthly reign. Yet, Howard Jacobson notes that the mere ability of Moses to see the entire cosmos does not necessarily mean that he is being depicted as ruling over the entire cosmos.[33] Instead, these details might be understood in terms of an exaltation of God's appointed earthly ruler. Again, certainty regarding the scope of the throne's significance remains allusive. What then in our estimation becomes decisive is the very interpretation of Moses's dream offered by Moses's father-in-law, Raguel. Raguel says nothing of a cosmic rule nor even hints at one. Instead, Raguel interprets the dream in terms of Moses causing a throne to rise, presumably the kingly throne of Israel, and Moses himself ruling over people. The interpretation specifically addresses the significance of Moses being able to see below the earth and above the heavens, claiming that this means Moses will see things in the present, past, and future. In light of this analysis, it seems unnecessary to conclude that the throne Moses sits on represents God's heavenly throne or the cosmic sovereignty that throne represents. Instead, it seems best to interpret the throne as the text of the Exagogue itself does, namely as a symbol of earthly rule.

What is to be made of the stars bowing down before Moses? Many have pointed out that stars at times represent or are identified with angelic beings, and as such, the text could be suggesting that astral angelic beings are offering worship or at least veneration to Moses.[34] If Moses is indeed receiving worship from angelic beings, the scene certainly seems to push the boundaries established by exclusive monotheists. But another referent for understanding the prostration of the stars is available. As noted above, this dream of Moses has striking parallels to the dream of Joseph in Genesis 37:9–11. In this dream, the sun, moon, and stars all bow down before Joseph, yet the interpretation of the dream makes it clear that these heavenly bodies are not angelic or supernatural beings, but rather, they represent Joseph's own family members. This obeisance performed by Joseph's family is certainly not regarded as worship, but reverence given to one in authority over them. If this dream of Joseph is an intentional referent of Moses's dream in the Exagogue, a conclusion that seems highly plausible, then there is good reason to believe that the heavenly bodies represent human figures, and their action of bowing is best understood as veneration rather than worship. Again, we would point to the interpretation of the dream offered by the text itself, which mentions nothing about Moses receiving worship, but instead specifically speaks of Moses ruling over humans. This interpretation seems to favor the background of Joseph's dreams, in which heavenly bodies bowing down represent human submission to human rule.

Ultimately, we believe the case that Moses's dream depicts Moses being granted an earthly rule in which humans will submit to him is ultimately stronger than the case that Moses is granted a cosmic rule in which heavenly beings will worship him. While the details of the dream can be interpreted in different ways, we contend the interpretation of the dream offered by the text itself, a factor too often neglected, should be decisive in the dream's interpretation.[35]

In light of this assessment, a case that Moses might in some way represent a divine being who is either included in prerogatives of Israel's God or is in fact a "second power" is weak.[36] The evidence that Moses sits on God's throne and receives worship is far from conclusive, and in fact, the text's own interpretation of the dream actually seems to point away from such conclusions. Yet, even if one were to push for such conclusions, so that the Moses of the Exagogue fits two of our criteria (sitting on the divine throne and worship), Moses's unambiguous human identity and role as a human agent seemingly works against the conclusion that he would be recognized as the "second power in heaven." In the Jewish traditions we have considered above, the human Moses encounters entities that we have already established as second power figures, including God's Word and the Angel of the Lord. Thus, if our assessments of those traditions are correct, the adherents of those traditions would not recognize Moses as the second power. Thus, while there are certainly traditions in which Moses is an extremely exalted and revered figure, he seems to be a decidedly human one, and contra Orlov, not best understood as a second power figure.[37]

While we reject the conclusion that the Exagogue depicts Moses as a divine figure or second power, we do wonder if the Exagogue might affirm a two powers theology in another way. As discussed above, Moses's dream includes a man sitting on a throne and holding a scepter. Though many conclude that this figure is the God of Israel, we wonder if such a conclusion might benefit from greater nuance. Within the Moses scriptural tradition and its interpretation, clear tensions exist between the visibility and invisibility of YHWH. In Exodus 33:20, YHWH tells Moses that he cannot see his face and live, a tradition that is repeated in Exagogue 101. If the figure that Moses sees in his dream is indeed Israel's God, then a tension exists within the Exagogue over God's visibility. Interestingly, this same tension exists in the Exodus tradition. In Exodus 33:11, the text claims that Moses spoke to YHWH "face to face," while only 9 verses later it claims no one can see God's face and live. Within the Second Temple period, this tension is at times solved by concluding that Moses spoke face to face with a mediating figure, such as the Angel of the Lord or God's Word, whom we have to this point identified as the "second power." We suggest that the same approach might explain the tension in the Exagogue, by which the embodied divine figure that appears to Moses in his dream is the second power, such as the Angel of the Lord or the Son of Man. While such a conclusion is indeed uncertain and thus not direct evidence of a two powers theology, we do believe it is consistent with and fits well within such a framework.

THE JEWISH HIGH PRIEST

In the Second Temple period, the role of the Jewish high priest becomes the object of significant theological speculation and imagination. The high priest is often closely connected with the notion of God's own glory and at times functions as a means by which that glory is revealed to God's people.[38] The priest's function as an attendant in God's Temple often takes on cosmic dimensions, as the earthly Temple is understood as a mirror of the heavenly Temple in which God is attended by angels.[39] By way of such an understanding of the earthly Temple, the high priest can be depicted as functioning in the midst of the angelic servants of Israel's God and even occupying the space between God's heavenly and earthly dwelling. In light of such Second Temple understanding of the Jewish high priest, some proponents of an inclusive monotheism have pointed to this figure as one who at times shares in what exclusive monotheists would regard as the prerogatives of Israel's God alone. Here we assess these examples and consider to what degree Israel's high priest might be included in divine prerogatives.

Recipient of Worship

In his *Antiquities*, Josephus recounts an episode in which Alexander the Great comes to Jerusalem on his way to battle King Darius of Persia. The high priest, Jaddua, along with a significant entourage of priests, went out to meet Alexander. Seeing the entourage of priests, Alexander approached them alone and "prostrated himself before the Name and first greeted the high priest (προσεκύνησε τὸ ὄνομα καὶ τὸν ἀρχιερέα πρῶτος ἠσπάσατο)."[40] This action surprises all who come with Alexander. Alexander's second in command, Parmenion, asks him why, when all men prostrate themselves before Alexander, Alexander "had prostrated himself before the high priest of the Jews (αὐτὸς προσκυνήσειε τὸν Ἰουδαίων ἀρχιερέα)."[41] To this Alexander replies, "It was not before him that I prostrated myself but the god (θεόν) of whom he has the honour to be the high priest."[42] Alexander then gives the following reason for his actions: "for it was he whom I saw in my sleep in the form that he is now, when I was at Dium in Macedonia and, as I was considering with myself how I might become master of Asia, he urged me not to hesitate but to cross over confidently, for he himself would lead my army and give over to me the empire of the Persians."[43] Crispin Fletcher-Louis has contended that this tradition offers an example in which the high priest of Israel shares in, or in some way is an actual recipient of, the worship offered to the God of Israel.[44] To make this case, Fletcher-Louis seemingly has to overcome two significant hurdles. First, the text specifically states that Alexander worshiped the "Name," a clear reference to the name of Israel's God, and only hailed the high priest. Second, when Parmenion asks why Alexander prostrated himself in worship before the high priest of the Jews, Alexander corrects him, explicitly saying that he did not prostrate himself before the high priest, but rather the god the high priest serves. Thus, Alexander seemingly excludes the high priest from his act of worship.[45]

While recognizing these challenges, Fletcher-Louis offers a number of arguments that the tradition indeed reflects the high priest's inclusion in the worship of YHWH. He begins by setting the entire narrative in the larger context of Greco-Roman ruler cults. While he concludes the episode is ultimately a polemic against such cults, he argues that many features within the narrative are best understood in light of this larger context.[46] For example, he contends that all of the priests hailing Alexander *might* be considered an affirmation of Alexander's divinity in some way.[47] He also notes that in the ruler cult, the ruler often dresses like a god. In light of this common feature of ruler cults, Fletcher-Louis makes much of the fact that the supernatural figure that appears to Alexander in his dream, presumably the God of Israel, shares the same appearance as the high priest himself. He argues that the narrative picks up the common feature of a ruler dressing as a god and intends to depict the high priest in just such a light. The priest's intentional depiction as a god is an important piece in Fletcher-Louis's case that the high priest is indeed a recipient of worship.[48]

Fletcher-Louis also notes that the episode is an example of the common *adventus* trope, in which a ruler visits his subjects.[49] A common feature of this trope is the bringing forth images of the city's god to meet the visiting ruler. The visiting ruler then offers worship to those gods when he encounters them. Fletcher-Louis contents that in this story, the priest himself functions as the image or idol of the God of Israel, and following the trope receives worship from Alexander.[50]

While the text appears to specify that worship is given to the "Name" and that the high priest is merely hailed by Alexander, Fletcher-Louis argues that the high priest himself would have been included in the worship of the "Name."[51] He notes that the high priest would bear this very name of Israel's God on his headgear, and also argues that the high priest's clothing functions to make him "the visual and ritual embodiment of Israel's God."[52] Fletcher-Louis also sees a precedent in Josephus in which the high priest is identified directly with the divine name. He offers the following translation of the description of the high priest Ananus's words in *The Jewish War* 4.164: "But wearing the high priest's vestments *and being called by the most honored of revered names* (ἀλλὰ περικείμενος τὴν ἀρχιερατικὴν ἐσθῆτα καὶ τὸ τιμιώτατον καλούμενος τῶν σεβασμίων ὀνομάτων)." From this text, Fletcher-Louis contends that Josephus understood the high priest of Israel to be called by the name of the God he represents, and thus, finds support for the notion that when Josephus claims that Alexander worshiped the name, the high priest himself would be included in such worship.[53]

Yet, there are a number of weaknesses that plague Fletcher-Louis's argument. While he is indeed correct that the episode takes place in the context of emperor worship, he seems not to take seriously his own recognition that the episode functions as a polemic against such worship. That is, the scene presents one of the most famously worshiped rulers, Alexander the Great, worshipping Israel's God. In a text that he recognizes as a polemic against ruler worship, it is baffling that he concludes it possible that the hailing by Alexander could be understood as worship, as this conclusion seems to run contrary to the very aims of the polemic.

Regarding the narrative's use of the *adventus* trope, Fletcher-Louis is indeed correct. Yet, we would contend that trope is cleverly "Judaized," so that it addresses the proper way in which a visiting king approaches and engages the God of Israel. Such an issue would be of great relevance for Jews living in a Greco-Roman milieu in which *adventus* was a common feature. Alexander is presented as a positive example of a king's visitation and engagement with Israel's God. He meets and reveres God's representative, he worships the God of Israel from a distance, and then under the guidance of the high priest he makes a sacrifice. Alexander thus stands in stark contrast to his distant successor, Antiochus IV, who defiled the altar of God and placed an altar to an idol over it. He also stands in contrast with the Roman emperor Caligula, who sought to erect a statue of himself in the Jerusalem Temple. Such a "Judaizing" understanding of the adventus trope, seems to adequately account for Josephus's use of it. There seems little need to conclude that Josephus uses the trope in order to depict the Jewish high priest as an idol that represents the God of Israel. As noted above, such intention would seemingly sit in conflict with the story's polemic against ruler worship. It would, at the very least, create confusion over which rulers can, in fact, receive worship, as the reader is left to somehow arrive at the conclusion that worship granted to Alexander is wrong, but that worship granted to the high priest, Israel's ruler, is acceptable.

Fletcher-Louis's case that the high priest would have been included in the worship of the "Name" is also problematic. While he may be correct in saying the visual appearance of the high priest finds parallels in visual depictions of Israel's God, that the high priest was understood as the visible and ritual embodiment of that God is debatable at best. Additionally, the degree to which such an identity would lead to including the high priest in the worship of Israel's God lacks a credible basis in the extant evidence. In making his case, Fletcher-Louis's argument rests heavily on his conclusion that elsewhere in Josephus, the high priest of God is called by the name of YHWH and thus in some way is identified with Israel's God. Yet, we contend there is an alternative interpretation of the text he relies on (*J.W.* 4.164). Fletcher-Louis misses what seems to be an intentional parallelism between two clauses of the passage he cites from Josephus. The first clause reads: ἀλλὰ περικείμενος τὴν ἀρχιερατικὴν ἐσθῆτα, which we would argue should be translated, "But wearing the highest priestly vestments." The second clause parallels the first, both in grammatical structure (passive participle followed by what might be called a "retained accusative") and, we would argue, in the use of intentional *priestly* superlatives. As such, we would interpret the second clause, καὶ τὸ τιμιώτατον καλούμενος τῶν σεβασμίων ὀνομάτων, "and being called by the most honored of revered names," to be referring to the realm of priests specifically and not to *all* names. That is to say, the text is claiming that the priest is called by the most revered name *among priests*, the high priest of Israel.[54] Thus, the priest who is speaking in the text is claiming to have the best priestly garments and the best priestly name of all other priests. He is not claiming to be called by the name YHWH. The fact that Second Temple Jews were already being very careful with the divine name by the first century CE (even avoiding it in speech and writing), it seems highly implausible that this text intends to communicate that the high priest of Israel was called by the personal name of Israel's God. Without additional evidentiary support, this interpretation of Josephus is untenable. Yet, even if one concluded that Josephus is claiming that the high priest is called by the name YHWH in *Jewish War* 4.164, the fact that in *Antiquities* 11.331 Josephus intentionally separates the "Name" and the "high priest," claiming that Alexander "worshipped the Name and hailed the high priest," suggests that he is not including the high priest in the worship of the Name. That he later intentionally depicts Alexander claiming that he did not worship the high priest but only the high priest's deity further supports such a conclusion.

Finally, what is to be made of the shared appearance between the "god" that appears to Alexander in his dream and the high priest? Fletcher-Louis understands this shared appearance in terms of the ruler cult motif, in which rulers who are worshipped often present themselves as one of the traditional deities. But again, we ask, whether such an interpretation makes sense of a text that is clearly a polemic against ruler cults? We find such a conclusion highly unlikely.

Here, we want to consider further the significance of the shared appearance between the high priest and the god that appears to Alexander. To this end, the nature of the shared appearance requires further explanation. Alexander's explicit comment that he does not worship the high priest but the God who appeared to him in a dream demonstrates that Alexander can discern between the appearance of the two. In other words, they are not identical in appearance. While Alexander says that he saw this God in the form in which the high priest currently now exists, a later detail seems to offer clarification on the nature of the shared form. Alexander adds, "Since, therefore, I have beheld no one else in such robes, and on seeing him now I am reminded of the vision and the exhortation."[55] This text seems to suggest that the similarity between the two figures is the priestly vestments that they wear, the distinguishable garments. If the priestly vestments are indeed that which is shared in appearance between the high priest and the God who appeared to Alexander, an interesting interpretive option emerges.

Alexander understands the figure that appears to him in a dream to be the God of Israel. We suggest there are a number of details that would be consistent with identifying this figure as an expression of a two powers theology. First, there is the shared appearance with the high priest, or more precisely they both wear the same priestly vestments. Such a shared appearance calls to mind Philo's depiction of the Logos as a high priest that mediates between God and his creation (*Her.* 205–6). A figure identified as the God of Israel that wears the vestments of the high priest would be consistent with such an understanding of the Logos. Second, Alexander states that the figure that appeared to him promised that he would lead his army and grant him success. This sort of language is reminiscent of the language of the Angel of the Lord (the Logos in Philo) leading God's people into battle or the pillars of cloud and fire that go before Israel (e.g., Exod 14:19–20; 33:1–3; Josh 5:13–15; Judg 2:1–5; 2 Kings 19:35). As we have argued above, these entities are interpreted by some Second Temple Jews in terms of a second power. That Alexander sees in his dream a figure that he identifies as the God of Israel is also suggestive. The invisibility of Israel's God is certainly engrained in a significant number of Jewish texts and traditions. We have shown how the visible appearance or manifestation of Israel's God could be understood in terms of a second power. Thus, the visibility of a figure identified as the God of Israel, might best be identified with the second power.

We contend the shared appearance between the high priest and the divine figure that appears to Alexander need not be explained in terms of the high priest having a divine identity or as being a recipient of worship. Instead, this shared appearance could be explained in terms of a two powers theology, in which the second power, one that functions as a high priest meditating between the transcendent YHWH and creation, appears wearing the same priestly vestments as the earthly high priest, for whom he serves as a heavenly pattern.

Even so, regardless of whether this Josephus tradition reflects a two powers theology, the biggest weakness of Fletcher-Louis's argument is the explicit claim made by Alexander in response to his general Parmenion, namely that he *did not prostrate* himself before the high priest, but rather before the god whom the high priest serves. There is no indication in these words that the high priest was included in the worship that Alexander offers to the God of Israel, and we contend that Josephus did not intend to portray the high priest as a recipient of such worship. As such, as it regards worship, the high priest cannot be regarded as a figure that is in some way included in the divine prerogative of worship.

Association with God's Wisdom

An argument regarding Israel's high priest that has particular significance for the present study is Crispin Fletcher-Louis's claim that the high priest is rightly understood as the embodiment or actualization of God's Wisdom.[56] Given our previous discussion of God's Wisdom and our conclusion that Wisdom is (at times) rightly understood in terms of the second power,[57] such a claim regarding the high priest is significant. Is the high priest truly understood as the embodiment of God's Wisdom by some Second Temple Jews? And if he is, should Israel's high priest himself be understood as an expression of this second power?

Fletcher-Louis provides numerous noteworthy parallels between the description of Wisdom in Sirach 24 and the description of the high priest Simon in Sirach 50.[58] The parallels are indeed numerous and noteworthy. Both Wisdom and the high priest are connected to ministering before God in the temple/tabernacle (24:10; 50:5). Both are compared to a cedar in Lebanon (24:13; 50:12), to a cypress (24:13; 50:10), to roses (24:14; 50:8), to a healthy olive tree (24:14; 50:10), and to a plant beside water (24:14, "as a plane tree beside water"; 50:8, "as lilies beside a spring of water"). Both are also connected to the incense burning in the temple (24:15; 50:9). These parallels certainly seem intentional and an attempt to establish a connection of some sort between Wisdom and the high priest Simon. From these parallels, Fletcher-Louis argues that the high priest is being depicted as the embodiment and actualization of God's Wisdom. Drawing on the notion that the earthly temple is not only an earthly representative of a heavenly temple but that it also represents the entire cosmos in miniature, Fletcher-Louis argues that the role Wisdom plays in relation to the cosmos is played by the high priest in the earthly representation of the cosmos, the temple.[59] But one wonders why the language of embodiment or actualization is needed. Instead, it seems that a relationship of representation might just as adequately account for the parallels between Wisdom and the high priest. As noted above, God's Word can be depicted as a high priest and one that mediates between God and his created order. Given the close association between the concepts of Word and Wisdom,[60] it seems plausible that Sirach is trying to convey a similar identity for Wisdom. In this way, the high priest could be understood as a human representative of God's Wisdom and thus an earthly expression of Wisdom's heavenly role. Therefore, while Sirach certainly seems to be communicating a connection between God's Wisdom and God's high priest, there does not seem to be any necessary reason to conclude that the priest is the embodiment of God's Wisdom, as Fletcher-Louis contends.

Association with Creation

Building on his argument that Sirach depicts the Jewish high priest as an embodiment of God's Wisdom, Fletcher-Louis also argues that Sirach depicts the high priest as engaging in the act of creation itself.[61] His argument contends that in Sirach 24:3–7, Wisdom is depicted as engaged in the act of creation.[62] In this argument, he sees a complex textual interplay between these verses in Sirach, Genesis 1 and Exodus 25–31. In Exodus 25–31, the seven speeches of Moses parallel the seven days of creation and contribute to the conclusion that the Tabernacle represents the entire cosmos, or the cosmos in miniature.[63] According to Fletcher-Louis, the author of Sirach is then drawing on these parallels in his presentation of Wisdom as an agent of creation.[64] Fletcher-Louis then contends that in Sirach 50 the author is drawing on all three texts (Sirach 24, Gen 1, and Ex 25–31), in an effort to present the Jewish high priest, the embodiment of Wisdom, as cocreator in his administration of his duties in the temple.[65] Here, we will address a number of potential problems for both his arguments and the ultimate conclusions he draws from them.

First, Fletcher-Louis's argument that Wisdom is depicted as an agent of creation in Sirach 24 is questionable. While commentators have noted a parallel between God creating through his Word and Wisdom in Sirach coming forth from the mouth of God as covering the earth like a mist (24:3), any explicit claim that Wisdom is being depicted as a creative agent is noticeably absent.[66] While Wisdom comes from God's mouth, the actions ascribed to it, on the surface, do not appear to be acts of creation. It covers the earth like a mist, but it is not described in any way shaping or organizing the cosmos. While it both compasses the vault of heaven and traverses the depth of the abyss (24:5), details Fletcher-Louis rightly identifies with the waters above and waters below that were created on the second day, the text never depicts Wisdom as the agent that separates or organizes these two spheres. If Sirach did indeed intend to present Wisdom as God's creative agent, one would expect Wisdom not only to occupy these spaces, but to be explicitly linked to their establishment. And it is not as though Sirach does not know traditions such as Proverbs 8 that are quite explicit in depicting Wisdom as God's agent in creation. As discussed previously, Wisdom of Solomon is a rather contemporary piece of Wisdom literature to Sirach that explicitly depicts Wisdom as an agent through whom God creates. If Sirach truly intended to present

Wisdom as an agent in creation, it is difficult to explain why it did not do so in a more explicit manner. One wonders if the reader of Sirach would be aware of the complex intertextuality used by Fletcher-Louis to make a case that Wisdom is depicted as God's agent in creation. Even when one does consider this intertextuality, it is hard to discern if Wisdom is depicted as an agent of creation or merely depicted as an entity that inhabits, reigns over, and provides blessing to all spheres of creation. If Sirach intended to present Wisdom as God's agent in creation, it has done so in an opaque manner that obscures this presentation for the reader.

Our assessment of Fletcher-Louis's argument about Wisdom has direct implications for his assessment of the Jewish high priest as an active agent in creation. As noted above, Fletcher-Louis's case that the high priest is an agent in creation is dependent on his case that the high priest is the embodiment of God's Wisdom, and that in the text of Sirach, he parallels the creative acts of God's Wisdom. Yet, if Sirach does not depict Wisdom as an agent of creation, whatever the parallels between Wisdom and the high priest signify, they cannot signify the high priest as an agent of creation. As with its depiction of Wisdom, if Sirach sought to depict the high priest Simon as an agent of creation, it certainly could have done so in a more explicit and obvious manner.

Yet, even if one accepted all of Fletcher-Louis's contentions, regarding Sirach depicting Wisdom as an agent in creation, and that Sirach presents the high priest as an embodiment of God's Wisdom making the high priest as in some sense a co-agent with God in creation, one still has to contend with the reality that the high priest does not actually create the cosmos or engage in that creative act. At best, one can say that the high priest participates in a temple ceremony that parallels the original act of creation. Such a ceremonial act may indeed convey the greatness of the high priestly role and the way in which this figure is a human representative of the God of Israel. However, it falls well short of the actual activity of participating in the creation of the cosmos. In other words, if Sirach intends to present the high priest engaged in an act that parallel's the creation of the cosmos, there is a significant difference between this act of the high priest and the actions of God's Word and Wisdom, which in many traditions (even if not in Sirach) *actually* participate in creating the cosmos.

The High Priest and the YHWH of Israel

In light of our analysis here, while there are indeed traditions in which the high priest is an exalted figure, perhaps even a figure that in certain ways shares in the glory of Israel's God, the high priest fails to meet unambiguously any of the criteria set forth for establishing an entity as a second power in heaven. The case that the high priest receives worship is relatively weak, and alternative explanations of the extant data remain more compelling. While Sirach might intentionally create a parallel between God's Wisdom and the high priest, there is no reason to go beyond the conclusion that both are being depicted as playing an intercessory role. Additionally, while the high priest might symbolically engage in the act of creation, unlike God's Word and Wisdom, he does not, in fact, create anything. Ultimately, all of the potential parallels that have led some interpreters to propose a potential divine identity for Israel's high priest fall short of establishing any sort of divine identification.

Thus far, the candidates for exalted humans, Adam, Moses, and the high priest, do not meet the criteria set for classifying an individual as divine and whether said individual could be understood as the second power of heaven. The next possibility, however, looks more promising, even if this figure is less easily identified and so offers very little about which to be certain. Nonetheless, it is worth comparing these previous exalted humans with one who is described in the Qumran text known as The Self-Glorification Hymn.

AN UNSPECIFIED FIGURE IN THE SELF-GLORIFICATION HYMN

In the Dead Sea Scrolls, there appears to have existed a hymn of glorification spoken by an unspecified figure about himself. The hymn exists in various fragments from different scroll texts, but there is strong evidence that these various fragments present a common tradition or various recensions of a single tradition.[67] To give a better sense of the hymn and its content, we offer Esther Eshel's translation of 4Q491 c frg 1, that largely comprises recension B.[68]

1. [let them praise him] in wonderful glorious things
2. [because of] the power of his might, the ri[gh]teous will praise and the holy ones will rejoice [because of . . .
3. [I]srael. He established his truth of old, and the secrets of his devising throughout all [generations
4. [] and the council of the humble for an everlasting congregation.
5. [for]ever a mighty throne in the congregation of the angels. None of the ancient kings shall sit in it, and their nobles shall not[
6. []shall not be like my glory, and none shall be exalted save me, nor shall come against me. For I have taken my seat in his [throne]in the heavens and none[

7. [] I shall be reckoned with the angels, and established in the holy congregation. I do not desire as a man of flesh[] everything precious to me
   is in the glory of
8. [the angels in the dwelli]ng place. Who has been despised on my
   account? And who can be compared with me in glory? Who [
9. [] who be[ars all] grief as I do? and who [suff]ers evil like me? []and
   (any) teaching will not be equal to [my teaching]
10. []who will stop me from speaking and who shall measure the flow of my
    speech, and who shall be my equal, and be like (me) in my judgement?
11. []For I shall be reckoned with the angels, and my glory with [that of]
    the King's sons. Neither refined gold, nor of Ophir
12. vacat
13. [rejoice] O righteous with the Lord [] in the holy dwelling, praise [him]
14. [l]et the music sound of the Hagu (lyre?)[] in everlasting joy, and no
    destruction
15. []to establish the horn of the Mess[iah [
16. [] to declare his hand in might [
17. [. . .]

Significant debate exists over the identity of the unspecified figure at the
heart of this hymn. A variety of solutions have been offered. Some have
argued for an angelic identity, particularly the angel Michael.[69] Others conclude that the figure is decidedly human, though a human who is clearly
exalted. Within this human option, a number of proposals have been offered,
including a royal messiah, the teacher of righteousness, a priestly figure,
Enoch, and Melchizedek.[70]

When we consider the features attributed to this figure, the reason for
such diverse identifications becomes clear. The figure claims a place among
the angels in heaven, which might suggest a heavenly angelic figure such as
Michael. Though some have responded that such a claim makes an angelic
identity less likely, as it may be intended to contrast a non-angelic figure
(i.e., a human) with angelic figures.[71] As an example of such a figure, we have
also seen that Enoch himself, whether identified with/as the Son of Man or
not, can be depicted as having a heavenly dwelling among the angels. And
given the connection between this Enochic Son of Man and the Messiah, a
place among the angels could also be fitting of a messiah figure. Such a place
among the angels might also fit the figure of Melchizedek as described in the
scrolls themselves.

This figure also seems to be enthroned in heaven and perhaps sits on God's
very throne. If the throne is indeed God's, the description would be unique
for an angel such as Michael, but as we have seen, not unique for a figure
like the Angel of the Lord or the Enochic Son of Man, the latter also being

identified as the Messiah. If the throne is not God's, then a heavenly throne could certainly belong to an angelic figure.[72] The comparison of this figure to kings and nobles, might suggest a royal messianic identity, one which both Enoch and Melchizedek might fit. But still also the text could be comparing an angel like Michael to lesser earthly kings. The detail regarding incomparable teaching fits well with either a figure like the sectarian teacher of righteousness or even a priestly figure, though it does not necessarily exclude either a messianic or angelic figure. That the figure distances itself from the desires of human flesh, might suggest a human who has moved beyond such carnal temptations, though on the contrary it might refer to an angelic figure for whom such desires were always foreign. In the speaker's questions about who has been despised more and who has suffered more than himself some see a clear allusion to the suffering servant of Isaiah, raising the question of possible messianic identity.

Given the descriptors in this text, the multiplicity among interpreters of the possible object of the hymn's glorification is not surprising. The text indeed brings together what seem like angelic, messianic, and priestly descriptors, making any one interpretation plausible. But the unity of all of these various descriptions might be telling in and of themselves, and a figure in which all such descriptors properly converge may provide the best interpretive option. We propose that we find just such convergence in the concept of a second power in heaven. As we saw in Philo, God's Word, best understood as the second power in heaven, is also identified as the Angel of the Lord that is active in Israel's scriptures and bears the name YHWH. Likewise, God's Wisdom is often closely associated with God's angels, as it dwells among them and rules over them, but it is also at times identified with the Angel of the Lord. Thus, it seems the second power could be understood in angelic terms and as both living with and reigning over all other angels. Such a description seems to fit Qumran's Hymn of Self-Glorification quite well, as the figure in the hymn both dwells with angels but also has a greater glory than the angels and possibly even reigns over them (see line 5 in which the figure has a mighty throne among the angels). Yet, we have also seen a connection between a second power in heaven and God's Messiah. The Enochic Son of Man is clearly identified as God's Messiah, and such an identity also seems closely associated with the Melchizedek of the Dead Sea Scrolls. Such an identity of the second power would make sense of the glorification hymn's contrast between the speaker and the ancient kings and nobles, as well as possible allusions to Isaiah's suffering servant. But not only have we demonstrated a connection between the second power and both an angelic and messianic identity, we have also demonstrated a connection between the second power and a priestly identity. The Logos is clearly portrayed as a high priest. And Melchizedek, if rightly identified as a second power, also is closely associated with a priestly (and kingly) identity. Thus, if we have a second power in heaven that is understood in terms of an angelic, messianic, and priestly identity, such a figure would seem to fit the object to the glorification hymn particularly well.

Yet, there are other indicators in the hymn that would seem to favor identifying the speaker as the second power over against merely a great angel, the messiah, or an exalted priestly figure. The hymn's use of superlatives in describing the speaker are quite striking and seem to parallel the use of superlatives in Hebrew scripture to describe the God of Israel. Twice the figure references his incomparable glory (line 6 and 8), a claim that would on its own seemingly point to the God of Israel. How could a figure lower than the God of Israel make such a claim? Yet more striking is the manner in which such a claim is made. The claim in line 8, "Who can be compared with me in glory?" a claim that seems to be, in particular, contrast with the glory of the speaker with the angels/gods (אלים), finds many striking parallels in the Hebrew Bible. Exodus 15:11 reads, "Who is like you, O Lord, among the gods?"[73] Similarly Psalm 86:8 declares, "There is none like you among the gods, O Lord, nor are there any works like yours." Psalm 89:6 asks, "For who in the skies can be compared to the Lord? Who among the heavenly beings is like the Lord?"[74] The speaker's question in line 10, "Who can be my equal?" finds a striking parallel in Isaiah 46:5, where YHWH says, "To whom will you liken me and make me equal, and compare me, as though we were alike?" These parallels are stark, and thus it is likely that the author and reader identified the speaker as none other than the incomparable YHWH of Israel. Yet, despite the strength of these parallels, virtually no scholars have identified the speaker as Israel's God![75] The reason for this is likely that the hymn seems to speak of God as distinct from the speaker, particularly in line 11 where the hymn references "the King," which is understood as a reference to Israel's God. While such a reference would indeed be problematic if the God of Israel was understood in terms of strict singularity, it is not problematic for a two powers theology. In fact, identifying the speaker of the hymn as the second power seems to fit the hymn better than all other options, as it seems to best account for the entirety of the data: the heavenly dwelling, sitting on a (God's?) heavenly throne, messianic imagery, priestly imagery, and striking parallels to the superlative language attributed to Israel's God in the scriptures. We have already contended that at least one scroll presents the figure of Melchizedek as a second power in heaven. Thus, Melchizedek might very well be the specific expression of a two powers theology that is found in this hymn of glorification.[76]

ASSESSING THE STATUS OF EXALTED HUMANS

While some have sought to demonstrate that certain exalted human figures share in divine prerogatives such as worship, creation, or sitting on God's throne, here we have demonstrated that the cases for figures with a clear and unambiguous human identity (i.e., Adam, Moses, and the high priest) are quite weak. Our analysis demonstrated that none of these figures fit the established criteria for being identified as a second power. In contrast to such characters, the ambiguous figure at the center of the self-glorification hymn is explained quite well as a second power in heaven. The various descriptors of this figure that have vexed scholarly attempts at identification actually find a unified explanation in a second power figure, and thus, we contend this figure is best understood as such. Now that we have reviewed the primary candidates for a second power figure in the Second Temple period, we can offer some additional reflections and conclusions.

NOTES

1. See Wis. 10:1–2; 1QS IV, 23; 1 QH IV, 15; Philo, *Opif.* 83; 1 En. 85, 90:37; T. Ab. 11.

2. For a thorough discussion of such depictions of Adam in Second Temple literature, see Kirk, *A Man Attested*, 44–77. In particular, see Kirk's discussion on kings of the Ancient Near East being associated with the image of their gods, Kirk, *A Man Attested*, 52.

3. See, for example, Fletcher-Louis, *All the Glory of Adam,* 97.

4. The account is found in the Latin, Armenian, and Georgian versions, with slight variations in the details. It is absent in the Greek version. For the most recent critical edition of the *Life of Adam and Eve*, see S. J. P. Pettorelli and J. D. Kaestli, *Vita Latina Adae et Evae*, vol. 1–2 (CC Series Apocryphorum 18; Turnhout: Brepols, 2012). The volume includes a synopsis of the Latin (two versions), Greek, Georgian, and Armenian versions, as well as translation of the Greek text in French.

5. Much of the discussion that follows regarding this tradition was first published in Adam Winn, "The Life of Adam and Eve and the Nature of Second Temple Religious Devotion: Can Satan Be Trusted Concerning the Worship of Adam?" *JSP* 33 no.3 (2024): 198–216. The material appears here in a modified form.

6. For all English translations, see Gary A. Anderson and Michael E. Stone, *A Synopsis of the Books of Adam and Eve* (SBLEJL 17; Atlanta: Scholars Press, 1999), unless otherwise noted.

7. Fletcher-Louis, *Jesus Monotheism*, 171–205 and 250–92.

8. Orlov, *The Glory of the Invisible God,* 24–27.

9. See, for example, Hurtado, *Lord Jesus Christ*, 13; and Bauckham, *Jesus and the God of Israel*, 203–4.

10. See Bauckham, *Jesus and the God of Israel*, 203–4; M. de Jonge and J. Tromp, *The Life of Adam and Eve and Related Literature* (Sheffield: Sheffield Press, 1997), 65–78. See especially page 74 in which they recognize the case for either Christian or Jewish origins is weak.

11. M. de Jonge, "The Christian Origin of the Greek Life of Adam and Eve" in *Literature on Adam and Eve: Collected Essays*, eds. G. A. Anderson, M. Stone, J. Tromp (Leiden: Brill, 2000), 347–63.

12. See Jean-Daniel Kaestli, "Le mythe de la chute de Satan et la question du milieu d'origine de la *Vie d'Adam et Ève*" in *Early Christian Voices: In Texts, Traditions, and Symbols. Essays in Honor of François Bovon*, ed. D. Warren, A. G. Brock, D. W. Pao (Biblical Interpretation Series 66; Leiden: Brill, 2003), 342–54.

13. See Kaestli, "La *Vie d'Adam et Ève*: nouveaux acquis et questions ouvertes" in *La Vie d'Adam et Ève et les traditions adamiques*, eds. F. Amsler, A. Frey, J. D. Kaestli, and A. L. Rey (Publications de l'Institut romand des sciences bibliques 8; Lausanne: Zèbre, 2017), 44–47; Jan Dochorn, *Die Apokalypse des Mose. Text, Übersetzung, Kommentar* (TSAJ 106; Tübingen: Mohr Siebeck, 2005), 117–18 and 345–46.

14. Dochorn, "Die Adamiegesen und das Neu Testament" in *La Vie d'Adam et Ève et les traditions adamiques*, eds. F. Amsler, A. Frey, J. D. Kaestli, and A. L. Rey (Publications de l'Institut romand des sciences bibliques 8; Lausanne: Zèbre, 2017), 73–74. John R. Levison, "1 John 3.12, Early Judaism and the Greek Life of Adam and Eve," *Journal for the Study of the New Testament* 42, no. 4 (2020): 453–71, at 460 sides with the earlier dating (of the Greek LAE).

15. Bauckham, *Jesus and the God of Israel*, 204.

16. Bauckham, *Jesus and the God of Israel*, 204.

17. Fletcher-Louis, *Jesus Monotheism*, 269–76.

18. Given the complexity of the textual history of the *LAE*, narrative analysis that seeks to assess the texts witness to the Second Temple period is challenging. In light of the rearrangement of events within the textual tradition and the certainty of added narrative details (and perhaps even entire episodes), making confident assessments of plot development and characterization is problematic. However, some aspects of narrative analysis are still possible. For example, if one relies on traditions/pericopes that are regarded as stable (or relatively so), general conclusions on character construction could be made.

19. For those who argue for somewhat of a coherent narrative for a leading supernatural opponent of God, see Thomas J. Farrar, "New Testament Satanology and Leading Suprahuman Opponents in Second Temple Jewish Literature: A Religio-Historical Analysis," *JTS* 70, no. 1 (2019): 21–68; Ryan Stokes, *The Satan: How God's Executioner Became the Enemy* (Grand Rapids, MI: Eerdmans, 2019); and Henry Kelly, *Satan: A Biography* (Cambridge: Cambridge University Press, 2006); idem, *Satan in the Bible: God's Minister of Justice* (Eugene, OR: Cascade Books, 2017). For a case against such a conclusion, see T. de Bruin, "In Defense of New Testament Satanologies: A Response to Farrar and Williams," *JSNT* 44, no. 3 (2022): 435–51.

20. This translation is my own, but for the Latin version in which it is found, see Pettorelli and Kaestli, *Vita Latina*, 2.840. This tradition is also found, with slight

variations in the Greek, Armenian, and Georgian versions, though only in one of two Latin versions. This wide attestation supports it textual stability.

21. This passage comes in the narration of Eve's penance and is found in the Latin, Armenian, Georgian, Slavonic, and some Greek versions. It is missing in what has long been regarded as the best Greek manuscripts, and in the manuscripts in which it is found, it appears in a different narrative location. However, with Jean-Pierre Pettorelli's newly discovered and published second Latin version, a Latin version that betrays existence of another and perhaps earlier Greek model, there is now greater confidence in the originality of narration of Eve's penance (see Pettorelli and Kaestli, *Vita Latina*). For a case for the originality of the penance narrative, see Stone, "The Fall of Satan and Adam's Penance: Three Notes on *The Books of Adam and Eve*" in *Literature on Adam and Eve: Collected Essays*, ed. G. A. Anderson, M. Stone, and J. Tromp (Leiden: Brill, 2000), 43–56.

22. See the previous footnote on the textual veracity of this pericope.

23. While some have argued for extant traditions in which Adam is the object of worship, these examples fall short of demonstrating that Adam is rightly worshiped by angels or human beings. One example is found in Philo, where the animals of creation bow down before Adam (*Opif.* 83). Yet, this tradition can hardly be equated with the tradition found in the *LAE*, as it is best understood as the animals of creation recognizing Adam as their king and ruler and not the offering of cultic devotion. Another example is found in rabbinic tradition. At least two rabbinic sources pass on a tradition in which angels mistakenly worship Adam because he is made in the image of God. This mistake is quickly remedied by God when Adam falls asleep and it becomes clear he is not God (*Gen. Rab.* 8:10 and *Eccl. Rabb.* 6:9.1). While some have argued that this tradition is a polemic against the tradition found in the LAE, such a conclusion is far from necessary (see Steenburg, "The Worship of Adam," 98; and C. R. A. Morray-Jones, "Transformational Mysticism in the Apocalyptic-Merkabah Tradition," *JJS* 43, no. 1 [1992]: 17). Yet, it is also quite possible that the *LAE* is drawing on the tradition reflected in these rabbinic texts and presenting Satan as distorting them.

24. While earlier scholarship sought to understand Moses of Philo and other Second Temple traditions as a θεῖος ἀνήρ (e.g., D. L. Tiede, *The Charismatic Figure as Miracle Worker* [SBLDS 1; Missoula, MT: Scholars Press, 1972], 101–240), the existence of the entire concept of such a figure has been widely rejected. See, for example, the influential work of Carl R. Holladay, Theios Aner *in Hellenistic-Judaism: A Critique of the Use of This Category in New Testament Christology* (SBLDS 40; Missoula, MT: Scholars Press, 1977). Yet, Fletcher-Louis has continued to read Moses as a divine figure in Philo (Fletcher-Louis, "4Q374: A Discourse on the Sinai Tradition: The Deification of Moses and Early Christology," *DSD* 3 [3 1996] 242). For a strong rebuttal to those who perceive in Philo a divine Moses, see John Lierman, *The New Testament Moses: Christian Perceptions of Moses and Israel in the Setting of Jewish Religion* (Tübingen: Mohr Siebeck, 2004), 194; see also, Kirk, *Man Attested*, 83–84; Hurtado, *One God*, 59–64. Fletcher-Louis has also sought to argue that a DSS fragment, 4Q374, could present a deified Moses ("4Q374"). Such a conclusion has

been embraced by few and is far from clear, with the fragment offering natural interpretations in which Moses is not understood as divine.

25. See Kirk, *A Man Attested*, 84–86, as one who understands this tradition in terms of an inclusive monotheism, as well as Fletcher-Louis, "4Q374," 245–46. The difference between Kirk and Fletcher-Louis is that the former understands Moses as an idealized human who is allowed to participate in divine prerogatives, whereas the latter understands Moses as a divinized human participating in divine prerogatives. See Orlov, *The Glory of the Invisible God*, 28–31, as one who understands this tradition in terms of a two powers monotheism.

26. Exagogue 69.

27. Exagogue 82.

28. For such a position, see Kirk, *A Man Attested*, 85; Orlov, *The Glory of the Invisible God*, 29; Kristine J. Ruffatto, "Raguel as Interpreter of Moses' Throne Vision: The Transcendent Identity of Raguel in the Exagoge of Ezekiel the Tragedian" *JSP* 17, no. 2 (2008): 121–23; Gregory E. Sterling, "From the Thick Marshes of the Nile to the Throne of God: Moses in Ezekiel the Tragedian and Philo of Alexandria," in *Studia Philonica Annual*, volume 26, eds. David T. Runia et al. (Atlanta: SBL, 2014), 129–33; Pieter van der Horst, "Moses' Throne Vision in Ezekiel the Dramatist," *JJS* 34 (1983): 21–29.

29. See, for example, Bauckham, *Jesus and the God of Israel*, 166–68; as well as Jacobson, "Mysticism and Apocalyptic in Ezekiel's Exagoge," *Illinois Classical Studies* 8 (1981): 273–93.

30. See Kirk, *A Man Attested*, 84–86; Fletcher-Louis, "4Q374," 242–46.

31. Even Bauckham (*God of Israel*, 166–69) and Hurtado (*One God, One Lord*, 57–59) recognize the throne as God's own, though Bauckham will conclude that in the dream, the divine throne is merely a heavenly representation of Moses's earthly rule.

32. See R. G. Robertson, "Ezekiel the Tragadian," *OTP* 2:812. For similar assessments, see Orolov, *Invisible God*, 29; Ruffatto, "Raguel as Interpreter," 121–23; Kirk, *A Man Attested*, 85; Fletcher-Louis, "4Q374," 245–46; van der Horst, "Moses' Throne," 25.

33. Jacobson, "Mysticism," 273.

34. See Hurtado, *One God, One Lord*, 59; Orlov, *The Glory of the Invisible God*, 31; Ruffatto, "Polemics within Enochic Traditions," 205; S. N. Bunta, "Moses, Adam, and The Glory of the Lord in Ezekiel the Tragedian: On the Roots of a Merkabah Text" (PhD diss; Marquette University, 2005), 167–83.

35. Bauckham notes the consistent failure on the part of interpreters to take seriously the given interpretation of the dream for understanding the nature and significance of the dream that is described (*God of Israel*, 166–67).

36. If one understands the "second power" in terms of simply another powerful agent, distinct from but representative of the God of Israel, such as Orlov's understanding (*Invisible God*, 128–32), then Moses's dream in the *Exagogue* may support such a view, as it is quite similar to that of an "inclusive monotheism." Though as noted above, we see such a position as unlikely.

37. While some might insist that traditions in Philo or the Exagogue suggest Moses received deification, i.e., is translated into an angelic or supernatural figure, he still clearly remains distinct from the God of Israel.

38. See, for example, Sir 50; T. Levi 18; Jub. 31.11–17; 1Q28b; 4Q400. For a thorough discussion of these texts, see Kirk, *A Man Attested*, 124–35; and Fletcher-Louis, *All the Glory of Adam*, 61–84.

39. See Kirk, *A Man Attested*, 124–35; and Fletcher-Louis, *All the Glory of Adam*, 61–68.

40. *Ant.* 11.331. This scene is also discussed in chapter 6 with regard to "the Name of God."

41. *Ant.* 11.333.

42. *Ant.* 11.333.

43. *Ant.* 11.334.

44. See Fletcher-Louis, "Alexander the Great's Worship," 71–102. In this work, Fletcher-Louis not only draws on the episode as recorded by Josephus, but on four other later accounts, accounts that post-date the Second Temple period. These include the account from a Judaizing version of the Alexander Romance (date of origin is highly questionable, but likely later than the fourth century CE), Babylonian Talmud tractate *Yoma* (c. fifth to sixth century CE), Josippon (tenth century CE), and the Samaritan Chronicle (thirteenth century CE). Because of the late date of these documents, they will not be treated here. Though we note that despite Fletcher-Louis's claim, that the high priest is presented as divine in any of these documents, is highly questionable (cf. Fletcher-Louis, "Alexander the Great's Worship," 78–79). It should also be noted that in this work, Fletcher-Louis relies heavily on the analysis of S. J. D. Cohen, "Alexander the Great and Jaddus the High Priest according to Josephus" *AJSR* 7–8 (1982–1983): 41–68.

45. See the next lines (*Ant.* 11.336), where Alexander accompanies the high priest into the temple, where he "sacrificed to God under the direction of the high priest, and showed due honour to the priests and to the high priest himself."

46. Fletcher-Louis, "Worship of the High Priest," 84–86.

47. Fletcher-Louis, "Worship of the High Priest," 85.

48. Fletcher-Louis, "Worship of the High Priest," 86–87.

49. Fletcher-Louis, "Worship of the High Priest," 89–90.

50. Fletcher-Louis, "Worship of the High Priest," 89.

51. Fletcher-Louis, "Worship of the High Priest," 87–89.

52. Fletcher-Louis, "Worship of the High Priest," 88.

53. Fletcher-Louis, "Worship of the High Priest," 88–89.

54. Note that this is the understanding of Whiston in his translation of this text, a point noted and critiqued by Fletcher-Louis. Yet, we feel that Whiston has rightly captured the sense of this passage conveyed by the structure of the text, contra Fletcher-Louis.

55. *Ant.* 11.335.

56. Fletcher-Louis, *All the Glory of Adam*, 73–74.

57. See in chapter 4.

58. Fletcher-Louis, *All the Glory of Adam*, 74.

59. Fletcher-Louis, *All the Glory of Adam*, 74.

60. See our discussion above in chapter 4.

61. Fletcher-Louis, *All the Glory of Adam*, 74–75.

62. Fletcher-Louis, *All the Glory of Adam*, 77.

63. Fletcher-Louis, *All the Glory of Adam*, 76–78.

64. Fletcher-Louis, *All the Glory of Adam*, 77–78.

65. Fletcher-Louis, *All the Glory of Adam*, 80–81.

66. See, for example, G. T. Sheppard, *Wisdom as a Hermeneutical Construct: A Study in the Sapientializing of the Old Testament* (BZAW 151; Berlin: de Gruyter, 1980), 22–27. And see our discussion in chapter 4.

67. For a thorough discussion of the various fragments of the hymn and reconstruction of its possible recensions, see Esther Eshel, "'4Q471B': A Self-Glorification Hymn," *RevQ* 17, no. 1 (1996): 175–203.

68. For this translation, see Eshel, "A Self-Glorification Hymn," 184–85. For the translations of 4Q471ᵇ and 4QHᵃ that comprise recension B, see Eshel, "A Self-Glorification Hymn," 178 and 187–88.

69. For the first to make such an identification, see Maurice Baillet, *Qumran grotte 4.III (4Q482-4Q520)* (DJD 7, Oxford: Clarendon, 1982); see also, A. S. van der Woude, "Discoveries in the Judean Desert, Band," volume 7, *TRu* 55, no. 3 (1990): 253–62; Hengel, "Zur Wirkungsgeschichte von Jes 53 in vorchristlicher Zeit" in *Der leidende Gottesknecht: Jesaja 53 und seine Wirkungsgeschichte*, eds. B. Janowski and P. Stuhlmacher (FAT 14; Tübingen: Mohr Siebeck, 1996), 90; F. García Martínez, "Old Texts and Modern Mirages: The 'I' of Two Qumran Hymns" in *Qumranica Minora I: Qumran Origins and Apocalypticism*, ed. E. Tigchelaar (STDJ 63; Leiden: Brill, 2007), 118–24.

70. For proponents of a priestly identity, see Joseph Angel, "The Liturgical-Eschatological Priest of the 'Self-Glorification Hymn,'" *RevQ* 24, no. 4 (2010): 585–605. Collins, *The Scepter and the Star,* 140–46, interprets this to be a priestly messianic figure. Bühner, *Messianic High Christology*, 45, sees this as an angelic messianic figure. Eshel, "4Q471B," 191–92, raises the possibility of a variety of human figures, particularly enthroned figures such as Enoch.

71. See, for example, Eshel, "4Q471B," 195.

72. Some apocalyptic texts even speak of "many thrones" in heaven (e.g., T. Levi 3.8). In such cases, however, there are numerous thrones, not simply one or two. When God's throne is in view, however, the case is different.

73. See this parallel noted by Eshel, "4Q471B," 180.

74. For this parallel, see Eshel, "4Q471B," 196. For additional parallels, see 1 Kgs 8:23; Ps 40:5; 113:5; Isa 40:18; 44:7.

75. See Bühner, *Messianic High Christology*, 32–33, who makes these very connections to Hebrew scriptures but falls short of identifying the object of the hymn as Israel's God. Similarly, Schäffer, *Two Gods*, 37, comes close by seeing this figure as a messianic figure "elevated to the status of a god."

76. Note that J. R. Davila understands this figure in terms of an apotheosis ("Heavenly Ascents in the Dead Sea Scrolls," in *The Dead Sea Scrolls After Fifty Years: A Comprehensive Assessment*, eds. P. W. Flint and J.C. VanderKam [Leiden: Brill, 1999],

2:475). We would contend that such a conclusion is not necessary or even merited. The text does not offer enough information to prove the ascent and apotheosis of a human. Perhaps more importantly, we contend that the divine features of this figure can be more naturally explained in terms of a second power figure than a human figure who experiences apotheosis.

Chapter 10

Conclusions and Looking Forward

Throughout the preceding chapters, we have analyzed a variety of entities and figures that are relevant to the discussion of Jewish monotheistic convictions in the Second Temple period. Through this analysis, we have argued that many Second Temple Jewish texts depict a second power of heaven under various titles and descriptors, and we have done so by utilizing a number of the criteria that were outlined at the outset of our study. Here, in our final chapter, after briefly summarizing our results, we will consider several relevant questions and issues. How might these various entities that meet our proposed criteria be related to each other? Do they represent a single reality, that is, a second power or many powers? Additionally, how do these figures relate to the "two powers in heaven" heresy that is prevalent in the later rabbinic period? And if these entities are rightly understood as the second power within a two powers paradigm, only under different titles and depictions, how might they be best understood? Are they merely the highest heavenly agents understood to stand in for and act on behalf of the one God of Israel? Or are they rightly understood as the God of Israel that engages both creation and Israel in Hebrew scriptures? After answering these questions, we will return to the notions of both inclusive and exclusive Jewish monotheism and how our proposed two power paradigm might relate to both. Finally, we will briefly consider the potential relevance of this study for assessing early Christian convictions regarding Jesus and the ways a two powers view might inform Christian commitments to the divinity of Jesus.

A BRIEF SUMMARY OF RESULTS

It will help if we briefly recap our findings in the previous chapters for the various figures we studied. In each chapter, we looked to Second Temple Jewish sources to see if the case in view is best understood as a distinct hypostasis, and if so, should this figure be understood as the second power in heaven.

God's Word: After making a case that God's Word is understood by many literary witnesses in the Second Temple period as a distinct entity, we noted that God's Word is depicted as engaging in the act of creation, reigning over the cosmos (at times seated on God's very throne), receiving cultic worship, sharing the divine name, and replacing YHWH in the interpretations and translations of YHWH texts from the Hebrew Bible.

God's Wisdom: After making a case that God's Wisdom is understood by many literary witnesses in the Second Temple period as a distinct entity, we noted that, like God's Word, God's Wisdom is depicted as engaging in the act of creation and reigning over the cosmos (at times seated on God's very throne). Yet, perhaps more importantly, we demonstrated that God's Wisdom, at least for some Second Temple authors, seems to function as a twin concept with God's Word, so that the two can be used synonymously with each other and appear to reference the same entity.

The Angel of the Lord: Our analysis of the Angel of the Lord from the Hebrew scriptures demonstrated that many Second Temple witnesses place the Angel of the Lord in the place of YHWH in their interpretations and translations of the Hebrew Bible. They also frequently equate the Angel of the Lord with God's Word, Wisdom, and other titles.

God's Spirit, Name, and Face: Several Second Temple sources speak of what at first appears to be an abstraction of God's presence, and yet upon closer inspection God's Spirit, Name, or Face, acts with its own agency so as to be a distinct hypostasis. In certain instances, the figure in question acts in creation, rules over the cosmos, plays the role of YHWH, and uniquely bears the divine name (which is obviously the case when a text speaks of the Name of the Lord as a distinct agent). In many cases, the figure in question is the Angel of the Lord, and there are also times where the figure is also called God's Word or Wisdom.

The Son of Man: The *Parables of Enoch* present a Son of Man figure who reigns over the cosmos as he sits on a heavenly throne, arguably God's very throne. Additionally, he receives cultic worship from humanity, has YHWH texts from the Hebrew Bible applied to him, and arguably is closely connected to the creation of the cosmos. We argued that this figure seems to be identified with God's Word and Wisdom. While this particular set of descriptors is unique to the Enochic Son of Man, we also noted that the Old Greek translation of Daniel 7:14 claims that the one like a Son of Man was "present as the Ancient of Days," a translation that suggests that the Son of Man is being understood as a divine figure. Additionally, this Son of Man figure seemingly receives worship. Likewise, in 4 Ezra, the Son of Man figure appears to be closely connected to YHWH texts and does what Hebrew scriptures attribute to YHWH.

Melchizedek and Enoch: While in most Second Temple traditions the ambiguous and mysterious figure from the Hebrew Bible, Melchizedek, seems to be understood strictly as a human being, in one text of Dead Sea Scrolls he appears to be something more. At three points, YHWH scriptures of the Hebrew Bible are directly applied to Melchizedek. We argued that while the Melchizedek of this scroll does not meet a significant number of our outlined criteria, he does meet this significant one. Additionally, he parallels the Enochic Son of Man quite strongly, as both serve as an exalted eschato-logical figure, have messianic attributes, and are closely tied to the God of Israel. We contended that a two powers theology offers a more compelling explanation for this figure than competing alternatives, and that Melchizedek might be for the Dead Sea Scroll community what the Son of Man was for the author of the *Parables of Enoch*. The character of Enoch, however, did not match any of the criteria. Instead, when later rabbinic sources spoke of Metatron in terms which echo the Angel of the Lord material from the scriptures, some offered a correction by insisting that Metatron was, in fact, Enoch exalted to a heavenly scribal role. This ensured that any conception of the Angel of the Lord as the second power of heaven could be denounced as heretical. This stance itself provides evidence that some rabbinic thinkers did believe in two powers in heaven.

Additional Exalted Humans: Finally, we determined that a number of human figures, whom many interpreters have perceived as sharing in divine prerogatives, upon further scrutiny do not, in fact, do so (or at least do not clearly do so). While the Life of Adam and Eve does include Satan's testi-mony to Adam that Adam was the object of worship from heavenly angels, we argued that Satan can hardly be trusted as a reliable narrator and that Satan's testimony is best understood as yet another attempt to destroy Adam. While the *Exagogue* of Ezekiel the Tragedian does present Moses sitting on a throne that reaches from earth to heaven and the heavenly bodies bowing down before Moses, we argued that the throne's identity is ambiguous and that it could be understood as an exalted depiction of the throne of Israel. We also argued that the bowing down of heavenly bodies may simply repre-sent human beings over whom Moses will rule, as such heavenly bodies are understood in the dreams of Joseph. The very interpretation of Moses's dream within the *Exagogue* understands the throne and the bowing of the heavenly bodies strictly in terms of human authority over Israel. Finally, while Crispin Fletcher-Louis has sought to argue that the high priest of Israel was included in both the worship of God and God's act of creation, we argued that his case for such positions lacks merit, and that the texts he relies on are better under-stood as the high priest functioning as a human representative of Israel's God.

The priest is never actually worshipped nor does he ever actually engage in the act of creation.

A SECOND POWER OR MANY POWERS?

We have identified a number of different entities that we believe could be recognized by many first century Jews as a second power in heaven. A question that one might ask is why we would conclude that there is merely a second power in heaven and not four, five, six, or many more? While we fully acknowledge that Second Temple Jews recognized many "powers" in heaven, much like their Greco-Roman neighbors, we also contend that in addition to the Most High God there was a belief in a second power, one greater than all other lower "powers." It is also our contention that this second power went by many different names and could be expressed in a variety of different ways. Thus, we do not see in the entities of God's Word, God's Wisdom, the Angel of the Lord, the Son of Man, or Melchizedek, many different mighty powers, but one single power being described in a variety of ways. The evidence for such a conclusion seems abundantly clear in the sources we have examined. For example, in Philo it is quite clear that God's Word and Wisdom are synonymous for the same entity. In fact, as we have demonstrated, Philo also understands God's Word to be one in the same with the Angel of the Lord found in Hebrew scriptures. At times, Philo even seems to identify God's Word with a heavenly man or heavenly Adam. Additional connections between God's Word and God's Spirit, Name, and Face, can be found in Philo. Thus, for Philo, the one Logos of God can be given many descriptors or names and yet it is still a single entity. The same pattern is found in the Targums, where God's Word (Memra) is clearly identified with the Angel of the Lord as well as God's Name. Again, only one entity is in view, but it bears many names. Additionally, we argued that the Enochic Son of Man should be understood as an embodiment of God's Word and Wisdom. That both Philo and the Targums can depict God's Word as taking the form of a human figure only lends greater credibility to the case that the *Parables of Enoch* are doing the same thing. With the case of Melchizedek, we contend that he should not be understood as a second human embodiment of the second power: one who stands beside a figure like the Enochic Son of Man, but rather that he is for the Qumran community what the Son of Man is for the Enochic community.

From this evidence, it seems quite clear that for many Jews, the second power could be described in a variety of ways or with a variety of names. All such names find clear precedents in the Hebrew scriptures, where a certain entity engages in the divine tasks of YHWH and looks quite like YHWH, or even is YHWH. The name or description that is used at any particular time could be influenced by a variety of factors, including function, literary genre, or audience. For example, it seems that when this second power is engaging in the act of creating the cosmos, the titles God's Word or Wisdom are preferred, a preference that likely has its origins in Hebrew scriptural tradition, wherein God creates via spoken word (Gen 1) or with the aid of wisdom (Prov 8). Yet, when depicting the second power sent for a specific errand, such as bringing a message to patriarch or aiding Israel against its foes, the title Angel of the Lord is preferable, with Hebrew scripture again being a guiding force. Son of Man or Melchizedek seem to be titles favored when depicting the second power's eschatological activity, particularly bringing about an age of blessing for the righteous and judgment for the wicked. Because the Jewish scriptures themselves gave a variety of potential names for what was interpreted by many to be a second power, it is not surprising that we see such variety in many Second Temple text's treatment of that power.

TWO POWERS AND THE RELATIONSHIP BETWEEN THE SECOND TEMPLE AND RABBINIC JUDAISM

In our first chapter on Jewish monotheism, we introduced the two power heresy of the rabbinic period. Here the literature is adamant that there is indeed only one power in heaven and that the God of heaven is one rather than two. We noted the significant work of Allen Segal who argued that while this two power heresy certainly would have included Christians and Gnostics, it also included Jews who were not Christian or Gnostic. Additionally, Segal argued that the two power heresy of the later rabbinic period originated not in the rabbinic period but in the late Second Temple period. Many have been convinced by these broad conclusions from Segal, and we would contend that the results of our analysis of Second Temple literature are consistent with Segal's findings, that is, the belief in a second power in heaven that is distinctly Jewish can be found throughout Second Temple literature.[1] Yet, an important question remains. What is the relationship between the two powers that we, Segal, and others have detected in Second Temple literature and the later belief in two powers of the later rabbinic period that was deemed a heresy?

In James McGrath's assessment of Segal's conclusion, McGrath describes Segal's position on the relationship between the "two powers" theology of both the Second Temple and rabbinic periods in terms of complete continuity, that is (1) continuity exists between the beliefs of the two powers proponents in both periods; and (2) continuity in the condemnation of two powers proponents by the authoritative teaching of both periods.[2] Yet, such a conclusion is far from clear. McGrath notes multiple alternative options. First, it may be that there is continuity of the belief in two powers within both periods but development in terms of condemnation. In other words, the belief that is being rejected by later rabbis is the same belief that existed in the Second Temple period, but that same belief was initially accepted by at least some Second Temple Jews, making its rejection a later rabbinic development.[3] Second, it may be that there is development in belief and, as a result, also in condemnation. In this scenario, the expression of two powers that we see in the Second Temple period was in some way different than the later expression found in the rabbinic period and that development led to the later condemnation, a condemnation that did not exist for the earlier and presumably more acceptable form of the belief. Schäfer sums up the state of the question: "For a long time scholars of rabbinic Judaism therefore considered it an unwritten law that binitarian ideas were useless for Judaism since they had been usurped by Christians. Today, however, we know better. Recent research has shown that they continued to live on also in rabbinic Judaism, and were adopted in certain circles and harshly rejected by others (undeniably the majority)."[4]

Here we assess these various positions in order to determine which one best fits the existing evidence and thus best describes the relationship between the noted "two powers" heresy of the later rabbis and the depiction of what appears to be a second power in the Second Temple period. We first consider the position of Segal, that which affirms continuity of both belief and condemnation. We start by assessing the continuity of belief. This position seems strong in many respects. There are a couple of strong points of contact between the rabbinic concerns regarding the two powers heresy and the descriptors of particular figures and entities that could be understood in terms of two powers within the Second Temple period. First, there is a rabbinic concern over the act of creation and who participated in it. Here the rabbis are clear that God created on his own, without the assistance of any other figure or entity. For example, in Mishnah Sanhedrin 4:5 one reads, "For this reason man was created one and alone in the world: . . . for the sake of peace among created beings that one man should not say to another, 'My father was greater than thine,' and that heretics (מִינִין) should not say, 'There are many ruling powers (רָשֻׁיּוֹת הַרְבֵּה) in heaven.'"[5] While this text says "many powers (רָשֻׁיּוֹת)" rather than only two powers, it still reflects a concern that God did not create with the help of any additional divine agents.[6] The same concern can be seen in the Tosefta Sanhedrin 8:7: "Man was created last. And why was man created last? So that the *minim* should not be able to say, 'There was a partner with him in his work of creation.'"[7] It seems that this tradition would find problematic Philo's Logos that both engaged in the act of creation and shared an identity with a heavenly Adam.[8] It might also find problematic the Parables of Enoch, in which a preexistent heavenly Son of Man is identified with an oath that is responsible for creating and sustaining the cosmos.

A second issue the rabbis seem concerned with are traditions in which one might discern conflicting appearances of God. Of particular interest is Daniel 7, which seems to depict at least two thrones in heaven, one occupied by the Ancient of Days and another presumably occupied by the Son of Man. In multiple places, the Talmud interprets this tradition in terms of the various ways the one God of Israel can be manifest, particularly as both a young man and an old one.[9] But perhaps most importantly, within the context of addressing this text, rabbinic interpretation explicitly rejects the notion of there being two powers in heaven. Such an interpretation strongly suggests that the two powers heresy that the rabbis are responding to reads Daniel 7 in terms of two distinct powers in heaven rather than one. It would seem the Parables of Enoch and their depiction of both the Head of Days and the seemingly divine Son of Man would be the type of heretical tradition these later rabbis are rejecting.

These two specific rabbinical arguments against the affirmation of two powers in heaven strongly suggest continuity of belief between the affirmation of two powers in both the Second Temple and rabbinic periods. Additionally, one is left questioning what sort of development could have taken place in a Jewish (non-Christian) commitment to two powers in heaven between the Second Temple and rabbinic period that would have moved the commitment from acceptable to unacceptable? While one might be tempted to point to Gnosticism as the change that might move a two powers commitment from acceptable to unacceptable, it is noteworthy that both of the examples considered above do not seem particularly tailored to address Gnosticism. In both traditions, the second power is seemingly understood as a complimentary figure to Israel's God, rather than antagonistic. For example, one tradition responds to the belief that God had assistance in the act of creation, a belief that is distinctly not Gnostic, as Gnostics are often accused of placing the creating demiurge in conflict with rather than cooperation with the one true God.[10] Gnosticism would then not be able to fully explain how an acceptable version of two powers became unacceptable. In fact, it seems highly unlikely that the later rabbis would have been comfortable with either Philo's Logos or with the 1 Enoch's Son of Man. If these two first century entities would have been condemned by the rabbis as a heretical belief in a second power in heaven, would any such expression be deemed acceptable? It seems highly unlikely. Thus, attempting to proffer an acceptable version of a "two powers" theology that later develops into an unacceptable version seems futile. The simplest and most plausible solution is that the "two powers" heresy of the rabbinic period is essentially what is represented in Philo's Logos, the Enochic Son of Man, and other second power entities. Thus, we agree with Segal and conclude that there does not appear to be evidence of any noteworthy development with regard to a Jewish "two powers theology" between the Second Temple and rabbinic period that would result in a development in censure.

Yet, what of Segal's contention regarding continuity in the condemnation of this heresy between the late Second Temple period and the rabbinic? On this issue, we contend that the evidence actually supports a different conclusion.[11] Perhaps the most significant argument to this end is the lack of any evidence to suggest that the depictions of the "second power" figures we outlined above were regarded as inappropriate or dangerous by Second Temple Jews. As we have argued above, there is no evidence that Philo's Logos theology was regarded as heretical. He never attempts to defend it against this accusation and, in fact, often uses the concept without explanation, a move that suggests his readers are both familiar and comfortable with it.[12] We also noted that there is nothing in the Parables of Enoch that suggest it be sectarian, let alone heretical. We have every reason to believe that the Parables (and the Son of Man depicted therein) represents a perspective that fit quite comfortably in the common Judaism(s) of the Second Temple period. That these "second power" entities are found in multiple Jewish sources across a variety of genres supports the conclusion that the thinking expressed about these figures was widely regarded as acceptable. We have also argued previously, that the Memra tradition in the Targums likely reflects the beliefs and interpretive traditions of the Second Temple period, as it is more likely to have coexisted alongside a prominent Logos tradition of Second Temple Hellenistic Judaism than it is to have originated in the early rabbinic period. This conclusion is all the more likely, given that most versions of Christianity were boldly declaring Jesus as a second power in heaven in at least the second century and beyond. As we see in rabbinic literature, the Jewish response to such Christian theology was to reject it in full, not offer up alternative versions. If then the Targums reflect a Second Temple Memra theology, we have yet another example that demonstrates the acceptability of, if not the widespread adherence to, a two powers theology. Significantly, even Segal himself seems to be inconsistent on this issue, as he both claims that the later rabbis would have recognized Philo as a heretical proponent of a second power in heaven, and that Philo was not regarded as heretical at the time of his writing.[13] Such a position seems more consistent with a discontinuity in condemnation of a two powers theology between the Second Temple and rabbinic periods respectively. Therefore, while we agree with Segal that the belief in two powers in heaven that is labeled a heresy in rabbinic literature did exist in the first century, we agree with Daniel Boyarin and James McGrath in concluding that in the Second Temple period a belief in a two powers theology was not heretical, but rather an acceptable belief within common Judaism.[14]

Our identification of Second Temple representations of a second power in heaven finds corroboration in our reconstruction of the origins and history of the two powers heresy that is clearly present, yet refuted, in the rabbinic period. When these pieces are put together, coherent progression of the thought surrounding a two powers theology becomes clear. Within the late Second Temple period there emerges a belief that in some way understands the one God of Israel and that God's activity as expressed in Hebrew scriptures in terms of two distinct powers, the second of which could be described in a variety of ways (e.g., Word, Wisdom, Angel of the Lord, Son of Man, etc.). This belief was acceptable within the common Judaism of the Second Temple period; that is, it was not seen as a violation of accepted Jewish praxis, belief, or identity. In fact, given our analysis above, the belief seems widespread, existing comfortably in Hellenistic Judaism, Palestinian Judaism, and quite possibly in the sectarian Judaism of the Dead Sea Scroll community. Yet, at some point in the centuries following the Second Temple period, this belief begins to receive challenge and censure within the emerging rabbinic movement. We believe that the likely catalyst for such censure was a response to the growing Christian movement and its affirmation of Jesus as a divine figure, one equated with the God of Israel. Gnostic challenges to Judaism may also have played a role. Rabbinic rejection of a two powers theology was thus an attempt to stamp out what was perceived as a dangerous belief, one that gave legitimacy to a rival religious movement and came from among adherents within the rabbis' own Jewish communities.[15] We contend that such a reconstruction explains the evidence far better than any alternative, and thus, strongly supports the existence of an accepted two powers theology within the late Second Temple period.

TWO POWERS AND THE ONE GOD

If, as we have argued, there was a non-heretical two powers theology within the common Judaism of the Second Temple period, the pressing question becomes the nature of this theology. How were these two powers understood and what was the nature of their relationship to each other? As we noted in our introduction, one interpretive option is to understand the first power as the God of Israel proper and the second as a powerful principal agent of the God of Israel who uniquely acts in God's place (e.g., this principal agent creates, reigns over creation, and is a worthy recipient of worship, etc.). Such a position is best represented by Andrei Orlov.[16] Yet, Orlov sees fluidity in the identity of this agent. For example, Orlov concludes that in the Life of Adam and Eve, the narrative depicts a change in the second power, one from Satan to Adam.[17] Thus, for Orlov, the second power is seemingly understood more as an office, one that can be filled by different entities, than the unchanging identity of a single entity. Thus, in Orlov's view, the second power is not

necessarily identified as Israel's God but as the greatest of the heavenly powers, at any given time, that are under that God. In many ways, it seems that
Orlov's understanding of a two powers theology is a variant of the inclusive
monotheism outlined in our opening chapter, with its distinction being that
special inclusion in divine prerogatives is granted to one figure who holds a
particular divine office, that of the second power.

While we believe it possible that some Jews could have perceived the second power as a distinct divine agent that acted in the place of God, we do not
see evidence supporting Orlov's understanding of this role being occupied by
different entities. As argued above, it seems quite clear that while the second
power can be identified by a variety of names or descriptors, it is understood
as a single entity that plays a distinct role, rather than a distinct role that can
be occupied by any number of entities. As we argue above, contra Orlov,
figures like Adam and Moses, fall short of being rightly identified as "second
powers," and it is largely the inclusion of these figures that undergird Orlov's
perception of the second power as a role that can be held by various figures.

A second option, that perhaps is best represented by Daniel Boyarin, is that
of a binitarian understanding of the second power, that is the understanding
of single "godhead" understood in terms of discernable duality, a first power
closely associated with transcendence and a second power closely associated
with immanence. Within such an understanding, the second power does not
just stand in the place of Israel's God in a unique way, but rather is rightly
understood and identified as the YHWH of Israel, as is the first power.

Here, we do not want to bring to the table any of the elements that will
dominate later Christian debates regarding the relationship between the persons of the trinity (e.g., co-eternality, consubstantiality, etc.). The existing
evidence does not answer such speculative matters or give evidence that such
issues concerned the possible proponents of such a two powers theology. We
simply contend that within the Second Temple period the two powers we
have identified here could be understood as the YHWH of Israel.[18] Since the
second power (variously named as God's Word, Angel, the Son of Man, etc.)
is unique in relation to the first power, many scholars speak of an implicit
binitarianism in ancient Judaism. We have avoided this concept where possible, since it has not been our aim to address how the two powers relate.
Instead, we have attempted to demonstrate that many Jews in the Second
Temple period understood there to be a second power in heaven in and
through whom the most high God of Israel is known and worshipped as Lord.

To make this case, we consider certain criteria met by the figures we have
identified as second powers. First, we consider interpretive traditions in which
the second power is read into a YHWH text or a YHWH text is applied to the
second power figure. If the second power is understood as a principal agent
of YHWH rather than YHWH, examples of the second power either being

read into YHWH texts or having YHWH texts applied to it then demand a particular hermeneutic. It must be concluded that the original Hebrew text is in some way mistaken or at least imprecise, and that the actual actor within the text is not YHWH but rather the principal agent of YHWH. Now certainly lying behind such a move may be the belief that the text is only technically mistaken, as YHWH does indeed act in all such texts, though he does so through the principal agent. Yet, even still, this interpretive move is offering an interpretive corrective to the text for the sake of improved precision. In other words, the text says YHWH, but more precisely, it is YHWH's principal agent. However, if the second power is rightly understood to be YHWH in some sense, or also called YHWH, then the interpreter is not offering any correction to the text, but merely a proper interpretation of it. That is to say, clarifying for the reader that it is the second divine power also called YHWH that is active in the text. With this approach, the Hebrew text is given greater authority and autonomy as it dictates for the reader the identity of the second power, rather than the reader offering a corrective to the text in identifying the second power as merely a principal agent. We suggest that this understanding is: (1) more consistent with the reverence that Second Temple Jews granted the Hebrew scriptures during the Second Temple period; and (2) it is the simpler and more straight forward way of reading the evidence. Thus, we find it more likely that this evidence supports the conclusion that the second power is best understood as the YHWH of Israel and not simply the highest agent of Israel's God.

Second, we considered the application of or close association with the name YHWH. As we have outlined above, we see already in the Second Temple period that Jews were becoming highly sensitive in their treatment of the personal name of their God. There is evidence that the name was no longer being spoken by certain Jewish communities.[19] The fact that no transliteration of the name can be found in the LXX and that it is consistently replaced by κύριος is strong evidence that the name was being treated with extreme caution. Given such sensitivity, we believe that second power figures that bear or are closely associated with the name YHWH are better identified as such than identified with the highest agent of YHWH.

Third, we look at the criteria regarding worship. As those like Hurtado, Casey, and others have demonstrated, there is significant evidence that Jews believed they were to worship the one God, YHWH, alone and by and large did so.[20] Initially, we were reluctant to affirm Hurtado's claim that worship functioned as hard boundary marker between the God of Israel and all other entities, given a number of possible exceptions that existed in Second Temple literature. However, in light of our assessment of potential second power entities/figures, the calculus related to such a boundary marker needs adjusting. If the exceptions to YHWH alone being worshipped can be identified as the second power, the boundary marker put forward by Hurtado would find new strength. Initially, those exceptions included Adam, Moses, the Son of Man, and possibly the Angel in Joseph and Aseneth (which we have identified as the Angel of the Lord). We have identified both the Son of Man and the Angel of the Lord as second power figures. Additionally, we have shown that the case for Adam and Moses as recipients of worship are highly suspect and that alternative explanations are preferable, meaning they are not sound examples of exceptions to the worship of YHWH alone. Thus, in our analysis, the only exceptions to YHWH alone being worshipped are second power figures.[21] We cannot from this evidence engage in circular reasoning (e.g., YHWH alone is worshiped; these second powers are worshiped; ergo they must be YHWH because YHWH alone can be worshiped) but it does allow us to ask the question about the nature of the second power with a sharpened focus. Given the abundant evidence in Second Temple Judaism that YHWH alone should be worshipped, we must ask what makes more sense regarding the nature of the second power: (1) to conclude that the second power figure who is decidedly not YHWH is worshipped; or (2) that the second power figure is rightly identified as YHWH and because of such an identification is worshipped? Again, while we cannot exclude the first option, we find the second option to be more consistent with the extant evidence as well as the simpler and more straight forward explanation.

Fourth, we consider the criteria involving creation. As Bauckham has argued, creation is an act that is closely associated with the God of Israel (at times this God alone) not only in the Hebrew scriptures but also in the literature of the Second Temple period.[22] While we were reluctant to follow Bauckham in establishing the act of creation as a hard boundary between the God of Israel and all other entities, our analysis of potential second power figures allows for a reconsideration. Bauckham's argument was that only the God of Israel could create. However, when he faced entities like God's Word and Wisdom, entities that are also depicted as participating in creation, Bauckham assumed that they must share in the divine identity with Israel's God. We faulted Bauckham on the circular reasoning of this position. Yet, now on the basis of much broader evidence, we have identified both God's Word and Wisdom as titles of the second power in many Second Temple Jewish sources. As such, the only exceptions that exist to Bauckham's claim to creation as a hard boundary line between the God of Israel and all other reality is the second power (depicted as God's Word, Wisdom, Spirit, Name, Face, and arguably the Enochic Son of Man). Such a development again sharpens our focus in assessing the nature of the second power of Second Temple Judaism. Given the widespread evidence within both the Hebrew scriptures and Second Temple Judaism that Israel's God alone creates, does it make more sense to identify a second power that creates as a principal agent of YHWH that is decidedly not YHWH, or to identify that power as the very YHWH that creates? Again, without excluding the possibility of the first option, we believe the second option to be more consistent with the existing evidence as well as the simpler explanation.

Here we bring together our assessment of all these criteria and ask the following question: If the second power is interpreted as acting in Hebrew scriptures as one that describes YHWH, and bears the sacred name of YHWH, and receives worship that is widely if not exclusively reserved for YHWH, and engages in the creation of the cosmos, an act widely associated with YHWH alone, shouldn't we must acknowledge the very real possibility, if not likelihood, that the second power figure is best understood as the YHWH of Israel and not merely a distinct and unique agent of Israel's God?

The one noteworthy factor that one might put forward to deny such a possibility is the thorough commitment in both Hebrew scripture and Second Temple literature that there is only one supreme God.[23] The proposal that the second power is also YHWH might appear to conflict with this basic and oft repeated commitment of Second Temple Judaism. Yet, we must clarify the Second Temple sources themselves, even those in which we find a second power, never affirm the existence of two distinct gods and that Second Temple literature is replete with a commitment to one and only one high God.[24] For this reason, we argue that two powers is a belief that is, for those who held it, distinct from ditheism and is rather a belief in the existence of two distinct entities that can both be understood as, and be called, YHWH.[25] In defense of such a position we offer a number of considerations. First, there is no Second Temple Jewish text that denies or precludes the possibility of plurality within Israel's one high God. Second, the Hebrew text itself could be read in a way that led some Second Temple Jews to just such a conclusion. We have demonstrated above the places where God's Word and Wisdom seem like distinct entities in the Hebrew scriptures, but also seem to be closely identified with the God of Israel. We have also noted places in which the Angel of the Lord and the Lord are used interchangeably without explanation. Daniel 7 could be interpreted as depicting two divine figures on two heavenly thrones (an interpretation that is evinced by rabbinic rejections of it), yet Daniel is clearly a book that affirms the existence of and devotion to the one supreme God of Israel. While in their original context passages like Genesis 1:26 and the use of first-person plural personal pronouns might refer to a heavenly council, they could be suggestive to Second Temple Jews of plurality in the one supreme God.[26] It is widely accepted that the Hebrew scriptures themselves reflect a history in which two distinct gods are blended into one.[27] That the traces of such a blending might lead some Jews of the Second Temple period to conceive of their one supreme God in terms of plurality seems plausible.

Finally, perhaps the most significant evidence is the existence of a move-ment that was birthed out of Second Temple Judaism and in a relatively short amount of time (if not immediately) conceived of the one supreme God of Judaism in terms of two distinct beings. While there was clearly diversity of thought within early Christian christological commitments, it is obvious that by the second century (see the examples of Justin Martyr in the introductory chapter) many Christians equated Jesus with the YHWH of Israel's scriptures while at the same affirming his Father also as YHWH. These Christians did this while clinging firmly to the conviction of Hebrew scripture that there is only one supreme God. Such obvious commitments of early Christians in the second century and the centuries that followed are widely recognized and impossible to deny. Yet, for some reason, scholars who can fully affirm that Christians held such convictions regarding the supreme God of Israel's scrip-tures refuse to believe that such convictions could exist in Second Temple Judaism, out of which the Christian movement was birthed. We contend that if Christians could affirm the existence of one God that in some way existed in two distinct entities by the second century, Jews of the first century could certainly do so as well. In fact, we would argue (and in a later volume will do so in full) that the Christian commitment to this understanding of the one God of Israel finds its most plausible explanation in a Judaism that already affirmed the same understanding.

In light of this analysis, we believe that the evidence supports the conclu-sion that at least some Second Temple Jews understood a two powers theol-ogy in terms of the one God of Israel existing in two distinct powers, the first associated with transcendence and the second with immanence. With this said, we recognize that it is quite possible that the two powers theology of the Second Temple period could have been understood in more than one way. While some may have understood the second power as the YHWH of Israel, others may have understood it in terms of a principal agent distinct from YHWH. Proving uniformity of thought within this two powers theol-ogy is unnecessary and not our goal. For our purposes, we simply want to affirm the likelihood that some, if not many, Second Temple Jews understood the one God of Israel in terms of two powers, both of which could be identi-fied as YHWH.

REVISITING THE INCLUSIVE AND
EXCLUSIVE PARADIGMS

In our first chapter, we considered both an exclusive and inclusive monothe-istic paradigm for understanding Israel's God in the world of Second Temple Judaism. After carefully analyzing the relevant evidence within Second

Temple literature and making the case for a new two powers paradigm, we now return to consider these two prominent ones. In some sense, both of these paradigms were explaining certain aspects of the evidence correctly. Proponents of an inclusive monotheism were at times correct in perceiving certain figures and entities as being included in the prerogatives of Israel's God. The Enochic Son of Man is indeed worshipped and exercises sovereignty over the cosmos. The unnamed angel of Joseph and Aseneth, best identified as the Angel of the Lord, does indeed receive devotion like that given to Israel's God. God's Word and Wisdom are often understood as distinct entities that both engage in creating the cosmos and reigning.

Similarly, proponents of an exclusive monotheism were indeed astute in their identification of certain boundary markers that set the God of Israel apart from other entities (e.g., receiving cultic devotion, creating the cosmos and ruling over it). The greatest weakness of their position was the existence of noteworthy exceptions to those boundary markers, exceptions that called into question just how firm of boundaries they created. Yet, if our analysis above is correct and the Enochic Son of Man, God's Word and Wisdom, and the Angel of the Lord are all seen as the second power in heaven, one rightly identified as the YHWH of Israel, these figures that were previously recognized as exceptions to the boundary markers can no longer be identified as such. Instead, they receive worship, create the cosmos, and reign over the cosmos because they are in fact the YHWH of Israel. Other oft noted exceptions, such as Adam, Moses, or the Jewish high priest are, after more careful analysis, not actually exceptions at all, as they do not transgress the proposed boundary markers. Thus, the assessment of the existing evidence by proponents of an exclusive monotheism is ultimately correct, when the evidence is assessed through the lens of a two powers paradigm.

Here, our conclusions must be circumspect to a certain degree. It is entirely possible that certain Jews were exclusive monotheists that rejected a two powers theology. It is equally possible that certain Jews affirmed the inclusion of certain entities, entities that were decidedly not YHWH, in what were widely regarded as the prerogatives of YHWH. Our conclusions do not attempt to determine *the* definitive understanding of the God of Israel during the late Second Temple period, as surely there were diverse views. Yet, we contend that the conclusions offered here regarding a two powers theology better explain the totality of the existing literary evidence than that of either the exclusive or inclusive models. In fact, when a two powers paradigm is employed, the strengths and weaknesses of both the exclusive and inclusive models find adequate explanations. In addition to offering a better explanation of the existing literary evidence, we contend that the two powers paradigm also provides a fruitful way forward for examining the earliest writings

of the Christian movement and assessing the christological commitments
found therein.

TWO POWERS AND EARLY CHRISTIAN
TEXTS: A CASE STUDY OF MARK

At the outset of our study, we noted that our ultimate purpose was to better
understand the earliest Christian confession, "Jesus is Lord," and to assess
how Christians of the second century and following centuries came to understand that confession to mean that Jesus was the God of Israel who acted in
Israel's scriptures. In this volume, by arriving at a two powers understanding of Second Temple Jewish monotheism, we have taken a monumental
first step in answering that question. The next step is considering how this
reconstruction of Jewish monotheism aids us in assessing the depictions of
Jesus found in the earliest Christian writings, primarily the writings of the
New Testament. Clearly this next step is an enormous task in and of itself,
and thus, its full undertaking will be reserved for our next, forthcoming volume. However, we wanted to briefly consider the explanatory power that our
reconstruction of Jewish monotheism might have for analyzing the earliest
Christian commitments regarding the divinity of Jesus. To this end, we consider two examples from the Gospel of Mark.[28]

The Gospel of Mark is widely regarded as having the lowest Christology of
the four canonical Gospels, with interpreters long concluding that the Markan
Jesus is an exalted messianic figure, but a decidedly human one.[29] When
compared to the Gospel of John, for example, it appears to lack any explicit
claims to preexistence or a divine identity. Its depiction of Jesus's death seems
to emphasize suffering, weakness, and possibly divine abandonment, while
John seems to depict the death in terms of Jesus's control, power, and even
glorification. But more recent studies of Mark's Christology have pushed
back on such claims and have argued that Mark's Jesus is every bit as divine
as John's, although the means of presenting him as such differs.[30] Yet, these
attempts include the weakness of being unable to explain how the Markan
Jesus can both be the agent of Israel's God (i.e., the Messiah), one who, in
fact, prays to that God, and yet, also be that very God.[31] Here we consider
two examples from Mark's Gospel and how a two powers understanding
of Jewish monotheism helps us better understand the Gospel's christological content.

Jesus Walks on the Water: Mark 6:45–52

In Mark 6:45–52, Jesus walks on the waves of the Sea of Galilee with the intent to pass by his disciples, as they are straining against the strong winds of a storm. Others have noted the christological significance of the details in this story.[32] The first significant detail is Mark's description of Jesus περιπατῶν ἐπί τῆς θαλάσσης ("walking on the sea"). This finds an almost parallel citation in Job 8:9, which describes YHWH *alone* περιπατῶν ὡς ἐπ' ἐδάφουω ἐπί θαλάσσης ("walking on the waves of the sea as on firm ground"). Apart from the clause ὡς ἐπ' ἐδάφουω the text of Mark reads as a citation of Job 8:9. Both Job 38:16 and Sirach 24:4–5 also connect YHWH with walking on the sea.

The second significant detail, one that many interpreters have noted as oddly placed, is the claim that Jesus intended to "pass by (παρέχομαι)" his disciples.[33] Matthew omits this detail and more naturally depicts Jesus as intending to help the struggling disciples. Yet, this Markan detail takes on great significance when considered in light of what are arguably the two greatest theophany stories of Israel's scriptures (esp. when reading the LXX). In Exodus 33 and 34, a scene is narrated in which Moses makes a request to YHWH that he might see his glory (33:18). To this request YHWH tells Moses that he will allow his goodness to "pass by (παρέχομαι)" him, while YHWH declares his own name. Yet, YHWH tells Moses that he can only see his back, for no one can see YHWH's face and live. In the following verses, YHWH reiterates what he will do, and in doing so tells Moses two more times that he will "pass by (παρέχομαι)" him. Then, in chapter 34, the text narrates what YHWH has told Moses of what will happen, and YHWH is described as "passing by (παρέχομαι)" Moses. Thus, in the matter of eleven verses in Exodus, the same word that Mark uses to describe Jesus's intent with relation to his disciples via walking on water is used four times to describe YHWH's act of self-revelation to Moses. The same word again appears in the account of YHWH appearing to Elijah on Mount Horeb in 1 Kings 19. Here Elijah is told to go stand on the mountain because the "LORD is about to pass by (παρέχομαι)." From these two texts, it becomes clear that the language of "passing by" plays a prominent role in the theophany stories of Jewish scriptures. Such prominence greatly informs the significance of what otherwise seems like an odd and superfluous comment in Mark's account of Jesus walking on the sea. Through this detail, Mark is again identifying Jesus with the actions of Israel's God, only with this detail, he is directly connecting Jesus to God's very act of self-revelation.

The final significant detail comes in Jesus's response to the disciples' terror when they see him. Jesus responds by saying, θαρσεῖτε ἐγώ εἰμι μή φοβεῖσθε, which is regularly translated "take courage, it is I, do not fear." Yet, this common English translation misses the significance of Jesus's words of self-identification, ἐγώ εἰμι. While these words can convey a simple self-identification (i.e., "it is I"), within the septuagintal tradition they take on far greater significance. This significance begins in Exodus 3 with Moses's encounter with YHWH in the burning bush. In this encounter, Moses asks YHWH what name he should give when the people ask for the name of the God who sent him (Exod 3:13). To this, YHWH says to Moses, ἐγώ εἰμι ὁ ὤν or "I am the one who is." Some have tried to argue that ἐγώ εἰμι should not be understood as a means of referencing this response of YHWH to Moses, on the basis that (1) it is only a partial citation of the response, and lacks ὁ ὤν; or (2) that the response in Mark 6:50 can and should be understood as a simple self-identification.[34] Regarding the first argument, it ignores the use of this part of YHWH's response to Moses as a means of YHWH's self-identification throughout the septuagintal tradition. In Leviticus, the phrase ἐγώ εἰμι κύριος ("I am the LORD") is used twenty-four times by YHWH to identify himself. YHWH uses the same phrase thirty-two times to identify himself in Ezekiel. Yet, the servant song of Isaiah (40–53) offers the most significant evidence for ἐγώ εἰμι as a form of YHWH's self-identification. In these chapters, ἐγώ εἰμι is used as part of a self-identification formula seventeen times. While some of these formulas include modifiers (e.g., "I am the Lord," "I am God," or "I am the first and I am the last"), on many occasions no modifiers are used at all and ἐγώ εἰμι alone is used to identify Israel's God: "so that you may . . . understand that I am" (Isa 43:10); "I am and there is no other" (Isa 45:18); "Until old age, I am, and until you grow old, I am" (Isa 46:4). At three points, the phrase is repeated twice in a move that closely ties it to the identity of YHWH: "I am, I am the one who washes away your lawlessness for your sake" (Isa 43:25); "I am, I am the Lord who speaks righteousness and announces truth" (Isa 45:19); and "I am, I am the one who comforts you" (Isa 51:12). The phrase is also used three times to describe the boastful claims to the king of Babylon that he is greater than Israel's God. The king declares, "I am and there is no other" (Isa 47:8; see also the phrase repeated twice in 47:10). These words parallel the very words of YHWH (Isa 45:18), and claims YHWH's identity for the king himself. From these examples it seems that throughout the septuagintal tradition, which is often likely drawing on the episode recorded in Exodus 3, that ἐγώ εἰμι is a phrase that was closely associated with YHWH's self-identification.

In response to the second argument, three pieces of evidence support our claim that Mark is intentionally drawing on this septuagintal tradition (and thus is offering more than a mere "it is I"). The first is Mark's virtual citation of Job 8:9 in his description of Jesus walking on the water, a text in which YHWH alone is described as walking on the water. The second is Mark's allusion to prominent theophany stories of the scriptures with his inclusion of Jesus's intention to pass by his disciples, closely associating Jesus's actions with YHWH's act of self-revelation. The third is closely tied to the Exodus theophany story. In the account of YHWH appearing to Moses on Mount Sinai, he tells Moses that he will pass by him while speaking his (YHWH's) very name. In this Markan episode, it is then significant that as Jesus is passing by his disciples, he speaks to them, ἐγώ εἰμι, thus drawing this form of self-identification even closer to YHWH's own self-identification.

Any one of these details on their own might not be enough to conclude that Mark intends to present Jesus as the YHWH of Israel's scriptures, but when all three are taken together, the case becomes virtually undeniable. The reader that was steeped in the septuagintal tradition would not miss the profound claim this story is making about Jesus's identity, that he is the YHWH of Israel. While many interpreters have identified all of these significant intertextual features, very few are willing to reach what seems to be the most obvious conclusion, namely that Mark narrates that Jesus is YHWH.[35] From this evidence, some will conclude that Mark depicts Jesus as acting like YHWH, but refuse to make the direct connection between the two. While such a conclusion might be adequate if Mark only depicted Jesus as walking on water, the inclusion of details that link Jesus to YHWH's acts of self-identification, that is, passing by while saying, "I am," yields such a position untenable. How is one able to merely act like YHWH while engaging in the acts of YHWH's self-revelation? By connecting Jesus with YHWH's acts of self-revelation, it seems no other conclusion is offered the reader other than to conclude that Jesus is YHWH.

The cause for hesitancy in reaching such a conclusion is no doubt scholarly presumptions about Jewish monotheism, namely, understanding the God of Israel in terms of strict singularity. In light of such presumptions, the fact that Mark depicts the God of Israel speaking to Jesus and Jesus praying to the God of Israel, precludes interpreters from concluding from Mark 6:45–52 that Jesus is being depicted as YHWH, despite the overwhelming evidence that supports such a conclusion. It is here that our revised understanding of Jewish monotheism and the belief in the one God of Israel existing in two distinct powers offers the elusive interpretive solution. In light of this view of monotheism, the evidence from Mark 6:45–52 can be followed to its logical conclusion, namely, that Jesus is the YHWH of Israel, or more particularly, the second power of heaven. And his prayer to the God of Israel, YHWH, need not contradict such a conclusion, because the God he prays to is rightly identified as the first power, the transcendent YHWH. Our interpretation of this passage can be further supported when taking into account the many other ways in which Markan Jesus is described as, acts as, and claims to be the "Lord" of Israel. For the sake of space in the present volume, we will limit ourselves to one more example.

Markan Exegesis of YHWH Scripture: Mark 1:2–3

Mark's Gospel opens with a citation of two texts from Hebrew scripture. The first cited text is Malachi 3:1 (and Exodus 23:20): "See, I am sending my messenger ahead of you, who will prepare your way." It is noteworthy that in this citation, Mark makes an editorial change. In the text of Malachi 3:1, the text claims "I am sending my messenger, who will prepare my way." In the original text of Malachi the messenger is preparing the way of the speaker, YHWH, yet in Mark, the messenger is preparing the way for someone seemingly distinct from the speaker: "ahead of you, who will prepare your way." This text of Malachi parallels Exodus 23:20 quite strongly, yet in the Exodus text, YHWH declares that he "will send his messenger before you (Moses and Israel)." Thus the Markan citation finds a verbal parallel with this Exodus text. However, within Mark's context, the "you" of the citation is clearly understood as Jesus, not Israel, which undermines the conclusion that Mark's editorial change is informed by the text of Exodus. The interpreter is then left with the question regarding the catalyst for this Markan editorial activity. Regardless of its origin, some note that this change by Mark creates a distinction between YHWH, the sender, and Jesus, the one for whom the messenger is preparing the way, and on this basis contends that the editorial change establishes an identity for Jesus that is decidedly distinct from YHWH.[36]

Such a conclusion runs into tension, however, with the next verse of Mark's citation, a citation of Isaiah 40:3: "A voice of one crying in the wilderness: 'Prepare the way of the Lord, make his paths straight.'" In this text from Isaiah, the text is describing a voice that prepares the way for YHWH. Yet when read within the context of Mark's narrative, the voice in the wilderness is clearly interpreted as John the Baptist, who clearly and obviously functions to prepare the way for Jesus. Thus, it appears that with the citation of this verse, Mark is applying this YHWH text of Hebrew scripture to the Jesus of the Gospel. In other words, Jesus is the Lord, YHWH, of Isaiah 40:3.

How, then, is the tension between these two Markan citations of scripture resolved, as the first text appears to distinguish Jesus from YHWH and the second text seemingly attempts to claim Jesus is YHWH? We contend that again, a two powers Jewish monotheism offers a way forward in resolving the tension. If Mark understands Jesus to be the second power, then the editorial move made in the citation of Malachi comes into sharper focus. Mark interprets the passage in terms of a two powers theology, in which the text describes the first or transcendent power (YHWH) sending a messenger before the second or immanent power (also YHWH). As such, Mark can bifurcate the text and reflect the presence of two powers with the simple change from "my way" to "your way," a change that is acceptable because both the first and second powers are rightly understood as YHWH. Jesus can then easily be identified with the YHWH of Isaiah 40:3, because he is indeed the YHWH of Israel's scriptures, who is preceded by John, the voice in the wilderness.

CONCLUSION AND FUTURE PROSPECTS

In sum, much more could be debated about these passages and about the best way to understand Jesus' divine status in Mark. Nonetheless, we have offered a thumbnail sketch of the possibilities that the two powers paradigm offers New Testament studies. Here, we can only mention other key examples that could be better understood in light of this approach, such as Paul's use of the monotheistic claims from Isaiah 45:23 in the Christ hymn of Philippians (Phil 2:6–11) so that Jesus is the "Lord" who has the "Name above all names"; Paul's ability to read the Shema of Deuteronomy 6:4 so that it includes the Father and Jesus (1 Cor 8:6); Jude's claim that it was Jesus who led the people out of Egypt and through the wilderness as a pillar of cloud (Jude 5); and Revelation's depiction of Jesus as "the first and the last" who looks like both Daniel's Son of Man and Daniel's Ancient of Days.[37] Again, such claims for these texts deserve a full exegetical analysis, which we cannot offer here, but it is something we will take up in a subsequent publication. For now, we have made a much more modest claim: we claim to have shown that the world of Second Temple Judaism included some, and perhaps many, Jews who believed there were two powers in heaven, both of which could be identified as the YHWH of Israel. Therefore, we believe that reading the New Testament descriptions about Jesus in light of this observation offers promising ways forward.

NOTES

1. Segal points to Philo as well as a number of the Second Temple traditions we have addressed above (Daniel, 1 Enoch, Sirach, Wisdom of Solomon, etc.) as evidence that the two powers heresy condemned in the rabbinic period had a precedent in the Second Temple period (*Two Powers*, 159–204). Segal concludes that Philo's teaching on the Logos would have been recognized by the later rabbis as a heretical proponent of "two powers in heaven" (*Two Powers*, 173).

2. See McGrath, *Only True God*, 82.

3. Segal also acknowledges this possibility (*Two Powers*, 28).

4. Schäffer, *Two Gods*, 66.

5. Translation from Herbert Danby, *Tractate Sanhedrin: Mishnah and Tosefta* (New York: MacMillan, 1919), 79.

6. McGrath argues that because this tradition says "many powers" rather than "two powers" it likely had in mind either the belief that angels were agents in creation or the gnostic belief that the evil demiurge created with the aid of lesser helpers (*Only True God*, 85). While McGrath might be right including these beliefs in those being critiqued, it seems his exclusion of any expression of a "two power" theology seems unnecessarily rigid. Because the concern seems to be God receiving aid in the act of creation, it seems the affirmation of two powers as well as many others would be problematic for the author of the critique.

7. Translation from Jacob Neusner, *The Tosefta: Translated from the Hebrew with a New Introduction* (Peabody, MA: Hendrickson Publishers, 2002), 2:1174.

8. Again, McGrath sees this tradition concerned specifically with a belief in Adam as an aid to God in the act of creating the cosmos and not a two powers theology (*Only True God*, 87). He notes that the connection in Philo between the Logos and the Heavenly Adam, a possible expression of a two powers theology, are not likely the object of this critique, as Philo places the creation of spiritual things (i.e., the heavenly Adam) on the first day, not the sixth. Yet, this conclusion does not allow for the possibility that other expressions of Judaism that affirmed a Logos/Heavenly Adam connection could not have associated these entities with the sixth day. We contend that the concern for God having a divine partner in creation would include concern for any second power figure, Adam or otherwise.

9. For the relevant rabbinic texts and discussion of them, see Segal, *Two Powers*, 33–59.

10. The debate over what the so-called Gnostics actually taught is too complex to cover here. For further discussion, see David E. Wilhite, *The Gospel according to Heretics* (Grand Rapids, MI: Baker, 2015), 61–86.

11. For recent examples of others who interpret the evidence contra Segal on this issue, see Boyarin, *Border Lines*, 112–127, McGrath, *Only True God*; Schäffer, *Two Gods*; Scott, "Binitarian Nature," 60; and Orlov, *The Glory of the Invisible God*, 5–9.

12. Indeed, Philo does deny that the existence of a "second god" means there are "two gods," as we discuss in chapter 2. Yet, we would argue here that Philo is clarifying the nature of the existence of "two powers" within the Jewish commitment to one God, i.e., two powers are acceptable, while two gods are not (see Philo, *Somn.* 1.229, in which Philo affirms both the one God and his Word).

13. Compare, for example, Segal, *Two Powers*, 159–160, 173, with 161. Ultimately, Segal seems unsure of how Philo's Logos would have been assessed by the first century precursors to the rabbis (see *Two Powers*, 261).

14. See Boyarin, *Bord Lines*, 130–134; McGrath, *Only True God*, 95–96.

15. For a similar conclusion, see Boyarin, *Border Lines*, 130–34.

16. Orlov, *The Glory of the Invisible God*, 9–10.

17. Orlov, *The Glory of the Invisible God*, 25–27.

18. The way in which both powers could be understood as the YHWH of Israel is beyond the scope of our inquiry. We recognize that a variety of ways of understanding the relationship between these powers could have existed, including, but not limited to, the one God of Israel being comprised of two distinct hypostases (as Boyarin claims, a binitarianism or dual Godhead), the second power representing a temporary

yet distinct avatar of the God of Israel, or the second power representing a younger YHWH or son-like figure of the elder YHWH.

19. See discussion in chapters 1 and 6.

20. See discussion in chapter 1.

21. In fact, in our analysis in this chapter, we demonstrated that God's Word was also depicted as an object of worship, both in Philo and the Targums. See chapters 2 and 3.

22. Neh 9:6 (possible claim to God alone); Isa 40:26, 28; 42:5; 44:24 (God of Israel alone); 45:12, 18 (possible claim to God alone creating); 48:13; 51:16; Hos 13:4 (LXX); Sir 43:33; 2 Macc 1:24; Bel. 5; Jos. Asen. 12.1–2.

23. See Deut 4:35, 39; 6:4; 32:39; 1 Sam 2:2; 2 Sam 7:22; Is 43:11; 44:6; 45:5, 6, 14, 18, 21–22; 46:9; Joel 2:27; Wis. 12:13; Sir 36:5; 1Q35; 4Q504; Let. Aris. 139; Philo, *QG* 4.8; *Decal.* 65; *Conf.* 170–75; *Leg.* 3.4, 82; Josephus, *Ant.* 3.91.

24. Cf. Philo: although he can call the Logos a "second god (δεύτερον θεόν)" (*QG* 2.62), he nevertheless also insists there are not "two gods (δύο . . . θεοί)" (*Somn.* 1.228), but "two powers (δυεῖν δυνάμεων)" (*Somn.* 1.162); discussed above in chapter 2.

25. This is one way in which our current project is distinct from that of Barker, *The Great Angel*.

26. At one point, Philo himself seems to understand the "us" in Genesis 1:26 to refer to the Logos and God (*Leg.* 3.96), though at other points, Philo explains the "us" in terms of a multiplicity of powers or something more akin to a divine council (*Conf.* 168–74; *Fug.* 68–70).

27. For an excellent discussion, see Mark S. Smith, *The Origins of Biblical Monotheism: Israel's Polytheistic Background and the Ugaritic Texts* (Oxford: OUP, 2001), 135–94.

28. These examples and many more can be found in Adam Winn, "A Case for Jesus as the YHWH of Israel," in *Christology in Mark's Gospel: 4 Views*, ed. Anthony Le Donne (Grand Rapids, MI: Zondervan, 2021), 211–40.

29. For those who perceive in Mark a "low" Christology, see Kirk, *A Man Attested*; Frank Matera, *The Kingship of Jesus: Composition and Theology in Mark 15* (SBLDS, 66; Chico, CA: Scholars Press, 1982); Donald Juel, *Messiah and Temple: The Trial of Jesus in the Gospel of Mark* (SBLDS, 31; Missoula, MT: Scholars Press, 1977), 78–82, 108–14; J. D. Kingsbury, *The Christology of Mark's Gospel* (Philadelphia: Fortress, 1989), 32, 65, 142; D. Rhoads and D. Mitchie, *Mark as Story* (Philadelphia: Fortress, 1982), 105; Paul Achtemeier, "Mark, Gospel of," *Anchor Bbile Dictionary* (1992): 4:541–57; E. Broadhead, *Teaching with Authority: Miracles and Christology in the Gospel of Mark* (JSNTSup, 74; Sheffield: JSOT Press, 1992), 125–26; Elizabeth Struthers Malbon, *Mark's Jesus: Characterization as Narrative Christology* (Waco, TX: Baylor University Press, 2009), 72, 134. For a review of scholarship on Mark's Christology, see Daniel Johansson, "The Identity of Jesus in the gospel of Mark: Past and Present Proposals," *CBR* 9:3 (2010), 371–82.

30. See, for example, Johansson, "'Kyrios' in the Gospel of Mark" *JSNT* 33, no. 1 (2010): 101–24; Timothy J. Geddert, "The Implied YHWH Christology of Mark's

Gospel: Mark's Challenge to the Reader to 'Connect the Dots,'" *BBR* 25, no. 3 (2015): 325–40.

31. Timothy Geddert raises these very questions at the conclusion of his argument for identifying Jesus as YHWH in the Gospel of Mark ("The Implied YHWH Christology," 338–40).

32. For example, see Eugene Boring, *Mark: A Commentary* (NLT; Louisville, KY: WJK, 2006), 189–90; Geddert, "The Implied YHWH Christology," 332–34; Francis J. Moloney, *The Gospel of Mark: A Commentary* (Peabody: Hendrickson, 2002), 134–35; Joel Marcus, *Mark 1–8: A New Translation with Introduction and Commentary* (AB 27; New York: Doubleday, 1999), 422–27; Winn, "A Case for Jesus as the YHWH of Israel," 226–29.

33. For this conclusion see R. T. France, *The Gospel of Mark* (NIGTC; Grand Rapids, MI: Eerdmans, 2002), 271. Morna Hooker notes that the detail would be incomprehensible if the story is taken as a mere description of Jesus coming to aid his disciples (*The Gospel according to Saint Mark*, [BNTC; Peabody: Hendrickson, 1991), 170 (cf. J. Marcus, *Mark 1–8*, 426).

34. For example, see J. R. Daniel Kirk, "Narrative Christology of a Suffering King" and "Kirk's Response to Winn" in *Christology in Mark's Gospel: 4 Views*, ed. Anthony Le Donne (Grand Rapids, MI: Zondervan, 2021), 159, 265–66; and France, *Mark*, 273, n.71.

35. See Hooker, *Gospel according to Saint Mark*,169–70; Moloney, *Mark*, 134–35; Boring, *Mark*, 258: Collins, *Mark*, 333–35.

36. See Kirk, *A Man Attested*, 182–83; France, *Mark*, 63–64; Boring, *Mark*, 37.

37. E.g., in Rev 1:14 (cf. 2:18) Jesus has hair like wool and flames around him, like the Ancient of Days in Daniel 7:9. In Rev 1:15 (cf. 2:18), Jesus's appearance like "bronze" and the sound of his voice are things said of the Son of Man in Dan 10:6.

Bibliography

Ahearne-Kroll, Patricia D. *Aseneth of Egypt: The Composition of a Jewish Narrative.* Atlanta: SBL Press, 2020.

Alexander, Philip S. "Jewish Aramaic Translation of Hebrew Scriptures." Pages 210–53 in *Mikra: Text, Translation, Reading & Interpretation of the Hebrew Bible in Ancient Judaism & Early Christianity.* Edited by Martin Jan Mulder. Peabody, MA: Hendrickson, 2004.

Allert, Craig D. *Revelation, Truth, Canon and Interpretation: Studies in Justin Martyr's "Dialogue with Trypho."* Supplements to Vigiliae Christianae 64. Leiden: Brill, 2002.

Aly, Zaki, and Ludwig Koenen. *Three Rolls of the Early Septuagint: Genesis and Deuteronomy.* Bonn: Rudolf Habelt, 1980.

Anderson, Gary A., and Markus Bockmuehl, eds. *Creation "Ex Nihilo": Origins, Developments, Contemporary Challenges.* Notre Dame: University of Notre Dame Press, 2018.

Anderson, Gary A., and Michael E. Stone. *A Synopsis of the Books of Adam and Eve.* SBLEJL 17. Atlanta: Scholars Press, 1999.

Andrade, Nathanael J. "The Jewish Tetragrammaton: Secrecy, Community, and Prestige among Greek-Writing Jews of the Early Roman Empire." *JSJ* 46, no. 2 (2015): 198–223.

Angel, Joseph. "The Liturgical-Eschatological Priest of the 'Self-Glorification Hymn.'" *RevQ* 24, no. 4 (2010): 585–605.

Arcari, Luca. "A Symbolic Transfiguration of a Historical Event: The Parthian Invasion in Josephus and the Parables of Enoch." Pages 478–86 in *Enoch and the Messiah Son of Man: Revisiting the Book of Parables.* Edited by Gabriel Boccaccini. Grand Rapids, MI: Eerdmans, 2007.

Aufrecht, W. E. "*Surrogates for the Divine Name in the Palestinian Targums to Exodus.*" PhD diss., University of Toronto, 1979.

Azuelos, Yaacov, and Francesco Giosuè Voltaggio. "The 'Angel Sent from before the Lord' in 'Targum Joshua' 5,14." *Biblica* 96, no. 2 (2015): 161–78.

Bacchi, Ashley L. *Uncovering Jewish Creativity in Book III of the Sibylline Oracles: Gender, Intertextuality, and Politics.* Leiden: Brill, 2020.

Baillet, Maurice. *Qumran grotte 4.III. 4Q482-4Q520.* DJD 7. Oxford: Clarendon, 1982.

Bampfylde, G. "The Similitudes of Enoch: Historical Allusions." *JSJ* 15 (1984): 9–31.

Barker, Margaret. *The Great Angel: A Study of Israel's Second God.* Louisville, KY: Westminster John Knox Press, 1992.

———. "The High Priest and the Worship of Jesus." Pages 93–111 in *Jewish Roots of Christological Monotheism: Papers from the St. Andrews Conference on Historical Origins of the Worship of Jesus.* Edited by Carey C. Newman, James R. Davila, and Gladys S. Lewis. JSJSup 63. Leiden: Brill 1999.

Barrett, C. K. *The Gospel according to John: An Introduction with Commentary and Notes on the Greek Text.* 2nd ed. Philadelphia: Westminster, 1978.

Bauckham, Richard. "Is 'High Human Christology' Sufficient? A Critical Response to J. R. Daniel Kirk's *A Man Attested by God.*" *BBR* 27, no. 4 (2017): 503–25.

———. *Jesus and the God of Israel.* Grand Rapids, MI: Eerdmans, 2008.

———. *Son of Man.* Vol. 1 of *Early Jewish Literature.* Grand Rapids, MI: Eerdmans, 2023.

Begg, Christopher. "Angels in the Work of Flavius Josephus." Pages 525–36 in *Angels: The Concept of Celestial Beings—Origins.* Edited by Friedrich V. Teiterer, Tobias Niklas, and Karin Schöpfin. Deuterocanonical and Cognate Literature Yearbook; Berlin: De Gruyter, 2007.

Behr, John. *The Nicene Faith: Part 1.* Vol. 2 of *Formation of Christian Theology.* Crestwood, NY: St Vladimir's Seminary Press, 2004.

———. *The Way to Nicaea.* Vol. 1 of *Formation of Christian Theology.* Crestwood, NY: St Vladimir's Seminary Press, 2001.

———. Behr, *The Nicene Faith: Part 2.* Vol. 2 of *Formation of Christian Theology.* Crestwood, NY: St Vladimir's Seminary Press, 2004.

Ben-Dov, Jonathan. "Exegetical Notes on the Cosmology in the Parables of Enoch." Pages 143–51 in *Enoch and the Messiah Son of Man: Revisiting the Book of Parables.* Edited by Gabriel Boccaccini. Grand Rapids, MI: Eerdmans, 2007.

Ben-Dov, Jonathan, and Eshbal Ratzon. "The Oath and the Name in 1 Enoch 69." *JSS* 60, no. 1 (2015): 19–51.

Bianchi, Ugo. *Le Origini dello Gnosticismo Colloquio di Messina 13-18 Aprile 1966.* SHR 12. Leiden: Brill, 1967.

Bird, Michael F. *Jesus among the Gods: Early Christology in the Greco-Roman World.* Waco, TX: Baylor University Press, 2022.

Black, Matthew. *The Book of Enoch or 1 Enoch: A New English Edition.* SVTP 7. Leiden: Brill, 1985: 181–222.

———. "The Throne-Theophany, Prophetic Commission, and the 'Son of Man.'" Pages 57–73 in *Jews, Greeks, and Christians: Religious Cultures in Late Antiquity.* Edited by Robert G. Hamerton-Kelley and Robin Scroggs. Leiden: Brill, 1976.

Bobichon, Philippe. *Justin Martyr, Dialogue avec Tryphon: edition critique.* Fribourg: Departement de Patristique et d'Histoire de l'Eglise de l'Universite de Fribourg. 2003.

Boccaccini, Gabriele. "Finding a Place for the Parables of Enoch within Second Temple Jewish Literature." Pages 263–89 in *Enoch and the Messiah Son of Man: Revisiting the Book of Parables.* Edited by Gabriele Boccaccini. Grand Rapids, MI: Eerdmans, 2007.

Bock, Darrell L. "Dating the Parables of Enoch: A Forschungsbericht." Pages 58–113 in *Parables of Enoch: A Paradigm Shift*. Edited by Darrell L. Bock and James H. Charlesworth. JCTCRS 11. London: T&T Clark/Bloomsbury, 2013.

Bockmuehl, Markus. "*Creatio ex Nihilo* in Palestinian Judaism and Early Christianity." *SJT* 65, no. 3 (2012): 253–70.

———. *Revelation and Mystery in Ancient Judaism and Pauline Christianity*. Tübingen: Mohr Siebeck, 1990.

Boring, Eugene. *Mark: A Commentary*. NLT. Louisville, KY: Westminster John Knox, 2006.

Böttrich, Christfried. "A New Approach to the Apocryphal Ladder of Jacob." *JSP* 28, no. 3 (2019): 171–81.

Bousset, Wilhelm. *Kyrios Christos: A History of the Belief in Christ from the Beginnings of Christianity to Irenaeus*. Translated by John E. Steely. Nashville, TN: Abingdon Press, 1970 (German original = 1913).

Bousset, Wilhelm, and Hugo Gressmann. *Die Religion des Judentums in späthellenistischen Zeitalter*, 3rd ed. Handbuch zum neuen Testament 21. Tübingen: Mohr Siebeck, 1926.

Boyarin, Daniel. *Border Lines: The Partition of Judeo-Christianity*. Philadelphia: University of Pennsylvania Press, 2004.

———. "Enoch, Ezra, and the Jewishness of 'High Christology.'" Pages 337–61 in *Fourth Ezra and Second Baruch: Reconstruction after the Fall*. Edited by Matthias Henze and Gabriele Boccaccini. JSJSup. Leiden: Brill, 2013.

———. "The Gospel of the Memra: Jewish Binitarianism and the Prologue of John." *HTR* 94, no. 3 (2001): 243–84.

———. "Is Metatron a Converted Christian?" *Judaïsme Ancien* 1 (2013): 13–62.

———. "The Quest of the Historical Metatron: Enoch or Jesus." Pages 153–62 in *A Question of Identity: Social, Political, and Historical Aspects of Identity Dynamics in Jewish and Other Contexts*. Edited by Dikla Rivlin Katz, Noah Hacham, Geoffrey Herman, and Lilach Sagiv. Berlin: de Gruyter, 2019.

———. "Was the Book of Parables a Sectarian Document." Pages 380–85 in *Enoch and the Messiah Son of Man: Revisiting the Book of Parables*. Edited by Gabriel Boccaccini. Grand Rapids, MI: Eerdmans, 2007.

Brandenburger, Egon. *Adam und Christus: exegetisch-religionsgeschichtliche Untersuchung zum Röm. 5, 12-21 (1. Kor. 15)*. WMANT 7. Neukirchen-Vluyn: Neukirchener, 1962.

Broadhead, E. *Teaching with Authority: Miracles and Christology in the Gospel of Mark*. JSNTSup, 74. Sheffield: JSOT Press, 1992.

de Bruin, T. "In Defense of New Testament Satanologies: A Response to Farrar and Williams." *JSNT* 44, no. 3 (2022): 435–51.

Bucur, Bogdan G. "'I Saw the Lord': Observations on the Christian Reception History of Isaiah 6." *ProEccl* 23, no. 3 (2014): 309–30.

Bühner, Ruben A. *Messianic High Christology: New Testament Variants of Second Temple Judaism*. Waco, TX: Baylor University Press, 2021.

Buitenwerf, Rieuwerd. *Book III of the Sibylline Oracles and Its Social Setting*. SVTP 17. Leiden: Brill, 2003.

Bunta, S. N. "*Moses, Adam, and The Glory of the Lord in Ezekiel the Tragedian: On the Roots of a Merkabah Text.*" PhD diss., Marquette University, 2005.

Burchard, Christoph. *Untersuchungen zu Joseph and Aseneth.* WUNT 8. Tübingen: Mohr Siebeck, 1965.

Burkitt, F. C. "Memra, Shekinah, Metatron," *JTS* 24 (1923): 158–59.

Calabi, Francesca. *God's Acting, Man's Acting: Tradition and Philosophy in Philo of Alexandria.* SPhiloA 4. Leiden: Brill, 2008.

Capes, David B. *The Divine Christ: Paul, The Lord Jesus and the Scriptures of Israel.* Grand Rapids, MI: Eerdmans, 2018.

————. "Jesus' Unique Relationship with YHWH in Biblical Exegesis: A Response to Recent Objections." Pages 85–98 in *Monotheism and Christology in Greco-Roman Antiquity.* Edited by Matthew V. Novenson. NovTSup 180. Leiden: Brill, 2020.

Carmignac, Jean. "Le document de Qumran sur Melchisédeq." *RevQ* 7 (1970): 343–78.

Casanellas, Pere. "The Use of the Expressions 'Prophetic Spirit' and 'Holy Spirit' in the Targum and the Dating of the Targums." *Aramaic Studies* 11, no. 2 (2013): 167–86.

Casey, Maurice. *From Jewish Prophet to Gentile God: The Origins and Development of New Testament Christology.* Louisville, KY: Westminster John Knox, 1991.

Chadwick, Henry. *Early Christian Thought and the Classical Tradition.* Oxford: Oxford University Press. 1984.

Charles, R. H. *The Apocrypha and Pseudepigrapha of the Old Testament.* Oxford: Clarendon, 1913.

Charlesworth, James H. "The Date and Provenience of the Parables of Enoch" in *Parables of Enoch: A Paradigm Shift.* Edited by Darrell L. Bock and James H. Charlesworth. JCTCRS 11. London: T&T Clark/Bloomsbury, 2013.

————, ed. *The Old Testament Pseudepigrapha.* 2 vols. Peabody, MA: Hendrickson, 1983.

Chavel, Simeon. "The Face of God and the Etiquette of Eye-Contact: Visitation, Pilgrimage, and Prophetic Vision in Ancient Israelite and Early Jewish Imagination." *JSQ* 19 (1 2012): 1–55.

Chester, Andrew. "Jewish Messianic Expectations and Pauline Christology." Pages 17–89 in *Paulus und das antike Judentum.* Edited by M. Hengel and U. Heckel. Tübingen: Mohr Siebeck, 1992.

————. *Messiah and Exaltation: Jewish Messianic and Visionary Traditions and New Testament Christology.* WUNT 207. Tübingen: Mohr Siebeck, 2007.

Clark, Earnest G. *The Wisdom of Solomon.* CBCA. Cambridge: Cambridge University Press, 1974.

Cohen, S. J. D. "Alexander the Great and Jaddus the High Priest according to Josephus." *AJSR* 7, no. 8 (1982–1983): 41–68.

Cohon, Samuel S. "The Name of God: A Study in Rabbinic Theology." *HUCA* 23, no. 1 (1950): 579–604.

Collins, John J. "Joseph and Aseneth: Jewish or Christian." *JSP* 14, no. 2 (2005): 97–112.

————. *The Scepter and the Star: The Messiahs of the Dead Sea Scrolls and Other Ancient Literature.* ABRL. New York: Doubleday, 1995.

————. "Sibylline Oracles." Pages 317–472 in vol. 1 of *Old Testament Pseudepigrapha.* Edited by James H. Charlesworth. Peabody, MA: Hendrickson, 1983.

Conzelmann, H. "The Mother of Wisdom." Pages 230–43 in *The Future of Our Religious Past: Essays in Honor of Rudolph Bultmann.* Edited by James M. Robinson. Translated by Charles E. Carlston and Robert P. Scharlemann. New York: Harper & Row, 1971.

Cox, Ronald. *By This Same Word: Creation and Salvation in Hellenistic Judaism and Early Christianity.* BZNW 145. Berlin: de Gruyter, 2007.

Crenshaw, James L. *Old Testament Wisdom: An Introduction.* 3rd ed. Louisville, KY: Westminster John Knox, 2010.

Dahl, Nils A., and Alan F. Segal. "Philo and the Rabbis on the Names of God." *JSJ* 9, no. 1 (1978): 1–28.

Danby, Herbert. *Tractate Sanhedrin: Mishnah and Tosefta.* New York: MacMillan, 1919.

Daniélou, Jean. *The Theology of Jewish Christianity.* Translated and edited by John A. Baker. Philadelphia: Westminster, 1978.

Davila, J. R. "Heavenly Ascents in the Dead Sea Scrolls." Pages 461–85 in vol. 2 of *The Dead Sea Scrolls After Fifty Years: A Comprehensive Assessment.* Edited by P. W. Flint and J.C. VanderKam. Leiden: Brill, 1999.

Davis, Carl Judson. *The Name and Way of the Lord: Old Testament Themes, New Testament Christology.* London: Bloomsbury, 1996.

Decharneux, Baudouin S. "Divine Powers in Philo of Alexandria's De opificio mundi." Pages 127–39 in *Divine Powers in Late Antiquity.* Edited by Anna Marmodoro, and Irini-Fotini Viltanioti. Oxford: Oxford University Press, 2017.

DeConick, April D. "Heavenly Temple Traditions and Valentinian Worship: A Case for First-Century Christology in the Second Century." In *Historical Origins of the Worship of Jesus Conference Volume, St. Andrews, Scotland 1998,* eds. J. Davila and C. Newman. Supplements to JSJ. Leiden: Brill, 1998.

Denzey, Nicola Frances. "Genesis Traditions in Conflict? The Use of Some Exegetical Traditions in the *Trimorphic Protennoia* and the Johannine Prologue." *VC* 55, no. 1 (2001): 27–28.

Di Lella, Alexander A., and Patrick W. Skehan. *The Wisdom of Ben Sira.* Anchor Bible 39. New Haven: Yale University Press, 1987.

Dillon, John. *The Middle Platonists, 80 B.C. to A.D. 220.* Rev. ed. Ithaca, NY: Cornell University Press, 1996.

————. "Philo's Doctrine of Angels." Pages 197–205 in *Two Treatises of Philo of Alexandria: A Commentary on* De Gigantibus *and* Quod Deus Sit Immutabilis. Edited by David Winston and John M. Dillon. Chico, CA: Scholars Press, 1983.

Dochorn, Jan. "Die Adamiegesen und das Neu Testament." Pages 57–76 in *La Vie d'Adam et Ève et les traditions adamiques.* Edited by F. Amsler, A. Frey, J. D. Kaestli, and A. L. Rey. Publications de l'Institut romand des sciences bibliques 8. Lausanne: Zèbre, 2017.

——. *Die Apokalypse des Mose. Text, Übersetzung, Kommentar*. TSAJ 106. Tübingen: Mohr Siebeck, 2005.

Dodd, C. H. *The Interpretation of the Fourth Gospel*. Cambridge: Cambridge University Press, 1953.

Dunn, James D. G. *Christology in the Making: A New Testament Inquiry into the Origins of the Doctrine of the Incarnation*. 2nd ed. Grand Rapids, MI: Eerdmans, 1989.

Ehrman, Bart. *How Jesus Became God: The Exaltation of a Jewish Preacher from Galilee*. San Francisco: HarperOne, 2014.

Eissfeldt, Otto. *El im ugaritischen Pantheon*. Berichte über die Verhandlungen der Sächsischen Akademic der Wissenschaften zu Leipzig. Phil. His. Klasse 98.4. Berk: Akademie, 1951.

Emerton, J. A. "The Origin of the Son of Man Imagery." *JTS* 9 (1958): 225–42.

Eshel, Esther. "'4Q471B': A Self-Glorification Hymn." *RevQ* 17, no. 1 (1996): 175–203.

Evans, Craig A., and Stanley E. Porter. *The Dictionary of New Testament Background*. Downers Grove, IL: InterVarsity Press, 2000.

Everson, David L. "Angels in the Targums: *An Examination of Angels, Demons, and Giants in the Pentateuch Targums.*" PhD diss., Hebrew Union College-Jewish Institute of Religion, 2009.

——. "A Brief Comparison of Targumic and Midrashic Angelological Traditions." *Aramaic Studies* 5, no. 1 (2007): 75–91.

——. "The Fish Grows Bigger: Angelic Insertions in Targums Neofiti and Pseudo-Jonathan." Pages 233–43 in *Aramaic in Postbiblical Judaism and Early Christianity*. Edited by Eric M. Meyers and Paul V. M. Flesher. Duke Judaic Studies Series 3. Winona Lake, IN: Eisenbrauns, 2010.

Falls, T. B., T. P. Halton, and M. Slusser. *St. Justin Martyr: Dialogue with Trypho*. Washington, DC: Catholic University of America Press, 2003.

Farrar, Thomas J. "New Testament Satanology and Leading Suprahuman Opponents in Second Temple Jewish Literature: A Religio-Historical Analysis." *JTS* 70, no. 1 (2019): 21–68.

Ferguson, Anthony. "The Elijah Forerunner Concept as an Authentic Jewish Expectation." *JBL* 137, no. 1 (2018): 127–45.

Fitzmyer, Joseph A. *Tobit*. Commentaries on Early Jewish Literature. Berlin: de Gruyter, 2003.

——. *A Wondering Aramean: Collected Aramaic Essays*. Chico, CA: Scholars Press, 1979.

Fletcher-Louis, Crispin. "4Q374: A Discourse on the Sinai Tradition: The Deification of Moses and Early Christology." *DSD* 3, no. 3 (1996): 236–52.

——. "Alexander The Great's Worship of the High Priest." Pages 71–102 in *Early Jewish and Christian Monotheism*. Edited by Loren T. Stuckenbruck and Wendy E. S. North. JSNTSup vol. 63. New York: T&T Clark/Continuum, 2004.

——. *All the Glory of Adam: Liturgical Anthropology in the Dead Sea Scrolls*. Leiden: Brill, 2002.

——. *Jesus Monotheism: Christological Origins: The Emerging Consensus*. Volume 1. Eugene, OR: Cascade, 2015.

Flowers, Michael. "The Two Messiahs and Melchizedek in 11QMelchizedek." *JAJ* 7, no. 2 (2016): 194–227.

Flusser, David. "Melchizedek and the Son of Man." Pages 186–92 in *Judaism and the Origins of Christianity*. Jerusalem: Magnes. Hebrew University, 1988.

Fossum, Jarl E. *The Name of God and the Angel of the Lord*. WUNT 36. Tübingen: Mohr Siebeck, 1985.

Fox, M. "World Order and Ma'at: A Crooked Parallel." *JANES* 23 (1995): 37–48.

France, R. T. *The Gospel of Mark*. NIGTC. Grand Rapids, MI: Eerdmans, 2002.

Fredriksen, Paula. "How High Can Early High Christology Be?" Pages 293–320 in *Monotheism and Christology in Greco-Roman Antiquity*. Edited by Matthew V. Novenson. NovTSup 180. Leiden: Brill, 2020.

———. "Mandatory Retirement: Ideas in the Study of Christian Origins Whose Time Has Come to Go." *SR* 35 (2006): 231–46.

Freedman, David Noel, ed. *The Anchor Bible Dictionary*. 6 vols. New York: Doubleday, 1992.

Frey, Jörg. "How Did the Holy Spirit Become a Person?" Pages 343–71 in *The Holy Spirit, Inspiration, and the Cultures of Antiquity: Multidisciplinary Perspectives*. Edited by Jörg Frey, John R. Levison, and Andrew Bowden. Ekstasis 5. Berlin: de Gruyter, 2014.

———. "Paul's View of the Spirit in the Light of Qumran." Pages 237–60 in *The Dead Sea Scrolls and Pauline Literature*. Edited by Jean-Sébastien Rey. STDJ 102. Leiden: Brill, 2014.

Frick, Peter. *Divine Providence in Philo of Alexandria*. Tübingen: Mohr Siebeck, 1999.

Gabrielson, Timothy A. "An Early Reader of James? Ethical Parallels between the Epistle and 2 Enoch." *JSNT* 43, no. 2 (2020): 226–47.

Geddert, Timothy J. "The Implied YHWH Christology of Mark's Gospel: Mark's Challenge to the Reader to 'Connect the Dots.'" *BBR* 25, no. 3 (2015): 325–40.

Gieschen, Charles A. *Angelomorphic Christology: Antecedents and Early Evidence*. Leiden: Brill, 1998.

———. "The Divine Name as a Characteristic of Divine Identity in Second Temple Judaism and Early Christianity." Pages 61–84 in *Monotheism and Christology in Greco-Roman Antiquity*. Edited by Matthew V. Novenson. NovTSup 180. Leiden: Brill, 2020.

———. "The Divine Name in Ante-Nicene Christology." *VC* 57, no. 2 (2003):115–58.

Goodenough, Erwin R. *By Light, Light*. New Haven, CT: Yale University Press, 1935.

———. *An Introduction to Philo Judaeus*. New Haven, CT: Yale University Press, 1940.

Goshen-Gottstein, Alon. *The Sinner and the Amnesiac: The Rabbinic Invention of Elisha ben Abuya and Eleazar ben Arach*. Stanford, CA: Stanford University Press, 2000.

Grierson, Fiona. "The Testament of Moses." *JSP* 17, no. 4 (2008): 265–80.

Gruen, E. S. *The Construction of Identity in Hellenistic Judaism: Essays on Early Jewish Literature and History*. DCLS 29; Berlin: De Gruyter, 2016.

———. *Diaspora: Jews amidst Greeks and Romans*. Cambridge: Harvard University Press, 2002.

Guggisberg, Frist. *Die Gestalt des Mal'ak Jahwe im AT.* Lyss: Dach Druck, 1979.

Günther, Eva. *Wisdom as a Model for Jesus' Ministry in the 'Lament Over Jerusalem' (Matt 23, 37–39 Par. Luke 13, 34–35).* WUNT 2/513. Tübingen: Mohr Siebeck, 2020.

Gurtner, Daniel M. *Introducing the Pseudepigrapha of Second Temple Judaism.* Grand Rapids, MI: Baker Academic, 2020.

Halperin, David J. *The Faces of the Chariot: Early Jewish Responses to Ezekiel's Vision.* Texte und Studien zum Antiken Judentum 16. Tübingen: Mohr Siebeck, 1988.

Hamerton-Kelly, Robert. *Pre-Existence, Wisdom, and the Son of Man: A Study of the Idea of Pre-Existence in the New Testament.* SNTSMS 21. Cambridge: Cambridge University Press, 1973.

Hannah, Darrell D. "The Book of Noah, the Death of Herod the Great, and the Date of the Parables of Enoch." Pages 469–77 in *Enoch and the Messiah Son of Man: Revisiting the Book of Parables.* Edited by Gabriel Boccaccini. Grand Rapids, MI: Eerdmans, 2007.

———. *Michael and Christ: Michael Traditions and Angel Christology in Early Christianity.* WUNT 2/109. Tübingen: Mohr Siebeck, 1999.

von Harnack, Adolf. *History of Dogma,* 7 vols. Gloucester: Peter Smith, 1976 (German original = 1894–1998).

Hayman, P. "Monotheism—A Misused Word in Jewish Studies?" *JJS* 42 (1991): 1–13.

Hayward, Robert. *Divine Name and Presence: The Memra.* Totowa, NJ: Allanheld, Osmun, 1981.

von Heijne, Camilla Hélena. *The Messenger of the Lord in Early Interpretations of Genesis.* BZAW 412. Berlin: de Gruyter, 2010.

Heiser, Michael S. "Co-Regency in Ancient Israel's Divine Council as the Conceptual Backdrop to Ancient Jewish Binitarian Monotheism." *BBR* 26, no. 2 (2015): 195–225.

———. "Deuteronomy 32:8 and the Sons of God." *Bibliotheca Sacra* 158 (2001): 52–74.

———. "Monotheism, Polytheism, Monolatry, or Henotheism? Toward and Assessment of Divine Plurality in the Hebrew Bible." *BBR* 18, no. 1 (2008): 1–30.

Hengel, Martin. *The Son of God: The Origin of Christology and the History of Jewish-Hellenistic Religion.* Philadelphia: Fortress, 1976 (German original = 1973).

———. "Zur Wirkungsgeschichte von Jes 53 in vorchristlicher Zeit." Pages 49–91 in *Der leidende Gottesknecht: Jesaja 53 und seine Wirkungsgeschichte.* Edited by B. Janowski and P. Stuhlmacher. FAT 14. Tübingen: Mohr Siebeck, 1996.

Hess, R. S. "Wisdom Sources." Pages 895–98 in *Dictionary of the Old Testament: Wisdom, Poetry and Writings.* Edited by Tremper Longman and Peter Enns. Downers Grove, IL: InterVarsity Press, 2008.

Hicks-Keeton, Jill. "Aseneth between Judaism and Christianity: Reframing the Debate." *JSJ* 49 (2018): 189–222.

Hillar, M. "The Logos and Its Function in the Writing of Philo of Alexandria: Greek Interpretation of Hebrew Thought and Foundations of Christianity: Part Two." *JRR* 7 (1998): 36–53.

Holladay, Carl R. Theios Aner *in Hellenistic-Judaism: A Critique of the Use of This Category in New Testament Christology*. SBLDS 40. Missoula, MT: Scholars Press, 1977.

Hombert, Marie. *Nouvelles recherches de chronologie augustinienne,* Collection des etudes augustiniennes, Série Antiquité 163. Paris: Institut d'Études Augustiniennes, 2000.

Hooker, Morna. *The Gospel according to Saint Mark*. BNTC. Peabody: Hendrickson, 1991.

Horbury, William. "Jewish and Christian Monotheism in the Herodian Age." Pages 16–44 in *Early Jewish and Christian Monotheism*. Edited by Loren T. Stuckenbruck and Wendy E. S. North. JSNTSup 63. New York: T&T Clark 2004.

———. *Jewish Messianism and the Cult of Christ*. London: SCM, 1998.

van der Horst, Pieter. "Moses' Throne Vision in Ezekiel the Dramatist." *JJS* 34 (1983): 21–29.

Howard, George. "The Tetragram and the New Testament." *JBL* 96 (1977): 63–68.

Hultgård, Anders. "The Ideal 'Levite,' the Davidic Messiah, the Savior Priest in the Testament of the Twelve Patriarchs." Pages 93–110 in *Ideal Figures in Ancient Judaism*. Edited by John J. Collins and George W. E. Nickelsburg. SBLSCS 12. Chico, CA: Scholars Press, 1980.

Hultgren, Stephen. "The Origins of Paul's Doctrine of the Two Adams in 1 Corinthians 15:45–49." *JSNT* 25, no. 3 (2003): 343–70.

Hurtado, Larry. "'Ancient Jewish Monotheism' in Hellenistic and Roman Periods." *JAJ* 4 (2013): 370–400.

———. *At the Origins of Christian Worship: The Context and Character of Earliest Christian Devotion*. Grand Rapids, MI: Eerdmans, 1999.

———. "First-Century Jewish Monotheism." *JSNT* 71 (1998): 3–26.

———. *Lord Jesus Christ: Devotion to Jesus in Earliest Christianity*. Grand Rapids, MI: Eerdmans, 2005.

———. *One God, One Lord: Early Christian Devotion and Ancient Jewish Monotheism*. 3rd ed. New York: Bloomsbury/T&T Clark, 2015.

Jacobson, Howard. *A Commentary on Pseudo-Philo's Liber antiquitatum biblicarum*. Leiden: Brill, 1996.

———. "Mysticism and Apocalyptic in Ezekiel's Exagoge." *Illinois Classical Studies* 8 (1981): 273–93.

Jobes, Karen H. "Sophia Christology: The Way of Wisdom?" Pages 226–50 in *The Way of Wisdom: Essays in Honor of Bruce K. Waltke*. Edited by James I. Packer and Sven Soderlund. Grand Rapids, MI: Zondervan, 2000.

Johansson, Daniel. "The Identity of Jesus in the Gospel of Mark: Past and Present Proposals." *CBR* 9, no. 3 (2010): 371-82.

———. "'Kyrios' in the Gospel of Mark." *JSNT* 33, no. 1 (2010): 101–24.

———. "'Who Can Forgive Sins but God Alone?': Human and Angelic Agents, and Divine Forgiveness in Early Judaism." *Journal for the Study of the New Testament* 33, no. 4 (2011): 351–74.

de Jonge, M. "The Christian Origin of the Greek Life of Adam and Eve." Pages 347–63 in *Literature on Adam and Eve: Collected Essays*, eds. G. A. Anderson, M.

Stone, J. Tromp. Leiden: Brill, 2000.Jones, L. *The Encyclopedia of Religion*. 2nd ed. 15 vols. 2005. Detroit, MI: Gale, 2005.

de Jonge, M. and J. Tromp. *The Life of Adam and Eve and Related Literature*. Sheffield: Sheffield Academic, 1997.

Juel, Donald. *Messiah and Temple: The Trial of Jesus in the Gospel of Mark*. SBLDS 31. Missoula, MT: Scholars Press, 1977.

Kaestli, Jean-Daniel. "La *Vie d'Adam et Ève*: nouveaux acquis et questions ouvertes." Pages 29–56 in *La Vie d'Adam et Ève et les traditions adamiques*. Edited by F. Amsler, A. Frey, J. D. Kaestli, and A. L. Rey. Publications de l'Institut romand des sciences bibliques 8. Lausanne: Zèbre, 2017.

———. "Le mythe de la chute de Satan et la question du milieu d'origine de la *Vie d'Adam et Ève*." Pages 342–54 in *Early Christian Voices: In Texts, Traditions, and Symbols. Essays in Honor of François Bovon*. Edited by D. Warren, A. G. Brock, D. W. Pao. Biblical Interpretation Series 66. Leiden: Brill, 2003.

Kaufman, S. A. "Dating the Language of the Palestinian Targums and their Use in the Study of First Century CE Texts." Pages 118–41 in *The Aramaic Bible: Targums in Their Historical Context*. Edited by D. R. G. Beattie and Martin McNamara. JSOTSup 166. Sheffield: Sheffield Academic, 1994.

Keddie, G. Anthony. "Judaean Apocalypticism and the Unmasking of Ideology: Foreign and National Rulers in the Testament of Moses." *JSJ* 44, no. 3 (2013): 301–38.

Kelly, Henry. *Satan: A Biography*. Cambridge: Cambridge University Press, 2006.

———. *Satan in the Bible: God's Minister of Justice*. Eugene, OR: Cascade, 2017.

Keener, Craig S. *The Gospel of John: A Commentary*. Vol. 1. Peabody, MA: Hendrickson, 2003.

Kelly, J. N. D. *Early Christian Doctrine*. Rev. ed. San Francisco: HarperOne, 1978.

Kingsbury, J. D. *The Christology of Mark's Gospel*. Philadelphia: Fortress, 1989.

Kirk, J. R. Daniel. *A Man Attested by God: The Human Jesus of the Synoptic Gospels*. Grand Rapids, MI: Eerdmans, 2016.

———. "Narrative Christology of a Suffering King." Pages 137–71 in *Christology in Mark's Gospel: 4 Views*. Edited by Anthony Le Donne. Grand Rapids, MI: Zondervan, 2021.

Kittel, Gerhard, and Gerhard Friedrich, eds. *Theological Dictionary of the New Testament*. Translated by Geoffrey W. Bromiley. 10 vols. Grand Rapids, MI: Eerdmans, 1964–1976.

Kloos, Kari. *Christ, Creation, and the Vision of God: Augustine's Transformation of Early Christian Theophany Interpretation*. Leiden: Brill, 2011.

Kloppenborg, John S. "Isis and Sophia in the Book of Wisdom." *HTR* 75 (1982): 57–84.

Knibb, Michael A. *The Ethiopic Book of Enoch: A New Edition in Light of the Aramaic Dead Sea Fragments*. 2 vols. Oxford: Clarendon, 1978.

———. "The Structure and Composition of the Parables of Enoch." Pages 48–64 in *Enoch and the Messiah Son of Man: Revisiting the Book of Parables*. Edited by G. Boccaccini. Grand Rapids, MI: Eerdmans, 2007.

Knox, W. L. "The Divine Wisdom." *JTS* 38 (1937): 230–37.

Kraemer, Ross Shepard. *When Aseneth Met Joseph: A Late Antique Tale of the Biblical Patriarch and His Egyptian Wife, Reconsidered.* Oxford: Oxford University Press, 1998.

Kratz, Reinhard G. "Deity and Divine in the Hebrew Bible and the Dead Sea Scrolls." Pages 636–54 in *Sibyls, Scriptures, and Scrolls: John Collins at Seventy.* Edited by Joel S. Baden, Hindy Najman, and Eibert J. C. Tigchelaar. JSJSup 175.1. Leiden: Brill, 2017.

Kugel, James L. *The God of Old: Inside the Lost World of the Bible.* New York: Free Press, 2003.

Kulik, Alexander. "On Traditions Shared by Rabbinic Literature and Slavonic Pseudepigrapha." *JSP* 28, no. 1 (2018): 45–67.

Kutscher, E. Y. "The Language of the Genesis Apocryphon." Pages 1–35 in *Aspects of the Dead Sea Scrolls.* Edited by Ch. Rabin and Y. Yadin. Scripta Hierosolymitana 4. Jerusalem: Magnes, 1958.

Kvanvig, Helge. "The Son of Man in the Parables of Enoch." Pages 179–215 in *Enoch and the Messiah Son of Man: Revisiting the Book of Parables.* Edited by G. Boccaccini. Grand Rapids, MI: Eerdmans, 2007.

Laato, Antti. *The Origin of Israelite Zion Theology.* Library of Hebrew Bible/Old Testament Studies, 661. Edinburgh: T&T Clark, 2018.

Legeay, D. Georges. "L'Ange et les théophanies dans l'Ecriture Sainte d'après la doctrine des Pères." *RThom* 10 (1902): 138–58, 405–24. and *RThom* 11 (1903): 46–69, 125–54.

Leonhardt-Balzer, Jutta. *Jewish Worship in Philo of Alexandria.* TSAJ 84. Tübingen: Mohr Siebeck, 2001.

Levison, John R. "1 John 3.12, Early Judaism and the Greek Life of Adam and Eve." *JSNT* 42, no. 4 (2020): 453–71.

———. "The Debut of the Divine Spirit in Josephus's *Antiquities.*" *HTR* 87, no. 2 (1994):123–38.

———. "Josephus' Interpretation of the Divine Spirit." *JJS* 46 (1996): 234–55.

———. "The Prophetic Spirit as an Angel according to Philo." *HTR* 88, no. 2 (1995): 189–207.

———. *The Spirit in First-Century Judaism.* Leiden: Brill, 1997.

Lierman, John. *The New Testament Moses: Christian Perceptions of Moses and Israel in the Setting of Jewish Religion.* Tübingen: Mohr Siebeck, 2004.

Lieu, Judith M. *Image and Reality: The Jews in the World of the Christians in the Second Century.* Edinburgh: T&T Clark, 1996.

Litwa, M. David. *Refutation of All Heresies.* Writings from the Greco-Roman World 40. Atlanta: SBL Press, 2016.

Lohmeyer, Ernst. "Die Verklärung Jesu nach dem Markus-Evangelium." *ZNW* 21 (1922): 188–89.

Longenecker, Richard. "Some Distinctive Early Christological Motifs." *NTS* 14 (1968): 526–45.

Longman III, Tremper. *The Fear of the Lord Is Wisdom: A Theological Introduction to Wisdom in Israel.* Grand Rapids, MI: Baker Academic, 2017.

Longman III, Tremper, and Peter Enns, eds. *Dictionary of the Old Testament: Wisdom, Poetry, and Writings*. Downers Grove, IL: Intervarsity Press, 2008.

Lust, J. "Daniel 7.13 and the Septuagint." *ETL* 54 (1978): 62–63.

Lys, Daniel. *"Ruach": Le souffle dans l'Ancien Testament*. Paris: Presses universitaires de France, 1962.

Macatangay, Francis M. *The Wisdom Instruction in the Book of Tobit*. DCLS 12: Berlin: de Gruyter, 2011.

Mach, Michael. "The Concepts of Jewish Monotheism during the Hellenistic Period." Pages 21–42 in *Jewish Roots of Christological Monotheism: Papers from the St. Andrews Conference on Historical Origins of the Worship of Jesus*. Edited by Carey C. Newman, James R. Davila, and Gladys S. Lewis. JSJSup 63. Leiden: Brill 1999.

———. *Entwicklungsstadien des jüdischen Engelglaubens in vorrabbinischer Zeit*. Texte und Studien zum Antiken Judentum 34. Tübingen: Mohr Siebeck, 1992.

———. "Justin Martyr's *Dialogus cum Tryphone Iudaeo* and the Development of Christian Anti-Judaism." Pages 27–48 in *Contra Iudaeos: Ancient and Medieval Polemics between Christians and Jews*. Edited by Ora Limor and Guy G. Stroumsa. Tübingen: Mohr Siebeck, 1996.

Mack, Burton L. *Logos und Sophia: Untersuchungen zur Weisheitstheologie im hellenistischen Judentum*. Göttingen: Vandenhoeck & Ruprecht, 1973.

Mackie, Scott D. "Seeing God in Philo of Alexandria: Means, Methods, and Mysticism." *JSJ* 43, no. 2 (2012): 147–79.

———. "Seeing God in Philo of Alexandria: The Logos, the Powers, or the Existent One?" *Studia Philonica* 21 (2009): 25–47.

Malbon, Elizabeth Struthers. *Mark's Jesus: Characterization as Narrative Christology*. Waco, TX: Baylor University Press, 2009.

Malone, Andrew S. "Distinguishing the Angel of the Lord." *BBR* 21, no. 3 (2011): 297–314.

Manzi, Franco. *Melchisedek e l'angelologia nell'epistola agli Ebrei e a Qumran*. AnBib 136. Rome: Pontifical Biblical Institute, 1997.

Marcus, Joel. *Mark 1-8: A New Translation with Introduction and Commentary*. Anchor Bible 27. New York: Doubleday, 1999.

Marcus, Ralph. "On Biblical Hypostases of Wisdom." *HUCA* 23, no. 1 (1950): 157–71.

Martínez, F. García. "Old Texts and Modern Mirages: The 'I' of Two Qumran Hymns." Pages 118–24 in *Qumranica Minora I: Qumran Origins and Apocalypticism*. Edited by E. Tigchelaar. STDJ 63. Leiden: Brill, 2007.

Martínez, F. García, and E. Tigchelaar, eds. *The Dead Sea Scrolls Study Edition*. 2 vols. Leiden: Brill, 1997.

Matera, Frank. *The Kingship of Jesus: Composition and Theology in Mark 15*. SBLDS, 66. Chico, CA: Scholars Press, 1982.

Mattila, Sharon Lea. "Wisdom, Sense Perception, Nature, and Philo's Gender Gradient." *HTR* 89, no. 2 (1996): 103–29.

Mattingly, Harold. "The Roman Virtues." *HTR* 30, no. 2 (1937): 103–17.

May, Gerhard. *"Creatio ex Nihilo": The Doctrine of "Creation out of Nothing" in Early Christian Thought*. Edinburgh: T&T Clark, 1994.

Mayer, G. "Logos." *Index Philoneus*. Berlin: de Gruyter, 1974.

McDonald, Nathan. *Deuteronomy and the Meaning of "Monotheism."* FAT 2/1. Tübingen: Mohr Siebeck, 2003.

McDonough, Sean M. *YHWH at Patmos: Rev. 1:4 in its Hellenistic and Early Jewish Setting.* WUNT 2/107. Tübingen: Mohr Siebeck, 1999.

McGrath, James F. *The Only True God: Early Christian Monotheism in Its Jewish Context.* Champaign: University of Illinois Press, 2009.

McNamara, Martin. *Targum and New Testament.* WUNT. Tübingen: Mohr Siebeck, 2011.

———. *Targum and Testament, Aramaic Paraphrases of the Hebrew Bible: A Light on the New Testament.* Grand Rapids, MI: Eerdmans, 1972.

———. *Targum and Testament Revisited: Aramaic Paraphrases of the Hebrew Bible.* 2nd ed. Grand Rapids, MI: Eerdmans, 2010.

Meier, Samuel A. "Angel of Yawheh." Pages 95–108 in *Dictionary of Deities and Demons in the Bible.* 2nd ed. Edited by Karel van der Toorn, Bob Becking, and Pieter W. van der Horst. Grand Rapids, MI: Eerdmans, 1999.

Michalak, Aleksander R. *Angels as Warriors in Late Second Temple Jewish Literature.* WUNT 2/330. Tübingen: Mohr Siebeck, 2012.

Milik, J. T. *The Book of Enoch: Aramaic Fragments of Qumran Cave 4.* Oxford: Clarendon, 1976.

———. *"Melkî-Ṣedeq et Melkî-Reša'* dans les anciens éscrits juifs et chrétiens (I)." *JJS* 23 (1972): 95–144.

Moloney, Francis J. *The Gospel of Mark: A Commentary.* Peabody, MA: Hendrickson, 2002.

Montgomery, James A. "The Religion of Flavius Josephus." *JQR* 11, no. 3 (1921), 277–305.

Moore, Carey A. *Tobit: A New Translation and Commentary,* The Anchor Bible vol. 40A. New York: Doubleday, 1996.

Moore, G. F. "Intermediaries in Jewish Theology: Memra, Shekinah, Metatron." *HTR* 15 (1922): 41–85.

Morray-Jones, C. R. A. "Transformational Mysticism in the Apocalyptic-Merkabah Tradition." *JJS* 43, no. 1 (1992): 1–31.

Mowinckel, Sigmund. "Hypostasen." Pages 2065–68 in vol. 2 of *Die Religion in Geschichte und Gegenwart.* 2nd ed. Tübingen: Mohr Siebeck, 1928.

Muñoa, Phillip. "Before Mary and Jesus There was Raphael: An Antecedent to the Angelic 'Incarnations' of Jewish Christianity and Its Gospels." In *The Open Mind: Essays in Honour of Christopher Rowland,* eds. Jonathan Knight and Kevin Sullivan. London: T&T Clark, 2014.

———. "Raphael, Azariah and Jesus of Nazareth: Tobit's Significance for Early Christology." *Journal for the Study of the Pseudepigrapha* 22, no. 1 (2012): 3–39.

———. "Raphael the Savior: Tobit's Adaptation of the Angel of the Lord Tradition." *Journal for the Study of the Pseudepigrapha* 25, no. 3 (2016): 228–43.

Murphy, Roland Edmund. *The Tree of Life: An Exploration of Biblical Wisdom Literature.* Grand Rapids, MI: Eerdmans, 2002.

Neher, Martin. *Wesen und Wirken der Weisheit in der Sapientia Salomonis.* BZAW 333. Berlin: de Gruyter, 2004.

Neusner, Jacob. *The Tosefta: Translated from the Hebrew with a New Introduction.* Peabody, MA: Hendrickson Publishers, 2002.

Newman, Carey C., James R. Davila, and Gladys S. Lewis, *The Jewish Roots of Christological Monotheism: Papers from the St. Andrews Conference on the Historical Origins of the Worship of Jesus.* Leiden: Brill, 1999.

Nickelsburg, George W. E. "Discerning the Structure(s) of the Enochic Book of Parables." Pages 23–46 in *Enoch and the Messiah Son of Man: Revisiting the Book of Parables.* Edited by Gabriel Boccaccini. Grand Rapids: Eerdmans, 2007.

Nickelsburg, George W. E., and James C. VanderKam. *1 Enoch.* Hermeneia. Minneapolis: Fortress, 2012.

Niehoff, Maren R. *Philo of Alexandria: An Intellectual Biography.* New Haven, CT: Yale University Press, 2018.

Nir, Rivka. *Joseph and Aseneth: A Christian Book.* Sheffield: Sheffield Phoenix, 2012.

Novenson, Matthew V. "The Universal Polytheism and the Case of the Jews." Pages 32–60 in *Monotheism and Christology in Greco-Roman Antiquity.* Edited by Matthew V. Novenson. NovTSup vol. 180. Leiden: Brill, 2020.

Olson, Daniel C. *Enoch: A New Translation.* North Richland Hills, TX: BIBAL Press, 2004.

Olyan, Saul M. *A Thousand Thousands Served Him: Exegesis and the Naming of Angels in Ancient Judaism.* Tübingen: Mohr Siebeck, 1993.

O'Neil, J. C. "If God Created Adam in His Own Image, in the Image of God Created He Him, How Is Christ the Image of God?" *Irish Biblical Studies* 21 (1999): 79–87.

Orlov, Andrei A. *Embodiment of Divine Knowledge in Early Judaism.* London ; New York: Routledge, 2021.

———. *The Enoch-Metatron Tradition.* TSAJ 107. Tübingen: Mohr Siebeck, 2005.

———. "Ex 33 on God's Face: A Lesson from the Enochic Tradition." *Scrinium* 3, no. 1 (2007): 323–36.

———. "The Face as the Heavenly Counterpart of the Visionary in the Slavonic Ladder of Jacob." Pages 59–76 in *Of Scribes and Sages: Early Jewish Interpretations and Transmission of Scripture.* Vol. 2. Edited by Craig A. Evans. London: Bloomsbury/ T&T Clark, 2004.

———. *The Glory of the Invisible God: Two Powers in Heaven Traditions and Early Christology.* JCTCRSS 31. New York: T&T Clark/Continuum, 2019.

———. "Praxis of the Voice: The Divine Name Tradition in the Apocalypse of Abraham." *JBL* 127, no. 1 (2008): 53–70.

———. "The Sacerdotal Traditions of 2 Enoch and the Date of the Text." Pages 103–16 in *New Perspectives on 2 Enoch: No Longer Slavonic Only.* Edited by Andrei Orlov, Gabriele Boccaccini, and Jason Zurawski. Studia Judaeoslavica 4. Leiden: Brill, 2012.

———. *Yahoel and Metatron: Aural Apocalypticism and the Origins of Early Jewish Mysticism.* TSAJ 169. Tübingen: Mohr Siebeck, 2017.

Paz, Yakir. "Metatron Is not Enoch: Reevaluating the Evolution of an Archangel." *JSJ* 50 (2019): 52–100.

Pelikan, Jaroslav. *"Canonica Regula:* The Trinitarian Hermeneutics of Augustine." Pages 329–43 in *Collectanea Augustiniana*. Edited by Joseph C. Schnaubelt and Frederick Van Fleteren. New York: Lang, 1990.

Peppard, Michael. *The Son of God in the Roman World: Divine Sonship in Its Social and Political Context*. Oxford: Oxford University Press, 2012.

Perdue, Leo G. *Wisdom Literature: A Theological History*. Louisville, KT: Westminster John Knox, 2007.

Pettorelli, S. J. P., and J. D. Kaestli. *Vita Latina Adae et Evae*. 2 vols. CC Series Apocryphorum 18. Turnhout: Brepols, 2012.

Pfeifer, Gerhard. *Ursprung und Wesen der Hypostasenvorstellung im Judentum*. Stuttgart: Calwer, 1967.

Philonenko, Marc. *Joseph et Aséneth*. SPB, 13. Leiden: Brill, 1968.

Piovanelli, Pierluigi. "'A Testimony for the Kings and the Might Who Possess the Earth': The Thirst for Justice and Peace in the Parables of Enoch." Pages 363–79 in *Enoch and the Messiah Son of Man: Revisiting the Book of Parables*. Edited by Gabriel Boccaccini. Grand Rapids, MI: Eerdmans, 2007.

Pitts, Andrew W., and Seth Pollinger. "The Spirit in Second Temple Jewish Monotheism and the Origins of Early Christology." Pages 135–76 in *Christian Origins and Hellenistic Judaism: Social and Literary Concerns for the New Testament*. Edited by Stanley Porter and Andrew W. Pitts. Early Christianity in its Hellenistic Context 2. Leiden: Brill, 2013.

Poirier, John C. "The Endtime Return of Elijah and Moses at Qumran." *DSD* 10, no. 2 (2003): 221–42.

Porzig, Peter. "The Place of the 'Treatise of the Two Spirits' (1QS 3:13–4:26) within the Literary Development of the Community Rule." Pages 127–52 in *Law, Literature, and Society in Legal Texts from Qumran*. Edited by Jutta Jokiranta and Molly Zahn. Studies on the Texts of the Desert of Judah 128. Leiden: Brill, 2019.

von Rad, Gerhard. *Deuteronomium-Studien*. Göttingen: Vandenhoeck & Ruprecht, 1947. (ET = *Studies in Deuteronomy*. London: SCM, 1953).

Radice, Robert. "Philo's Theology and Theory of Creation." Pages 124–45 in *Cambridge Companion to Philo*. Edited by Adam Kamesar. Cambridge: Cambridge University Press, 2009.

Rainbow, Paul. "Melchizedek as a Messiah at Qumran." *BBR* 7 (1997): 179–94.

Reed, Annette Yoshiko. "From Asael and Šemiḥazah to Uzzah, Azzah, and Azael: 3 Enoch 5 (§§ 7–8) and Jewish Reception-History of 1 Enoch." *JSQ* 8, no. 2 (2001): 105–36.

Reese, James M. *Hellenistic Influence on the Book of Wisdom and Its Consequences*. AnBib 41. Rome: Biblical Institute Press, 1970.

Reiterer, Friedrich V., Tobias Nicklas, and Karin Schöpflin, eds. *Angels: The Concept of Celestial Beings—Origins, Development and Reception*. Berlin: de Gruyter, 2007.

Reynolds, Benjamin. "The 'One Like the Son of Man' according to the Old Greek of Daniel 7,13-14." Pages 70–80 in *Son of Man Problem: Critical Readings*. Edited by B. Reynolds. London: T&T Clark, 2015.

Rhoads, D., and D. Mitchie. *Mark as Story*. Philadelphia: Fortress, 1982.

Richter, Sandra L. *The Deuteronomistic History and the Name Theology: Leshakken Shemo Sham in the Bible and the Ancient Near East*. Berlin: de Gruyter, 2014.

Ringgren, Helmer. *Word and Wisdom: Studies in the Hypostatization of Divine Qualities and Functions in the Ancient Near East*. Lund: Håkan Ohlssons, 1947.

Rowland, Christopher. "A Man Clothed in Linen: Daniel 10:6ff. and Jewish Angelology." *JSNT* 24 (1985): 100–110.

———. "The Vision of the Risen Christ in Rev. i.12ff.: The Debt of an Early Christology to an Aspect of Jewish Angelology." *JTS* 31, no. 1 (1980): 1–11.

Royse, James R. "Philo, Κυριος, and the Tetragrammaton." *Studia Philonica Annual* 3 (1991): 167–83.

Ruffatto, Kristine J. "Raguel as Interpreter of Moses' Throne Vision: The Transcendent Identity of Raguel in the Exagoge of Ezekiel the Tragedian." *JSP* 17, no. 2 (2008): 121–39.

Ruiten, Jacques V. "Angels and Demons in the Book of Jubilees." Pages 585–609 in *Angels: The Concept of Celestial Beings—Origins, Development and Reception*. Edited by F. V. Reiterer, T. Nicklas, and K. Schöpflin. Deuterocanonical and Cognate Literature Yearbook. Berlin: de Gruyter, 2007.

Runia, David T. *Exegesis and Philosophy: Studies on Philo of Alexandria*. Hampshire: Aldershot, 1990.

———. "Logos." Page 528 in *Dictionary of Deities and Demons in the Bible*. 2nd ed. Edited by Karel van der Toorn, Bob Becking, and Pieter W. vad der Horst. Leiden: Brill; Grand Rapids, MI: Eerdmans, 1999.

———. *On the Creation of the Cosmos according to Moses*. PACS 5.1. Atlanta: SBLPress, 2005.

———. *Philo in Early Christian Literature: A Survey*. Minneapolis: Fortress, 1993.

Schäfer, Peter. *Die Geburt des Judentums aus dem Geist des Christentums: Fünf Vorlesungen zur Entstehung des rabbinischen Judentums*. Tübingen: Mohr Siebeck, 2010.

———. *The Jewish Jesus: How Judaism and Christianity Shaped Each Other*. Princeton: Princeton University Press, 2012.

———. *Synopse zur Hekhalot-Literatur*. Tübingen: Mohr Siebeck, 2020.

———. *Two Gods in Heaven: Jewish Concepts of God in Antiquity*. Translated by Allison Brown. Princeton: Princeton University Press, 2020.

Schremer, Adiel. "Midrash, Theology, and History: Two Powers in Heaven Revisited," *Journal for the Study of Judaism* 39 (2008): 230–54.

Schrenk, G. "Lego." *TDNT* 4 (1967): 88–90.

Scott, S. R. "The Binitarian Nature of the Book of Similitudes." *JSP* 18, no. 1 (2008): 55–78.

Segal, Alan F. *Two Powers in Heaven: Early Rabbinic Reports about Christianity and Gnosticism*. SJLA 25. Leiden: Brill, 1977.

Sekki, Arthur E. *The Meaning of Ruaḥ at Qumran*. Atlanta: Scholars Press, 1989.

Sellin, Gerhard. *Der Streit um die Auferstehung der Toten. Eine religionsgeschichtliche und exegetische Untersuchung von 1 Korinther 15*. FRLANT 138. Göttingen: Vandenhoeck & Ruprecht, 1986.

Siegert, Folker. "The Philonian Fragment *De Deo*: First English Translation." *Studia Philonica Annual* 10 (1998): 1–33.

Simkovich, Malka Z. "Echoes of Universalist Testament Literature in Christian and Rabbinic Texts." *Harvard Theological Review* 109, no. 1 (2016): 1–32.

Sheppard, G. T. *Wisdom as a Hermeneutical Construct: A Study in the Sapientializing of the Old Testament*, BZAW 151. Berlin: de Gruyter, 1980.

Skehan, Patrick W., Eugene Ulrich, Judith E. Sanderson, and P. J. Parsons, *Qumran Cave 4: IV, Palaeo-Hebrew and Greek Biblical Manuscripts*. Oxford: Clarendon Press, 1992.

Smith, Mark S. *The Origins of Biblical Monotheism: Israel's Polytheistic Background and the Ugaritic Texts*. Oxford: Oxford University Press, 2001.

Snaith, John G. *Ecclesiasticus or the Wisdom of Jesus, Son of Sirach*. CBCA. Cambridge: Cambridge University Press, 1974.

Sommer, Benjamin D. *The Bodies of God and the World of Ancient Israel*. New York: Cambridge University Press, 2009.

Steenburg, D. "The Worship of Adam and Christ as the Image of God." *JSNT* 39 (1990): 95–109.

Sterling, Gregory E. "From the Thick Marshes of the Nile to the Throne of God: Moses in Ezekiel the Tragedian and Philo of Alexandria." Pages 129–33 in *SPhiloA XXVI*. Edited by David T. Runia, et al. Atlanta: SBL, 2014.

———. "Philo." in *The Dictionary of New Testament Background*. Edited by Craig A. Evans and Stanley E. Porter. Downers Grove, IL: InterVarsity Press, 2000.

Stokes, Ryan. *The Satan: How God's Executioner Became the Enemy.* Grand Rapids, MI: Eerdmans, 2019.

Stone, Michael E. "The Fall of Satan and Adam's Penance: Three Notes on *The Books of Adam and Eve*." Pages 43–56 in *Literature on Adam and Eve: Collected Essays*. Edited by G. A. Anderson, M. Stone, and J. Tromp. Leiden: Brill, 2000.

Stone, Michael E., and Frank Moore Cross, *Fourth Ezra: A Commentary on the Book of Fourth Ezra*. Hermeneia. Minneapolis: Fortress, 1990.

Stone, Michael E., and Matthias Henze, *4 Ezra and 2 Baruch: Translations, Introductions, and Notes*. Hermeneia. Minneapolis: Fortress, 2013.

Strack, H. L., and P. Billerbeck, *Das Evangelium nach Matthäus erläutert aus Talmud und Midrash*. Vol. 2. München: Beck, 1922.

Strickert, Fred. "On the Cherubim." *Studia Philonica Annual* 8 (1996): 40–57.

Struthers Malbon, Elizabeth. *Mark's Jesus: Characterization as Narrative Christology*. Waco, TX: Baylor University Press, 2009.

Stuckenbruck, Loren T. *Angel Veneration and Christology: A Study in Early Judaism and in the Christology of the Apocalypse of John*. Tübingen: Mohr Siebeck, 1995.

———. "'Angels' and 'God': Exploring the Limits of Early Jewish Monotheism." Pages 45–70 in *Early Jewish and Christian Monotheism*. Edited by Loren T. Stuckenbruck and Wendy E. S. North. JSNTSup 63. New York: T&T Clark, 2004.

———. "Melchizedek in Jewish Apocalyptic Literature." *JSNT* 41, no. 1 (2018): 124–38.

————. "'One Like a Son of Man' in the Old Greek Recension of Daniel 7:13: Scribal Error or Theological Translation." Pages 497–507 in *Son of Man Problem: Critical Readings*. Edited by B. Reynolds. London: T&T Clark, 2015.

Sullivan, Kevin P. *Wrestling with Angels: A Study of the Relationship between Angels and Humans in Ancient Jewish Literature and the New Testament*. Leiden: Brill, 2004.

Suter, David Winston. *Traditions and Composition in the Parables of Enoch*. SBLDS 47. Missoula, MT: Scholars Press, 1979.

Tal, Abraham, ed. *Tibåt Mårqe/The Ark of Marqe: Edition, Translation, Commentary*. Studia Samaritana 9. Berlin: De Gruyter, 2019.

Talbert, Charles. *The Development of Christology during the First Hundred Years: And Other Essays on Early Christian Christology*. NovTSup 140. Leiden: Brill, 2011.

Tanner, Norman P., ed. *Decrees of the Ecumenical Councils: Nicaea I to Lateran V. Volume 1*. London and Washtington, D.C.: Sheed & Ward; Georgetown University Press, 1990.

Teselle, Eugene. *Augustine the Theologian*. New York: Herder and Herder, 1970; Repr., Eugene, OR: Wipf and Stock, 2002.

Tiede, D. L. *The Charismatic Figure as Miracle Worker*. SBLDS 1. Missoula, MT: Scholars Press, 1972.

Tilling, Chris. *Paul's Divine Christology*. WUNT 2/323. Tübingen: Mohr Siebeck, 2012.

Tobin, Thomas H. *The Creation of Man: Philo and the History of Interpretation*. CBQM 14. Washington, DC: The Catholic Biblical Association of America, 1983.

van der Toorn, Karel, Bob Becking, and Pieter W. van der Horst, eds. *Dictionary of Deities and Demons in the Bible*. 2nd ed. Grand Rapids, MI: Eerdmans, 1999.

Tov, Emanuel, R. A. Kraft, and P. J. Parsons. *The Greek Minor Prophets Scroll from Nahal Hever (8HevXIIgr)*. Oxford: Oxford University Press, 1990.

Turner, Max. *Power from on High: The Spirit in Israel's Restoration and Witness in Luke–Acts*. Journal of Pentecostal Theology Supplement Series 9. Sheffield: Sheffield Academic, 1996.

Tuschling, R. M. M. *Angels and Orthodoxy: A Study in their Development in Syria and Palestine from the Qumran Texts to Ephrem the Syrian*. STNC, 40. Tübingen: Mohr Siebeck, 2007.

Uhlig, S. *Das äthiopische Henochbuch*. JSHRZ 5.6. Gütersloh: Gütersloher Verlagshaus, 1984.

VanderKam, James. "The Angel of the Presence in the Book of Jubilees." *DSD* 7, no. 3 (2000): 378–93.

————. *The Dead Sea Scrolls Today*. Grand Rapids, MI: Eerdmans, 1994.

————. "Righteous One, Messiah, Chosen One, and Son of Man in 1 Enoch 37-71." Pages 179–82 in *The Messiah: Developments in Earliest Judaism and Christianity*. Edited by James H. Charlesworth. Minneapolis: Fortress, 1992.

Van de Water, Rick. "Michael or Yhwh? Toward Identifying Melchizedek in 11Q13." *JSP* 16, no. 1 (2006): 75–86.

Vialle, Catherine. "Ange et Compagnon de Route: Le Personnage de Raphaël Dans Le Livre de Tobie (texte Court)." *ETR* 89, no. 2 (2014): 145–56.

Waddell, James. *The Messiah: A Comparative Study of the Enochic Son of Man and the Pauline Kyrio*s. JCTCRS 10. London: Bloomsbury, 2011.

Waetjen Herman C. "Logos προς τον θεον and Objectification of Truth in the Prologue of the Fourth Gospel." *CBQ* 63, no. 2 (2001): 265–86.

Wasserstein, Abraham. "Notes on the Temple of Onias at Leontopolis." *ICS* 18 (1993): 119–29.

Wedderburn, A. J. M. "Philo's 'Heavenly Man.'" *NovT* 15, no. 4 (1973): 301–26.

Weeks, Stuart, Simon Gathercole, and Loren Stuckenbruck, eds. *The Book of Tobit: Texts from the Principal Ancient and Medieval Traditions with Synopsis, Concordances, and Annotated Texts in Aramaic, Hebrew, Greek, Latin, and Syriac.* Berlin: de Gruyter, 2004.

White, Stephen L. "Angel of the Lord: Messenger or Euphemism?" *TynBul* 50 (1999): 299–305.

Wilckens, U. *Weisheit und Torheit: Eine exegetisch-religionsgeschichtliche Untersuchung zu 1Kor und 2.* Tübingen: Mohr Siebeck, 1959.

Wilhite, David E. *The Gospel according to Heretics.* Grand Rapids, MI: Baker Academic, 2015.

Wilkinson, Robert J. *Tetragrammaton: Western Christians and the Hebrew Name of God.* Leiden: Brill, 2015.

Williams, M. H. *The Jews among the Greeks and Romans: A Diasporan Sourcebook.* London: Bloomsbury, 1998.

Winn, Adam. "A Case for Jesus as the YHWH of Israel." Pages 211–40 in *Christology in Mark's Gospel: 4 Views.* Edited by Anthony Le Donne. Grand Rapids, MI: Zondervan, 2021.

———. "Identifying the Enochic Son of Man as God's Word and Wisdom." *JSP* 28, no. 4 (2019): 290–318.

Winston, David. *Logos and Mystical Theology in Philo of Alexandria.* Cincinnati: Hebrew Union College Press, 1985.

———. "Philo Judaeus." Pages 7105–8 in vol. 10 of *The Encyclopedia of Religion.* Edited by L. Jones. 2nd ed. 15 vols. 2005.

———. *The Wisdom of Solomon.* Anchor Bible 43. New York: Double Day, 1979.

Wolfson, H. A. *Philo: Foundations of Religious Philosophy in Judaism, Christianity and Islam.* 2 vols. Cambridge: Harvard University Press, 1947.

Worthington, Jonathan. "*Creatio ex Nihilo* and Romans 4.17 in Context." *NTS* 62, no. 1 (2016): 49–59.

van der Woude, A. S. "Discoveries in the Judean Desert, Band," volume 7VII. *TRu* 55, no. 3 (1990): 253–62.

———. "Melchisedech als himmlische Erlösergestalt in den neugefundenen eschatologischen Midraschim aus Qumran Höle XI." *Oudtestamentische studiën* 14 (1965): 354–73.

Xeravits, Géza G., ed. *Dualism in Qumran.* London: T&T Clark, 2010.

Yarbro Collins, Adela. *Mark: A Commentary.* Hermeneia. Minneapolis: Fortress, 2007.

Young, Frances. "*Creatio ex Nihilo*: A Context for the Emergence of the Christian Doctrine of Creation." *SJT* 44 (1991): 139–51.

Zucker, David J. "A Jubilee (50) of Fascinating Facts about the Book of Jubilees." *BTB* 50, no. 2 (2020): 92–96.

Scriptures Index

Ancient Sources Index

PSEUDEPIGRAPHA

Eccl. Rabb.
  6:9.1, 223n23

PLATO

Republic *(Rep.)*
  6.e, 69n91

Timeaus (Tim.), 69n95
  29e, 64n26

ANCIENT CHRISTIAN WRITERS

Athanasius

Defense of the Nicene Definition (Decr.)
  25, 69n91

Epistle of Barnabas (Barn.), 8n17
  5, 69n91

(Ps.-)Hippolytus

Against Noetus
  11.1, 69n91

Refutatio omnium haeresium (Haer.)
  10.22, 194n1
  10.24.1, 194n1
  10.29, 194n1

10.30.1–7, 194n1

Irenaeus

Against Heresies (Haer.)
  2.13.5, 69n91

Justin Martyr

Dialogue with Trypho (Dial.)
  128, 69n91

Origen

On First Principles
  4.28, 69n91

In Psalmus
  2, 150n49

Commentary on John (Comm. Jo.)
  2.7, 150n53
  2.25, 154n114

Shepherd of Hermas (Herm.Sim.)
  9.6.1–2, 131n107
  83.9.6.1–2, 131n107
  90.9.12.7, 131nn107–8

Tertullian

Against Praxeas (Prax.)
  8.5–7, 69n91

Apology (Apol.)
  33.4, 67n64

General Index

About the Authors

David E. Wilhite is professor of historical theology at Baylor University's Truett Seminary. His research focuses on early Christian developments, and his publications include *Tertullian the African* (2007), *The Gospel According to Heretics* (2015), *Ancient African Christianity* (2017), and *The Cambridge History of Ancient Christianity* (coedited with Bruce Longenecker, 2023).

Adam Winn holds the Louis and Ann W. Armstrong Chair of Religion and is both chair and professor for the Department of Biblical and Religious Studies at Samford University. His research focuses on early Judaism and the New Testament. His publications include *The Purpose of Mark's Gospel* (2007), *Mark and the Elijah-Elisha Narrative* (2010), *An Introduction to Empire in the New Testament* (ed., 2016), and *Reading Mark's Christology under Caesar* (2018).